DATE DUE

DEC 0 7 1989			
GAYLORD			PRINTED IN U.S.A.

COUNTRY TO CITY
The Urbanization of a Japanese Hamlet

COUNTRY TO CITY
The Urbanization of a Japanese Hamlet

By EDWARD NORBECK

University of Utah Press

Salt Lake City

1978

For Katherine

Table of Contents

INTRODUCTORY NOTE   ix

TAKASHIMA   xiii
    Table of Contents   xv
    Preface   xix

TAKASHIMA URBANIZED   237
    Table of Contents   238

Introductory Note

This study of a Japanese community is in fact two related studies. The first consists of a detailed ethnographic description of a rural hamlet in central Japan as it existed in 1950–51, an account originally published under the title *Takashima: A Japanese Fishing Community* (University of Utah Press, 1954). The second study describes and discusses the same community as it existed late in 1974, giving special attention to changes that had occurred in the twenty-three years since the original study was conducted. During this span of more than two decades, Takashima had undergone many changes, of which the most radical took place in the 1970s. As a result, this book concerns two different kinds of communities, one rural and the other urban and industrial.

The Takashima of 1950–51 was a small, isolated, impoverished hamlet of fisherfolk on an island bearing the same name. By 1974, it had become a well-integrated suburb of a growing industrial city of 400,000 people, and, as the result of a government project to "reclaim" land by filling part of the sea, Takashima was no longer an island but part of the mainland that fronted the sea only on what had formerly been its most distant shore. The erstwhile fisherfolk, who had drawn their water from wells, lighted their homes with kerosene lamps, cooked with pine twigs as fuel, and lived a life that revolved principally about fishing and affairs of the family and hamlet, had become relatively prosperous suburbanites following industrial occupations and living urban lives.

By 1975, familial and community organization and relationships had changed in adaptation to economic and other changes, and other aspects of life had become similarly altered. The cumulative effect of the many changes may accurately be called enormous, a statement that must be qualified by a note of caution to avoid creating the impression that the new consists of a group of revolutionarily different elements entirely displacing the old. The transition occurred swiftly and without bringing pronounced or disorganizing stress to the human beings concerned, a seemingly remarkable condition that has not been characteristic of all industrializing communities and nations of the world. Paradoxically, one of the keys to gaining an understanding of the speed and relative ease of the transition in Takashima is stability, that is, cultural continuity. Despite many genuine and seeming discontinuities, certain fundamental attitudes, values, and ways of perceiving and putting order into human relations vigorously persist. Their durability and elasticity have been important factors in easing the process of change.

ix

To understand these continuities and their role in the process of transition, it is necessary to know the conditions that existed long before 1975. Even the best of informants have fleeting memories, and it is certain that many of the circumstances existing in 1950–51 could never be recorded — or recaptured — today. For this reason, the original publication of 1954 is here reproduced in its entirety. The present study may then be described as consisting of two parts: a detailed ethnographic account of a rural community in times gone by that serves as a necessary base for understanding later developments; and an account of subsequent industrialization that also concerns events and processes of social change, noting continuities as well as discontinuities.

So described, the present book concerns a large class of human settlements, the industrializing or recently industrialized communities of the world. Many other such communities exist in Japan. Although unique in its particulars, Takashima represents them in fundamental features, old and new. Elsewhere in the world, the process of industrialization has followed different courses and has often been troublesome to the people whose lives are undergoing change. I hope that this account of the Japanese circumstances will have relevance in our attempt to gain a general understanding of the problems as well as the processes of change in culture brought on by rapid industrialization.

In the preparation of this study, I am once again grateful to the people of Takashima for their kindness and patience. Special thanks are due Minoru Matsui for her unfailing and generous aid as an informant and for her rewarding friendship. I am thankful also to Akira Ōyama, Shōichi Watanabe, and Shiro Moriwake and their families, to Professor Takaaki Sanada of Shizuoka University, and, once again, to Professor Hiroshi Mannari of Kansei Gakuin University. I am indebted and grateful to the National Science Foundation for a grant-in-aid that allowed me to conduct research in Takashima for six months ending late in December 1974. Thanks are also due to *Urban Anthropology* for permission to reprint material from my "Changing Associations in a Recently Industrialized Japanese Community (Vol. 6, No. 1, 1977).

TAKASHIMA
A Japanese Fishing Community

TAKASHIMA
A Japanese Fishing Community

By EDWARD NORBECK

University of Utah Press

Salt Lake City

1954

Table of Contents

Chapter		Page
I.	INTRODUCTION	1
II.	GAINING A LIVELIHOOD	12
	Fishing	12
	Farming	28
	Other Occupations	38
	Incomes	41
	Budget and Finance	43
III.	THE HOUSEHOLD AND HOUSE LIFE	48
	The Family and the Household	48
	The Dwelling	55
	Building a House	63
	Household Arts and Crafts	67
	Diet	68
	Dress	73
	Sickness and Health	79
	Recreation and Entertainment	83
IV.	THE *BURAKU* AND THE COMMUNITY	93
	Introduction	93
	Buraku Organization	96
	Buraku Cooperative and Uniting Mechanisms	100
	Buraku Property	100
	Buraku Cooperative Activity	102
	The *Buraku* and the City	104
	Relations with Outside Communities	112
	Social Distinctions and Interpersonal Relations	112
V.	RELIGION	119
	Introduction	119
	Popular Beliefs and Deities	121
	Household Gods	122
	Buraku Gods and Shrines	126
	Gods and Beliefs of the Sea	129
	Outside Shrines and their Gods	132

TABLE OF CONTENTS—*(Continued)*

Chapter		Page
V.	RELIGION (Continued)	
	Religious Practitioners	134
	Priests	134
	Faith-healers and Mediums	134
	Geomancers	137
	Spirits, Ghosts, and Devils	139
	Defilement and Taboo	140
	The Ceremonial Calendar	142
	The Abandoned Customs	159
VI.	THE LIFE CYCLE	161
	Sex and Reproduction	161
	Childhood and Adolescence	167
	Marriage	174
	The Bad Years	185
	Maturity and Old Age	187
	Death	188
VII.	THE IMPACT OF WESTERNIZATION	195
	APPENDIX	223
	GLOSSARY	223
	BIBLIOGRAPHY	225
	INDEX	227

List of Tables

Table		Page
1.	Species of Marine Fauna Commonly Taken	13
2.	Fishing Chart	16
3.	Major Crops Raised in 1949	31
4.	Estimated Household Budget	44
5.	Foreign Words in the Adult Vocabulary	202-206

TABLE OF CONTENTS—*(Continued)*

List of Illustrations

MAPS

		Page
I.	Takashima	3
II.	Mae, Dwellings and Outbuildings	6
III.	Subana, Dwellings and Outbuildings	7
IV.	Takashima and Neighboring Communities	8
V.	Sketch of Kojima City	94

FIGURES

1.	House Plan	59

PHOTOGRAPHS

Plate

1.	The Island of Takashima	xxii
2.	Beach Scene at Mae	15
3.	Mending Nets, Summer	15
4.	Motored Fishing Boat	22
5.	Hauling in a Net, Man and Wife	22
6.	Hand-line Fishing, the Occupation of Poor Fishermen	27
7.	Gathering Pine Needles and Twigs for Firewood	27
8.	After Sweet-potato Harvest, Cutting Up the Vines — Mother and Daughter	33
9.	Digging Clams	33
10.	Terraced Fields, September	37
11.	Carrying Night-soil to the Fields	37
12.	Average House, One-story, with Attic	56
13.	Better-than-average House, Two-story	56
14.	Summer Clothing, Adult Male	75
15.	Summer Clothing, Children	75
16.	Girls in Western Dresses — "Good" Clothes	75
17.	Young Men Dressed in Their Best Clothes for the Autumn Festival	75
18.	Priest and Female Assistant Conducting Faith-healing Prayers to O-Fudō-sama	158
19.	Children and Adults Toasting *Mochi* Around Bonfire Inside Shrine at Ōtsumogori	158
20.	New Year's Decorations Before the Shelf Dedicated to Ebisu and Daikoku	189
21.	Ceremonial Offering of Food to Child on Its Naming Day	189
22, 23, 24.	Two Brides, Photographed in Ordinary Clothes and in Wedding-day Attire with Wigs	180

Preface

IN THE PAGES which follow an attempt is made to present an ethnographic description, with emphasis upon aspects of Westernization, of a rural Japanese fishing community. Few accounts of life in rural Japan, and none dealing with fishing communities, have been published in any European language. It is hoped that this study will in some measure serve the purpose of providing ethnographic data on rural Japan and at the same time serve to point out some cultural trends which apply in considerable measure to all of rural Japan. An attempt is also made herein to offer suggestions concerning factors which underlie these cultural trends.

The rural settlements of Japan, whether lowland farming, highland farming, coastal fishing or open-sea fishing, are all part of a national culture which is everywhere much the same. There are local variations in custom and differences correlated with types of economy, but there is throughout a high degree of cultural homogeneity. Takashima, the fishing community upon which this study is based, is thought to be to a considerable extent representative — although by no means "typical" —of rural Japan as a whole. There have been vast changes in Japanese culture during the past eighty years, most of which appear to point to one thing, the effects of contact with the West. The rate of change has not been uniform in all rural areas, but the conditions which obtain in one rural area today are those which in broad outline now exist, have recently existed, or will in all likelihood soon come into existence in other rural areas. When all of rural Japan is considered, Takashima is perhaps slightly more "advanced" than the average.

This study is one of a series made under the auspices of the Center for Japanese Studies of the University of Michigan. Field work in Japan was done during the period from June, 1950, through April, 1951. Study of the community of Takashima began in August, 1950, and ended late in April, 1951. Initially, the gathering of data was done by commuting daily from living quarters in Okayama City, 21 miles away. Later, as the opportunity presented itself, the author and his wife remained in part-time residence in Takashima.

Selection of Takashima as the community for study was made after a survey of all fishing communities of the Okayama Prefecture coast. At the time, under Occupation ruling foreigners in Japan were not permitted to rely upon Japanese economy for subsistence. It was thus necessary to choose a community within reach of an urban center (Okayama City) where imported food might be obtained through channels approved by the military government. A small community was considered most desirable for intensive study. It was also considered desirable to select a community which had no special features to set it apart from others and one sufficiently isolated from other rural communities and from any large urban center to form a unit of its own.

Nearly all adults of the community of Takashima as well as many of the adolescents and children served as informants. Serious attempt was made to check all data with several informants. Material presented herein on pre-natal and post-natal care, childbirth, child rearing, and taboos was drawn from at least one woman in every household of the community, and a number of men were also consulted. Some comparative material was gathered in nearby communities and during visits to other, more distant areas of Japan. Comparative data were also drawn from Japanese publications, and from conversations with native scholars and other researchers of the Center for Japanese Studies. All "interviewing" of informants done by the author consisted of informal conversation in the Japanese language, in which the author has a modest competence. Valuable aid was given by the author's wife in interviewing women on women's affairs. For these interviews a Japanese woman usually served as interpreter, and sometimes the author acted as interpreter for his wife. The cooperation of Takashima residents was warmly and gratifyingly whole-hearted.

Expressions of appreciation are due to many persons for aid in connection with the field work upon which this study is based and in the preparation of the manuscript. Gathering of the field data was made financially possible through a grant from the Social Science Research Council. It was made physically possible through the facilities and good offices of the Center for Japanese Studies of the University of Michigan which provided, among many other things, a place to live and a car for commuting.

First, thanks are due to the people of Takashima for their warm friendship, thorough cooperation, and patience in the face of protracted although informal interrogation. The list of Japanese nationals to whom the author feels gratitude for aid and advice is long, too long for recounting here. Mention must, however, be made of the Japanese professors and scholars Eiichirō Ishida, Katsunori Sakurada, Tsuneichi Miyamoto and Jirō Suzuki. Thanks must also go to Seiko Miyakawa, Hisashi Hasegawa, and, warmly, to our good friends and aids in Takashima, Minoru and Kashirō and their families. The officials of Okayama Prefecture are to be given thanks for their kind reception, aid, and encouragement.

I wish also to express my gratitude to Dr. Robert B. Hall, Director of the Center for Japanese Studies and moving spirit behind that organization; to Dr. Robert E. Ward, Dr. Joseph K. Yamagiwa, Dr. Mischa Titiev, and to other members of the Okayama field station of the Center for Japanese Studies. Included among these are the unsung wives of my fellow researchers there, who not only contributed much toward making domestic life tenable but were also useful sources of ethnological information on Japan. To Dr. Richard K. Beardsley and Dr. John B. Cornell go special thanks for aid of many kinds.

In the preparation of this report I wish to express thanks to Dr. Richard K. Beardsley, Professor Volney H. Jones, Dr. Mischa Titiev, and Dr. Joseph K. Yamagiwa. To Dr. Leslie A. White must go special thanks for aid in preparing the study and for other counsel. For matters connected with publication, I am warmly grateful to Dr. Jesse D. Jennings. Mrs. Louise Okada was very helpful in typing the manuscript.

Last, but far from least, I want to thank my wife for direct aid in this study and for other things too numerous and personal to be mentioned here. Without her aid this study would truly have been impossible.

PLATE 1.—*The Island of Takashima, photographed from adjacent mainland.*

CHAPTER I

Introduction

TAKASHIMA, literally "high island," is a small fishing and farming community located upon an island bearing the same name in the Inland Sea within the boundaries of Okayama Prefecture in Japan. To reach Takashima one proceeds by bus or train from the city of Okayama southeasterly to the smaller city of Kurashiki, a distance of twelve miles. He transfers there to a crowded, charcoal-powered bus which churns and bumps over the gravel and dirt roads, and rides one uncomfortable hour to traverse the eleven remaining miles to Shionasu, on the westerly side of Kojima Peninsula and the place of embarkation for Takashima. An alternate route recommended for those whose stomachs become queasy, as well they might, on the rural buses of Japan, runs from Okayama City to Ajino by a tiny *matchibako* (match-box) train and by bus for the remaining three miles to Shionasu.

The trip, by either route, is punctuated with frequent stops at villages along the way, where a few persons squeeze their ways out of the bus or train and a somewhat larger number squeeze their ways in. The bus and the train are small, as are the people, their houses, and their fields. The Western traveler marks the narrowness of the roads. He notes the manner in which buildings are compressed together so that as much productive land as possible may be used for raising crops. The Westerner is also likely to be impressed by the sight, seldom missing from the Japanese rural scene, of male bicyclists stopping unconcernedly along the road to urinate.

The Island of Takashima lies approximately one-quarter mile offshore, in shallow water. The sheltered Inland Sea is seldom rough enough to prohibit traffic of even small craft, and one can usually reach Taka-

1

shima within a few minutes at any season of the year in one of the small flat-bottomed, stern-sculled boats used for such transport. There is no commercial boat, and no necessity for one, as each household of Takashima owns its own small boat for transport to Shionasu and back. Passage between Shionasu and Takashima is frequent. Anyone who wishes to go to Takashima usually need stand expectantly on the stone breakwater at Shionasu for only a short time before one of the returning islanders will obligingly take him across.

The fanning strokes of the heavy stern scull cause the boat to rock from side to side in short, jerky movements so that the passenger's head and upper trunk are in constant, wiggling motion. If the person sculling is a child or woman, the stranger will often feel obliged to offer his aid. A few minutes' attempt by the novice will, however, succeed only in unseating the scull, propelling the boat in a circle, and producing polite, sympathetic comment from the islander. The stranger soon resumes his seat as a passenger and the boat jerks steadily onward, in the proper direction.

From the shore of the mainland Takashima is a picture island, heavily wooded in part, neatly and carefully cultivated in the less precipitous areas, with clusters of dwellings tucked in the protected lee of the island. The surface of the surrounding water, as far as the eye can see, is dotted with islands of various sizes, some heavily grown with pines, others stripped of their forest or with young new growth, and still others — wave-washed rocky islets — devoid of vegetation. On a clear day the tops of the mountains of the large island of Shikoku can be seen in the far distance. Viewed from a height the panorama is unreal. There are too many picturesque islands. No such tranquil sea could exist. It is a Japanese painting.

Approaching the island, one's eye is struck by a large pine tree, gnarled and handsome, in the center of the main group of dwellings, which spreads its twisted branches over several of the surrounding houses. A stone and concrete breakwater-pier projects a slim arm into the water from the settlement, and to it are anchored the unpainted fishing boats and smaller transport craft of the people of Takashima. At the base of the pier stands a small shrine to Ebisu, a god of fishermen, on which lumps of coral, pine branches and other offerings can be seen. Tile-roofed dwellings, jammed together seemingly at random with narrow, twisting paths between them, extend to the edge of the sandy beach, just out of reach of high tide. Additional boats are pulled up on the beach in front of the houses so that their prows almost touch the long rows of fishing nets suspended from bamboo poles to dry in the sun.

At low tide there are wide expanses of yellow sand, clean and inviting from a distance, but often found to be littered with refuse upon closer

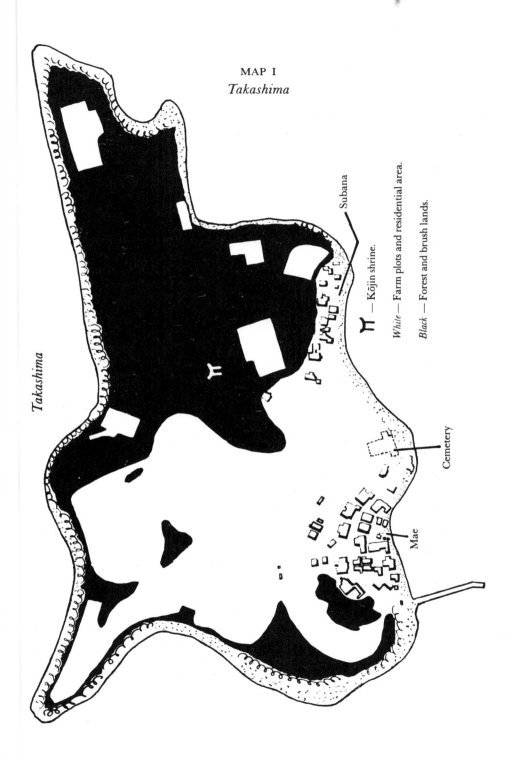

MAP I

Takashima

Subana

Ⴤ — Kōjin shrine.

White — Farm plots and residential area.

Black — Forest and brush lands.

Cemetery

Mae

Takashima

view. A number of women, girls and young children may be seen any day
at low tide on these sandy stretches digging their daily supplies of clams.
Digging clams, women's work, continues throughout the year, but the
work of men is more seasonably variable. Dependent upon the season
and the habits and vagaries of the fish, the men will be off fishing, at their
homes making or caring for nets, sleeping, or simply resting.

A narrow strip of sand between the most seaward of the dwellings
and the net racks on the beach forms the main thoroughfare of the community, and is the center of community activities. Along this path are the
communal vats for treating nets, the community hall, and the largest
uncultivated open area in the community. From this path, narrow and
twisting branch paths lead off to the dwellings which extend on up to the
edge of the hillside. For children, the main path is a gathering place
where, noses running twin viscous streams from chronic colds, they play a
variety of games. For adults the path is a convenient spot to place vegetables and grain in the sun for drying, the scene of work with the nets,
and the place where greetings and gossip between neighbors is exchanged.

Takashima is a quiet and peaceful spot, sheltered from wind by the
hillside behind the settlement, and removed from noise except that of the
motors of passing water craft and of children at play. On certain days the
sound of the radios of Shionasu carries clearly across the water to Takashima. It is said that the voices of Shionasu schoolteachers raised in reprimand can occasionally be heard, and the returning schoolchild is sometimes mystified when asked by his parents about misdeeds at school.

The area of the island is approximately thirty acres, nearly half of
which is non-irrigated farm land, and the balance predominantly pine
and bamboo-grass forest. The island, irregular in outline, rises toward the
north to a peak approximately 250 feet above sea level which is known as
the "mountain." The peak slopes to the south, forming a saddle, and rises
in the southern extremity to a rounded eminence. The saddle and southern end comprise the principal area of farm lands, and the peak and its
northern and western slopes form the forest land. Several small farm
patches are scattered throughout the forest area.

The climate is, as a whole, kind. Rainfall is adequate to keep the
wells full and the farm plots growing with no fear of crop failure. The
summer is hot and humid, but the sticky heat is somewhat ameliorated
by breezes from the sea. Days of below-freezing temperatures during the
winter are few in the low-lying areas of Okayama Prefecture, and Takashima, protected from cold winds by the hill behind the settlement, is said
to be several degrees warmer than the adjacent mainland. Nearby Shionasu is reportedly one garment-thickness colder in the winter months.
An inch or two of snow may fall once or twice during the winter season,

but it usually melts within a few hours. Winters are, however, uncomfortable for lack of adequate heating devices, and summers are disliked because of their humid warmth. Spring and autumn, favorite seasons, are periods of very nearly ideal temperatures.

From archaeological evidence Takashima was inhabited or at least utilized for burial from a period beginning before the birth of Christ. Amateur archaeologists have in the past excavated a number of burial mounds and cists on the island which have produced a variety of objects ranging from hammerstones and stone arrow-heads to Iron Age swords, pottery and ornaments. According to the *Nihongi*, one of the oldest (720 A.D.) extant accounts of Japanese history, the perhaps legendary Emperor Jimmu, first ruler of Japan,[1] stopped at a place called Takashima in the country of Kibi to prepare for further military conquest in his campaign to subjugate all of Japan. Takashima is an extremely common place name in Japan and several communities bearing this name lie within the confines of the old country of Kibi. There have been claims by local scholars that the Takashima of this study is the place in question. Such arguments are, however, of little concern to the residents of the present Takashima, and belong to a scholarly world far removed from their lives.

Although there is no written history of Takashima, according to oral traditions the island, dry-farmed by commuting Shionasu residents from a period beginning several centuries earlier, was first settled about three hundred years ago. At that time three households of Shionasu residents, thought to have been genetically related, built dwellings and settled down permanently on Takashima as farmers. Such fishing as was done at that time was for table use only. The great pine is said to have been planted by the first settlers shortly after their arrival. As the years went by and the people increased in number, branch households with new dwellings came into being and a graveyard was established by the side of the settlement. About one hundred years ago every dwelling and building burned down: only the big pine escaped destruction. New houses were soon built and seventy years ago the community, still dependent principally on farming, had grown to about twenty-five households. Since the sheltered hollow which formed the only residential area of that time had become too cramped for additional buildings, the community began spreading to the other side of the graveyard, forming there a subdivision of the settlement. At the present time there are thirty-three households, twenty-two of which are in the original settlement area, called Mae, "front," and eleven in the newer area, Subana, "sandspit." The present population is 188 persons, precisely evenly divided in number by sex.

1. According to traditional Japanese chronology, Jimmu had completed his conquests and established himself as ruler in 660 B.C. Modern scholars place the date as several centuries later.

MAP II
Mae, Dwellings and Outbuildings
1:600 (Approx.)

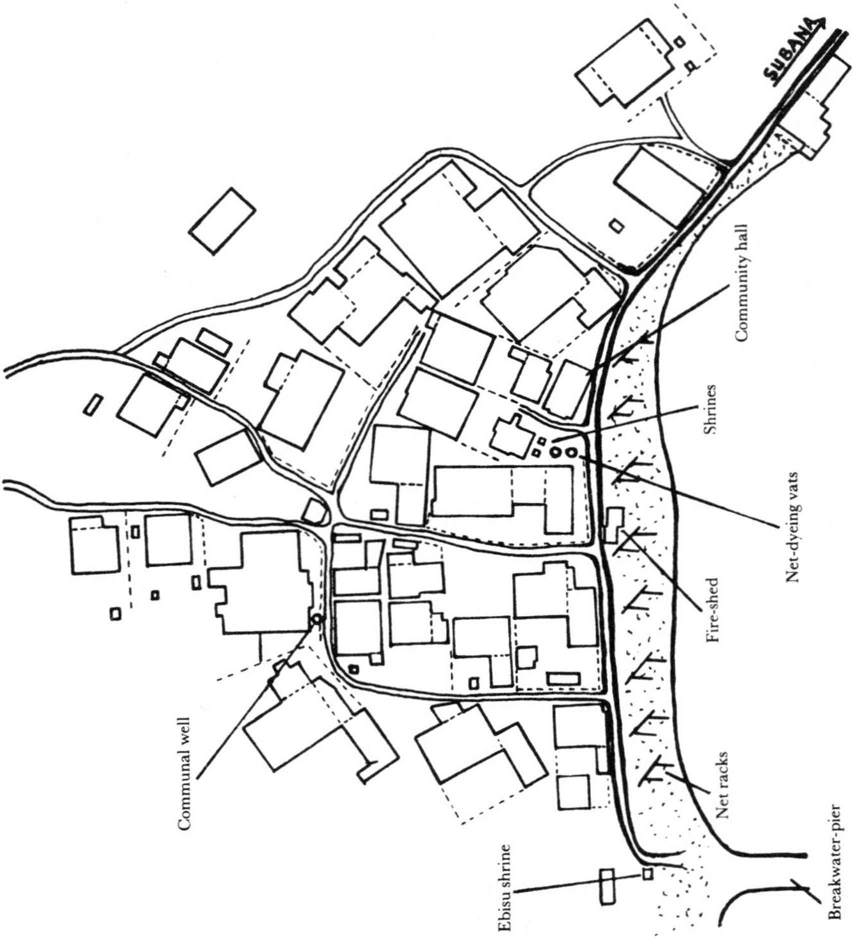

MAP III

Subana, Dwellings and Outbuildings

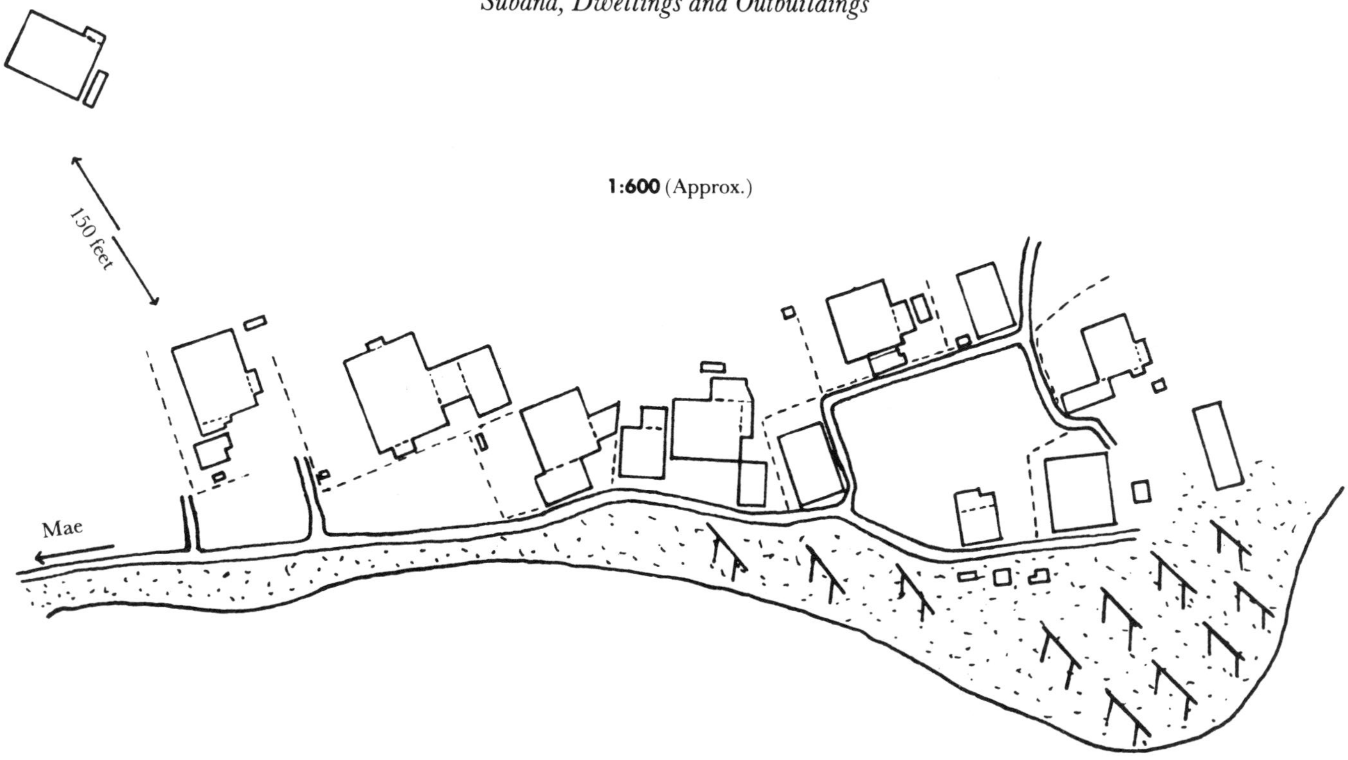

1:600 (Approx.)

150 feet

Mae

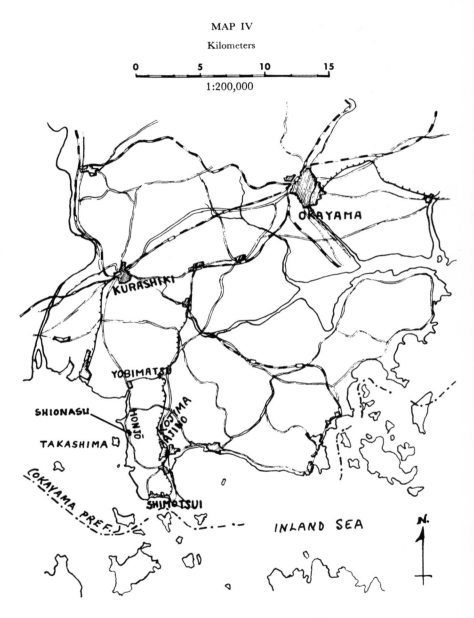

MAP IV

Kilometers

0   5   10   15

1:200,000

Takashima and Neighboring Communities

Takashima is today known as a fishing community, which means that most of the adult males engage in fishing for a livelihood. Conversion to a predominantly fishing economy began about seventy years ago and seems to have been a rapid process after the introduction to Takashima at that time of large and effective nets. In a period of about ten years the males of Takashima turned almost exclusively from farming to fishing, and the responsibility for cultivation of the land was left to the women. Although regarded locally as a fishing community, Takashima is perhaps best described to Westerners as a fishing-farming community.[2] Livelihood is gained chiefly from fishing, but farm plots are important, supplying household needs and also contributing a small percentage to household cash revenue through the sale of farm produce.

Takashima is officially and administratively a part of Kojima City, a loose aggregation of farming, fishing and industrial communities which amalgamated for purposes of administrative economy in April, 1948 to form a city. Kojima is referred to by local Japanese, because of its sprawling, rural aspect, as a city in name only. Takashima is a *buraku* (a small residence community which is not always a political or administrative unit but which may, and in the Kojima area almost always does, coincide with an administrative unit), and a subdivision of Shionasu. Shionasu is in turn a part of Honjō, one of the four formerly independent communities which amalgamated to form Kojima City. Honjō residents are primarily farmers; only one other *buraku* besides Takashima within Honjō engages predominantly in fishing. Honjō, like much of the rest of Kojima City, is rural, and there has been little change in the rural tenor of the lives of most of its residents since the formation of the city.

In matters of daily living Takashima is closely tied, as it always has been in the past, with Shionasu. Nearly all purchasing of necessary foodstuffs and other commodities is done there. A branch office of the Kojima city hall is located in Shionasu, as are the elementary school and the fishing and agricultural cooperatives for Honjō. One of the two Buddhist temples in Honjō is also located in Shionasu. For ordinary purposes there is little reason for Takashima residents to go farther afield than Shionasu and they seldom do so.

Genetically, most of the residents of Takashima are related. The bulk of the *buraku* population is comprised of persons bearing the surname of Matsui, all of whom acknowledge themselves to be at least distantly related to one another. They divide themselves, with varying degrees of

2. Fishing communities where no farming is done can be found in Japan, but are uncommon. Takashima is not to be confused, however, with the Japanese concept of a fishing-farming community called *hannō-hangyo*, "half agriculture, half fishery." This means a community in which approximately half of the males fish and half of them farm or in which the same males both fish and farm as their primary means of livelihood. The term *hannō-hangyo* does not apply to Takashima, which relies principally upon fishing.

agreement, into three lines as descended patrilineally from the original three households which settled on Takashima in the seventeenth century. Persons peripheral to any one of these three branches are ordinarily not considered as relatives although they bear the same surname, live in the same *buraku,* and are thought or known to be distantly related. Although relationships can be traced in many cases as far as third and fourth cousins, there has been much adoption and distant relationships are often very confused. According to the Japanese custom obtaining until Meiji times (1868-1912), commoners bore no surnames. During early Meiji the people of Takashima, along with the rest of Japan, took surnames, and all residents of the *buraku* assumed the name of Matsui, for reasons now forgotten.

No outside and non-related males, excepting a number of adopted husbands (see Chap. VI, Marriage) and adopted male children, are said to have joined the community from its inception until sixty-five years ago. Then a strange household established itself on the island. Shortly afterwards two additional non-Matsui families were added to the community, one of them by means of an outside male's marrying a Matsui daughter and taking up residence there. Today there are seven non-Matsui households, composed of the three original non-Matsui households and their descendants.

There is no general conformity among the people to physical types as set up by physical anthropologists.[3] There is something of a preponderance of squat, sturdy persons, but others are of more delicate and linear construction. Curly or wavy hair is very rare. Hair is usually black and straight, but there are occasional brown-haired persons. Facial and body hair is usually very sparse. The massive-jowled, heavily bearded, Ainu-like Japanese is not to be found on Takashima.

Speech is sub-standard Japanese: that is, it does not conform in all respects with Standard Japanese (based on Tokyo dialect) as taught in the public schools of Japan. There are local variations in phonemes, and a moderate number of colloquial words and local idioms. The variation from Standard Japanese is, however, not extremely marked and speakers of Standard Japanese can maintain conversations with Takashima people with little difficulty. Young people and most middle-aged persons can speak Standard Japanese and use it when conversing with obviously city-reared strangers.

Life on Takashima revolves about work, the household, and the yearly cycle of festivals and celebrations. For the majority of the people there is little contact with people of outside communities with the excep-

---

3. See F. S. Hulse, "Physical Types Among the Japanese," *Papers of the Peabody Museum of American Archaeology and Ethnology* (Cambridge), XX (1943), pp. 122-133.

tion of Shionasu. Trips to Shionasu for purposes of marketing or attending meetings of the various Honjō associations to which Takashima people belong are frequent, almost daily occurrences for many persons. Children must go there to attend school. The average standard of living is comparatively high for rural Japan.[4] There are, however, a few extremely impoverished households, and the range of variation in wealth from the richest household to the poorest is fairly wide.

Takashima has no electricity since it is a small island community. Financial loss would result for the electric company because of the high cost of installation of power facilities as against a very small return. Kerosene lamps are used in the homes for illumination. Whether rich or poor, all residents join in stating with conviction that their greatest hardship is the lack of electricity and their most fervent wish is for its installation.

4. Based upon the author's observation of other communities and upon the statements of Jirō Suzuki, Japanese sociologist.

CHAPTER II

Gaining a Livelihood

FISHING

O F THE thirteen *buraku* in Honjō only Takashima and one other rely principally upon fishing for a livelihood. People of the other *buraku*, most of whom are farmers, frequently refer to Takashima by the term customarily translated as "village," as a *jungyoson* (pure fishing village). Takashima fishermen, however, seem to think of themselves as farmers turned fishermen. To have been once a farmer seems to carry with it at least a trace of social prestige, and traditional fishermen are very low in the general social scale of Japan.

Twenty-six of the thirty-three households on Takashima are primarily fishing households. Three households farm; three operate small freight boats, and one operates a small shop selling miscellaneous merchandise. Fishing, then, is by far the most important means of livelihood, more important than the figures above indicate, as the freight boat operators may go out as fishermen in between freight runs, and two of the three farming households are composed of only one adult person each, a widow and a widower.

Fishing techniques utilized in Japan are extremely varied. A publication of SCAP states "Almost every type of fishing gear known to man is used in Japan. . . . The most primitive to the most modern types of gear were used by the 1,500,000 Japanese fishermen who caught 3,000,000 to 5,000,000 metric tons of fish and other marine products annually from 1936-1942."[1] Techniques may vary widely from village to village within a limited area, and there is also marked specialization in species of marine fauna and flora taken. Takashima fishermen, for example, take no shrimp whereas some of the fishermen of nearby Shionasu and Yobimatsu rely

1. *Japanese Fishing Gear* (Tokyo: General Headquarters, SCAP, Natural Resources Section, Report No. 63, 1946), pp. 4-5.

principally upon them. In Shimotsui, about four miles from Takashima, fishing techniques and species taken vary from *buraku* to *buraku*.[2] Much of the variation and specialization is based upon traditional practices. There is legally nothing to prevent Takashima fishermen from purchasing shrimp nets and adding shrimping to their fishing techniques. Permission must, however, be secured from the Marine Products Department of the prefectural government, which relies largely upon the recommendations of officials of the local fishing cooperative organizations *(gyogyō kumiai)* to which all fishermen belong. Without "buttering up" the channels, officials of the *kumiai* are reluctant to establish a precedent, and tradition rules.

TABLE 1

Species of Marine Fauna Commonly Taken

COMMERCIAL SPECIES

Local Name	English Equivalent	Scientific Name
Akō	Red rock cod	*Sebastodes matsubarae*
Chinu	Black porgy	*Sparus swinhonis*
Ika	Squid (several species)	
*Ine, teppo, bora**	Striped or gray mullet	*Mugil cephalus*
Karei	Flatfish (several species)	
Mamakari	?	*Sardinia melanostica (?)*
Managatsuo	Butterfish or harvest fish	*Stromateoides argenteus*
Mebaru	Gray rock cod	*Sebastodes inermis*
Okoze	Scorpion fish	*Inimicus japonicus*
Sawara	Mackerel	*Sawara hiphonia*
*Se, hane, suzuki**	Sea bass	*Lateolabrax japonicus*
Tanago	A shiner	*Acheilognathus moriokae*
Tsunashi	A herring	*Clupanodon punctatus*

SPECIES TAKEN FOR HOME CONSUMPTION

Local Name	English Equivalent	Scientific Name
Asari	A clam	*Paphia philippinarum*
Fuku or *fugu*	A globefish	*(Species uncertain)*
Hamaguri	Common shield clam	*Meretrix meretrix*
Haze	A goby	*(Species uncertain)*
Mategai	Jackknife clam	*Solen gouldi*
Mogai	A species of arkshell	*Anadera subcrenata*
Shiofuki	A clam	*Mactra veneriformis*
Tairagi	Fanshell	*Atrina pectinata japonica*
Tako	Octopus	*(Three undetermined species)*

* Name varies with age and size; e.g., immature fish called *ine,* and fully mature fish, *bora.*

2. For numerous examples of variation and specialization within closely situated areas see K. Sakurada, *Gyonin* (Tokyo: Rokuninsha, 1942) and K. Yanagida (ed.,) *Kaison Seikatsu no Kenkyū* (Tokyo: Nihon Minzoku Gakkai, 1942). Both works are in Japanese.

There is a bewildering variety of names for fishing gear and species of marine flora and fauna, names which vary from one locality to another. Although there are extensive scholarly publications in Japanese giving local terms, it is often still difficult to determine Western scientific designations without the aid of a biologist. Names of fish may also vary with their stage of growth so that in some cases the same species of fish may have three or four different and unrelated names dependent upon its age and size.

The species of fish of greatest commercial importance to Takashima fishermen is mackerel, which, although taken for a period of only about five weeks beginning early in May, represents about 50% of the annual income from fishing. Butterfish, caught during July and August, represents another 10%. The remaining 40% is divided principally among mullet, black porgy, sea bass, rock cod, flounders, several species of small herring-like fishes, and crabs. Most of the fish are seasonal and leave the local fishing waters entirely or remain in only small numbers during the winter months. Since all fish are sold fresh, there is no problem of storage.

The annual fishing cycle starts slowly in March with the fishermen lowering their nets perhaps one or two days of the week until early May, when night fishing for mackerel begins. For the five-week period of the mackerel run fishermen ordinarily take no rest days unless they are forced to do so to repair damaged nets. To fall ill or become otherwise incapacitated during the mackerel season is a tragedy.

After the end of the mackerel season fishing continues on an average of three or four days a week until early October, reaching a minor peak of activity during the butterfish season in late summer, and dwindling to a stop in December as catches decrease in size and it becomes unprofitable to use the nets and boats. Mackerel and butterfish can be taken only at night with the nets and netting techniques used by Takashima fishermen. Although some other species may also be netted after dark, they are usually caught during the daylight hours. During the mackerel and butterfish seasons fishermen sleep uncomfortably during the heat of the day and snatch naps as they can on their boats at night during the waiting period after the nets have been laid until they are ready to be drawn in. Although every day possible is devoted to fishing during the mackerel season, it is impractical or impossible to continue fishing every day throughout the whole fishing season. Human bodies tire, and if nets are to be effective they must be repaired and treated from time to time with tannin solution to make them rot-resistant. The annual round of traditional holidays provides a welcome change from work, and additional rest days are taken as circumstances allow. There are lazy fishermen and industrious fishermen, but even the most industrious take days of rest.

PLATE 2.—*Beach scene at Mae, the larger settlement on Takashima.*

PLATE 3.—*Mending nets, summer.*

Fishing techniques may be classified into three types: netting, hook and line fishing, and pot or jar fishing. Of these techniques, netting predominates almost to the exclusion of other techniques. Hook and line fishing *(ippontsuri)* is done habitually and professionally by only a few impoverished fishermen who do not own suitable boats or equipment for the more profitable net fishing. Net fishermen and old men occasionally use the hook and line method, but the catches are for household consumption. Pot or jar fishing is limited to a few households during the brief run of a type of goby in May and to the catching of octopus through the summer months. Goby and octopus are caught in such small quantities that they are seldom offered for sale.

TABLE 2

Fishing Chart

COMMERCIAL FISHING

Fishing Technique	No. of Nets in Buraku	Chief Species Taken	Principal Season
Nagashi-ami	6	Butterfish	Aug.-Sept.
"	14	Mackerel	May
Karisashi-ami	11	A herring	Apr.-Nov.
"	9	Sea bass	Oct.-Dec.
"	2	A herring	Oct.-Dec.
Tate-ami, one-fold mesh	6	Crabs	Sept.-Oct.
" , three-fold mesh	13	Various small fishes, squid	Apr.-Dec.
Tsubo-ami	3	Various small fishes	Apr.-Dec.

NON-COMMERCIAL FISHING

Fishing Technique	Chief Species Taken	Principal Season
Ippontsuri (hand-line)	Mullet, black porgy	Apr.-Dec.
Haze-game (goby pot)	Goby	May
Tako-tsubo (octopus pot)	Octopus	July-Oct.
Kai-tori (clam digging)	Several species of clams	Throughout year

Nagashi-ami: A submerged, drifting gill net. Length may go up to 2,000 feet, depth about 20 feet. Butterfish and mackerel nets differ principally in size of mesh.

Karisashi-ami: Floating gill net. Three types, varying in size of mesh and overall dimensions. Length is from 1,000 to 1,500 feet, depth from about 12 to 30 feet. Surface of the water is ordinarily beaten with bamboo poles and bottoms of boats beaten with sticks to frighten fish into these nets.

Tate-ami: Stationary gill net. Vary in length in accordance with the number of sections used, commonly about 1,000 to 1,200 feet. Depth of nets is about six feet. Three-fold nets have three plies of mesh placed together, attached to each other only at upper and lower borders, so that all three sets of mesh billow freely in water. Outer two plies are coarse and inner ply is fine mesh.

Tsubo-ami: Set or trap net. Fish are guided by long projecting sections of mesh into roughly circular central portion of net, from which they enter one of several cylindrical pockets *(tsubo)* and are there entrapped. Pockets only are lifted to remove catch.

There is a large variety of sizes and types of construction of nets and of methods of use. Nets may, however, be divided into two types, gill nets and set nets. Set nets, permanently fixed in place and designed to entrap fish, are only three in number for the whole *buraku* and all are owned and operated by one household. Gill nets, designed to capture fish and other marine fauna by entangling them in the meshes, are the device in general use, and the livelihood of most of the residents of Takashima depends upon the successful operation of these nets. There are three general types of gill nets in use, which may be further classified into several sub-types differing in size of mesh, number of folds, pattern of construction, and technique of use (see Table 2).

Although nets are made on Takashima, no single type or sub-type of net is of Takashima origin. All nets used in commercial fishing were introduced from surrounding areas within the memory of presently living persons, with the first of these commercial nets coming in about seventy years ago and the latest a post-war innovation. The local source of introduction is well known but the ultimate provenience may be very distant areas. Mesh sections for some of the fine-mesh nets are machine-made of silk cord and must be purchased. With rare exception, all other meshes are woven on Takashima. Final assembly of nets, the attaching of weights and floats, is always a home process.

Materials required in the manufacture of nets are cotton and ramie cordage for the meshes, twine and rope of hemp or palm fiber, paulownia wood for floats, and net weights of terra cotta. Silk cord is also required for the repair of damaged silk meshes, but most nets are made of cotton or ramie. There are a few paulownia trees on the island, all privately owned and in number far from adequate to meet the demand. A little palm fiber cordage, which is durable and resistant to rot in sea water, is also made from locally grown *shuro* palm *(Trachycarpus excelsus)*. Except for limited quantities of these two home-produced items, however, all raw materials for nets must be purchased, usually through the local fishing cooperative. Net floats are made in the home from raw paulownia wood. In addition, netting accessories such as waterproof casks of wood and bamboo for net buoys, kerosene lanterns, gaffs, dip nets, rubber aprons, and net anchors must be purchased.

The manufacture and repair of nets continues throughout the year, repair as required and the manufacture of new nets principally during the slack season and on days unsuitable for fishing for one reason or another. In winter, when there are few fish and the sea is considered too rough for the small fishing boats, there is little for men to do but repair and manufacture nets. Net work is, however, not confined to males. Women and adolescent children of both sexes also aid.

Equipment required in net making is simple and inexpensive, consisting of a home-made revolving spool, several sizes of bamboo netting needles, an awl-like implement for securing one edge of the net so that it may be drawn taut during the weaving operation, and short-bladed knives for cutting cords. Small blocks of wood are used for measuring the size of meshes. Bare toes are also extremely useful devices, and in the repair of nets are much utilized in place of the awl-like *kiri* to hold sections of mesh taut. Only one type of knot is used for the weaving of all nets, with two additional knots to attach floats and weights. While weaving, progress is measured by counting the number of mesh knots tied. Ten thousand knots in one day is said not to be uncommon. To be a fast and efficient net weaver is an accomplishment which entitles one to modest prestige.

During the life span of a fisherman more time is devoted to the care and manufacture of nets than to any other task including actual fishing operations, for not only are the manufacture and repair of nets time-consuming, but there is also the vital need to clean, dry and treat the nets with preservative solution. The better the care given to nets, the longer they last, of course, and even the laziest fishermen treat nets which are in use at intervals of at least once every two weeks. The tannin preservative (*kachi*) used in treating nets is purchased in solid form and made into a dark brown solution by mixing with fresh water. The solution is brought to a boil in the communal steel vats located near the community hall and is then transferred to large flat-bottomed wooden vats. Nets, after they have been freed of seaweed and dried, are dipped into the solution, emerging dark brown in color. They are then hung up to dry on long racks of bamboo poles on the shore. New nets must also be treated before being put to use, and silk nets require special handling and treatment directly in the boiling solution in the steel vats. Crab nets are allowed to retain the natural white color of the cotton cord used in their weaving, as nets darkened by preservative catch few crabs. Untreated nets rot quickly, however, and crab nets must usually be replaced annually whereas other nets last an average of three years.

The making and care of nets is something of a social enterprise. Members of a household work together when they can, and neighbors will sometimes cooperate. Because net work is monotonous, the presence of other persons and conversation make it seem less a task.

In many of the fishing communities of Japan the average fisherman owns no nets but works for an *ami-moto*, a rich net owner, and receives in payment for his work a share of the catch. Communally owned nets and equipment are also common, especially for types of fishing which require the united effort of many men. There are no *ami-moto* on Takashima and no communal nets. All nets are owned by the households which use them, but there is considerable inequality in ownership. The poorest fisherman owns only one net, a small *tate-ami* (see Table 2), suitable for catching only small and relatively non-profitable species of fish. The richest man owns nets of every kind in use on the island, but he is, nevertheless, no *ami-moto*. Nets are operated by members of individual households, with rare aid from outsiders. Exception is made during the mackerel season when a few households employ outside help, often related persons, by the day. The employment of such outside help is avoided as much as possible. Wages, 300 yen[3] per day plus keep in 1950, are considered high, and the outlay of cash is always begrudged.

Like the nets, Takashima fishing craft are all individually owned and individually operated—by household. A minor exception is the operation of a few *tate-ami* in which two boats are required, when the net owner usually relies upon the aid of members of a related household if there are insufficient boats or fishermen in his own household. In such cases, the catches may be shared.

In addition to the small unmotored craft owned by each household and used for commutation to the mainland, there are 29 fishing boats owned by the 26 fishing households, all except five of which are motored. The average motored craft, made principally of cryptomeria wood, is about thirty feet in length and six feet in greatest width. Within the boats are wells for transporting live fish, a hatch for storage of clothing, bedding, and food, and a recessed area in which a *konro*, a type of charcoal brazier for cooking, is placed.

Motors are ordinarily used only to proceed to and return from fishing grounds. For short movements and during the lowering and raising of nets, boats are propelled by sculling from the stern or side with the heavy, two-piece Japanese oar. All Takashima fishing craft are purchased, usually ordered from ship carpenters in Shionasu. The first motored fishing craft on Takashima was purchased in 1924; by 1926 almost every fishing household in the *buraku* either possessed a new motored craft or had motors installed in boats formerly propelled by sail. Early engines were intended for general farm use, and the first motors built especially for fishing boats were introduced in 1930. Most motors are six horsepower and have an average life of ten years. Sails are no longer used on even the non-motored craft, which are sculled and used only in nearby waters. Battery lights for night fishing replaced gas lamps shortly after the end of World War II. Old craft still in use have long, slim and projecting prows, but those constructed within the last ten years lack this now purely ornamental feature, long traditional to Japanese fishing boats. The fishing

3. Official rate of exchange in 1950-51 was 360 yen to the dollar.

boat of present-day Takashima is, in short, motor-powered, battery-lighted, and functional in shape and design.

Until recent years considerable ceremony was connected with the construction and launching of a fishing boat. Carpenters offered prayers before beginning work that all go well during the construction, and also prayed for the welfare of the people who might use the boat after its completion. When a boat was completed and ready to be launched, a boat-launching ceremony *(shinsui-shiki)* was conducted. After the carpenter or carpenters had again offered prayers, the owner of the boat and members of his household then stood inside the boat on the beach at the edge of the water and threw rice cakes *(mochi)*, specially prepared for the occasion, to friends and relatives gathered about the boat. Male members, in order of seniority, first threw large *mochi,* and were followed by females and children of the household, who flung smaller cakes. As an offering to the gods of the sea, metal coins wrapped in paper were tossed onto the sand at the same time, where they were allowed to disappear through action of the waves and the tide. After the ceremony, a feast for the carpenters and for relatives followed at the dwelling of the household which owned the boat.

Partly for lack of the foodstuffs required for the ceremony, no *shinsui-shiki* has been held since the early part of World War II. Both food and money are now available in quantity sufficient to prepare the cakes and give the feast associated with the ceremony, but the practice, in a state of gradual decline before the war, appears to have permanently died. The expense is now considered unworthy of the occasion, and all that now remains of this old custom are (usually) the preliminary prayers by the carpenters.

Like the nets, boats require a good deal of care. They must be scrubbed down carefully after every fishing operation so that the succeeding catch of fish may remain fresh and saleable. The noisy engines require frequent tinkering to keep them in operation, and barnacles and sea worms cause further work. The bottom of all fishing craft must be treated every few weeks when in use to avoid serious damage by these pests. Boats are beached on the sand at high tide, and as the water recedes leaving the boats stranded, small straw fires are built beneath them. The heat and smoke cause barnacles to drop off and kill the marine worms. Coal tar *(kōru taru)* is sometimes used as a preventive, but rice straw is either free or very cheap and coal tar costs money.

The treatment of boats with fire is called *funatade.* It is said that during *funatade* the Funadama-sama, the god of the boat (see Chap. V, Gods and Beliefs of the Sea), steps out of the craft and waits nearby. When the treatment is completed, it is customary to tap the boat twice on each side with a stick or pole to notify the Funadama-sama to return. This custom is common throughout Japan, with some variation in detail and regional variations in name.[4] In some areas, the rudder is removed and placed with one edge resting on the sand in such a manner that it forms a gang-plank for the convenience of the Funadama-sama in disembarking, and boats are tapped both before and after firing. All Takashima fishermen, including those who express disbelief in the Funadama-sama, tap the sides of their boats when the fire has died out.

Becoming an experienced fisherman is not a quick process. Centuries of lore of the sea, the weather, and the habits of fish must be assimilated. Sculling the boats and handling the nets require experienced coordination which is gained only from long experience at sea. Takashima fishermen estimate that it takes a boy of eighteen about four years before he can scull a boat and handle nets during fishing without supervision or aid. For most young men, learning is a gradual process beginning in late childhood when they are given simple tasks. From instruction and observation they gradually assimilate knowledge of the location and habits of fish. Even a boy who begins helping with nets and going out in the boats in his early teens (full-time fishing generally begins between the ages of 16 and 18) is usually not considered a full-fledged fisherman until he is 19 or 20.

Fishing waters, which vary with the season, are defined by prefectural law, and for the most part conform with traditional assignments of fishing waters which have come down from the centuries. There are fairly elaborate regulations covering fishing operations, which are also largely a heritage from the past. Permission must be secured from the Marine Products Department of the prefectural government to operate certain kinds of nets and fishing equipment. In such cases, it is necessary to transmit through the fishing *kumiai* application to the prefectural office for five-year permits, which usually go through in routine fashion upon the payment of a small fee. Permits for fishing in the waters of neighboring prefectures may also be secured in the same manner by applying to the prefecture in question. Prefectural boundary lines in the Inland Sea are irregular so that in some instances nearby islands are in foreign waters and distant points are within one's own prefecture. Poaching is practiced to some extent but does not reach large proportions. Robbery of returning fishing boats at sea occasionally occurs, and this is treated as a serious crime. Such offenses are reported to local police and to officers of the *Kaijō Hōanchō*, the marine patrol organization, and the culprits are usually soon taken into custody. Fishermen themselves sometimes bring in rob-

4. See Kagawa-ken Minzoku Chōsakai, *Takami, Sanagi-shima Minzoku Chōsa Hōkoku* (Takamatsu: Kagawa-ken Kyōiku Iinkai, 1950) (in Japanese), and K. Sakurada, *op. cit.*

PLATE 4.—*Motored fishing boat.*

PLATE 5.—*Hauling in a net, man and wife.*

bers or habitual poachers by force, and turn them over to police officers.

Securing permission to operate the various types of nets in use on Takashima, as stated, is not usually a difficult problem, but to use these nets effectively a fisherman must have a motored craft. Securing a permit for a new boat is an extremely difficult and time-consuming process unless the applicant is simply replacing an old boat with a new one. All fishing boats must be registered and licensed, and there is a fixed quota for the Inland Sea allocated by prefecture. Prefectural quotas are almost constantly full so that it is necessary to wait until one of the presently registered craft is for one reason or another withdrawn from registry before a new or additional craft may be licensed. Transfer of registry from one person to another within a household, such as upon the death or retirement of the male head, is, however, routine. A new fisherman, or a fisherman who wishes to purchase additional boats, must have influence behind him, as there is considerable concern in official circles about the future of fishing in the Inland Sea, where the supply of fish is endangered by over-fishing.

For the efficient operation of most types of nets used in the *buraku*, a crew of three is required, two of whom handle the nets while the third person sculls the boat. Some types of nets can be managed by two fully skilled fishermen, and husband and wife combinations are not uncommon. On a typical butterfish netting trip the crew, after sleeping and resting during the day, eats a hearty meal about five o'clock in the evening and is ready to leave for the fishing grounds by five-thirty. A noisy ride of two hours takes the boat to the fishing grounds for this species of fish, an area approximately twelve miles from Takashima, just as the sun is setting. The engine of the boat is stopped, and one man begins sculling the craft from the stern while the other two handle the nets. A waterproof wooden keg to the top of which a kerosene lamp has been fastened is first attached to the end of the net by a rope and dropped overboard to serve as end marker. To lower the long series of net sections into the sea it is necessary that two men work together. One man grasps the wooden floats and rope on the upper edge of the net and gradually pays them over the side. The second man at the same time seizes the mesh at the bottom of the net with one hand and the weights with the other. He throws the weights with an outward motion, so that the net will not foul on the side of the boat, and releases the mesh simultaneously. It is vital that all crew members be in coordination. Inexpert sculling will foul the net on itself or lay it in an irregular and thus not fully effective pattern.

A second buoy and lantern are attached to the middle of the net, and, after the netting has all been paid out in a straight line, a third buoy and lantern are attached to the end. The end of the net is then secured to the boat by a rope, and the operation of net laying, which requires about thirty minutes, is completed. Since it is usually dark by the time the net has been laid, illumination is by means of battery-powered lights.

Both net and boat now drift with the current for several hours, usually until after the change of the tide. During fishing season the Inland Sea is full of craft, fishing boats of many kinds, freighters, and the occasional passenger ship, so that it is necessary to maintain watch to prevent collision or damage to nets. Watch is usually alternated; two men rest, talk, or sleep while one serves as lookout. For reasons of economy, the battery light is usually extinguished during the waiting period. Pilots of Inland Sea craft are thoroughly familiar with the bobbing kerosene lanterns, which ordinarily serve as adequate warning of the presence of fishing boats and nets.

The surface of the sea is seldom rough during butterfish season, and the boat bobs gently as it floats with the current. On the land it is hot summer, but out here on the surface of the sea there are cooling breezes, cool enough so that light cotton shirts or jackets are necessary. Lights of dwellings on nearby islands, of the buoys of neighboring fishermen, and of the many passing watercraft twinkle on all sides. It is comfortable, peaceful, and beautiful, but to most fishermen it is dull and routine, with nothing to break the monotony. Occasionally a fire is started in the recessed earthenware brazier to prepare tea, and a light snack may be eaten, but ordinarily little or no food is consumed during the night.

When the tide has changed, perhaps four hours later, the net is ready to be lifted, and the battery lights are again turned on. While one man sculls the boat from the rear the other two pull in the net, grasping it by the rope borders at each edge and folding it into the bottom of the boat in concertina fashion. Rubber or home-woven straw aprons are worn by the net handlers to prevent getting excessively wet from the dripping net. Fish are few and far between. They are disentangled by the net handler closest to them as they are encountered and thrown onto a low shelf out of the way of the nets. Since the butterfish net is a gill net, most of the fish have drowned and are already dead at the time the net is lifted, so that there is little delay or inconvenience from flopping fish. The few live fish which come in are stunned or killed by striking their heads against the gunwale of the boat. When the net has been completely lifted, an operation which usually takes about one hour, the fish are placed in covered holds (filled with water and used as live wells for certain other types of fish and for crabs). The net is now ready to be lowered again. Catches are small, the total for one netting operation averaging about thirty butterfish of approximately two-pound weight each, perhaps a stingray or a crab or two, and a few smaller fish of miscellaneous species.

Unless the catch from the first netting has been exceptionally good, it is customary to move to another area. The net is again lowered into the sea and raised at dawn. When the catch has been stored in the fish hold, the fishermen return to Takashima, for no butterfish can be caught during the daylight hours with these nets. Upon return to Takashima at about seven o'clock in the morning, the nets are cleared of seaweed and debris and hung up to dry. The catch is sold at this time, either to waiting independent buyers who charge no commission or to the fishing *kumiai* at Shionasu which charges a commission of 6% of the total value of the catch (see Chap. IV, The *Buraku* and the City).

The total catch averages about ninety pounds of butterfish (morning catches are usually smaller than those of the first netting of the night). In the summer of 1950 butterfish brought a revenue to the fisherman of 500 yen ($1.39) per unit of 8.27 pounds (one *kan*), a total in cash for an average catch of about $15.00. The cost of gasoline and oil for the night's operation is thirty or forty cents. A fishing boat costs about $150.00, the engine about $300.00, and both last approximately ten years. The butterfish net, which must be replaced every three years, costs about $140.00 for the materials required in its manufacture. Salvage of weights, buoys and rope is usually possible, however, which brings the cost down somewhat. A gross of $15.00 for one day is considered good. Butterfish netting is, however, more lucrative than many other kinds of fishing, even though this species of fish is sometimes elusive and empty nets are not uncommon.

Types of netting engaged in during daylight hours usually produce smaller catches. On a good night during mackerel season the catch may run as high as 10,000 yen ($27.80), but other types of fishing generally bring much smaller returns. A full day of netting smaller herring-type fishes may yield a catch of only twenty-five pounds or less, and a gross return of two or three dollars. When catches dwindle to this size, fishing is unprofitable, as operating expenses exceed the revenue.

During the major part of the fishing year netting is done in nearby waters for various fish smaller in size than mackerel or butterfish. Fishermen may, however, go to grounds ten or more miles distant for daylight or night fishing and stay for two or three days, selling their catches at the closest markets en route. Except during mackerel season it is unprofitable to use nets for more than three or four days of continuous operation without repairs, cleaning, and sun-drying. On long trips, stores of food are brought along, and rice and hot fish and onion stews are prepared on the boats. Some types of netting require far greater exertion of physical effort than others. Nets for herring-type fishes are light, but they must be lowered and raised frequently, and the fish must be frightened into the nets by beating the surface of the water with long bamboo poles and drumming on the bottom of the boat with wooden sticks. The sun is hot and enervating.

Hand-line (hook and line) fishing, the occupation of only those fishermen without equipment for netting, yields little profit. Catches are small and expenses high. This type of fishing requires, in quantity, both patience and expensively purchased bait. Boats are anchored at spots known to be frequented by mullet and black porgy, the only fish taken commercially by hand-line. For porgy the surrounding area must be sprinkled liberally with balls of a compound made of imported clay and decomposed, foul-smelling silkworm cocoons, also imported. A compound of the same clay mixed with rice bran is used for mullet. Two lines, one for mullet and one for porgy, are usually operated at the same time. The procedure is simple still-fishing with shrimp, caught by the fisherman himself in the shallow water at low tide, as bait for porgy and balls of the clay-rice bran mixture for mullet. The hand-line fisherman who in one day catches thirty fish totalling twenty pounds in weight considers himself fortunate. Cash returns are at best low, as the cost of the bait consumes nearly half the proceeds from the sale of the fish.

A fish is a precious thing. It is good to eat and nutritious. It makes a fine and always acceptable gift, and it can be sold for money. But it is a hard thing to catch. Commercially saleable fish are seldom taken home for food unless no damaged fish or fish of low selling price happen to have been caught. The household may instead eat clams, which have a very low selling price and may be dug at no expense. Saleable fish are as good as money and less desirable fish are quite as filling and nutritious although they may be a little wanting in flavor. The cash realized from the sale of butterfish, for example, will buy many things, whereas the few mixed small fish taken in the same net have little or no market value.

Non-commercial fishing, although it yields no money, is of great importance, especially the digging of clams. Several species of clams may be dug in the sand and sand-gravel beaches of Takashima during low tide. Some species are seasonal, but one or more species may be dug at any season of the year. Although seldom relished, clams are consumed more frequently and in greater quantity than any other animal protein. A few households which do no fishing rely almost entirely upon clams for animal protein, and most households rely heavily upon them during the winter months when there is no fishing. Octopi are taken in small quantity for home consumption by means of terra cotta pots resembling flower vases. Thirty or more of these pots are attached to a long rope at evenly spaced intervals and lowered to the bottom of the sea. No bait is used. The octopi enter the darkness of the unbaited pots and do not attempt to escape when the pots are raised.

A goby is also taken during the month of May by means of a twin-mouthed jar or pot operated in the same fashion as the octopus pot. Small

PLATE 6.—*Hand-line fishing, the occupation of poor fishermen.*

PLATE 7.—*Gathering pine needles and twigs for firewood.*

balloon fish are often caught during the summer months by hook and line, carefully cleaned to remove their poison sacs, and suspended from stringers to dry in the sun before being cooked and eaten. Octopi and balloon fish drying in the sun on stringers attached to long bamboo poles stuck in the crevices of the breakwater-pier or in the sand are a standard part of the summer scene. When clams are available in large quantity they are occasionally cooked, removed from the shell, and dried in the sun for later consumption.

FARMING

Fish are precious and not easily come by, but cultivable land is even more precious and almost impossible to acquire except by inheritance. Arable land is security: it produces food through good times and bad times. Without a plot of land a fishing household is in dire straits as a large share of all food consumed ordinarily comes directly from the household plot. No one wishes to sell land of any kind, and all desire to buy.

Land for dwellings is begrudged, as they must be located in the sheltered lee of the island; to erect a new building in that area means the sacrifice of agricultural land. So difficult is it for a non-landowner to acquire even a plot large enough to build a house that it was necessary for one landless household head, one of several sons of a household grown too large for its dwelling, to utilize a beach refuse dump as house site. Beaches are national property, but with the erection of a retaining wall and filling with beach sand, the area became reclaimed land. Upon explanation and petition to the government, title to the plot was granted to the applicant and a dwelling built, almost into the sea and at high tide surrounded on three sides by water.

The total area of cultivated land on Takashima, all of it in dry farm plots *(hatake)*, is approximately thirteen acres. Until fifty or sixty years ago additional plots totalling perhaps five acres were under cultivation, all of them land of poor quality located on ridges or steep inclines where the soil is thin, poor and rocky, and drainage overly rapid. These were abandoned as economically unprofitable after Takashima became a fishing *buraku,* and are now heavily overgrown with pines. To prepare the land again for farming is impractical because of the work and expense involved in clearing these plots, which could at best produce only poor crops. The pine trees themselves are of greater economic value than non-productive *hatake* as their fallen branches, needles, and cones provide firewood which must otherwise be purchased, and the trunks provide material for building. Most areas of pine forest present a very tidy appearance as the ground is under a never-ending process of raking to gather firewood for fuel in cooking and heating. Stones mark the boundaries of individual household plots so that the housewife does not gather fuel from the floors of forest land which is the property of someone else.

Forest and brush lands total approximately sixteen acres, of which about half became part of the prefectural forest preserve about thirty-five years ago. Needles and cones are, by regulation, not to be removed from preserve land and, in fact, seldom are taken as private holdings are usually adequate to supply fuel. For the few households which own no forest there is a small communal plot about one-quarter acre in size. This communal plot is said to have originated in early Meiji times, when only landed persons had the right to vote. Official registry of the plot under the names of all household heads is said to have entitled them, whether landed in their own right or not, to the franchise.

Distribution of both forest and *hatake* among households is highly inequitable. The largest land holding is about two and one-half acres, whereas average holdings are less than one-half acre. Four households own no land but cultivate tiny plots owned by others. A number of households rent small patches of *hatake* to other, often related, households. Rental is done for a variety of reasons. In some cases, a small piece of land is troublesome for the owner household to work because of its location, far from home or well, so that the night-soil and water mixtures used for fertilizer must be transported a long distance. Sometimes the land holdings of one household are more than adequate to fill needs whereas the holdings of others are inadequate. Rental is sometimes done out of a spirit of friendliness and kindness to aid those who are lacking in planting space. Rentals are occasionally free and never involve cash payment. As a rule, they are based upon payment of a share of the produce. The ratio of payment varies from one *to* (approximately one-fourth bushel) of barley for one *se* (approximately 1/40th of an acre) of land of good quality down to less than half this quantity for a *se* of poor land. The rental fee is usually in barley only, although the rented land is farmed the year around and other crops also raised. Arrangements on rental are seldom made for short periods. Agreements are verbal and may extend over periods of many years.

For lack of adequate water, no rice is grown on Takashima, but six households own tiny paddy plots, averaging one-fourth acre in size, in Shionasu, to which household members commute as required for cultivation. These plots are cultivated for rice only during spring, summer and fall, and are rented on a verbal share-cropping basis to Shionasu farmers during the winter months for the raising of barley or rape.

Hatake land is divided into extremely small plots, partly because of the nature of the terrain and partly because of repeated division through inheritance. Most of the agricultural land lies on slopes, and a large proportion of it is terraced. The holdings of the average land-owner are composed of a number of small plots, often widely separated and thus necessitating long walks transporting heavy tools, fertilizer, and produce. Equitable exchange of plots to bring about centralization of holdings is never considered. The soil is light and sandy, and easily turned with hand tools. Soil fertility varies greatly with location. Yields from the most productive areas, usually low-lying, may triple yields from the poorest plots.

The land reform instituted by the American Occupation has had slight effect on Takashima. Under the regulations limiting the holdings of absentee landlords a small fraction of an acre of land, owned by former residents who had moved away, changed ownership. All land except one infinitesimal plot, which is owned and worked by a former resident who lives in a nearby community, is now owned by Takashima residents. Cultivation of the land owned by fishing households is done almost entirely by women. Only two adult males, the heads of farming households, are full-time farmers. A few men regularly, or when the exigencies of fishing will allow it, aid the women of their households with agricultural duties. Most men give aid during harvest time when the work is too heavy for women alone. During the sweet potato and barley harvest in October, which coincides with the rice harvest of the mainland, every able-bodied member of the household works in the fields, and the schools are closed so that children may help.

Farm plots, through sale of produce, contribute about 10% of the annual cash income of the average fishing household as well as providing a large part of household food. Vegetables and sweet potatoes are the chief cash crops. During 1950 chili peppers were raised for the first time on Takashima as a cash crop upon the recommendation of the prefectural agricultural department. The peppers, intended for export, had brought a high price the preceding year, but because of overplanting throughout the prefecture in 1950 prices sank far down, and the crop represented a loss to many farmers. Sales of produce are made either directly to buyers or through the medium of the agricultural *kumiai,* with headquarters in Shionasu, of which all land-owners with holdings of over five *se* (approximately 1/8th of an acre) are members.

Crops are raised throughout the whole year, and the soil, never allowed to go fallow, is seldom unplanted for more than a few days at a time. There are no official restrictions upon the types of crops which can be raised except tobacco, which is a government monopoly and requires a permit, and other narcotics. Crops differ little from those of the past several decades. The principal additions in recent years have been a few new vegetables, a new sweet potato, tomatoes, and American varieties of peas and onions. Sweet potatoes and barley, which alternate in the same fields by season, are the principal crops, and about 50% of the total acreage is devoted to them. Other grains planted in limited quantity are wheat, maize, and varieties of millet. Maize, when young and tender, is a favorite of children, and when mature it is used as chicken feed. It is never considered suitable food for adults. Three varieties of sugarcane or sorghum are also raised, principally as a confection for children, who chew peeled sections of the green stalks. The quantity raised is always small and the juice is seldom expressed for the manufacture of sugar or molasses. Vegetables include several varieties of onion, giant radish *(daikon)*, cucumbers, tomatoes, Irish potatoes, squashes, a small pumpkin, garlic, several varieties of beans and peas, eggplant, a dry-land taro, burdock, carrots, cabbage, Chinese cabbage, and spinach. Peanuts and strawberries are also occasionally grown in very small quantity. Many households raise small patches of sesame, the seed of which is used in the cooking of many dishes as a sort of condiment. Sesame seed oil is one of the most common cooking fats in Japan, but plantings of sesame on Takashima are so small that use is seldom made of the seed for expressing oil.

TABLE 3

Major Crops Raised in 1949

	AREA[1]			
Crop	*Chō*	*Tan*	*Se*	*Bu*
Barley	3	1	6	12
Sweet potatoes[2]	3	1	2	9
Giant radish *(daikon)*[3]	1	..	..	..
Peas	..	7	7	..
Millet	..	2	..	..
Beans	..	1	7	24
Onions	..	1	..	21
Potatoes	..	1	..	6
Wheat	..	..	8	9
Spinach	..	..	7	..
Cucumber	..	..	2	27
Cabbage	..	..	2	9
Squash	..	..	1	24
Garlic	..	..	..	12
Miscellaneous, including carrots, burdock, taro, maize, Chinese cabbage, and sugarcane	1	5	..	..
Total (see note [1])	10	3	7	3

(Approximately 25½ acres, including double-cropping)

Note: The above figures are based upon records maintained by a *buraku* official as required by government regulation during the war years and through 1949. Figures are only approximate. No record of crops except barley, wheat and sweet potatoes were kept after 1949.

[1] 30 *bu*–1 *se*; 10 *se*–1 *tan*; 10 *tan*–1 *chō*; 1 *chō*–2.45 acres.

[2] Double-cropped, for the most part, as an alternate with barley.

[3] Double-cropped with other vegetables. Smaller scale double-cropping of other plants is also practiced.

Government requisitions of barley, wheat, and sweet potatoes began during World War II, and were felt by *buraku* people to be extremely onerous. Under the regulations covering the requisitioning, householders were allowed to keep a formula percentage based upon acreage, estimated yields, and the number and age of household members. The balance was purchased by the national government at fixed prices. The requisitioning of sweet potatoes ceased in 1950, much to the relief of Takashima residents, but the requisitioning of barley and wheat continued. Requisitioning is disliked because government-fixed prices are low and because it is felt that the quantities left in the hands of raisers for household use are skimpy. Requisitioning also entails the irksome task of keeping fairly accurate records of areas planted and yields.

There is no season of the year free from agricultural tasks, and few months in the year when some crop is not planted. The heavy and dreaded seasons are November, when the sweet potatoes are harvested and barley planted, and May, when the barley is harvested and sweet potatoes set in. Of the two, the barley harvest is considered the more unpleasant because of the heavy work and the dust and chaff.

Agricultural implements are all of a hand type. Beyond simple traditional machines, there is no mechanization for Takashima agriculture. Motor-driven machines of various sorts are used to some extent in the surrounding rice-growing areas, but farming on Takashima is on such small scale that the expense is not thought to warrant the gain. Turning, working, and levelling of the soil is done by means of the *taguwa*, a three- or four-tined spading fork used in the manner of a hoe. The soil is light and sandy and can be easily worked. Steel hoes of various sizes, sickles, and *taguwa* comprise the principal implements used in plowing, cultivating, and gathering crops. Western style shovels and the *joren*, a scoop-like implement, are used to move large quantities of soil, such as in digging storage pits for sweet potatoes, but are seldom used in the *hatake*.

Baskets of rice straw, made in the home, are used to carry field produce. Home-made cordage of rice straw is attached to the upper edges of the loosely woven baskets, and, if the load is great, two such baskets are suspended from a carrying pole placed over one shoulder. Wheelbarrows with sinuous backs called *nekoguruma*, "cat carts," are used where the terrain will allow, but many sections of *hatake* are too steep or the trails leading to them unsuited for the wheelbarrows.

Techniques of agriculture vary little from household to household. Chief differences are in degree of thoroughness of ground preparation and of cultivation during the growing period. In sweet potato culture, a steel device *(kaibakiri)* on the principle of a paper cutter, commonly used in other sections of Japan for cutting up straw for cattle feed, is used by

PLATE 8.—*After sweet-potato harvest, cutting up the vines —*
mother and daughter.

PLATE 9.—*Digging clams.*

some Takashima farmers to chop up old sweet potato vines. The vines are then spread over the soil or plowed under. Other persons simply turn the vines under the soil in furrows without cutting them up several days before the planting of barley. Seeds for sowing are commonly carried in the fields in square wooden boxes ordinarily used for measuring rice. For some types of planting the soil and planted seeds are watered with a sprinkling can. With the exception of the water in the night-soil mixtures used as fertilizer and the sprinkling of newly-planted vegetable seeds, no irrigation is practiced.

Night-soil is by far the most important of the fertilizers, and is the only fertilizer ordinarily applied in quantity. Night-soil is dipped with long-handled wooden ladles from the toilet receptacles into wooden buckets, where it is mixed with waste bath and kitchen water, and carried off for aging to the fields by means of carrying poles. The mixture is there dumped into earthenware vats sunken in the ground at the edges of farm plots. Bath houses and toilets usually adjoin, and the toilet receptacle serves also to catch drain water from the bath. The supply of water is adequate but not abundant so that none is wasted. In any event, waste bath water must be disposed of before drainage receptacles overflow and the waste water seeps into the wells.

The usual mixture is said to be about 40% night-soil and the balance water. It is considered the best practice to allow the mixture to remain in the field receptacles for a week before applying it to the *hatake*. If left for a week, there is relatively little odor. In actual practice, however, there is much variation in the period of aging, and raw and extremely malodorous mixtures are frequently applied to the fields because it is convenient in the working schedule. The mixture is ladled into furrows in the fields, and since it is felt that there is always a shortage, it may be further diluted with water so that all planted areas may be covered. There are no definite rules of application. Night-soil is used as available with little or no change in practices of utilization because of the agricultural season, and, since the amount available is always insufficient, there is no fear of over-application. When it becomes difficult to apply the mixture to crops such as barley which have grown tall and dense, the practice is stopped and the fertilizer used more heavily on other crops.

Other fertilizers of home provenience are small quantities of chicken and rabbit manure. Barnacles removed from ropes or marine gear may occasionally be pulverized and sprinkled on fields, and the few households which raise rice in Shionasu may apply *sukomohai,* rice hulls charred by a slow fire. A type of seaweed cast up on the shores in great abundance is used by all as fertilizer for sweet potatoes, but is used for no other crops. This seaweed is eagerly sought after by island farmers of Hiroshima

Prefecture, many of whom come in boats twenty or more miles to gather loads from the sea surrounding Takashima. Joint *buraku* sales, with the proceeds held as *buraku* funds, are occasionally made to outsiders of seaweed washed up on the shores. The plant, however, is not held in great esteem on Takashima. Composting, standard practice in the nearby rice-growing communities, is not done on Takashima for lack of composting materials.

Commercial fertilizers of various types, rationed during the war and until late 1950, are known and esteemed but are too costly for extensive use. Most households use limited amounts of sulphate of ammonia, and some use is made of nitrogenous lime. Households with large land holdings, and thus insufficient night-soil, make greater use of commercial fertilizers. Sulphate of ammonia is regarded as the most effective.

Insecticides are seldom used although damage from insects, particularly to *daikon,* Chinese cabbage and beans, is fairly extensive. Insects may be picked off by hand. A Japanese-made DDT preparation, new since the end of the war, has been utilized by a few households on *daikon* and Chinese cabbage, but it is considered too expensive. Before the advent of this DDT compound no insecticides were used, and no one considers past or present damage by insects to growing crops as serious.

When grain begins to head, scarecrow devices of several types are utilized. Strips of cloth tied to poles or attached to long ropes and suspended over the tops of plots of grain so that they flutter in the breeze are common. The paper carp flown on Boys' Day (see Chap. V, The Ceremonial Calendar) also sees frequent use to frighten hungry birds. Fine-meshed fishing nets are placed over plots containing heading stalks of barley and other grains.

Reaping is done with small hand sickles. A simple comb-like implement with steel teeth is utilized to remove grain from heads by pulling the heads between the projecting teeth. Long-handled flails with revolving steel heads are also used. Straw winnowing baskets and sieves with wire mesh of various sizes are found in every household. The most common threshing machine is the ancient *tōmi,* a paddle-wheel device operated by a hand-crank. Grains of the small quantities of sesame and millet raised are customarily separated from the heads after sun-curing by rubbing with the hands or by beating the stalks by hand into a container.

A few households own hand mills, and most households have a *kara-usu,* a foot-operated mortar and pestle for milling rice and other grains, but they are now seldom used. It is much simpler to take the grain to one of the home refineries in Shionasu, which take as a fee only the inedible hulls. The hulls are later sold by the refinery to persons who wish to use them as packing to prevent decay in the storage of sweet potatoes, as filler for pillows, or for the making of mullet bait. The few households which raise rice in Shionasu have additional equipment, all of it hand-operated. Most machines are old, having been in use for decades. A few households still own and use rotary stone mills operated by a push-and-pull hand lever and also upright sieving devices with wooden hoppers and slanting metal screening. These are said to have been replaced in surrounding agricultural communities by more efficient machines, and their manufacture is reported to have stopped.

Green vegetables are gathered from the fields as required for household use. *Daikon* is preserved in whole, sliced, and shredded form by drying, and is also pickled in rice vinegar. An edible gourd is sliced in the manner that an apple is peeled into thin six- to twelve-foot strips about one-half inch in breadth, which are thoroughly dried in the sun. The strips are then cut into short pieces, two or three of the pieces tied together in a simple knot, and the whole stored in this form for future use. Beans and peas are dried in the sun on straw mats for a few days and stored in containers of various sorts. Householders are frequently plagued with worm infestation of both beans and peas. The remedy is to place the beans or peas in the sun again for a few days and the worms die or disappear, only to reappear some time later. Onions are hung in bunches from eaves to cure, and are used as required. Sweet potatoes are briefly cured in the air and stored in earthen pots lined with rice hulls and rice straw, where they rarely spoil but are sometimes gnawed by rats and mice. Pits are often permanent and are usually located in the earthen floor of the entrance room of the dwelling or in an outbuilding. To prevent rodent damage concrete and stone storage pits have been constructed in recent years, but spoilage in these pits is thought to be greater.

The cultivation of fruit trees is haphazard and very limited in scale. Most households have a fig tree or two growing in the yard or near the house, and there are a number of citrus trees of several varieties scattered about the *buraku*. A few peach, plum, loquat, and persimmon trees and the rare pomegranate bush complete the list of fruit. No fruit is raised for sale, and little attention is given to its cultivation. Fruit is a luxury little indulged in as the trees require ground space better utilized for higher-yielding garden crops.

Shuro palm, from the fibers of which rot-resistant cordage can be made, is occasionally planted, as are paulownia trees, valuable as fishing floats for their light wood which is impervious to water for long periods. Pines seed themselves. A bamboo grove once grew densely in the vicinity of Mae, the principal settlement, but as the housing area expanded the thicket dwindled in size to a very small patch at present. No attempt at cultivation of this bamboo is made or necessary.

PLATE 10.—*Terraced fields, September.*

PLATE 11.—*Carrying night-soil to the fields; one of the
two full-time male farmers.*

Other agriculture is limited to the occasional raising of *hechima (Luffa petola)*, a type of spongy gourd, the fibrous inner core of which is used as a scrub brush, and the semi-cultivation of *dokkeshimame,* a leguminous medicinal plant. Shrubs used in connection with religious ceremonial are planted in yards or near houses but, once planted, receive little or no cultivation. *Shikibi* (Chinese star anise, *Illicium religiosum*) is used in Buddhist ritual, and *naruten* or *nanten (Nandia domesticus Thumbergia)* as an offering to Shinto deities. *Sakaki (Cleyera japonica),* also known as *sasaki,* may be used in either Buddhist or Shinto ritual. A shrub called *babe* is used only once a year to build a fire for the roasting of beans at the end of winter (see Chap. V, The Ceremonial Calendar).

As in fishing, there is almost no cooperative effort in Takashima farming. Cultivation of *hatake* holdings is almost entirely restricted to the members of each household with occasional aid, and payment for such aid in produce, from a few married daughters who live in Shionasu. The average adult woman spends perhaps one-third of her working time throughout the year in agricultural tasks, either directly in the fields or in the preservation of produce. Infants are frequently carried on the back while working and nursed as required in the fields.

OTHER OCCUPATIONS

The operation of small freight boats occupies a position of third importance in livelihood, but is relatively unimportant as compared with fishing and farming. Two of the three households which own and operate freight boats turned to this occupation within the last decade. Freighting has been the occupation of the third household for approximately one hundred years. Freight boats are small, two of them of 30 ton and one of 40 ton capacity, and all are powered by 25 horsepower engines. Operation is limited to Inland Sea waters and the nearby Asahi River, which is navigable by small craft from its mouth to Okayama City, a distance of about ten miles.

A crew of three is required for operation of the boats, and crews are usually drawn entirely from the owning household. Two of the households are large, with married sons whose young wives accompany them as crew members, doing all of the cooking and aiding in the handling of the boats. Infant children are also taken on the boats, but are left at home in the care of female relatives when they are mature enough to walk for fear of injury or falling overboard. Older children remain on Takashima, where they are usually cared for by their grandmothers when their parents are away.

There are many freighters of the same type in adjacent communities which vie for the loads suitable for these small, slow craft. The poorest of the Takashima boats is in service only three or four months of the year, and the best boat sees fairly continual service. When at Takashima the boats, whose draft is too deep for the shallow water of the *buraku* break-water-pier, are anchored in deeper water to the protected lee of the island.

Ordinary care and maintenance tasks are usually performed while the boats are in operation or waiting for loads. Paint is a luxury which these blackened, dilapidated craft seldom are given. Little work is said to be necessary on the ships while they are at anchor at Takashima, and crew members may engage in fishing. Time must be taken to treat the bottoms of the boats once monthly during the warmer weather against invasion by marine worms. Treatment is the same as for fishing craft except that larger fires, of pine needles instead of straw, are built.

Trips are usually of short duration, averaging four or five days each, so that crew members participate in most *buraku* activities. Effort is made to be at home during the *buraku* festivals, at New Year's, and during *Bon,* the Buddhist Festival of the Dead. Freight most commonly hauled is table salt, commercial acids, and rock for building. Boats are registered and licensed through the prefectural government, but operation of the boats is through a freight boat *kumiai,* which serves as an agency for the rationed issuance of gasoline and also provides assignment and notification of loads to be hauled (see Chap. IV, The *Buraku* and the City). Young men of the *buraku* occasionally work as crew members on outside-owned freighters. A few men have made such work their professions and have moved to other communities. The livelihood gained by the households engaged in freighting is no better than that of *buraku* fishermen or farmers. One household is considered well-to-do, one average, and one poor.

There are few specialists on Takashima, and the *buraku* depends upon Shionasu for many special services. There are no full-time carpenters on the island, although three young men repair boats during free time from fishing. Barbering is done by a young man, crippled from birth and the member of a large household with many sons, as well as by his wife, as the primary means of support for themselves and their children. The barber also aids his household in fishing from time to time.

Kojima City owns a motored boat for transporting school children to and from Shionasu during the school year. A salary is paid to the head of one of the Takashima households as operator of this craft, but the salary received, although comprising a large part of the annual household income, is inadequate for full support and this man supplements his income by fishing.

A small home shop provides the total support for one household of five, the master of which was crippled in childhood by infantile paralysis.

Stocks of merchandise carried are small, confined principally to food-stuffs, confections, bottled soda water, and a few household implements. An aged man, formerly a fisherman but now retired, and his wife sell tobacco in their home.

A full-time specialist is an eighty-year-old woman from an impover-ished household, who has supported herself for ten or more years by weaving sandals and coarse baskets of rice straw for sale through mer-chants in Shionasu. A war widow weaves nets by piecework for other households as a part-time occupation, as do two other women of poor households. This work, done as a means of getting extra cash, is limited, and the pay, averaging 50 yen (about 14c) for a full day's work, is insuffi-cient to maintain life for even one person. When time is available and money is not, even starvation wages are better than none at all.

Three young unmarried girls are employed outside in nearby towns, two in a printing press and one as clerk in a garment factory, and com-mute daily by boat and bus. Garment manufacture is one of the major industries of the larger communities of Kojima Peninsula. There are a few fairly large factories and many small home sewing industries in which only a few machines are operated. Most young women of Takashima have in recent years received or are now receiving instruction in Shionasu or Ajino in the fashioning of both Western and native style clothing. Some of the girls work from time to time in home factories in Shionasu, a privilege for which, during their student training period, fees must be paid. One unmarried *buraku* girl who finished courses of training in Shionasu does part-time sewing for other households.

Chickens and rabbits contribute a small part to the earning of a live-lihood. Most households raise two or three chickens of Leghorn type, and eggs, considered a luxury, are sold from time to time. Several households have pairs of rabbits, which earn their way from the sale of their young and from the manure for the fields which they provide. Rabbit and chicken coops are usually tiny affairs placed beneath the raised floors of houses, and the animals quickly become regarded as pets. There is a great reluctance to eat rabbits or chickens raised by the household so that they frequently die of old age and are buried. On the rare occasions when rabbit or chicken is eaten, it must have been raised by some other house-hold and be purchased or received as a gift.

The *buraku*, once nearly self-sufficient in most matters (except the very important matter of securing rice), is now strongly dependent upon outsiders. There is little development of specialization beyond the major occupations. For carpentry, the milling of grain, and many other services the residents of Takashima rely upon specialists in Shionasu and other nearby communities.

The basic rule in the division of labor is that men fish and women take care of the home and children and practice agriculture, but there are a good number of exceptions to the rule. Most *buraku* fishermen feel that farming is an honorable occupation but a little distasteful. There are only two full-time male farmers, but a few fishermen whose *hatake* plots are relatively large frequently help their wives with farm tasks. It would be necessary otherwise to hire help—and spend money. In households lacking in men, women habitually go out in the boats as fishermen and do men's work. This has always been the practice on Takashima, and at the present time nine women, four of whom are young and unmarried, do the work of men on the fishing boats.[5] For the types of fishing which require a crew of only two, a man and wife usually do the work if there are no sons or other able-bodied males in the household. A daughter or the grandmother is responsible for housework and agricultural tasks during the absences of the mother. For a woman to fish is not shameful.

Weaving and repair of nets are joint household work, but the care of children, cooking, washing, cleaning and other housework are done by women only. Even during the winter off-season when men can easily take a day or a few days off from net making, it would be considered an unreasonable (not to mention unheard of) request for a wife to ask her husband or any male past adolescence to look after young children. To ask a man to do cooking or housework is unthinkable. Children are frequently seen with their fathers or grandfathers, who sometimes carry them on their backs, but such care is usually only for short periods and does not involve the feeding, dressing, and answering all needs and wants of children throughout a day.

INCOMES

There is great variation within the *buraku* between the highest and lowest annual incomes, as there is between the greatest and smallest land holdings and the finest and poorest homes. The highest income is several times greater than the lowest. Although the income of a neighboring household may be fairly accurately estimated, there is considerable reluctance to discuss incomes even among persons of related households. A man with a high income does not want the figure known for fear that he will be approached for loans. A man with a very low income is usually ashamed.

There is an even better reason for reluctance to discuss earnings with outsiders—the matter of taxation. Fishermen are notorious among local tax officials for their habit of under-declaring earnings. A farmer's income

---

5. In some fishing communities of Japan, women are rigidly prohibited from entering fishing boats (cf. K. Sakurada, *op. cit.*) Until recent years the fishermen of nearby Yobimatsu are said to have laughed at the idea of women serving as crew members of fishing boats, and very few Yobimatsu women work on fishing craft today.

can be computed with a fairly high degree of accuracy because land holdings are known and approximate yields are easily determined. It is impossible, however, to determine the quantity and species of fish caught
during the year by a fisherman. During the war years, sales of fish could
be made legally only through the fishing *kumiai,* so that accounting was
possible through the *kumiai* records. Some fish seem always to have gone
to the black market even during that period. Regulations covering the
sale of marine products were changed in early 1950, and sale of fish on
the open market became legal. Most fishermen are reluctant to sell more
than perhaps a third of their catches through the *kumiai* because of the 6%
commission charged and because records of the *kumiai* are open to inspection by tax officials.

The income tax returns of fishermen are rarely accepted at face
value but instead serve only as working bases upon which to attempt to
determine actual or taxable income. It is assumed, with considerable
justification, that all fishermen underestimate their earnings as much as
they dare. The procedure of the tax office is to consult the records (since
1950 of little value for this purpose) and the officers of the *kumiai.* The
kumiai officials, fishermen themselves, have a good idea of the annual
incomes of each member of the cooperative whether or not sales are made
through the cooperative. Consultation with the *kumiai* officials is said at
least to yield a fairly good indication of relative incomes of fishermen
within the cooperative. The total taxable earnings finally decided upon
by the tax office usually represent an increase varying from 30% to 100%
above the amounts declared. Each case has individual handling. If a
fisherman feels that he is being overcharged, vociferous complaint usually
results in a reduction of his tax.

Despite the raising of income figures by the tax office, Takashima
fishermen are still far ahead of the official rates. The average fisherman
paid income taxes on net earnings of 60,000 yen during the fiscal year
1949. Average actual net earnings far exceed this figure, running somewhat over 100,000 yen (equivalent to $278 in American currency). The
largest income declared was 87,100 yen. This amount was raised by the
tax office to 135,700 yen, upon which an income tax of 24,430 yen was
levied. The actual net income in this case is estimated to have exceeded
250,000 yen. The household in question also had additional income from
farming and other sources bringing the actual total to perhaps 300,000
yen. The poorest household receives government aid of about 3,000 yen
monthly under a welfare program instituted by the Occupation. The
head of this household was injured and also contracted tuberculosis while
in service during the war so that he is able to fish only part of the time.
The total cash income of this household does not exceed 50,000 yen

annually, a sum inadequate to maintain the household. In this case, the father and a brother of the ailing household head give modest aid.

Excluding the household receiving public welfare aid, the lowest actual income in 1950 for an able-bodied male household head was approximately 60,000 yen. For the tax year 1949, fourteen household heads, some of them aged or infirm, were legally exempted from the payment of income tax, but of the households represented by these fourteen men only three are considered, by *buraku* consensus, to be in want.

In addition to income taxes, a variety of city and prefectural taxes are levied, which include house and building, land, bicycle, and head taxes. Tax formulas are complex and beyond the comprehension of most *buraku* residents. There is, as a whole, little awe of tax officials and *buraku* persons have upon occasion successfully refused the payment of certain taxes upon the grounds that they were exorbitant. As a rule, however, tax payments are made fairly promptly.

When individuals are delinquent in payment, the tax office, which is empowered to confiscate property in settlement of arrears, usually sends out employees to talk with, cajole and threaten those who are remiss. Such persuasion usually bears fruit, and no confiscation of property has ever been made. The policy of the Kojima City tax office is tolerant, and confiscation would require most extreme circumstances.

Total sums paid in taxes, which by formula computation should exceed 20% of the income of the ordinary household, actually average somewhat less than 10% because of successful tax evasion. Freight boat operators and the sole farming household with adequate produce from its land to fall within income tax brackets are less able to evade taxes, and must expend a larger proportion of their incomes for this purpose. Young unmarried men, unless employed outside, seldom appear on the income tax rolls as all household earnings are ordinarily declared under the name of the household head.

BUDGET AND FINANCE

Gross incomes of fishermen far exceed net incomes, for over 50% of annual earnings must be expended for nets, gasoline, boat equipment, and repairs. With the exception of one household, no accounting of expenditures is maintained. Major expenses are, however, known, as are approximate total expenditures, but monthly or annual costs of individual items such as foodstuffs are difficult for *buraku* people even to estimate. A survey of the opinion of household heads and their wives indicates that to supply minimum needs a net income of from 8,000 to 9,000 yen monthly is required for a family of five or six persons. Income of the average Takashima household slightly exceeds this figure, and it has been possible to put away savings since the end of the war (see Table 4). Such savings as were made before that time were swept away by the post-war inflation of the yen.

Rationing of food items except rice, sugar, and barley, which is cooked together with rice as a measure of economy, ceased by 1950. The sugar ration of 1950-51 was considered adequate, and the barley ration was not always taken by households which qualified for it, i.e., those which do not raise barley or which raise a quantity below the year's ration. The rice ration, if supplemented with other foods, is adequate to provide caloric requirements but inadequate to appease all appetites. Most households regularly purchase small amounts of black-market rice to supplement the ration. No one likes barley, which is considered rude fare and a substitute for rice. Pure rice (with no barley added) is eaten regularly if a household can afford to purchase enough black-market

TABLE 4

*Estimated Budget for Average Household of 5.7 Persons**

INCOME

	Yen
Gross earnings	240,000
Less fishing expenses (nets, gasoline, boat expenses), deductible for income tax computation	130,000
Net income	110,000

EXPENDITURES AND SAVINGS

Rice, including about 6,000 yen black-market rice	45,000
Foodstuffs and household supplies, including: sugar, tea, *shoyu* (soy bean sauce), *miso* (bean paste), cooking oil, *sake* and *shōchū* (alcoholic drinks), vinegar, noodles, bean curd, seaweed, dried fish, lamp oil, soap, charcoal, matches, and miscellaneous special foods	12,000
Clothing	10,000
Tobacco	10,000
Taxes	9,000
School (boat fee, lunches, books, etc.)	8,000
Gifts and donations	2,000
Entertainment (principally spending money for children. Holiday foods are entered with foodstuffs)	2,000
Miscellaneous, including organization fees	3,000
Savings	9,000
Total	110,000
	$305.80

* Based upon estimates made by 12 informants.

rice. During 1950-51, the black market of rice existed more or less openly all over Japan. Even residents of remote island or mountain hamlets were able to secure illegal rice, the purchase of which was hardly considered an offense in either popular or, apparently, official opinion.

Excluding boat and fishing expenses, the purchase of rice is by far the most costly single item. Home garden produce and fishing keep costs for other foods low. Forest plots provide fuel, and expenditures for firewood or charcoal are either nil or very small.

The purchase of clothing is the great problem. Woolen clothing is beyond financial reach, and, for the past decade, the purchase of fine silk clothing has been as a rule reserved only for brides. A single modest dress without accessories for a bride, even if made in the home, will cost at least 10,000 yen. Best clothing for the middle-aged and aged is, for the most part, the best clothing of ten or more years ago. Work clothing and clothing for children are necessities and comprise the major part of clothing purchases.

In the opinion of most *buraku* residents, present-day living conditions are in many respects as good as if not better than those which existed prior to the war. The purchase of clothing is difficult, and rice is still rationed, but there is little shortage of other merchandise and commodities. During 1950-51 Japanese shops were full of merchandise of all kinds, and rationing had almost ceased. Prices were high, but fishermen were fortunate as fish prices were also high. Some old and middle-aged persons state that they now enjoy luxuries which they had formerly thought could never be within their reach. In the old days, they say, the smooth rush floor mats of today were rare indeed on Takashima, and in their place coarse, home-made grass mats were used. This is not to say that all of Japan enjoys conditions as good as those before the war. The actual circumstances seem far from it. The lot of men who work with their hands seems, however, to have improved, and perhaps the lot of most fishermen has improved. With the motorizing of fishing craft twenty-odd years ago, the fortunes of Takashima fishermen began to grow better. Fish have dwindled in number since then, but fishing techniques in use have steadily improved and fish prices have risen. There is, however, some worry about the future as it seems inevitable that catches, now smaller than in the past, will decrease progressively. The Inland Sea is small and fishermen are very numerous.

Fishermen have the reputation in Japan of being carefree and spendthrift, with little thought for tomorrow.[6] Compared with the people

6. A publication (in English) of the Japanese government states: "Fishermen are as a rule lacking in the spirit of diligence and are prone to be improvident. They work at sea for only a limited time, while for the rest of the time they stay at home doing nothing." *The Rural Life of Japan* (Tokyo: Home Department, Bureau of Local Affairs, 1914), p. 9.

of farming communities, the fishermen of Takashima are perhaps a little improvident, but many traditions of farming life remain with them. Compared with the residents of other fishing communities of the Kojima area, however, Takashima fishermen are cautious and frugal. Almost every household has savings of some kind. The most common form is postal savings, in small amounts. Every household which belongs to the farming *kumiai* has small interest-bearing savings and also shares in that organization, and all fishermen own shares in the fishing *kumiai*. Several households have savings accounts in Kojima City banks. At least one member of nearly every household has inexpensive government insurance, usually 10,000 yen policies, and members of three households hold insurance policies for much larger amounts with commercial companies. Insurance is limited to that against accident or loss of life; there are no fire insurance policies held.

The number of households and individuals holding savings accounts and insurance policies has grown greatly in the past few decades. Savings and policies which existed before and during the war were, however, rendered almost valueless by inflation. An example is the case of a 1951 bride, whose provident parents had taken out an endowment policy in her name in the amount of 700 yen in 1941. Upon its maturation in early 1951 the policy, which was intended to cover all of the heavy bridal expenses, served to purchase one pair of medium quality *geta*, a type of footgear, for the bride. Policies of smaller face value were not worth the postage stamps and trouble required to complete payments and redeem them.

Loans, almost invariably intra-*buraku*, are made from time to time and are kept secret. Neither the lender nor the recipient usually wishes to let others know, for it reflects upon the status of the borrower and suggests that the lender is willing to make further loans. To become known as a man vulnerable to a request for money is to extend open invitation to those who desire to borrow, and something to be avoided. One man of moderate means and kind heart, after granting several loans, found it necessary to shutter his house while at home and pretend to be away in order to evade further importunate requests. Another reason for secrecy is that interest is sometimes charged on loans, an illegal practice except for licensed firms or individuals. Money is occasionally borrowed, at low rates of interest, from the agricultural and fishing cooperatives, but a man must usually be in fairly solvent financial condition to obtain such a loan. No one has ever attempted to secure money from a bank or commercial loan firm for the stated reason that fishermen are considered poor risks and it is felt that there is very little likelihood of loans being granted. In any event, commercial rates of interest are higher than those customarily charged by relatives or friends.

Men control the purse-strings. Women have small sums of money on hand at their disposal for incidental expenses, but for any larger expenditure they must first consult with their husbands. Larger sums of money are usually kept in dwellings but, although women are well aware of the hiding places, none of it is spent without first consulting husbands.

CHAPTER III

The Household and House Life

THE FAMILY AND THE HOUSEHOLD

T HE basic social unit on Takashima is the household. The average household embraces three generations and includes the household head, his wife, two or three children, and the retired parents of the household head. A fourth generation, the children of the eldest son, is not uncommon. By mathematical computation the average household is composed of 5.7 persons, but several households consist only of older persons whose children have died or moved away. Ten per cent of the *buraku* population is composed of persons over seventy years of age. This percentage of aged persons is said to exceed the average for Japan.

In rural Japan the household is in common terminology and in many official records the unit by which the size of communities is judged. A very common reply to a question regarding the population of a village, even when the questioner specifically asks regarding the number of persons, is to state the number of households. In all *buraku* affairs the household is the unit of primary importance, and representation at most non-social gatherings is by one person only from each household, whether the household is comprised of one person or twelve persons.

Within the household there are commonly two pairs of spouses, the household head and his wife and the eldest son and his spouse. If the household head is an eldest son, his parents (the retired grandparents) may form a third couple. In accordance with the former Japanese custom of primogeniture, now officially banished by postwar legislation, the eldest son and his wife remain in the household. Younger sons move away or establish separate households within the *buraku* which are regarded as branches *(bunke)* of the original household. In some areas of Japan the relationships between the head or main household *(honke)* and branch

households are institutionalized and involve formalized patterns of behavior. *Honke-bunke* relations receive little stress on Takashima. Daughters
marry out. The household is thus a continuing unit averaging about six
persons in number because of the practice of marrying out or moving
away of siblings of the male successor. No effect of the abolishment of
primogeniture is as yet evident.

The size of the household is sometimes dependent upon the size of
the dwelling. If there is adequate room, a second son with wife and children may also be members of the household. Within the household there
are thus two or three nuclear families, but they are seldom distinguished
as significant units by the members of the households themselves.

Household pets of no economic value are limited to a fair number of
cats and caged birds and a few dogs. Rabbits and chickens, kept primarily because they are of economic value, also have the status of pets.

Only one household, the richest in the *buraku,* has servants. This
household some years ago took in a non-related man of sub-par mentality
in the capacity of an unpaid menial. This man is regarded by no one in
the *buraku* as a member of the household in question. He is treated with
good-natured tolerance but is outside the circle of most human relations.
The household which "hires" him also hires outside labor, one or two
men, to aid with fishing a few weeks of the year. These are employees and
are not regarded as servants.

There is a strong feeling of unity among members of a household.
A grandfather is not "my grandfather," but *uchi no ojiisan,* "the grandfather of our house(hold)." A mother may refer to her son as the *wakai
mono* (young person) of our household. So common is the usage through
all Japan of the term *uchi no* ("of our house," or "of our household") that
it is commonly translated into English simply as "my" or "our."[1]

The household head is the supreme authority within the household,
but if the retired grandfather is not senile, care is taken to consult him at
least nominally in matters of importance to the whole household such as
the marriage of a younger sibling or daughter. Master's wives are, as a
rule, pliant and abide by the decisions of their husbands. They have,
however, somewhat more freedom of speech and action than wives in
farming communities and, within the home, often express their opinions.
Takashima men themselves state that fishermen's wives ordinarily have
more freedom than wives of farmers for the reason that they must run the
households and make decisions on at least small matters much of the time
while the men are at sea. Women, as the operators of the vital household
farm plots, are economically very important. But there is truth in an old

1. In some rural areas of Japan, *uchi* has come also to be used as the personal pronoun, first person singular, "I" or "me."

saying that women when young obey their husbands and when aged obey their children.

Daughters married out and sons who have moved away or set up independent households within the *buraku* may be thought of as a complement which forms an extended household. This group of relatives is of little social importance except at the time of *buraku* festivals and on the occasions of weddings, funerals, and memorial services, when those who are not members of the central household make serious effort for at least a number of years after separation to return to their original homes. Time and the adjustment to new households weakens the ties of the extended household, and as the years go by, the composition of the group which actually comes together changes. Married daughters, in particular, soon cease to be members in fact of the extended household. Daughters, by marrying into other households, develop new ties and incur new familial obligations which serve eventually to exclude them from the households of their procreation. The young bride may visit the household of her birth during *buraku* festivals, but the middle-aged woman seldom does so. A middle-aged woman does not always return to her native household for even such important events as funerals or weddings. Older women rarely visit their native homes. The extended household appears clearly to be waning in importance as a social unit. Increased reliance is being placed upon the resources of the immediate household.

The mother-in-law is the traditional terror of the new bride in Japan, but on Takashima there is now reported to be little discord between brides and mothers-in-law. It is said that there was much ill-feeling about thirty years ago between the brides and mothers-in-law of the time, occasioned by the jealousy of the mothers-in-law, then nearly all illiterate, of the elementary school education of brides. The word of the mother-in-law supersedes that of the bride, but the custom, reported from various other sections of Japan, of the ceremonial "turning over of the rice spatula" to the bride after the master's wife has begun to age does not exist.[2] According to this custom, a bride was not allowed access to the household rice supply until this ceremonial transfer of authority was made. Takashima brides, although subservient to their mothers-in-law, quickly take over the work and responsibility for most of the household cooking and serving of food as well as many other duties. The considerate household, if there is a young wife among its members, is careful to see that all traditional holidays are taken, since the good young wife works hard and does not rest unless all others rest.

2. This custom still exists among more isolated communities of Japan. See Kagawa-ken Minzoku Chōsa-kai, *op. cit.*, and also Ōmachi Tokuzō, *Ceremonial Practices in Japan* (Tokyo: Nippon Bunka Chuo Renmei, 1942).

The bride is theoretically the most insignificant member of the household, but all are usually careful to treat her well, for discord with her will lead to difficulty and strained relations with her husband. Traditionally, the husband supports his mother in cases of disagreement between wife and mother. If he is considerate, he later consoles his wife, who is well aware of the traditional pattern he is observing. In actual practice, this course of action is not always followed.

Considerable emphasis is placed upon age. Traditionally, grandparents are greatly revered and given the seats of greatest honor during banquets and other social gatherings. Again this is a tradition which is not always followed. The attitude toward the aged is usually one of tolerant affection and respect, but it is not carried to an impractical degree. Older siblings supersede younger ones of the same sex in authority, and male siblings by and large dominate female siblings. During childhood boys are subservient to their older sisters, but once they have reached the age of about ten, little heed is paid to them. Males — especially the oldest son or successor — receive somewhat preferential treatment over females. If there are two married sons in the household, the status of the wife of the younger son is somewhat lower than that of the spouse of the older son. The emphasis upon age appears to be linked with a day long past when age-grades existed. Age-class systems are reported as late as 1940 for isolated communities.[3]

Quarreling between members of the same sex, except among young children, is uncommon, but verbal quarrels between spouses are considered a part of normal life by most persons. The usual course in such quarrels is that the wife eventually gives in, but often not until she has had her say. Standard causes for quarrels are disagreements over treatment or rearing of children and over money. Gambling on the part of men is also a frequent cause of domestic strife. Quarrels which go beyond the verbal stage are extremely rare. Quarreling is shameful and kept as secret as possible, but dwellings are close together and walls are so thin that domestic relations within most households are usually common knowledge.

Despite quarreling, there is a strong feeling of attachment between most couples and a dislike for divorce. Divorces are uncommon and said

3. Sakurada reports the existence of a full-fledged age-grade system for males in Kunizaki village, Mie Prefecture, with six classes, and suggests that age-grading also formerly existed among women of the village (K. Sakurada, *op. cit.*). A coming-of-age ceremony upon reaching the age of sixteen is still reported for isolated Inland Sea communities (Kagawa-ken Minzoku Chōsa-kai, *op. cit.*). Numerous other examples may also be quoted. Cf. K. Segawa, "Dōrei Shūzoku ni tsuite," *Minzokugaku Kenkyū*, XII, no. 2 (1947), pp. 46-52, and Ōmachi Tokuzō, *op. cit.* The distinction of young persons' associations and work groups at the present day in many rural areas of Japan, the traditional practice of retirement at the age of sixty-one, and terms used in address also suggest that more or less clearly defined age groups once existed.

to be far below the national average for Japan. There has been only one case of divorce within the past twenty years. Three of the present wives, however, entered marriage with Takashima men as divorcees coming from other communities. The stated reason for divorce in three of these four cases was incompatibility between spouses. In the fourth case, the wife was deserted by her husband. Unions which are dissolved before official entry is made in city records (see Chap. VI, Marriage) are not ordinarily considered as divorces. Only one case of this sort is remembered by persons up to middle age. A Takashima girl who had married out returned to her home after a few weeks because she disliked both her husband and her mother-in-law.

In view of the high birth rate in Japan, the number of child-less couples is surprising. Of the thirty-three couples which comprise the household heads and their wives, five have no children of their own. So that the lineage may continue unbroken and so that ancestors may be given due care in accordance with Buddhist doctrine, the usual course is to adopt a son who will become the successor and bear the household name. The adoption of daughters is also common, and in cases where a female child is adopted, a husband is also adopted (see Chap. VI, Marriage) for her later in life and assumes the household name. In 1950-51 there were nine adopted persons living within the *buraku,* two of them female and seven male. Of the seven males, five were adopted husbands. Within the past two decades, seven children have been adopted out and no longer live on Takashima.

Young children taken in adoption are usually relatives, but adopted husbands are ordinarily not related or only distantly related. No attempt is made at concealment of the fact that children are adopted, nor, in such a small and intimate community, is concealment possible. The relationship between foster children and foster parents is said to be not quite so close as that between parents and natural offspring, but there is little or no stigma attached to being an adopted child. Adopted husbands are, however, under something of a stigma, and, although adopted husbands are common enough, most men speak of entering a union of this sort as something to be avoided (for further details, see Chap. VI, Marriage).

Adoption out of children is ordinarily done only if there are many children and the household is economically pressed. The adoption out of male children is easier to arrange than that of female children, and there is greater reluctance to give boys in adoption. Two sons in the household are an economic asset for a fisherman, and there is little objection to three. If the house becomes crowded upon their maturity and after the marriage of the eldest son, one or both younger sons can be financed to set up separate households or given in adoptive marriage. Until younger sons reach the age of marriage, when it is difficult to accommodate another family in the small dwelling, they are valuable assets in fishing operations.

Daughters are less desired than sons, for they are of less economic value and the lineage does not continue through them. A great deal of money must also be expended on them at the time of their marriage. Women usually desire at least one female child, and a balanced family of both male and female children is welcomed by both parents. No *buraku* daughter is said to have been sold as prostitute or *geisha* for a great many years, and the practice, though once common among impoverished people of some sections of Japan, is regarded with distaste as a thing of the *yaban* (uncivilized) past.

Adoptions are not uncommonly dissolved, and may sometimes be re-entered. Dissolution is usually caused by economic pressure. Friction between adopted husbands and household heads is said to be a further cause of the dissolution of adoption in other communities. Although there have been a number of dissolved adoptions in *buraku* history, within the memory of living persons there has been no instance of the dissolution of the adoption of a husband. One boy had gone through three adoptions by the time he reached adolescence. In each of the two instances of dissolution the reason was economic, the incurable illness of a foster father in one case, and the reduction to abject poverty of the foster parents in the other.

Adoption is sometimes very complex. In one instance a distantly related girl was adopted by a *buraku* couple during her adolescence. A few years later the sole natural male sibling of the girl died, and since she was the only unmarried child of her natural parents, the adoption was dissolved by request. At the same time, however, it was arranged that the younger brother of her former foster father enter into marriage with her as an adopted husband, taking her native family name. In another household, the master was adopted as a boy by a childless couple. After attaining maturity he married in due course but the union was childless, and the couple adopted a related infant female for whom it was necessary to secure an adopted husband when she became of marriageable age. In former years a custom called *junyōshi* consisting of the adoption by childless household heads of much younger brothers is said to have been known. There is now no instance of this practice among *buraku* households and it is said to have become rare in the surrounding community.

There is no ceremony or legal process connected with adoption except recording the event in the official records at the branch city hall office in Shionasu. Dissolution is accomplished by another entry into the records. After adoption, the break between parents and their offspring is usually fairly final, even when adoption is within the *buraku* and blood relationships are known to the children involved. Adopted children have all the rights and prerogatives of natural children and, after a period of adjustment to the new household, patterns of relationship with foster siblings and foster parents appear indistinguishable from those with natural siblings or parents.

Speech and behavior within the household are ordinarily highly informal. In direct intercourse older persons of the household are called by terms indicative of relationships, such as "mother," and "older sister." To these terms are added the suffix *-san,* a term of respect usually translated as "Mr.," "Mrs.," or "Miss,' or, more commonly, the more intimate suffix *-chan.* There is no close English equivalent for the suffix *-chan*; it might best be thought of as similar to English diminutives or nicknames such as Robert—Bob and John—Johnny. Children and younger siblings are usually addressed by their given names with the suffix *-chan.* For young children the suffix is ordinarily attached only to the first syllable of given names. Thus Eiichirō becomes, in speech used in daily life, Ei-chan. The dropping of all except the first syllable is also extended to terms of relationships, with some phonetic modification, so that *otō-san* (father) becomes *totchan.* The more formal *otō-san* is normally used only in the presence of strangers or persons with whom the speaker is not well acquainted. In stating the number of one's siblings *(kyōdai),*[4] the speaker must include himself as one of the number.

Husbands and wives frequently address each other with the familiar terms meaning mother and father. The term *anata* (you), more often spoken only in private because of its affectionate or amorous connotation, is occasionally heard. Husbands may also address wives as *o-mae,* an abrupt and familiar term meaning "you," or may use the even more abrupt *oe,* which is said to be a contraction of *o-mae.*

Older persons within the *buraku,* whether or not related to the speaker, are also addressed and usually referred to by terms of relationship. Old men and women are called *ojii-san* and *obaa-san* (grandfather and grandmother) and middle-aged persons, *oji-san* and *oba-san* (uncle and aunt) by their juniors. A woman addresses another woman a few years her senior as *ne-san* (older sister), and a woman several years her senior as *oba-san.* This practice is also extended to include total strangers, particularly those advanced in age, to whom the terms for grandparent are chronologically appropriate. A bride is addressed within the house-

4. The word *kyōdai* is at times difficult to translate. It may, according to context, be translated as "brother(s)," "sister(s)," or "sibling(s)." When a person states, in Japanese, that he has five *kyōdai,* the normal English translation is "I have four brothers and sisters." Perhaps the most accurate although unwieldy translation for *kyōdai* is "children of the same parents."

hold by given name but referred to by household members as *uchi no yome-san*, "the bride of our household." Age distinctions remain important and terms of reference may become fixed as one grows old. A grandmother may refer to the middle-aged wife of her middle-aged son, with whom she has lived for twenty or more years, as *uchi no yome-san*, and may refer to the middle-aged son as *uchi no wakai mono*, "the young person of our household."

Being related, most persons bear the same surname, but even when surnames differ they are seldom or never used as terms of address for other persons in the *buraku*. Given names to which the suffix -*san* is added are the rule in direct address among persons of approximately the same age, and are also frequently used as terms of reference.

Geographical terms are sometimes used to designate neighbors. *Mikan-yama no oba-san*, literally "the aunt of tangerine mountain," is the middle-aged woman whose house is located on a slope where a few tangerines were once raised. A number of households bear traditional *yagō*, house names, terms which apply to both house and household. The types of names are various: *Kome-ya*, "rice house," is a household which once sold rice; *Eifuku-ya* is taken from the name of the series of freight boats, all bearing the same name, owned by one household during the past century; *Moto-ya*, "original house," is so named because the present dwelling is said to be on the site of one of the three original dwellings of the *buraku*. Members and possessions of households bearing *yagō* are referred to in terms of the house name, such as "the Kome-ya grandfather," and "the Eifuku-ya dog." Not all houses bear *yagō* nor are all *yagō* in frequent use. A little prestige seems attached to the possession of house names, but the custom of attaching and using the names appears to be disappearing. Of the eight *yagō* in common use thirty years ago only three are frequently spoken now. The three households represented by these names have always been well-to-do and possess houses larger than the average.

THE DWELLING

There is a large variety of patterns of dwellings in rural Japan, but all hold certain features in common, the dirt or concrete floored storage room and kitchen, and rooms with raised wooden floors which are covered with mats and used for sleeping, resting, and the entertainment of guests. These rooms form a basic square or rectangle to which other rooms may be appended. The arrangement of rooms and their nomenclature vary from section to section of the country.[5] Within the *buraku* of Takashima there is also considerable variation in houses, but basic plans and nomen-

5. See *Nihon Minzokugaku Jiten* (Japanese Ethnographic Dictionary) (Tokyo: Tōkyōdō, 1951) for figures illustrating several different types of rural dwellings.

PLATE 12.—*Average house, one-story, with attic.*

PLATE 13.—*Better-than-average house, two-story.*

clature are uniform. Chief differences are in size. A few dwellings have only one *tatami* room (a room with raised wooden floor covered with *tatami,* woven grass matting), whereas others have as many as six or eight. A few houses have two stories, but the average house is one-story. Roofs are usually of slate-grey tile, but a few of the very poor have thatched roofs.

The usual house is a one-story structure with four *tatami* rooms, a narrow porch, a combined entrance and storage room, a combined kitchen-dining room, and an attic under the peaked roof (see Figure 1). The framework of the house is of wood, and outside walls are of bamboo and mud wattle. Projecting eaves of tile protect porches and entrances from the splashing of rain. Outside walls are often protected and reinforced with pine boards, charred on the outer surface to resist rot and insect infestation. Exposures are always in the direction of the sea, to the south or east. Exposures to the west would have the entrance facing the hillside and away from the usual avenue of approach, and northern exposures are traditionally unlucky as the dead are buried with their faces to the north.

Entrance to the house is through the dirt or concrete floored *soto-niwa,* which is used as an entrance hall and as a storage room, into the kitchen, or by means of a wooden step *(itaba)* into the *tatami* rooms. A rear entrance opens into the kitchen. It is possible to enter a house directly into two of the *tatami* rooms, the *kaminoma* and *shimonoma,*[6] but this is rarely done. According to traditional practice, only brides or adopted husbands on their wedding day may enter or leave the house by this direct route, passing over the porch into or out of the *kaminoma,* the best room of the dwelling. Bodies of the dead also leave the house by this route, directly from the *kaminoma* into the yard. A narrow wooden porch, the *ama-en,* extends along the *kaminoma* and *shimonoma* and has solid wooden shutters to enclose it at night and during inclement weather.

Sliding wooden shutters of light wood and paper or glass separate the four *tatami* rooms from each other and from the *soto-niwa* and kitchen. Additional sliding shutters of heavier construction serve to close the front and rear entrances; i.e., the *soto-niwa* and kitchen entrances. Footgear is used in the *soto-niwa* and kitchen, but must be removed before entering the *tatami* rooms.

Dwellings in Japanese fishing *buraku* are traditionally dirty, but Takashima is above average among fishing communities of at least the Kojima area in cleanliness and tidiness. Some dwellings and yards are almost always dirty and littered; others are always clean. The American

6. *Kami* means "upper," and *shimo* "lower." If two or more objects are in a line, the one to the extreme left is *kami.* The *kaminoma* is sometimes also called *zashiki,* the Standard Japanese term for the parlor or best room of a house.

housewife would, however, be horrified at the appearance of most Takashima *soto-niwa* and kitchens. The *soto-niwa* and, in particular, the kitchen are considered by *buraku* householders to be inherently dirty places, rooms which do not really enter into the scheme of living, and which are not a part of the house proper. It seems probable that these rooms were once detached structures. Many persons habitually use the term *niwa*[7] to include both the entrance-storage room *(soto-niwa)* and the kitchen,[8] which are separated from each other by a partition with an open passageway. When it is necessary to make a distinction, the kitchen is called *oku-niwa*, "inner" *niwa*, as opposed to *soto-* ("outer") *niwa*. In a few houses the kitchen, i.e., the cooking place, is a small detached structure or a lean-to attached to the main dwelling. The simple facilities in the kitchen are not conducive to a tidy appearance. The floor is usually of hard-packed soil, less frequently of rough-surfaced concrete. Utensils are placed on shelves and hang from nails on the walls, or are simply stacked in piles. A water container stands on the floor, and one corner of the room is dominated by the *kudo*, an earthenware cooking device, and a fuel container. The fuel includes many pine needles, which scatter easily. Although a few of the richer households have hand pumps, water must usually be drawn from a well so that lavish use is difficult. Most of all, the untidy appearance is the result of tradition; kitchens are not meant to be clean places.

The four *tatami* rooms are extremely simply furnished, and if not actually clean appear to be so because of their barrenness. The *shimonoma* sees perhaps the most frequent use, for resting, talking, children's schoolwork, for the greeting of guests, and occasionally for dining. The *kaminoma* is reserved for the entertainment of guests and ordinarily sees little other use. The *naka-e*[9] and *nando* are always sleeping rooms, the *nando* usually serving as bedroom for the household head and his wife and as the accouchement room during childbirth. All *tatami* rooms may be used as bedrooms, but the *kaminoma,* as the parlor, is not utilized if other rooms are unfilled. Infants may sleep in the same bed as their parents; older children frequently sleep in separate beds in the same room with their parents, and there is usually a sleeping room in a detached building for grandparents or bridal couples.

7. In Standard Japanese the term *niwa* is used to designate the yard in front of dwellings, called on Takashima the *kado*.

8. Terms applied to this room are varied and the word "kitchen" is used as a matter of convenience here. As noted above, *oku-niwa* is sometimes used, and *niwa* may also be used. Additional terms are *daidokoro*, "elevated place," and *kamaba*, "stove place." *Daidokoro*, the Standard Japanese term used for the cooking room and usually translated as "kitchen," may refer only to the raised wooden platform in this room on which the household eats its meals sitting about a low table. *Kamaba* may mean only the area adjacent to the stove, and is the term invariably applied to a cooking place if it is a detached structure.

9. *Naka-e* is a local variant of the term *naka-oe* (also a local term). Both *shimonoma* and *kaminoma* are occasionally referred to collectively as *oe*. *Naka* means inside or middle.

FIGURE NO. 1
House Plan

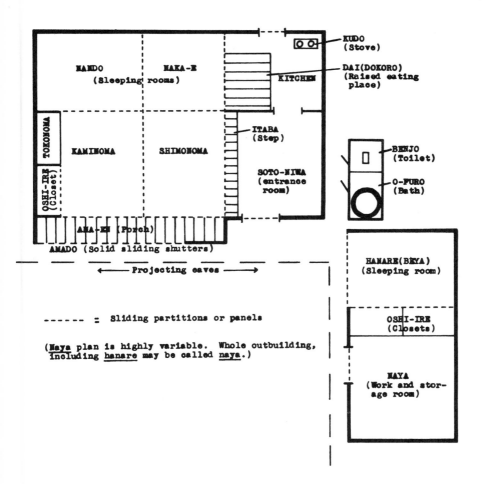

MANDO
(Sleeping rooms)

NAKA-E

KITCHEN

KUDO
(Stove)

DAI(DOKORO)
(Raised eating place)

TOKONOMA

KAMINOMA

SHIMONOMA

ITABA
(Step)

OSHI-IRE
(Closet)

SOTO-NIWA
(entrance room)

BENJO
(Toilet)

O-FURO
(Bath)

AMA-EN (Porch)

AMADO (Solid sliding shutters)

← Projecting eaves →

HANARE(BEYA)
(Sleeping room)

OSHI-IRE
(Closets)

- - - - - - = Sliding partitions or panels

(Naya plan is highly variable. Whole outbuilding, including hanare may be called naya.)

NAYA
(Work and storage room)

The *tatami* rooms are considered the center of the dwelling. As such they are given better care than *soto-niwa,* kitchen, or outbuildings, and are little used during the daytime except in cold weather. Children usually play outside, and if rain makes it necessary for them to come in, an attempt is made to confine them to one room. Dwellings of households with young children are easily identified by the ragged appearance of the thin white paper sections of the sliding panels between rooms, punctured by exploring childish fingers.

The manufacture and repair of nets is usually done in the *naya,* one of the two outbuildings of the ordinary household. The *naya,* which is usually of fairly solid construction, contains a storage and work room with wooden or earth floor and often has a small separated *tatami* room. This room is called the *hanare* or *hanare-beya,* and if there are retired grandparents in the household it is used by them as a sleeping room.

Bathroom *(o-furo)*[10] and toilet *(benjo)* adjoin each other in another outbuilding. Because the housing area is cramped and lots are of odd sizes, the outbuildings may be located in various places but are rarely placed to the rear of the house, where it would be necessary to go around or through the kitchen to reach them. Ordinarily, outbuildings are placed to the left of the *soto-niwa,* looking out from the entrance. Old persons say it is bad luck to have a toilet in the area in front of the *tatami* rooms, for if there is an offensive thing like a toilet in the way, the gods of good fortune will not enter the house and the household will always be poor.

The floors of the building containing the *o-furo* and *benjo* are always elevated to avoid excessive dampness from bath water, which drains from the floor of the bath to the joint bathwater-toilet receptacle beneath, and to allow access to the receptacle for the removal of night-soil.

To take a bath one first cleanses the body with soap and hot water dipped out from the bath with a hand basin, rinsing off the soap with clear water. It is customary to maintain a crouching position while doing this. All soap is to be removed and the body theoretically clean before entering the tub. The bath continues with a soaking in the hot water of the tub, a steel receptacle which rounds to a pointed or egg-shaped bottom. To conserve water and fuel the tub is small, and it is necessary to crouch with knees drawn up under the chin while inside it. The tub is heated from the bottom by a bricked-in fire-pit in which pine needles, branches, trash, and sometimes split pine-wood are burned. Atop the water in the tub floats a circular lid-like structure made of wood. The bather places his feet on this lid and by his weight forces it to a position about one-fourth of the distance from the bottom, where it lodges. By resting his feet on this lid the bather is able to avoid discomfort or injury

10. The "o" of *o-furo* is an honorific prefix habitually attached to many words.

from the more intense heat of the bottom of the tub, which is reached by the flames from the fire beneath. Baths are taken in water near the scalding point; on cold winter days one can remain comfortably warm for two or three hours after a bath.

Several households do not have baths and use those of their neighbors. To save fuel and the work of carrying water, it is a common practice for two neighboring households with baths to take turns in preparing tubs. Thus one tub of water may be used by as many as ten or twelve bathers. Old bath water is occasionally re-used for bathing to avoid carrying heavy pails from the well. Daily bathing throughout the whole year is the exception rather than the rule; the average is perhaps three or four baths a week. A bath is always prepared for guests.

The toilet is separated by a partition from the bath, if both are in the same building. A simple rectangular hole cut in the floor with a slanted wooden guard projecting from one end serves as the toilet. Glazed pottery or porcelain devices are sometimes fitted into the rectangular openings, but their purpose seems to be chiefly ornamental. They are not seats; one crouches. For the convenience of males there is frequently a urinal, of metal or earthenware, attached to the outer wall of the toilet and draining into the toilet receptacle.

Attics are reached by ladder or stairway from the kitchen or *naka-e,* and are used for storage of miscellaneous items for which there is no immediate prospect of use.

In the front of most houses is a small yard, in one corner of which there are usually a few weary flowers or flowering shrubs, always in need of cultivation. Among the commonly planted flowers are dahlias, cosmos, cannas, and zinnias, all of which are usually called by the Japanese rendition of their English names, *daria, kosumosu,* etc. Native chrysanthemum and iris are also common. Old octopus pots encrusted in a pleasing pattern with oyster shells, large lumps of coral or oddly shaped stones are frequently placed among the plants for their decorative value. A number of yards have no flowers whatever, and many yards are chronically littered with implements and rubbish. On sunny days the yards serve as drying areas for grain, beans, and various other foods, which are spread thinly on mats laid on the soil or placed on low, wide benches. If the household has a well of its own, it is usually located somewhere within the yard, but wells (none have been dug in recent years) are dug upon the advice of geomancers and positions vary. The boundaries of the yard are marked by an ill-cultivated hedge, a line of stones, a wooden fence, or a wall of mud or stone. Dwellings of wealthier households may have walls around their yards made of stone and concrete with tile covering like miniature roofs. Somewhere within the front yard, or in other positions to the side and rear of the house where the sun will reach them, are two or three trees, usually a fig tree or two and a *mikan* (generic term for citrus fruit, and specific term for tangerine).

Furnishings within the dwelling are extremely simple. The *shimonoma* may in summer be bare of any furnishing except the household shrine shelves, an inaccurate wall clock, and shrine talismans. During winter a charcoal brazier for heating is usually present. Standard furnishings for the *kaminoma,* the finest room of the home, are a low table placed in the approximate center of the room and two cheap framed prints of Western-style paintings (a Swiss lake scene is very common). These are hung on walls above the sliding panels, one on the *nando* wall and the other opposing it. In the recessed alcove called the *tokonoma* (in ordinary speech more frequently referred to as *o-toko*), the traditional beauty spot of the Japanese home, hangs a paper scroll bearing a formalized version of the ideographs used in writing the name of the sun goddess, Amaterasu-ō-mikami. An arrangement of flowers may also occasionally be placed in the *tokonoma,* and if the household is well-to-do, scrolls with painted scenes of waterfalls, birds, or flowers may be used and changed with the season of the year. Bedding and *zabuton,* thin cushions stuffed with cotton batting which are used as seats, are stored in a shelved closet with sliding paper and wood doors which adjoins the *tokonoma.*

The *nando* and *naka-e* contains chests of drawers for storage of native clothing, which is folded when put away, and wardrobes for the storage on hangers of Western-style clothing. A miniature dresser with mirror is always found, and, if the household owns a sewing machine, phonograph, or Western desk, they are placed in one of these two rooms. An additional shelved closet may be located in the *nando.*

The votive places of household gods are distributed through the dwelling. There are two god shelves in the *shimonoma,* and one in either the kitchen or in the *soto-niwa.* The *tokonoma* is dedicated to Amaterasu-ō-mikami, and the Buddhist *Butsudan,* "Buddha altar," is placed in the *naka-e.* If the household is well-to-do the *Butsudan* is an elaborate cabinet-like affair covered with black lacquer and gilt. A few poor households make a simple board shelf serve as the *Butsudan.* Additional household shrines are located outside the dwelling. (For further details on household gods, see Chap. V, Household Gods.)

Houses are invariably chilly during cold weather and there is no device in use for effectively warming all rooms or even a single room. Heating is regarded as necessary only during about three months of the year although temperatures may be uncomfortably chilly for a much longer period. Even then heating devices are ordinarily reserved only for mealtimes and evening hours. Partly to save fuel, it is the usual practice simply to don additional clothing during daylight hours when not at meals. Winter cold is one of the expected discomforts of life. Charcoal braziers *(hibachi)* of several types are the principal heating device. A few pieces of glowing charcoal half-buried in ashes inside an *hibachi* burn for a long period and suffice to keep hands, at least, comfortably warm if they are extended over the coals. *Hibachi* are always put into use for guests and, although not considered as cooking devices, are also utilized to prepare tea or to keep it hot.

Small portable lidded devices of earthenware, or sometimes of metal-lined wood *(kotatsu),*[11] into which burning charcoal is placed are wrapped loosely with bedding and placed in beds on cold nights. It is also customary to make use of the *kotatsu* when one becomes thoroughly chilled during daylight hours. A padded cotton blanket is placed over the wrapped *kotatsu*. One takes a sitting position on the floor, placing his feet under the blanket against the warm *kotatsu* and pulling the blanket on up to his waist or armpits. Hands may then also be warmed by placing them under the blanket.

Another bed-warming device, used in the same manner as the *kotatsu* and said to be especially liked by old people, is a flattened oval of galvanized iron *(yutampo)* into which hot water is poured through a screw-topped opening.

One sleeps on the floor on a pad *(futon)* resembling a thick comforter made of cotton cloth stuffed with cotton batting. One or more additional *futon* of somewhat larger dimensions serve as covers. Pillows are small rectangles made usually of scrap cloth, cotton, rayon, or silk, and stuffed with the hulls of barley or other grains. Although far from soft, they yield somewhat to the pressure of the head. *Futon* are heavy and not very warm. On winter nights it is necessary to sleep beneath two or three of them and the weight becomes oppressive. *Futon* are seldom washed, as this would require taking them apart, and in many households are lumpy, dirty, and stale-smelling.

BUILDING A HOUSE

Construction of houses is always done by professional carpenters, hired from outside the *buraku*. Erection of dwellings as a communal *buraku* enterprise was the custom in times past, but for thirty or more years construction has been on an individual household basis. The one exception is that relatives and neighbors (in former days, a representative from each household of the *buraku*) aid with the setting up of the heavy central beam. A feast for *buraku* people was formerly given upon the completion

11. *Kotatsu* in recessed pits in the floor, common in mountain and more northerly areas, are not found on Takashima nor are the open fire-pits *(irori)* of the mountain areas.

of the framework of a house, but this practice, slowly dying before the war, went out with the wartime shortage of food (several new houses were built during and after the war).

There is still a good deal of ceremony and some feasting connected with the erection of dwellings and other major structures. A house is an important place. It not only provides shelter and some degree of warmth, but it is also the focal point for all activities of the household and is inhabited by various supernatural beings who strongly influence the lives of the human beings who dwell within it. Care must be given to the selection of a site and to the date when construction is to commence. The supernatural beings must be consulted and appeased through the medium of specialists and votive offerings.

The first step in the erection of a house is to select an appropriate site within the always limited plot of land available. There are many rules, little known to the average person, which must be followed, and so a *kasōmi* (geomancer)[12] must be consulted — and paid for his services. After talking with the household head and determining his wishes, the *kasōmi* examines the plot of ground and reserves decision until he has had time to work matters out, as there are many contingencies. The *kasōmi* bases his decisions largely upon the horoscope and the location of Konjin-sama, a deity who moves about the world in a fixed orbit (see Chap. V, Konjin-sama and the Lunar Calendar). The age of the head of the household and the lunar day and year of his birth are of importance. Certain directions are to be avoided for the erection or facing of a house or outbuilding because they are inauspicious.

After some days of deliberation the *kasōmi* delivers a sketch of the house plan, similar to a blue-print. Superimposed on the sketch are twelve lines extending outward from the *Daikoku-bashira* (the pillar near which the household shrine shelf to the god Daikoku-sama is located, and the so-called central pillar of a dwelling). These lines and the intervals between them represent the ancient Chinese zodiac and bear the zodiacal signs. Sketches are invariably drawn to have dwellings face south or east, as is both traditional and practical. The *kasōmi* recommends auspicious days to begin construction and may have special recommendations of dates for the erection of outbuildings and the *Daikoku-bashira*.

Either before or after consulting the *kasōmi,* but long before construction is begun, the whole area of ground upon which the dwelling, outhouses and yard are to be located must be ceremonially prepared. This procedure is called *yashiki-dori,* "grounds taking," and is usually said to be a form of appeasement or appeal to the supernatural beings so that no

---

12. *Kasō*mi, literally translated, means "seeing the aspect of houses." The field of knowledge of the *kasōmi* covers geomancy in general, and includes lore on auspicious and inauspicious times for any venture.

harm will befall the eventual occupants of the dwelling or the carpenters who construct it. There is considerable vagueness concerning this ceremony. Some persons state that it is toward no specific deity but to all. Still others do not know the significance of the ceremony. Tall stalks of bamboo, with branches and leaves allowed to remain on the growing tips, are placed upright in the ground at each of the four corners of the plot. Between them are stretched *shichigosan*, Shinto talismans, the origin and significance of which are now forgotten.[13] *Shichigosan*,[14] literally "seven-five-three," consist of lengths of rice-straw cordage to which loose strands of rice straw are attached at intervals in groups of seven, five, and three. No prayers are offered at this time, and there is no restriction as to which household members may perform *yashiki-dori*.

Before beginning to build a house, the carpenter or head carpenter leads a prayer to Jijin-sama in which household members silently participate. The prayer informs Jijin-sama that a house is to be built and asks his forgiveness and blessings. There is no further ritual until the framework of the house has been completed and the roof tiles put in place, at which time a ceremony called *muneage*,[15] "ridgepole-raising (ceremony)," is performed on the roof. Before the ceremony, relatives present the household concerned with quantities of disc-shaped *mochi* including a number of large cakes eight or more inches in diameter called, for this occasion, *sumi-mochi*, "corner (i.e., direction) cakes." Relatives may also make presents of rice wine *(sake)* and various other foodstuffs. Large quantities of food are also prepared by the household concerned, and additional *sake* may be purchased if the quantity received as gifts is thought to be inadequate.

A scaffolding of long planks is erected on one of the sloping sides of the roof to form a series of three or four long steps. The tools of the carpenters or head carpenter are placed on the highest step together with three paper *gohei*, Shinto talismans symbolic of an offering of cloth. Ceremonial wooden stands containing the *mochi* and all *sake* and food received as gifts are placed on the second level. The carpenters, male members of the household, and close male relatives, all dressed in their best clothes, stand on the third level. If there is room, female household members and close female relatives may also stand on the third level. Sometimes a fourth step is constructed for the use of females. Friends and relatives gather on the ground below the roof on all four sides of the house.

13. The origin of the custom of *yashiki-dori* appears to be very ancient. See K. Florenz, "Ancient Japanese Rituals, Part IV," *Transactions of the Asiatic Society of Japan*, XXVII, Part 1, (1900), pp. 1-112.

14. *Shichigosan* is also the name applied to a ceremony for seven-, five- and three-year-old children held on November 15th in many parts of Japan. This ceremony is not observed on Takashima.

15. Also known, to a few people, by the more elegant term *jōtō-shiki*. The term *muneage* is often translated as "framework."

The officiating carpenter makes a prayer to Itsubashira-no-kami-sama, god of carpenters, offers him the food and *sake,* and pours a ceremonial cup of the wine for each of the males assembled on the roof. After the food and wine have been offered to the *kamisama* (god) there is no restriction as to who may consume it. Anyone may, but in actual practice the food is eaten by members of the household concerned, their relatives, and the carpenters. When the prayer has been said and offerings have been made, *mochi-maki ("mochi* sowing")* begins. The head of the household, and sometimes other males, throw one of the large cakes in each of the cardinal directions, following this with the throwing of many smaller cakes of the usual table size. Women and children of the household also join in the festivities, throwing the small *mochi.* Women are occasionally also allowed to participate in the sowing of the large cakes. *Mochi* are much liked and are eagerly caught by the waiting hands of those gathered below to be taken home and eaten. A few old people say that these *mochi* and any other used in ceremonial carry good fortune with them. Tangerines are also thrown if they are in season, but all other food is kept for later consumption by those on the roof. The quantity of *mochi* or tangerines thrown varies with the wealth of the family and the generosity of relatives and close friends. When the last of the *mochi* and tangerines set aside for this purpose have been thrown down, the ceremony is concluded inside the house with an informal feast for those who were assembled on the roof. Most males are soon maudlin with drink, and there is much laughter, singing, and dancing which continues from late afternoon or early evening until about midnight.

Because of the rationing of rice, the holding of a *muneage* ceremony is contingent upon both the generosity of relatives and friends and upon the amount of money available for the black-market purchase of the glutenous rice of which *mochi* are made. It is desirable to keep such ceremonies from the notice of officials, although no official action has ever been taken on Takashima or in surrounding areas in consequence of household celebration of the sort. The annual ration of the special glutenous rice for *mochi* is received at New Year's and is usually all consumed at that time. Whenever a banquet is held it is accepted as a foregone conclusion that the rice and glutenous rice used are largely from the black market. If it is at all possible to hold a *muneage* ceremony and feast, however, it is still usually done, but guests, formerly one representative from each household, are now restricted to the carpenters and close relatives.

The house is by no means completed as yet. Interior finishing, plastering, and many small tasks remain to be done. The plastering of walls is done with a compound of local mud-clay and chopped rice-straw, and usually requires the services of a professional plasterer. For a house built in 1949-50, work began December 25th and the framework, built by two carpenters with the aid of household members, was completed January 15th. The *muneage* ceremony was held at this time, and is said to have been on a grand scale. The house was ready for occupancy on February 15th although some of the several coats of plaster had not yet been applied. On April 25th the house was considered completed, but there were still small finishing touches to be done. The house in question was a two-story structure and more elaborate than the average. Time required for ordinary houses is said to be considerably less.

A fine and large house reflects prestige. The finest and largest on Takashima are the *mi-ma-nagare* (three-rooms-running), which have six *tatami* rooms instead of the usual four. These rooms are arranged so that when the sliding panels between rooms are opened there are two parallel series of three rooms each stretching away from the *soto-niwa* and kitchen. There are two houses of this type in the *buraku*, one of which, the grandest in the community, has a second floor with additional rooms. Two-story houses, uncommon in Takashima, are usually of the standard four *tatami* room style on the ground floor with four additional rooms, *tatami*-covered or bare, on the second story. Any two-story house is grand.

HOUSEHOLD ARTS AND CRAFTS

Fishing, farming, housework and the care of children occupy most of the waking hours of Takashima men and women, leaving little time during the ordinary day for other activities. For men, work associated with fishing comprises almost the sum and total of economically gainful activities during waking hours of the normal day. A few men do a little home carpentry, and almost all are capable of making minor repairs to building or boat. Men have more leisure time than women, especially during the winter.

In the woman's world there are a number of tasks connected with fishing, farming, and the care of children and dwellings which require special training or skills. A woman must be able to sew. Ready-made clothing of both native and Western styles is available in town shops but it is expensive and only the rare household purchases ready-made clothing of native style. Sewing is usually done by unmarried girls or young brides who have received professional instruction. Their mothers and mothers-in-law, fingers now usually too thickened and stiff from labor for delicate work, learned sewing at home and in elementary school. The grandmothers, as a rule incapable of handling anything as delicate as a needle, received home training in their girlhood.

Young women sew clothing of both Western and traditional style, but the knowledge of older women is confined to native styles. Western clothes, principally garments for women and children, are usually made by means of following purchased patterns. Men's Western clothes must, as a rule, be purchased. Bedding is made at home, as are the tiny pillows. Knitting, with rayon yarn as wool is too expensive, is a common winter occupation for young women, who make sweaters, cardigans and knitted underclothing. Most middle-aged and younger women have learned cro-cheting and embroidery at school, but the skills are usually confined to the making of two or three pieces during girlhood, mirror covers for the small dressers or covers for trays to be used in connection with the marriage ceremony.

Most women know the rudiments of flower arrangement *(ikebana)*, but there is little time for such activity, and vases and other necessary equipment are often lacking. The rare privileged daughter of a financially fortunate household may have a few lessons in *cha-no-yu*, the tea ceremony, but this is regarded as a grace of the wealthy. The rare woman may have somewhere picked up the rudiments of the playing of native musical instruments, but no one is musically skilled. One lone woman in the *buraku*, her children now grown and no longer making demands on her time, has resumed the water-color painting learned at school during her childhood. According to the statements of Takashima women, the *buraku* is a place devoid of arts, the pursuit of which requires both time and money.

Arts and crafts are for the most part of a much homelier nature. The weaving of rice-straw baskets and grass or straw mats to be used for dry-ing farm produce or for protecting bundled nets from sun and sudden showers is known and practiced by every housewife. Occasionally rice-straw sandals *(waraji)* and straw aprons for use while pulling in fishing nets are still made, but machine-made substitutes are gradually replacing them. Straw and *shuro* palm fiber cordage are made by both men and women. A primitive home-made weaving frame is utilized for the weav-ing of baskets. Rounded beach stones attached to the ends of the straw weft insure tightness of weave.

DIET

With the exception of purchased rice, the diet of *buraku* residents is confined principally to the products of field and sea, raised or secured by themselves. The greatest single source of animal protein is not fish but clams, as most fish are sold. During the winter and spring months, when there is no fishing, clams are the staple in the average household. Among the purchased items considered essential are rice vinegar, soy bean sauce *(shoyu)*, *miso*, a paste made from beans, and several varieties of noodles. Polished rice—often mixed with barley—is served at every meal and comprises the bulk of the diet; other items of food are called *o-kazu*, "side dishes."[16] The average adult eats two or three bowlfuls of rice or rice and barley at each meal, about the amount required to fill a quart jar. The quantity of *o-kazu* eaten is small.

Cooking may be divided into three categories: boiling or steaming; broiling and toasting; and frying. Baking is not possible with the cooking equipment now in use. For boiling, steaming, and occasionally for frying, the *kudo* is used. The earthenware *kudo,* which stands about two and one-half feet in height, has two and sometimes three separate fire pits with apertures on their surfaces for the insertion of flanged pots. It is not suitable for the broiling or toasting of foods. Small, round, portable charcoal braziers of earthenware *(konro)* are used for broiling, toasting, and frying. Most ordinary fare is either boiled or broiled. To avoid the expenditure of money for charcoal, the usual fuel for the *konro* is *keshi-zumi,* "put-out charcoal," made at home by pouring water onto burning coals within the fire-pits of the *kudo* after *kudo* cooking is finished. The coals are then dried and saved for future use in the *konro. Keshi-zumi* is inferior to purchased charcoal, but it serves satisfactorily and is free. It is also used in *hibachi* for heating.

Pots and pans are made of aluminum or of a yellow aluminum-brass alloy, and are little different from those in use in the Western world. Flanged pots used on the *kudo* may be of either aluminum or cast iron. Frying pans *(furai pan)* are common. Kitchen implements such as graters and peelers are mostly of traditional Japanese design. Stainless steel, called "stainless," is known and desired but is as yet relatively uncommon among household utensils. Thin wire grills, some of single construction and some double with handles so that fish may be clasped between the two meshes and easily turned, are used on the *konro* for broiling and toasting. Chopsticks are used for handling broiling foods, and either chopsticks or large metal spoons are used for dishes which are boiled. Firewood, except large and heavy pieces, and *keshi-zumi* are handled with long, slim, chopstick-like metal fire tongs attached at the upper ends by a ring. These are used in the same manner as chopsticks.

Three meals and one or two snacks are eaten daily. Waking hours of the average day are from 6:00 A.M. to 9:00 P.M. Variation between summer and winter is slight. In winter the evening meal is prepared a little earlier so that it may be eaten before dark and people may sleep a little later in the morning. The ordinary breakfast consists of sliced, pickled *daikon,* rice, and soup made of *miso* and water in which a little onion and perhaps a small piece of fish are placed. The only normal

16. The diet of Americans and Europeans is frequently referred to by Japanese as *pan-shoku,* "bread diet," with the idea that bread is the mainstay and that Americans and Europeans consume bread in quantities equivalent to the amount of rice eaten in Japan.

variation in the breakfast menu is the soup, which may be made with *shoyu* instead of *miso* and contain pieces of *tōfu,* the white and nearly tasteless soy bean curd.

Rice, pickled *daikon,* and fish or clams with vegetables are served for the noon meal, which is the heaviest meal of the ordinary day. Fish is served in only small portions. It may be broiled, but is more commonly boiled, as are clams, with onions and other vegetables into a sort of stew. Vegetables vary with the season and are usually served either boiled or pickled. In some households cooked *daikon,* spinach, Chinese cabbage or carrots may serve as a substitute or alternate for fish for the noon meal when fish are not available. Sesame seed is used liberally with many vegetables to give them flavor, and certain vegetables, such as *daikon,* cucumbers, and Chinese cabbage, are frequently shredded and served with vinegar. Certain combinations of foods, such as persimmon and crab or octopus and green plums, are thought to produce gastronomic upsets and are avoided.

The evening meal, eaten around six o'clock, is again rice and usually such other food as has been left over from the noon meal. During the season of night fishing the evening meal is heavier and usually includes broiled or stewed fish. A large pot of rice is ordinarily cooked only once during the day and made to last for all meals; it is served cold for two of the three meals.

Unless the household is extremely poor, sweet potatoes are seldom served during regular meals. Although important in the diet, they are regarded as a food to be eaten, boiled with a little salt or deep-fried in fat, in between meals. The social status of sweet potatoes is very low; to offer them to an honored guest, if not insulting to the guest, is embarrassing to the host. Fruit is also ordinarily eaten only in between meals, although it serves as the last item at feasts and elaborate holiday meals. Fruit is often referred to as *kuchi-naoshi,* "mouth corrector," i.e., eaten as a last course, after salty fish and vegetables or sticky rice, it refreshes and leaves a pleasant taste in the mouth. Well-to-do households may eat purchased sweet cakes made of flour and filled with colored, sweetened bean paste as mid-morning and afternoon snacks. Tea, or sometimes simply hot water, is served at all meals and snacks. Fresh water is seldom drunk and school-children are frequently warned by their teachers of the dangers of drinking unboiled water.

The average Takashima housewife will tell you, laughing apologetically, that ordinary cooking within the *buraku* is hardly worthy of the name. Meals are as a rule hastily prepared, hastily served, and hastily eaten. Places at the low table on the raised wooden *daidokoro* in the kitchen are fixed. There is, however, usually no special seating arrangement except that the woman or women doing the cooking and serving are seated on the side closest to the *kudo*. When the master of the household is away, no one may occupy his place. Servings are individual, in cheap porcelain dishes placed on varnished or lacquered wooden trays. Finer trays and lacquer and porcelain dishes are reserved for guests and special occasions. The front entrance of the house, usually left open during the day, is closed when the members of the household are at meals.

A number of variant dishes are served from time to time. During winter holidays rice cakes are made and served in soup or toasted on the *konro*. Deep-fried foods *(tempura)* are frequently made, particularly deep-fried slices of sweet potatoes for in-between-meal snacks. *Tempura* is first dipped into a batter made of water and *Meriken-ko* ("American flour"), a refined white wheat flour, and immersed in boiling sesame or rape seed oil, the only cooking oils in ordinary use. A number of types of noodles cooked in broth are frequently eaten, especially when there is no fish, and are traditional during *Bon* (see Chap. V, The Ceremonial Calendar). Almost all food except soup and noodles in broth or stew-like dishes is served cold. "Hot" food is often prepared long beforehand and, in any event, is invariably allowed to become cold before being served. Hot food is relished, but cold is the standard.

Traditional and special dishes are served on holidays and other special days throughout the year if the household can meet the expense (see Chap. V, The Ceremonial Calendar). For unexpected guests, a hurried trip is made to the small shop in the *buraku* and small sweet cakes of a number of varieties purchased. Fruit or hard-boiled eggs also have sufficient status to be served to guests, and tea is always offered. Candy, which is lumped with sweet cakes under the term *o-kashi,* is much liked and a great variety, much of it Western in inspiration, is available in local shops. Sliced raw fish *(sashimi),* served with *shoyu* and mustard, is a perennial favorite, but since it requires better and larger species of fish than those normally taken for home use by fishermen, it is usually reserved for occasions of note. The rice wine, *sake,* is both rationed and expensive and its use is as a rule confined to special occasions, when quantities above the ration may be purchased through the black market. *Shōchū* is the standard liquor in drinking households and is acceptable for ordinary guests. It is made variously from sweet potatoes or grain, and is both stronger and cheaper than *sake*. *Shōchū* is often referred to as *sake*. Both drinks are served hot. Beer has long been known and liked, but is considered too expensive. Not all men drink. There are a number of teetotalers in the *buraku,* and women, in theory at least, do not drink. The occasional matron, however, gets carried away with the spirit of the occasion at wedding feasts or other banquets and consumes *shōchū* or *sake* with gusto, although never to the point of intoxication.

Reactions to alcohol are usually rapid. For many persons the first obvious reaction is a flushing of the face; often only a few of the tiny cups of *sake* or *shōchū* will produce a vivid glow. This quick and intense flushing is considered both embarrassing and ugly, but it is also amusing and the subject of friendly jokes. Continued drinking soon results in good-natured drunkenness, camaraderie, laughter, jokes, songs and dances, which are considered the inevitable result if not the objective of continued drinking.

Feasts revolve around fish. The king of all fish is the *tai* (sea bream), which is seldom taken by Takashima fishermen and must be purchased when the occasion, such as a wedding, demands it. At an elaborate feast, six or seven kinds of fish will be served, as *sashimi,* broiled, and boiled in broth with vegetables, taro, mushrooms and bamboo sprouts. No single household owns enough fine dishes and trays for a large feast, and it is customary to borrow from related households. Lacquered chopsticks, which are washable and will last indefinite periods, are used for ordinary meals. For guests, and for everyone at banquets, plain wooden chopsticks wrapped in paper are purchased and burned as fuel after a single using.

For a fishing *buraku,* the quantity of fish consumed is surprisingly small. Since non-fishing households receive gifts of fish from neighbors and relatives only occasionally, it is necessary for them to purchase almost all fish used. A certain type of small dried fish is purchased by all households and used in soups as a flavoring. Impoverished households buy very little fish but rely instead upon clams and, during the winter months, upon a species of octopus which can be dug from the sands at low tide. Whale meat, available at Shionasu at extremely low prices, is used by some of the poorer households but is seldom liked. Although chicken is esteemed, it is eaten upon very rare occasions. Other meat is also rare, for it must be purchased. The well-to-do household may purchase poor quality beef, sliced very thin, two or three times a year during the winter months, which is served in the form of *sukiyaki,* i.e., fried with fat, sugar, *shoyu,* and vegetables. There is something of a prejudice against pork, but on the very rare occasions that *buraku* persons eat in a town restaurant, breaded pork cutlets *(katsuretsu,* i.e., "cutlets") are popular if they can be afforded.[17] Meat is never eaten during summer months as it is then regarded, with some justification, as dangerous.

Garbage presents no problem. Fish are cooked with their heads on, and bones and entrails given to the household cat or to the neighbors' cat. The most common type of table refuse is clamshells, which are easily disposed of by throwing them onto the beach. The peelings of vegetables

17. Pork cutlets are also called *tonkatsu,* a word of curious origin. *Ton* is a China-derived reading of the ideograph (the ideographs used in writing Japanese are borrowed from the Chinese) for "pig." *Katsu* is the Japanese version of the "cut" of "cutlet."

and fruits are also thrown on the beach (all fruits are peeled; even the skins of grapes are removed). A trash pile composed principally of straw and materials which do not decompose readily is located at the edge of the beach in the center of Mae, the main settlement area, and serves as a landing point where one can disembark from boats during high tide without having to clamber up the stony sides of the breakwater-pier and without the danger of wet feet and garments. Trash is burned now and then on the beach, but, for the most part, the ocean serves as a garbage disposal system. If the tides do not carry the refuse completely away they at least succeed in distributing it more thinly over a greater area.

DRESS

The standard dress for ordinary wear is *yōfuku*, "Western clothing," i.e., clothing of American or European inspiration or derivation. An exception is the clothing of infants and aged women, which is usually of native style. Western clothing did not, however, become common until fifteen or twenty years ago, beginning with school children and spreading rapidly upward to the middle-aged. Western clothes have become increasingly common and increasingly popular since the beginning of the Occupation. They are cheaper and are said to be more comfortable and better suited for work. Until the end of the war nearly all Western clothing for women in use on Takashima was purchased. At that time an unmarried *buraku* girl, in face of strong opposition from her father, who thought Western clothing unbecoming and immodest, began taking lessons in one of the home sewing factories in Shionasu in the sewing of Western clothing. Once precedent had been established, other disapproving *buraku* fathers quickly became adjusted and, currently, all young women learn both native and Western sewing and make clothing of both types for themselves and other members of their households. The new art has enriched the English vocabulary of Takashima women to include words such as "snap," "fastener," and "style book."

Ordinary hot weather garb for male children consists of short trousers and shirts, and for females, cotton dresses. Boys of ages two or three may occasionally be seen naked during the summer, but more frequently wear shorts or a diaper. Infants of either sex, before they are able to walk, are almost invariably clad in native clothing of the type we call "kimono," but may wear only diapers during the heat of the day. Adult males wear cotton shorts or trousers and t-shirts or cotton shirts with open collars. A few aged men habitually wear long native style clothing. During extremely warm weather, and often while out on the fishing boats, men wear only loin cloths, but, although done, this is considered a little shameful within the *buraku* when outside one's own home. Older women, who

wear long Japanese clothing during both summer and winter, frequently
strip to the waist during hot weather but only within the confines of their
own homes. Girls and middle-aged women wear cotton dresses of Western style.

Some sort of headpiece is always worn in the heat of the sun. Men
wear soft cloth or straw hats, many of them of Western inspiration, and
sometimes a band of cloth or a piece of thin Turkish toweling *(hachimaki)*
is tied about the forehead. *Hachimaki* of red or white are traditionally
worn by young men during community festival parades. When tied with
the knot in front they are said to give the wearer strength and courage.[18]
Women use cloths or towels tied about their heads, so that most of the
face is covered, and sometimes add broad-brimmed straw hats.

The common working clothes of women are *mompei,* long and baggy
cotton pants tightly secured at the ankles, which became standard garb
throughout urban as well as rural Japan during the war. Long Mother
Hubbard-like aprons, head coverings, and footgear complete the visible
outfit. A fair skin is prized and efforts are made to cover the face while
working outside to prevent darkening from the sun. During the war a
new type of headgear which has no special name came into common use
and is much liked. This is a stringed cotton bonnet with a frilled hood,
very much like an unstarched sunbonnet. Slacks (called *suraksu*) are also
in use. They are more commonly worn by unmarried girls, for work and
also for "better" wear.

Footgear is ordinarily the Japanese straw or wooden sandals *(zōri*
and *geta),* and in wet and cold weather the *chika-tabi,* ankle-height rubber
and canvas shoes with a separation for the great toe. *Zōri* and *geta* are
made to stay on the feet by means of straps which pass between the great
and other toes. Stockings of native style *(tabi),* ankle-length and made of
flat cotton fabrics, open on the side and are secured by snaps or buttons.
Like *chika-tabi,* they have a separation for the great toe, and may thus be
worn with *zōri* and *geta. Tabi* and *zōri* are ordinarily used only for special
occasions. *Geta,* or sometimes rough, home-made straw *waraji,* on stock-
ingless feet are the standard for everyday wear. Bare feet are not uncommon during summer months. While inside homes or on fishing boats,
footgear is removed.

All young men and women and most middle-aged men also own
shoes and stockings of Western type, but they are reserved for dress-up
wear and are seldom worn in the *buraku.* Men, women and children may
frequently be seen dressed completely in Western clothes except for footgear, which is Japanese.

18. For an account of the history and use of *hachimaki* see M. Jōya, *Japanese Customs and Manners* (Tokyo: The Sakurai
Shoten, 1949).

PLATES 14, 15.—*Summer clothing. Use of the loin-cloth, normally worn only within the confines of one's own yard or on fishing boats, is declining.*

PLATES 16, 17.—*Girls in Western dresses, "good" clothes. Young men dressed in their best clothes for the Autumn Festival.*

Western clothes are as a rule better liked than native clothing but considered less attractive. The finest clothing of women of all ages, from infants to aged grandmothers, is of Japanese style and worn only on special occasions. Young women have "good," but not "best," clothing of Western style. Until the time of their marriage young men usually possess little native apparel and no fine native clothing. If they are fortunate, "best" clothing is a Western suit; otherwise it is trousers and an unmatched coat or jacket. Middle-aged men usually have one or two outfits of good Japanese clothing which has served them from the time of their marriage, and some also have Western suits. When the occasion demands that middle-aged or older women dress up, it is considered unbecoming for them to wear Western clothing.

During winter there is likely to be more Japanese clothing in evidence, as Western garments suited for cold weather are far too expensive. Padded cotton garments with long sleeves are frequently worn by persons of either sex and of any age. During cold weather a square-cut padded garment with sleeves, normally a winter sleeping garment, is frequently worn on the fishing boats at night and at any other time except when handling the dripping nets. Knitted undergarments of rayon or cotton yarn similar to union suits are worn extensively in winter. Schoolchildren wear purchased uniforms, sweaters, and light overcoats. A woolen overcoat *(ōba,* the Japanese rendition of "over") is the wish, usually ungranted, of every young girl.

Children are carried on the back by means of *itsuke,* roughly rectangular pieces of cloth, padded or unpadded, with tapes at each corner for tying around the body of the bearer. During colder weather a loose outer garment, with or without sleeves, called *oeko* or *nenneko,* is donned over the infant and *itsuke* and around the body of the transporter, leaving only the head of the child exposed to the air.

Sleeping garments, padded in winter and of a single thickness in summer, are entirely native, and again are of a cut which we call "kimono."[19]

For ceremonial occasions traditional native style clothing prevails. Brides are always dressed in traditional costume, expensive and elaborate silk gowns, white *tabi,* and elaborately embroidered *zōri,* basically white in color. Occasionally, a groom of recent years has worn *sebiro* (sack suit of Western derivation), and the richest man in the *buraku* owns morning clothes (called simply *moruningu,* i.e., "morning") for such occasions as weddings. The standard clothing for the groom and for all older males of a wedding party is, however, the *montsuki,* a native garment with an embroidered crest,[20] usually dark in color. Clothing worn by adults at

---

19. *Kimono* is a generic term meaning clothing. There is a great variety of specific names for articles and types of clothing.

20. During Meiji times, when sumptuary laws came to an end and crests became permissible for the first time for commoners, most Japanese households adopted them. The paulownia, used by many Takashima households, is very common throughout Japan.

funerals and memorial services is also predominantly native, often the same clothing as is worn for weddings and other happy occasions. Burial is usually in Japanese clothing, although children and young men may be dressed in clothing of Western style.

For most persons, the type of clothing worn is that which happens to be in their possession. Clothing is expensive, particularly fine Japanese clothing and woolen goods. The high cost of Japanese clothing has contributed a good deal toward making the less costly Western clothing predominant. Work clothing and everyday clothing, whether Western or native, is likely to be threadbare and ragged.

Clothing colors follow traditional rules. The native clothing of infants and young girls is bright in color, most frequently red, and continues to be bright for girls until marriage, when the colors gradually become more subdued. Red figured prints on a pink ground are very popular for female children. As a woman matures, her clothing becomes progressively somber in color. According to ancient Japanese tradition, persons who have retired may once again wear bright colors, but this is a tradition which now probably exists in speech only throughout all of Japan. There is an old saying, *"Rokujū mitsugo,"* "sixty-year-(old) three-year-old," which is said to refer to this tradition. Western garments are more conservative in color, as is the clothing of all males except infants. Young men avoid red neckties lest they be thought effeminate, since red is a girls' color.

Styles in native clothing as well as in Western dress for women change from time to time, but changes in Japanese clothes are usually slight and consist principally of fabric pattern variations and color variations rather than cut. Young girls are very conscious of style changes in Western clothing. All clothing and all fabrics are utilized for one purpose or another until they are worn beyond repatching.

Most households allow clothes to become quite dirty before washing them. Washing is done in wooden or metal tubs in which clothing is rubbed by hand or upon corrugated wooden washboards, an innovation of about twenty years ago. Soap, seldom used on work clothing, is purchased; no household has made its own for twenty-five or more years. The ordinary method of drying a wash is to lay articles over bamboo poles which are suspended in the air by resting their ends in the crotches of fruit trees or on fences. Poles are inserted through the sleeves of garments to prevent their being blown down by wind. Seams are removed from native clothes before laundering so that they become long, narrow strips of cloth after removal of the stitches. The strips of cloth are starched and smoothed out while still wet on long, flat boards to dry flat and wrinkle-free. A device consisting of a series of many pins or clamps attached to two parallel cords is also utilized for the wrinkle-free drying of silk fabrics.

Wheat flour is ordinarily used for starching, but is considered inferior to a seaweed which is gathered at low tide during the springtime and washed, dried, and stored for use as needed. This seaweed may also be purchased in shops. When boiled, it produces an almost colorless solution.

Clothes, such as Western dresses, which require ironing are pressed with heavy charcoal irons, called "iron." These appear to be an adaptation of Western flat-irons. Seam-folds and other hard-to-reach places of fine clothing are ironed after the clothes have been reassembled by means of small, long-handled chromium plated native irons. These irons are shaped like flattened shoe-trees and are heated over charcoal braziers. Ironing is done upon thin cardboard and cotton devices, many of which fold like screens. These are placed on the floor, and one kneels to iron.

Unmarried girls and young brides wear make-up, which is available in tremendous quantities in the shops of any town. Lipstick, rouge, and powder, all packaged in containers modeled after those in use in the Western world, are the property of every young female but are ordinarily used only in moderation and seldom while working in the fields. Other cosmetics such as cold cream *(kuriimu)*, vanishing cream, cologne, and perfume are the possessions of only a few. One advance-guard maiden rounds out her collection with eye shadow (called "eye shadow"). The lavish use of cosmetics is frowned upon except for a bride on her wedding day, and there are few offenders.

Excessive facial and body hair is disliked, and most men keep their lightly bearded faces shaved with straight or safety razors. For special occasions, both men and women have professional shaves in which all visible parts of the face and neck are shaved of whatever fuzzy growth they might bear. Eyebrows of young women and often of young men, if they are abundantly hairy, are shaved or plucked to a narrower and more attractive conformation. All unmarried girls and most women up to the age of forty have permanent waves, a relatively new fashion. The first permanent wave in the *buraku* was in 1940, and the practice became general after the close of the war. Permanent waves are not unusual among young men in towns and even rural areas of Japan, but no Takashima boy has yet ventured to have his hair treated. Older women wear their hair long and straight, parted in the middle, and arranged to form a bun in the back. A greying woman may occasionally dye her hair, but women who have been married for a few years, as a rule, give little attention to their day to-day appearance. Long hair is not to be found among unmarried girls, and it is necessary to rent elaborately coiffed wigs for the modern bride so that she may appear on her wedding day wearing traditional, if artificial, hairdress. Few ornaments are ever worn. Young girls regard brooches, pins, rings, and earrings, all foreign to Japanese tradition, as attractive, but such luxuries are beyond *buraku* purses.

Little attention is given to the brushing of teeth, although white, shiny teeth are admired. Schoolchildren are instructed in practices of dental hygiene by their teachers but, as a rule, little heed is given. A few battered and unsavory-looking tooth brushes of both Western and native style may be found hanging from nails on the outside wall by the kitchen door of nearly all houses, but they are ordinarily utilized only before making ceremonial calls or before special events. Such dental care as is practiced is for aesthetic, not hygienic, reasons.

A beautiful woman is a combination of the classical and the modern. From the classical tradition, she must have an oval "melon-seed" face, fair skin, coal-black hair, small lips, small eyes set close together, a small but high-bridged nose, and a gracefully shaped neck. The beautiful young *buraku* woman of today should also have a permanent wave. Teeth should be straight and white; the gold or imitation gold teeth affected by some persons of the present generation of parents have been passé for fifteen or more years. A young man should be straight, vigorous, and tall. His face should be fairly narrow, teeth straight, complexion fair, and nose high-bridged. Beauty in either male or female is, however, not a matter of supreme importance (see Chap. VI, Marriage).

SICKNESS AND HEALTH

The state of health of the residents of Takashima appears, as a whole, to be good. *Buraku* people commonly attribute their good health and long life-span (one man reached the age of ninety-five in 1951) to the "good air." It is perhaps better explained by the fact that the ocean serves as a fairly effective system for disposal of possibly harmful waste and garbage, and that the islanders spend most of their lives out in the open and are to some degree isolated from other settlements.

Deaths of infants and children have been fairly common in *buraku* history, but they have rarely been diagnosed. Deaths of adults are usually from old age. Serious illness caused by disease is uncommon. Within the past several decades there have been a few deaths from typhus, but none in recent years. There has been no death from tuberculosis, one of the great scourges of Japan, for a great many years. At the time of this writing, however, one *buraku* man suffers from tuberculosis which he contracted during military service, and there is possibly a second case. Neither of these persons can afford medical treatment by private practitioners, and no attempt is made to secure treatment through government institutions because they are away from home, crowded, difficult of access for visiting relatives, and because *buraku* people believe that they would never be able to secure admission. One man, now middle-aged, was crippled during childhood by poliomyelitis. An aged woman who became slightly crippled during childhood, long before she came to Takashima as a bride, may also have been a victim of poliomyelitis. Beyond minor ailments, however, there is relatively little illness in the normal course of life of the average person.

The ailments of children are those which are most noticeable. During the summer and continuing until early winter, many children are afflicted with a pustulant skin disease. Skin disease is, however, rarely evident on older children or adults. Colds prevail among children during much of the year, and children with noses running thick streams of a curious yellowish color are a permanent part of the scene. Some child always has ringworm of the scalp during warm weather, and all children as well as many adults are said to have intestinal worms. An infection of the eyes called *hayarime,* "running eye," is endemic and reaches mild epidemic proportions occasionally during the summer. But these are all normal illnesses, to be expected, and not regarded as serious.

With the exception of the mentally sub-normal male who acts as unpaid servant for one household, there is no obvious evidence of mental aberration. One woman is regarded as peculiar because of her occasional habit of injecting extraneous topics into conversation. Insanity is feared and attempts are said to be made to conceal it. No prospective bride or groom wishes to become allied with a lineage in which there is a record of insanity.

Flies, mosquitoes, and fleas are present in abundance during much of the year and are regarded as one of the inevitable and minor annoyances of life. Toilets seethe with maggots in the summer. No preventive measures are ordinarily taken against any of these pests, although a few households have in postwar years utilized a DDT compound sprinkled on *tatami* to eradicate fleas. Large mosquito nets of cotton mesh are used at night while sleeping by everyone during six or seven months of the year.

Rats and mice abound, in dwellings, outbuildings, and in the rocky crevices at the base of the breakwater-pier. A few households regularly take positive measures to eradicate them from their dwellings and outhouses, using poisons (the name of one poison, in translation, is "Cat Unnecessary") and traps. Household cats also help to keep the number of rodents down. The attitude of most persons toward both rats and mice, however, is one of affectionate irritation, and no one attempts to do anything about the breakwater-pier, the home of most of the rats.

Among the young and middle-aged, who have attended school, theory of disease is modern for the most part. Treatment of disease is also largely modern, if not thorough. Medications are almost entirely commercially prepared compounds purchased at drugstores or from house vendors. Common home medical supplies are ammonia for use on hands punctured by the spines of fish; mercurochrome, gauze bandage, and absorbent cotton for first aid; and vaseline for burns, bruises, and cracking of the skin. Most of these items are known by their English names.

Treatment for ordinary ailments is casual home therapy. Commercially prepared medications are administered for skin disease, worms (Santonin is a standard remedy for worms), and colds. If the skin disease lingers for many months because effective attention is not given, it is no serious matter. Children will recover from this ailment, given time.

Every household has a supply of medicines: it is almost impossible to avoid having one because of the persistence and attractiveness of the sales methods of door-to-door peddlers. Several vendors, each representing a different company, visit Takashima once annually, leaving large, flat paper sacks of medications at each house. The outer surface of the sack is printed with advertising in bright colors, and bears the names of twenty-odd medicines which are available by this method of distribution. Small packets of several different types of medicines for common ailments are left within the bag, which is marked to indicate its contents. Vendors return the following year, examine the sacks, and charge the householder only for medications used. Replenishments are made with presumably fresh preparations. So persuasive are the salesmen that it is difficult to refuse to accept a medicine bag. The argument that payment is to be made only for medicines used is appealing, and it is good to be prepared for emergencies. Ailments for which the drugs are advertised to be specific include headache, stomach upsets, rheumatism, itching, frost-bite, and worms. As a rule, a good deal of faith is placed in the effectiveness of these preparations.

A few home remedies are known and sometimes used. The beans of a semi-cultivated plant *(dokkeshimame,* "poison-removing bean"), boiled and eaten, are considered effective in cases of food poisoning or stomach-ache.[21] A small wild plant *(mikoshigusa)*, the whole plant dried and then steeped in hot water, is also used in the treatment of stomach disorders. An infusion made by boiling dried green figs in water is prescribed by older people for fevers, and an infusion made in the same manner from the stems of eggplant is said to relieve the pains of appendicitis. With the exception of *dokkeshimame,* these home remedies now see little use.

Moxa *(mogusa)* is known to all, but the incidence of its use is declining. Most individuals over the age of fifteen have been subjected to moxa

21. In other parts of Japan an infusion called *habucha* is made from these beans.

treatment *(o-kyū)*[22] during childhood; many persons under that age have not. Treatment consists of burning on the skin a pinch of moxa, an inflammable tinder made of the leaves of *Artemesia indica*. Moxa is considered both a therapeutic device and a punishment, and is most commonly used for the cure of worms and fretfulness in children. The first administering of moxa is usually done by a professional in nearby Ajino; later treatments are given by the mother. Moxa may be given to children as young as two years of age, and three applications, the last when a child is six, are considered most effective. Moxa — or the threat of its use — may be resorted to when children misbehave, and is said to achieve excellent results. Most persons, however, still regard moxa more as a form of therapy than as a punishment. Middle-aged and older women say that the use of moxa, and particularly the first application by a professional, "makes children healthy." Young mothers do not as a rule subscribe to its use, relying instead upon commercial vermifuges for worms, and other punishments for misbehavior. Older persons use moxa occasionally for aches and pains and "to soothe nerves." Professional specialists in the use of moxa are also usually specialists in Japanese massage *(amma)* and acupuncture *(hari)*, the puncturing of the skin with needles to relieve pain. Only the old have faith in acupuncture, and little resort is made by even the aged to treatment by either acupuncture or massage, in part because it is considered expensive.

In case of extremely serious illness or injury a doctor is called from Ajino, the nearest town with a physician and hospital, by means of telephoning from Shionasu. Office visits to physicians are occasionally made, but medical bills are avoided as much as possible. Confinement in Japanese hospitals works a hardship on the household of the patient as the only equipment provided in patients' rooms is bedsteads and springs. Bedding, cooking utensils, dishes, food, and someone to cook and take care of the ordinary wants of the patient must be provided by the patient. Crowded buses are unsuitable for the ill and impossible as conveyances for all the equipment needed. The only recourse is to call a taxi from Ajino, thereby incurring the expenditure of a large sum of money. Unless the physician insists, treatment of the sick and injured is at home.

Under the national public health program, schoolchildren have for some years received various inoculations and vaccinations, and under the post-war public health program preventive therapy is being extended to pre-school children and adults.

Religious and magico-religious treatment of illness exists (see Chap. V, Faith-healers and Mediums), but for younger persons, who are prone

22. Moxacautery is said to have come to Japan from China. The term *mogusa* may be used to mean either the preparation burned on the skin or moxacautery. *O-kyū* means only moxacautery. For a more detailed description of Japanese moxacautery see M. Jōya, *op cit.*, pp. 136-138.

to rely upon commercial medications and the services of physicians, such treatment is confined principally to prayers at shrines. Older people place faith in traditional beliefs and practices including the services of faith-healers and mediums and the reliance upon talismans, at which many young people scoff silently.

A few old beliefs expressed in the form of folk sayings and bearing no connection with religion are remembered, but little or no credence is placed in them; a strained or sore wrist can be cured by having a child of opposite sex from the afflicted person tie a string about it; drinking a cup of cold water before the sun comes up will cure nervous ailments; a metal ring worn on the finger—a practice sometimes still followed—will remove pain from a stiff neck or aching shoulders.

RECREATION AND ENTERTAINMENT

During the ordinary day of adults there is little activitiy which *buraku* people regard as recreation. Men, however, talk as they make, mend, or treat nets, and occasionally several men do their work in the company of one another. Women have the odd moment in the fields for gossip, and the women of the several households with no wells have an opportunity for exchanges of greetings and tidbits of news as they draw water at the communal well. It is a workaday world, although the work may some-times be accomplished at a leisurely pace with time out, for men at least, to rest or sleep a little.

The children's world is one of school and play. Card games are a favorite pastime for both boys and girls. A card game based upon the scoring rules of baseball is popular with older boys. Older girls like a game called *baba-nuki* ("draw the grandmother"), similar to Old Maid, and very young boys and girls like to play *patchi* (called *pachin* in various other areas of Japan). This is a simple game involving the throwing of cards which bear pictures of Japanese heroes and of Western figures, including Western dolls and comic strip characters. The sandy path by the beach is the scene, for both boys and girls, of various hopscotch-like games, and for marbles, which are propelled by placing the marble between the extended thumb and forefinger and squeezing until it shoots forward.

Games and amusements for children are likely to be seasonal and to follow cycles of fad. There is greater indulgence in games during the cooler winter months, when girls jump rope, bounce bean bags, play with dolls and ornament the backs of their hands with bright decalcomanias of dolls (a kewpie-doll is common). Girls, inspired by school training, may amuse themselves during fine autumn and spring weather by drawing outdoor scenes with crayons and water colors. In the summer there is less heightened game activity. Children are allowed to play on the sandy beaches close to their homes if there is an older child among them, but children of any age are seldom allowed to go swimming, with the result that many adults cannot swim or swim only poorly. When the fashion strikes, usually in cooler weather, boys are much addicted to playing with tops and rolling hoops, generally old bicycle rims, with sticks. A favorite pastime for ten- and twelve-year-old boys during autumn and spring is the catching of *mejiro (Zosterops japonica)* with bird-lime. The small, white-eyed birds are placed in cages and kept as household pets. Small wooden and metal toys—trucks, trains, and airplanes—are the proud possessions of the fortunate. Toys are available in great abundance in the shops of any town, and children are usually indulged as much as it is thought the budget will allow. Most small children have rattles, scooters, and wagons, often inherited from older siblings. Chewing gum (called "chewing gum") of the ordinary soft variety is popular, and the chewing of bubble-gum, a post-war innovation, was perhaps the favorite amusement of young Takashima children for a period of several months during the year 1950. Children with impetigo presented a particularly noteworthy scene while chewing bubble-gum. As the big bubbles broke and the rubbery matter adhered to pustules about the mouth, it was gathered promptly back into the mouth for rechewing.

Entertainment for adults revolves about the household, the rearing of children, and traditional religious observances, which are occasions more in the nature of enjoyable festivals than serious obeisances to the supernatural.

For the average married person, the only commercial entertainments are the several annual visits of traveling *Naniwa-bushi* performers, who come to Takashima with little advance notice. Performances are given at the community hall *(kōkaidō)* and performers rely for payment upon donations made after performances are concluded. *Naniwa-bushi* is a type of chanting-singing recital of traditional tales; it is said to have originated in Osaka (formerly called Naniwa). Performers who come to Takashima are often a family group of man, wife, and one or two children. Their singing and elaborately dramatic story-telling vary between the extremes of broad comedy and heavy-handed tragedy. A little obscenity is both permissible and desirable, for it is amusing.[23] Besides traditional tales, stories and songs of topical interest are always included, and the performance is sometimes like a variety or vaudeville show.

Naniwa-bushi is, however, little enjoyed by most young and many middle-aged adults; instead, it is the amusement of the grandparents,

23. To quote an example, a character in one of the comic tales heard by the author refers scornfully to a small amount of money as being infinitesimal, not even equivalent to *neko no shoben*, "a cat's piss." This quip produced hearty laughter.

who sit in happy attendance through the three-hour performances. *Naniwa-bushi* is also a respite for mothers, as young children, who are interested by the noise, the crowd, and the make-up and bright costumes of the performers, can be sent off with their grandmothers, where they usually fall asleep before the long performances are concluded.

There is no longer any purely social gathering in which all *buraku* people participate. In the past, until perhaps thirty years ago, communal work projects and feasts at the times of weddings and house building saw the assembling of at least one representative from each household.

Athletic contests and other affairs of the elementary school at Shion-asu are frequent, and attendance of parents, particularly mothers and grandmothers, is strong. Track meets draw nearly everyone, and the one great track meet of the year has become an unofficial village holiday when none but essential tasks are done. The attendance at school plays and other school entertainments featuring dancing and singing is heavy, but it does not approach the all-out attendance of the one major track meet of the year.

Pilgrimages to shrines are at least partly a non-secular pleasure for adults, and are pure entertainment for the young. The annual trip to Kotohira Shrine on Shikoku is unadulterated adventure for children. The annual calendar of traditional and religious holidays may be re-garded as a series of occasions for light-hearted enjoyment and rest. The two annual watches maintained at the shrine of the tutelary god of the *buraku* approach the status of a general gathering of the *buraku* and mark a time for light conversation and stories. For children, these are events not to be missed. Funerals for the aged, whose deaths have long been expected, are likely to be somewhat light in character, and funeral masses, held upon the anniversaries of death, are often happy occasions. (See Chap. V for further details on religious entertainment).

The modern-minded young men and women, unhampered as yet by marriage and parental responsibilities, find the attractions of Ajino and other nearby towns enticing. Movies are great favorites, but because of the distance and the expense, three or four visits a year are the usual quota. American movies are now shown everywhere as well as Japanese productions, but *buraku* young people prefer movies in the native lan-guage for the stated reason that although American films have sub-titles (more properly, side-titles) they are ineptly executed and difficult to fol-low. *Shakai dansu* ("social dancing," i.e., Western style dancing), is admired by unmarried girls and young men, but it is still a little new and bold for the *buraku* and not all young persons have attempted it. Western style dancing is learned from friends, or, rarely, in the dance halls at Ajino, which young people attend in the company of members of their own sex. Popular styles of Western dancing are the *tango, trotto* (fox-trot), *burūsu* (blues, considered a style of dancing as well as a type of music), *warutsu* (waltz), and *jiruba* (jitterbug) — the latter is regarded as a little *gehin* (vulgar). For the young people of Takashima, Western dancing is a wholly postwar development.

Newspapers are read by nearly all literate adults, which group comprises the young and middle-aged, although a single newspaper will often serve two households. There is a fair amount of interest in local events as reported in newspapers and a lesser degree of interest in national and international affairs. Magazines, because they are expensive, are uncommon and confined principally to those purchased in connection with school work. Comic books, some of them of Western origin, are popular among the young as are magazines depicting the lives of Japanese film stars, but can rarely be afforded. Mickey Mouse *(Miki)* and Popeye are favorites. Blondie, which appears as a strip in one of the newspapers, is not comprehended nor liked, although it is very popular among the more Westernized and sophisticated residents of Okayama City. An issue of the Japanese edition of *Reader's Digest* appears now and then in the hands of young men or women. Young women, single and married, like the various "women's magazines" of national circulation, which appear to be of American inspiration. America is currently a favorite topic in many if not most magazines which reach Takashima.

Few persons have hobbies. Two young men display some interest in collecting and mounting the small number of stamps upon which they are able to lay their hands. Some young women regard sewing, knitting and crocheting as hobbies, but these are usually considered tasks to provide clothing for themselves and other members of the household.

Gambling, with dice and with cards, is a pastime which many men relish and which all women and old persons hate and fear, for it can and sometimes has meant ruin to financial security. It is said that Jizō, a Buddhist deity whose stone statues appear in the graveyard and scattered about the *buraku,* is the only male who does not gamble, and this is because he is deaf and blind. Gambling is *haji,* something to be ashamed of, and something to be done covertly so that wives, *ojii-san* and *obaa-san* do not see. Everyone will soon know, but until it is discovered the pleasure can be enjoyed. Gambling, nearly always intra-*buraku,* is said always to represent a loss as winners are expected to be extravagant with their easily gained money and are chided by their opponents into spending if they are not liberal in the purchase of *shōchū* or *sake.* For this reason, gambling runs in cycles; for a year or so most men gamble frequently until all find that they are in financial need because of their losses or extravagances. The disapproval of aged parents and wives is also a deterrent. The gambling fever then dwindles for a time, to spring up again when there is a little available cash.

Tobacco is considered a necessity rather than a luxury by most men. The average adult male smokes heavily, both cigarettes and pipes with tiny bowls which contain only a pinch of tobacco. It is bad form for a woman to smoke as this is a habit said to be confined to *kurōto* (literally, "professionals," i.e., women who are regarded as professionally promiscuous, such as waitresses, prostitutes, and *geisha*). A few women, nevertheless, smoke, but never in the presence of strangers and usually only within their own homes.

Feasts, and particularly wedding feasts, are the most pleasurable social occasions of life, for even during difficult times strong effort is made to have food and liquor available in liberal quantities at these times. All feasts to which guests are invited begin formally, with the exchange of careful, deep bows performed between host and guest. Bows are exchanged while guest and host and hostess kneel on the *tatami* of the *shimonoma*. Gifts are presented to the household at this time, and are acknowledged with many bows and profuse thanks. It is considered rude to open a gift in the presence of the donor.

If the party is small, guests are ushered into the *kaminoma*. If there are many guests, the sliding panels between the *kaminoma* and *shimonoma* are removed to make them into one large room. Guests also usually exchange bows with other guests before taking their seats. If the party is large, several cross-currents of bows may take place at one time. Seating is arranged according to prestige. The seat of highest honor is a position in front of the pillar by the *tokonoma*. Seats decrease in honor in proportion to their distance away from the *tokonoma*. Guests sit on the finest and thickest cushions in the house.

Food and hot *sake* and *shōchū* are served by young girls of the household and of related households. Ceremonial rounds of drinks are exchanged during the feasting, always initiated by the host, who starts things off by handing his own *sake* cup to a waitress and directing her to fill and present it to the most honored guest. The guest acknowledges the compliment with a bow, drinks the cup, and returns the compliment. As the party becomes more informal, guests dispense with the services of the too-busy waitresses and pour toasts for each other. When stomachs are comfortably full of banquet food[24] and the liquor has begun to evince itself, the gathering becomes highly informal. Men quickly abandon the traditional and formal kneeling postures and lean against the walls or sit with their legs crossed (the usual sitting position for men). Both Taka-

---

24. In surrounding farming areas it is a common custom at feasts to eat very little of the food but, instead, to wrap it up and take it home when the festivities are over. This is not usually done on Takashima and is never done at big feasts.

shima men and women state that the traditional Japanese kneeling
position soon becomes uncomfortable for them because they do not often
sit in this formal fashion. Women continue to kneel but do so in a relaxed,
informal manner. With informality comes conviviality. A common form
of conviviality is to call upon everyone in turn to render a song. There is
hesitation at first until someone bolder than average or someone with
confidence in the reputation of his voice has sung a song. From that point
there is no difficulty, and even the most unaccomplished singers take
their turns. Applause follows every turn, and as the party spirit waxes,
someone rises and dances to his own singing or to that of others. The party
has now reached its height, and several dancers may perform at once.
Men, usually careful to avoid bodily contact with other persons, throw
their arms affectionately about one another in an excess of friendliness.
Women are more restrained; those talented at singing perform, but their
drinking is limited and they seldom dance.

A huge platter containing a whole baked *tai* or a large flounder resting upon a great mound of noodles is the last main course (fruit may follow), and is the traditional sign that the party has come to an end. The
platter is placed in the middle of the floor where it can be seen and
admired, and while singing, drinking, and dancing continue, the noodles
and fish are served to each guest.

Feasts begin before nightfall and continue until midnight or shortly
after midnight. Guests who have come from a distance are bedded down
for the night at the house of the host or in the homes of neighboring relatives of the host. Drunken guests returning to the mainland must be
carefully shepherded by their wives and the more clear-headed men for
fear of falling from the small boats and drowning during the crossing to
Shionasu. Departing guests, after a sometimes weaving exchange of bows
with the host and hostess, leave the house carrying with them gift boxes
of fish and other delicacies. These boxes are placed beside the food trays
of guests sometime toward the end of the feasting. A wealthy household
ties the gift boxes in *furoshiki,* square pieces of cloth which serve as customary carry-alls when traveling or marketing, but this is a luxury rarely
seen on Takashima. The *furoshiki* in which guests have brought gifts are
always returned to them and, on the occasion of big feasts, are utilized
for wrapping the gift boxes of food. A *furoshiki* is, under any circumstances, seldom returned empty.

There is no obscenity in dance and little in song. Individual para-
phrases, fairly obscene, are occasionally heard, but pronounced obscenity
is *yaban* ("uncivilized," a word which sees frequent use) and the custom of
the far past. There are no songs peculiar to Takashima and, for lack of
musicians and instruments, there is rarely any musical accompaniment

to singing. Party songs are, for the most part, popular songs learned from recordings or well-known folk songs of the central Japan and Inland Sea area which the singers have heard and learned at other parties or from records. A favorite song at parties for both singing and dancing is *Tankō-bushi,* a coal miners' song which came into vogue throughout all Japan during the war. Themes of old songs and folk-songs are the doings of traditional heroes and eulogies extolling the virtues of a town, region, or mountain. The popular songs (as opposed to traditional songs) which the average guest sings are those which were current in Japan during his youth. Some of these songs are humorous. A humorous song entitled *Sarari-man* (Salary Man)[25] is said to have been nationally popular about twenty years ago, and is still sometimes sung (although considered just a little vulgar) by middle-aged persons:

SALARY MAN

I am a salary man.
I have just received my monthly salary
And it is a lot of money.
I must go home and confer with my wife
Whether to buy a *geisha* or a prostitute.

Songs sung for dancing at *Bon,* a presumably religious occasion, are seldom religious in character (but doubtless once were). Tales of heroes and sad stories of the sufferings of the virtuous are common themes for *Bon* dancing songs. Among popular *Bon* songs is one entitled *Ishidō-maru,* which recounts the well-known and traditional tale of a feudal lord and his illegitimate son:

The concubine of a feudal lord who ruled over five countries bears him a son named Ishidō-maru. The barren wife of the lord, overcome with jealousy, orders a retainer to kill the concubine. The retainer, feeling pity for the concubine, kills a beggar woman instead and shows her head to the lord's wife as evidence of the slaying. When the true facts become known to the lord, he grows to despise his wife and becomes despondent. The jealous wife soon loses her mind, and the lord then retires into the mountains to become a priest.

When Ishidō-maru, the illegitimate son, turns seventeen he decides to go seek his father. Strapping on his father's sword he sets out on his quest accompanied by his mother, the concubine, whom he leaves at the foot of the mountains. The young man eventually comes into contact with his father, who recognizes him by his sword but who in no way acknowledges the relationship.

After long wanderings through the mountains Ishidō-maru abandons his unsuccessful search and returns to the hut where he had left his mother, only to find her dead. He then returns to the mountains to enter the priesthood and becomes a disciple of his father, who treats him kindly but goes to his death without informing Ishidō-maru of their relationship.

25. "Salary man" refers to salaried white collar workers of urban communities.

Another favorite song for parties is a version of an old *minyō* (folk-song) about the nearby fishing community of Shimotsui, a way-stop for feudal lords traveling by sea to Edo (Tokyo) in Tokugawa (1603-1868) times. This song is said to have originated as a rowing song, sung by boatmen of the feudal lords.

Shimotsui-bushi

Shimotsui minato wa yo! Hairiyote deyote yo,
Matomo makiyote magiriyote yo!
Tokohai tonoe nanoe sore-zore.

Shimotsui minato ni yo! Ikari o irerya yo,
Machi no ando no hi ga maneku yo!
Tokohai tonoe nanoe sore-zore.

Washūzan kara yo! Matsushima mireba yo,
Uzumaku koshio ni tsuki ga uku yo!
Tokohai tonoe nanoe sore-zore.

Shimotsui yoi toko yo! Ichido wa oide yo,
Haru wa tai-ami, aki wa tsuri yo!
Tokohai tonoe nanoe sore-zore.

* * *

Shimotsui harbor is easy to enter and to leave,
Straight on, or with sails full or aslant.
Tokohai tonoe nanoe sore-zore.

In Shimotsui harbor we lower our anchors,
And the lights of lamps beckon from the town.
Tokohai tonoe nanoe sore-zore.

From Mt. Washū we look down on the island of Matsushima
While the moon floats in the ebb-tide whirlpools.
Tokohai tonoe nanoe sore-zore.

Shimotsui is a fine place; come visit it sometime,
In spring for sea-bream netting, in autumn for line fishing.
Tokohai tonoe nanoe sore-zore.

Songs of children are ancient onomatopoetic jingles and lullabies learned from mothers and older sisters, and songs learned at school. The latter are frequently of Western derivation and include *Oh, Susannah, Auld Lang Syne,* and *Old Black Joe* with Japanese lyrics. *Turkey in the Straw,* played repeatedly on the school phonograph, provides lively background music for the activities of a track meet. Not-yet-married young people prefer tunes learned from the recordings of Japanese professionals or heard on the radio. Included among these are a number of adaptations of American popular songs. *Buttons and Bows* and *You Are My Sunshine* were favorites in Okayama City in 1950 and known to a few young people in the *buraku*.

Dancing during the *Bon* festival season was common until about fifteen years ago, and is still occasionally done in the *buraku*. *Bon* dancing styles are traditional. Dancers take positions beside or behind each other to form a circle. Routines involve simple forward and backward movements of the feet, and the movement of hands and arms to the right, left, above, and in front of the body in time with the rhythm. Clapping of the hands to the beat of the vocal music is an integral part of the dance.

In former days there were always several evenings of dancing which might continue intermittently over a period of a month at *Bon* season, but for many years dancing has been half-hearted and in recent years sometimes omitted. Dances begin informally. A few persons who are gathered together in the evening begin and others, hearing the singing, come to watch and join in. Several men and women are known for their skill at singing and their services are always happily given. Kerosene lanterns and a few paper lanterns may be set up for illumination and for the feeling of well-being which their lights contribute. Dancing, in the old days, continued until past midnight. Today it may continue for two hours and participation is seldom strong or whole-hearted. The middle-aged, the principal participants in *buraku* dancing in recent years, blame the apathy upon the younger generation, who regard *Bon* dancing as old-fashioned and must be cajoled into joining. Young people of the present generation who are persuaded to join the dancing do so in a self-conscious and embarrassed manner, and are ready to stop at any moment.[26]

During the war there is said to have been much joint village dancing, religious in nature, in honor of the war dead. These dances were held in the elementary school grounds in Shionasu. Dancing by adults is sometimes one of the events of the program of the big annual school track meet. During the fall of 1950 the women of the Honjō *Fujinkai* (Women's Club, see Chap. IV, The *Buraku* and the City), including young and aged persons and a number of Takashima women, danced in the schoolyard as part of the program of the track meet to the rhythm of *Tankō-bushi*.

Native dancing and particularly *Bon* dancing has been dying a slow death in Japan for several decades. Many, or perhaps most, communities no longer have *Bon* dancing. Some rural communities have, however, deliberately perpetuated *Bon* dancing and perfected it to a semi-profes-

26. For a collection of folk-songs of Okayama Prefecture, see *Folk Music of Japan*, Ethnic Folkways Library (LP disc).

sional degree. This is done partly because of pride in local achievements and partly because expert dancing is a great attraction for persons of other communities, including urban residents, who will travel many miles to watch renowed performers — and incidentally spend money in the community for food, drink and souvenirs.[27]

There are a few *geisha* and many prostitutes in the nearby larger communities, Ajino, Kojima, Shimotsui, and Kurashiki. The entertainment of *geisha* is, however, always expensive and is far beyond the world of Takashima fishermen, whose only contact with them is through the rare festivals which they may attend in the larger communities where *geisha* give public performances of singing and dancing. Prostitutes, usually those in Ajino, three miles away, are occasionally patronized by young, unmarried *buraku* men.

27. An example is the *Bon* dancing of the Island of Shiraishi (Hiroshima Prefecture) in the Inland Sea. The residents of Shiraishi have intense pride in the polished, near-professional performance of their *Bon* dancers, singers and musicians. Shiraishi dancing and singing is famous in at least its home and neighboring prefectures. During 1951 Shiraishi performers were invited to Tokyo to participate in a *Bon* dance recital as one of the finest thirteen community groups in all Japan.

CHAPTER IV

The *Buraku* and the Community

INTRODUCTION

Prior to 1889, when the seventy thousand villages of Japan were amalgamated by national order into approximately ten thousand villages, the *buraku* of Takashima was part of the village *(mura* or *son)*[1] of Shionasu. At that time Shionasu and three neighboring *mura* were consolidated to form Honjō-son. The old village areas were given the name *ōaza,* a geographical term, and two of them were combined into one *ōaza* (Shionasu). *Ōaza* (great *aza*) were further broken down into smaller units called *koaza* (small *aza*). Communities or groups of households, usually somewhat isolated from other clusters of dwellings and possessing a tradition of communal action, were then known, as they are now in common speech, as *buraku.* Within Honjō-*son, buraku* and *koaza* coincided; i.e., the geographical area *(koaza)* in which a *buraku* was located and the *buraku* itself were known by the same proper name. The Island of Takashima was thus Takashima *koaza* of Honjō-*son,* and the community of dwellings on the island, Takashima *buraku.*[2] Between the *buraku* and the *mura* were political units, composed of two or more *buraku,* and called *ku,* which may or may not have coincided with *ōaza* boundaries.

Beyond the village level, the *gun* (commonly translated "county") was formerly the next larger government division. The hierarchy went from the *gun* to the *ken* (prefecture) and on to the national government. After the abolishment in 1926 of the *gun* as a political unit, there was no intervening body between the *mura* and the *ken,* nor any between *shi* (city) and *ken.* The political units were then the *buraku, ku, mura,* and *ken.* Geographic units within the *mura* were *koaza* and *ōazu.* In addition, numerous non-official geographical terms and traditional names existed and still

---

1. *Mura* and *son* are alternate pronounciations for the same ideograph. When spoken together with the proper name of a village as a suffix, *son* is usually used; i.e., Honjō-*son.* When used non-specifically to mean village or when the referent village is understood (and its proper name omitted), the word is usua lly *mura.*
2. Although *buraku* and *koaza* coincide in Honjō, this is by no means the case in all other areas. A *buraku* may be located partly in one *koaza* and partly in another.

93

MAP V
Sketch of Kojima City
(Showing *Chiku*)

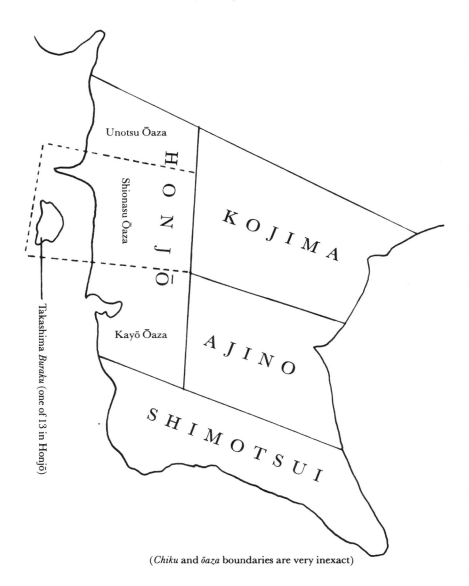

Unotsu Ōaza

HONJŌ

Shionasu Ōaza

K O J I M A

Takashima *Buraku* (one of 13 in Honjō)

Kayō Ōaza

A J I N O

S H I M O T S U I

(*Chiku* and *ōaza* boundaries are very inexact)

remain in common use to identify areas within *aza* or physical conformations, such as mountains, which might overlap *aza*.

Kojima City (Kojima-*shi*) was created on April 1, 1948 by the amalgamation, by means of a plebescite and petition to the prefecture, of three towns *(chō)*, Kojima, Ajino and Shimotsui, and the village of Honjō (see Map V). The four components are now officially designated as *chiku* (usually translated as "area"), but this is a term seldom used in common speech. Official designations for further subdivisions have not been officially set, and the old terms which were current before the amalgamation are those still in normal use. Honjō-*son* has now, however, come to be called Honjō-*chō*, an unofficial designation.

Thirteen divisions corresponding with the former *ōaza* and 94 divisions corresponding with the former *buraku* are recognized within the four *chiku* of Kojima City. *Koaza* have tended to become identified with *buraku*.[3] In 1951 the city administrative plan was still in the process of organization, and at that time the chain of political command went upward from *buraku* to *ōaza, chiku* and *shi,* with the *ken* as the next step. The chain is, however, a broken one, for *buraku* and *ōaza* officials ordinarily have no direct official contact with city officials, who are headed by an elected mayor and council. A number of local problems are left entirely to the handling of the *buraku* and *ōaza*.

Because the *chiku* which comprise Kojima City are separated, one of the conditions of the amalgamation was that the then existent village or town offices remain as branch offices of the city for the convenience of the people in transacting business. Contact between *buraku* and *ōaza* officials and those of the city is usually through the medium of the salaried heads of these branch offices. The former town hall of Kojima, about three miles from Shionasu, serves in a double capacity as the city hall and is also the branch city office for the *chiku* of Kojima.

The total population of Kojima City in July, 1950 was 33,602 persons. Both Kojima and Ajino, which adjoin each other, are primarily industrial and shopkeeping *chiku,* drawing their incomes chiefly from spinning and sewing. Shimotsui is a preponderantly fishing *chiku* with some farming and a little development of industry. Honjō is largely dependent upon farming, with a fairly strong development of fishing and home sewing industry on a very small scale. A common police force serves all *chiku,* and each *chiku* serves as a fire district.

The formation of Kojima City has as yet had little effect upon the lives of Takashima residents. Official business is, as ever, conducted through the office in Shionasu and there is rare occasion to go to the city office in Kojima.

---

3. It is to be remembered in the discussion that follows that *buraku* and *ōaza* are not official designations. They are utilized here of necessity, because there are as yet no other terms.

BURAKU ORGANIZATION

Elective officials within the *buraku* are a *buraku* head called *sōdai* and an official concerned with agriculture, called *jikō kumiaichō*. The *sōdai* is responsible for the planning and carrying out of all *buraku* affairs which do not come directly under city management. The office of *sōdai* has existed for a great many years although the official designation for the position has changed from time to time. In common terminology the *sōdai* is known by a variety of other names including *buraku-chō*, "*buraku* head," and *sewa-nin*, "responsibility-assuming person." The office is not onerous nor does it exact much time. Authority is seldom or never wielded by this official, who confines his *buraku* activities to planning and management rather than giving orders of any kind. The annual cleaning and repair of communally used paths is a responsibility of the *sōdai*, who discharges his duty by setting a date and notifying all households. There is little or no bossing during the actual work. One member from each household participates, and, as the work is familiar and simple, all fall to with a minimum of direction from the *sōdai*.

An important duty of the *sōdai* is in connection with the serious illness or death of a *buraku* resident. The *sōdai* is careful to keep informed of the condition of persons stricken with illness. If he and the household concerned feel that the sickness is grave, the *sōdai* organizes a joint *buraku* shrine pilgrimage to pray for the welfare of the sick person (see *Daisan*, this chapter). In case of death, the *sōdai* sees that all households are notified at once so that the *kōrenchū*, the communal funeral organization, may go into action to aid the bereaved household (for further details on the joint pilgrimage and on the funeral organization, see *Buraku* Uniting and Cooperative Mechanisms, this chapter). The *buraku* has a small fund of money, kept by the *sōdai*, which is derived from the occasional sale to outsiders of seaweed drifted onto Takashima shores, the rare sale of pines from communal land, and the more frequent solicitation of contributions. Such sales and solicitations are handled by the *sōdai* after agreement is expressed by all households. Expenditures are usually in connection with the maintenance of *buraku* property. In addition, the *sōdai* participates in the several annual meetings of all *ōaza* (Shionasu) *sōdai*, which are presided over by an elective official called *kuchō*, and at which matters of *ōaza* interest are discussed.

In most *buraku* affairs the *sōdai* is theoretically the leader. In the *buraku* of Takashima, however, there is a special situation. Most Takashima residents speak of the *buraku* as having two *sōdai*. The term *sōdai*, perhaps best translated as "leader," is itself ambiguous, and the actual situation is that there are two "leaders" in the *buraku*. The second "*sōdai*" is the richest man in the *buraku*. He has always been prominent in local political matters and since the formation of Kojima City has served as an elected city council member. His influence and prestige are great. In his capacity as city councilor, he is charged with official duties relating to the *buraku*. He brings to the attention of the city repairs and maintenance work required for the breakwater-pier, the main beach path, and the fire equipment, the upkeep of which are the responsibility of the city. So great is the prestige and fear of this man that he virtually runs the *buraku* and in recent years has, with no show of opposition, often conducted many of the *buraku* meetings (usurping the place of the elected *sōdai*). Feelings of other residents toward him are ambivalent. He is feared and disliked for his aggressiveness and selfishness, but he is also openly acknowledged as the most intelligent, influential, and capable person in the community. The execution of *buraku* affairs is greatly expedited through his skilled although atypically bossy handling and he remains in power as a necessary evil.

Agricultural affairs are handled by the *jikō kumiaichō*, an office created during the war to assume tasks connected with the requisitioning of agricultural products. Prior to that time, the *sōdai* or an appointed official of the agricultural cooperative held this office, which consisted at that time primarily of liaison with the cooperative. The *jikō kumiaichō* is charged with maintaining records of all land holdings, types of crops planted, and yields, a task leading to considerable acrimony during the war and early post-war years. This job has, however, involved little effort since the fall of 1950, when sweet potatoes were removed from the list of requisition crops, leaving, for Takashima, only barley and a little wheat with which to contend. It is assumed by *buraku* residents that the requisitioning of barley and wheat will also soon be abandoned, and that the office of *jikō kumiaichō* will be dropped or confined simply to liaison with the agricultural cooperative.

Terms of office of both *sōdai* and *jikō kumiaichō* are four years. Elections are conducted by secret ballot at the one fixed annual *buraku* meeting, which is held on January 7th by the lunar calendar. Qualifications for office are adequate ability in reading and writing, a reputation for competency, and an ability to speak in public. Voters always give thought to whether or not prospective officials have adequate leisure time to fulfill their duties. There are no candidates; one simply writes the name of the person of his choice on a ballot. *Sansei-in,* "approvers," persons who out of politeness are known to express approval of the ideas and plans of others whether or not they regard them as acceptable or feasible, are undesirable. *Sansei-in* and persons judged incapable of accepting official responsibility are numerous so that the field of choice is narrow. *Sōdai* are invariably chosen from among well-to-do men of the *buraku,* the only men who normally possess the desired qualifications. An exception is the incumbent *jikō kumiaichō,* the crippled and extremely impoverished man who operates the *buraku* shop. This man is respected for his intelligence and it is felt that he is the only person in the *buraku* with sufficient free time for the office, who can also handle complex accounts. Furthermore, since his own land holdings are extremely small and not subject to requisition, it is thought that he is less influenced by personal motives in arriving at the estimates of crop production upon which requisitioning is based. Neither of these offices, both of which are without stipend, are welcomed, but once a man has been voted in he accepts the responsibility with good grace. If a man discharges the duties of his office without serious error, he is likely to be voted into office for several continuous terms.[4]

Until January, 1950, when erection of the community hall was completed, *buraku* meetings were held in one or another of the homes. Non-scheduled meetings are now held in the community hall as deemed required throughout the year. Word is usually disseminated beforehand by the *sōdai,* but the signal for actual convening is always the ringing of a hand bell. In the normal year there are three or four such meetings at which matters pertaining to the whole *buraku* are discussed, such as repair of paths damaged by tidal action or matters related to requisitioning. Issues are frequently put to vote, and balloting is always secret so that no personal offense will be given to others holding dissenting or different views. Participation in these meetings is limited to one representative from each household. During the absence of household heads from the *buraku,* representatives may be women or young men but are almost never unmarried girls. In their own households women and young men may discuss issues with some freedom with household heads, but during meetings they take the seats of least prestige and seldom speak. These seats are usually those nearest the entrance, and women occupy positions of less prestige than those of young men.[5] Since advance notice of issues at hand which require voting or the statement of opinion is nearly always given, women and young men usually come to the meetings with their decisions and votes predetermined by household discussion.

The fixed annual meeting is much more than a convening for business purposes. Despite the existence of the new community hall, this meeting is held in accordance with ancient tradition in the home of the new caretaker of the shrine of the tutelary god of the *buraku.* The origins of

4. Methods of election and terms of office of *buraku* officials vary from *buraku* to *buraku.* Duties also vary with local circumstances.
5. One female informant states that the places where women sit at any gatherings are always regarded as *shimo* (the lowest in prestige), even when, as may happen on occasion because of the size or shape of a room or the order of arrival, seating is unorthodox.

the office of shrine caretaker *(tōban)* and of the practice of holding an annual meeting at the home of the caretaker are both lost in antiquity. The office of *tōban* is assumed for one-year periods by rotation among the *buraku* households in accordance with a list retained by the *sōdai,* which is revised from time to time as households change or are added. The annual meeting is both a social and a business occasion. Traditionally, it is for the mutual expression among the households of good wishes for the new year and for the joint expression of wishes for the welfare of the shrine care-taker and his household. Food and *shōchū* or *sake,* the quantities fixed by custom, are always served to the assembled persons by the household of the *tōban. Buraku* affairs dealt with at this meeting are all-embracing and include the drawing of lots for the selection of a household to serve as *buraku* representative in a pilgrimage to a fairly distant shrine (see Chap. V, Outside Shrines and their Gods).

The meeting begins with a reading by the *sōdai* of a financial report covering all revenue and expenditures during the past year and the pre-sentation for discussion and approval of a proposed budget for the coming year. The *sōdai* then brings up any and all matters he thinks deserving of attention. These may embrace subjects as varied as tardiness of children in meeting the school boat, erosion of land in the *hatake,* or use of the community hall for entertainment. It is an open meeting and household representatives may speak freely and bring up for discussion any addi-tional matters of *buraku* concern. Discussion and debate are traditionally polite and, in theory, no one contradicts or opposes others; in actual prac-tice there is occasional open opposition between individuals. Such be-havior is frowned upon and leads to strained relations among households but is occasionally indulged in while other householders try to soothe the troubled waters. The failings such as short temper, stubbornness, and argumentativeness of the persons assembled are known to all others, and efforts are made to circumvent animosity. During the 1951 meeting there was an open flare-up between two household heads over damage to *hatake* holdings. One man blamed the damage to his fields from heavy run-off of rain water to the poor farming practices of the householder who owned the adjoining and higher land. Attempts were made to placate the two men, but no joint *buraku* action was taken. Such incidents are, however, uncommon and the usual conduct of the annual meeting is smooth even between acknowledged enemies.

Supervision of *buraku* fire equipment is in the hands of the *buraku* members of the Honjō *(chiku)* fire association (see The *Buraku* and the City, this chapter), one of whom serves as *buraku* chief. Duties, almost non-existent, consist of the occasional checking of fire equipment; there has not been a fire in the *buraku* for several decades.

Maintenance of the main *buraku* shrine consists of sweeping the small building and its grounds before important festivals and placing offerings of pine branches and incense on the altar. The *tōban* is nominally responsible, but the work is done by women of his household. He, however, makes occasional inspections and is responsible for bringing needed repairs to the attention of the *sōdai*.

A new *buraku* official called *kusei-iin*, a liaison agent between the city and the *buraku*, was added through city ordinance in 1950. *Kusei-iin* are appointed by the city council for a term of two years and receive small annual allowances based upon the number of households in the *buraku*. Duties of *kusei-iin* are "to promote efficiency, democracy, understanding, and cooperation through informing *buraku* residents of city action and explaining the basis for such action." Appointment of a *kusei-iin* in every *buraku* was duly made in 1950, but at the time this field work ended in the spring of 1951 the services of these officials had never been called upon. The actions and orders promulgated by the city government, as they had in the past, continued to come to the attention of *buraku* people through their branch city offices or through publication in the Kojima newspaper. Free copies of the paper are distributed to city residents when something of particular importance, such as new tax regulations, arises.

BURAKU COOPERATIVE AND UNITING MECHANISMS

Cooperative effort is well-developed and traditional throughout rural Japan. In rice-growing areas cooperation in the management of irrigation is a necessity. The tradition of cooperation is also well marked in fishing communities, especially those which engage in types of fishing which require the combined efforts of many men. Although communal enterprises have grown increasingly less important in the past several decades in the *buraku* of Takashima, a strong feeling of *buraku* unity still exists and a number of communal activities are still engaged in. Common residence, common property, traditions and institutions, as well as the bonds of blood and common interests, serve as important unifiers. There are enmities and intra-*buraku* discord, but these are of a personal nature and so regarded, and have no major effect upon united action by the *buraku*.

BURAKU PROPERTY

Property of communal use owned and maintained by the *buraku* consists of the community hall, shrines, net dyeing vats, wells, a plot of forest land, and the graveyard. The community hall, a small, one-room wooden structure built in 1949 beneath the spreading pine in the main settlement, is more than a place for conducting *buraku* business. It was erected with *buraku* funds, and partly by *buraku* labor, and is an object of community pride. It is the place in which traveling theatrical troupes perform, and the place in which the farewell party for the author and his wife was given. For young men and women it is a place to play ping-pong during festivals and at New Year's, using equipment purchased by the *buraku*. In former days the site of the present building was the community square,[6] where much of the work with nets was done and where *Bon* dancing was held. The sandy area adjoining the community hall, considerably narrowed since the erection of the building, still remains the center of the community for work and play activities of both children and adults.

In the remaining area of the old square are located the two steel vats used in treating nets. They were purchased with *buraku* funds and are for common use with no order of precedence. One must, however, provide his own fuel to use in the stone and concrete firepits above which the round vats are placed. Two or more households may work together in the use of vats to save time and, particularly, to conserve fuel.

Of the several joint *buraku* shrines, two are located in the square by the meeting hall. These are tiny shrines of what has been called the "wayside" type, miniature wooden shrines or simply small stone statues. An additional small shrine is located at the foot of the breakwater-pier. The major shrine edifice, to the tutelary god of the *buraku,* is located on the "mountain" beneath the pine trees, and, although seeing little use in recent years, it is strongly felt to be joint property and a joint responsibility. There is no priest associated with the shrine and it is never visited by residents of other *buraku*. (For additional details on shrines, see Chap. V, *Buraku* Gods and Shrines).

Two wells, used by the women of the half-dozen households which have no wells of their own, are considered community property. When repairs have been necessary in recent years, however, they have been made by the households enjoying the use of the wells. Like the wells, the communal forest is used only by households who have none of their own.

The graveyard, gradually encroaching upon *hatake,* is also communally owned by the *buraku*. Plots are tiny, and to avoid the use of valuable farm land at its borders, reburial over old burials has sometimes been made.

Other properties of community use, now legally the responsibility of the city administration, are the breakwater-pier and fire-fighting equipment, which consists of a hut on the beach in which are stored a hand-pump, cart, and reel of hose, never used in the twenty-odd years since

6. A breakwater-pier with a shrine to the god Ebisu near its foot, a large pine tree close to the shrine, a community square, and a shrine to the tutelary god at some distance from the clustered settlement of dwellings, are cited by Sakurada as typical of Inland Sea fishing communities (cf. K. Sakurada, *op. cit.*, p. 193 ff.). This description also applies to Takashima.

their installation. Since the formation of Kojima City, responsibility for
the maintenance of these properties, formerly under the *mura*, rests upon
the city. The breakwater-pier and beach are for common use with no
assignment of position or special privileges accorded to any household.
Bamboo poles used on the beach in drying nets are private property and
bear simple property marks.

BURAKU COOPERATIVE ACTIVITY

Certain forms of cooperative activity which existed in former days
have now disappeared. Among these are all-*buraku* participation in wedding feasts and in house-building and house-building feasts, already
mentioned. Until about twenty years ago, joint activity during holidays
and festivals was also common. The pounding of *mochi* for New Year's
was once a social affair in which everyone joined, but it has for twenty
years been on an individual household basis. Formerly, too, everyone in
the *buraku* assembled to toast *mochi* over open bonfires on the beach during
New Year's (see Chap. V, The Ceremonial Calendar), and there was
greater joint participation in other religious events.

Although the idea of individual action appears to be growing, the
tradition of communal action is still fairly strong. The repair of roads and
other *buraku* property is always accomplished through joint effort. Decisions on matters within *buraku* jurisdiction are joint decisions, not simply
those of the *sōdai*. The average resident is quite unwilling to bear the
responsibility for an individual decision on matters which affect others
than himself and his own household. *Buraku* residents still participate
jointly in weddings to some extent. Following ancient custom they gather
to watch the bridal procession to the house in which the marriage is to be
performed and in the yard they observe the marriage ceremony going on
within the house, from which all shutters and screens have been removed
or opened for this purpose. Some of the traditional religious meetings still
have fairly wide if not full attendance and shrine pilgrimages, although
dwindling in number, still represent communal action.

Joint work projects are limited principally to repairs and maintenance of common property and aid in erecting the heavy beams of houses.
In recent years aid in house-building has come to be the informal aid of a
number of relatives and nearby neighbors rather than a *buraku* project.
With the exception of occasional joint sales of farm produce, there is felt
to be neither occasion nor need for communal work projects connected
with agriculture. Emergencies such as fires or typhoon damage would
undoubtedly produce cooperative action, but such calamities have not
occurred for decades.

Gift exchange is also an important form of cooperation. No one attends a party or banquet without presenting a gift. If a household receives a gift, such as upon the occasion of the birth of a child, the donor or his household is sure to receive a gift in return. The receipt of any favor or present entails a keenly felt obligation to reciprocate.

Serious illness and death are the emergencies which produce unfailing cooperative aid, in the form of the *daisan* pilgrimage and the *kōrenchū* funeral organization.

Daisan:

In case of serious illness which does not yield to medical attention, the *sōdai,* who is careful to watch the progress of the ill and injured, notifies each household that he believes a *daisan,* "great pilgrimage," should be made. When all households agree, as is always the case, he sets a date. Representatives of each household gather at an appointed spot after breakfast on the morning of the selected day, dressed in good clothing and carrying lunches. The pilgrimage requires six or more hours and involves traveling to five shrines, four of them in outside communities. The party first visits the island shrine to the *buraku* tutelary god and then crosses over to Shionasu to visit one shrine there. The pilgrimage continues another mile by foot to Kayō to another shrine, and on three miles farther to two shrines in Shimotsui before returning to Takashima. Prayers are offered at each shrine, and small amounts of money and a few grains of rice are placed in shrine offertories. A talisman is purchased at one of the shrines in Shimotsui and brought back to the household of the ailing person. Lunch is eaten somewhere en route. In ordinary years one or two such pilgrimages may be made. Most persons for whom *daisan* have been conducted have died, which is to say that the pilgrimage is made only in serious cases.

The Kōrenchū:

When someone within the *buraku* dies, the *sōdai* is notified at once. He in turn notifies all households, which each furnish one representative, either male or female, to form the *kōrenchū,*[7] an organization whose purpose is to aid the bereaved family in matters pertaining to the death and to the funeral. The members of the *kōrenchū* gather at the house of the deceased the first evening following death, usually about 7:00 P.M., and maintain a wake until midnight. During this period the assembled people decide upon the assignment of duties *(yakuwari)* connected with the death which non-relatives can fulfill. Someone is assigned to make contact with the Buddhist priest in Shionasu or Kayō and arrange between him and the household of the deceased the time of the funeral. Others notify rela-

7. Also called *kōuchi.*

tives, personally if possible. Assignments involving departure from the *buraku* are usually made to two persons who travel together. If no doctor has been in attendance one must be called at once, as a certificate of death signed by a physician is required by law before the funeral can be held. The branch city office in Shionasu must be notified and a permit for the funeral secured there, upon the authority of the death certificate. A number of women take care of all cooking and housekeeping for members of the stricken household, who are to do no work during this period except the preparation of the body for burial. One person of the *kōrenchū* serves as accountant, recording all gifts of money and food received from friends and relatives and all expenditures for food and funeral paraphernalia.

The *kōrenchū* performs other tasks, which include operating boats to transport outside relatives, digging the grave, carrying certain Buddhist ceremonial paraphernalia during the funeral procession, and reading Buddhist sutras at the home of the deceased. There is no compensation for the *kōrenchū* beyond a light meal which is at the expense of the household of the deceased but which is prepared and served by female members of the organization. Rather, membership in the *kōrenchū* entails the expenditure of time and effort and also the outlay of a small amount of cash, as each member presents the household with small sums varying in amount according to individual circumstances.

THE *BURAKU* AND THE CITY

The branch city office, staffed by salaried employees of the city, serves as a transmission agency through which nearly all city business is conducted. It is the agency which handles the *kōseki,* the official register of births, deaths, marriages, divorces, and adoptions. Distribution of ration coupons, collection of taxes, and all ordinary official business is transacted through this office. The branch office also serves as liaison agency between the three *ōaza* of Honjō and the city, which is governed by a mayor and a council, all elected officials.

Remnants of the old *ku* system, established about thirty years ago, still remain. Within each *ōaza* an official called *kuchō* is elected for a term of two years by vote of one representative of each family in the *ōaza*. Duties of the *kuchō* are principally in connection with matters for which the city does not accept responsibility, such as the dates of opening and closing of irrigation ponds, repairs to the irrigation system and non-city roads, and the supervision of *ōaza* property, which includes forest lands and arable land reclaimed by clearing forest plots. The *kuchō* meets with the *sōdai* of the various *buraku* four or five times annually for decision on these and other matters under *ōaza* jurisdiction. When it is necessary to carry matters to the city, liaison is made through the branch city office. There is no official *chiku* head to replace the former *mura* mayor, but the chief of the salaried employees of the branch office serves in effect as head of the *chiku*. A general meeting of the *ōaza* in which one representative of each household in the *ōaza* participates is held annually to discuss matters of general interest, usually irrigation problems. Election of the *kuchō* is also conducted at this general meeting. Open *chiku* meetings which anyone can attend have also been held periodically, upon the inspiration of the city administration, for the discussion of matters between the *chiku* and the city.

The separate *mura* which were united in 1889 to form Honjō-*son* were more or less self-sufficient units for purposes of ordinary living. Contact between these *mura* was often expressed in the form of rivalry. *Mura* festivals were individual and held on different dates. During the festival period rivalry is said to have reached the point of physical violence, when youths of rival *mura* sought to capture or overturn the portable shrines carried during festival processions. A feeling of unity has grown slowly but progressively among the old *mura* since the time of their consolidation into one *mura*. Rivalry is little thought of during the present day, but the old separatistic traditions remain to some extent, partly because the old *mura* (now *ōaza* of the *chiku* of Honjō) remain somewhat separated geographically. In day to day life, contact is with people of one's own *buraku* and *ōaza,* and less frequently with persons in other sections of the *chiku*. Takashima remains close to Shionasu, as it always has in the past.

In the old pre-Honjō days the residents of one *mura* seldom knew more than a few people in other separated communities of the same *mura*. Today there are many ties, most of them inherited from the period when Honjō was a *mura,* which unite the people of the *chiku* so that acquaintance is usually fairly broad. Important among these are the various cooperative organizations, the elementary school, shrines and temples, the fire brigade, the young people's association, and the branch city office.

Temples and Shrines:

There are two Buddhist temples of the Shingon sect in Honjō, both under the jurisdiction of the great Ninnaji Temple in Kyoto. One of these two temples is subsidiary to the other. The main temple, said to have been established in 698 A.D., is located in Kayō, a mile from Shionasu, and has nine branch temples in communities located within a radius of six or seven miles. Under ordinary circumstances, the nearest temple is the one utilized; Kayō persons go to Kayō temple and Shionasu and Unotsu people to the one in Shionasu. The Kayō temple and priest, however, have greater prestige, and well-to-do persons of outside *chiku* may call upon the Kayō priest or upon both the Shionasu and Kayō priests to officiate at funerals. In such an instance, the Kayō priest officiates and the Shionasu priest, coming from a subsidiary temple, serves as assistant. Most persons in Honjō have at some time or another visited both temples.

The largest shrine edifice in Honjō is that of Hachiman, the god of war, located on a picturesque promontory near Kayō. A Shinto priest is in part time attendance. Two other shrines larger than the "wayside" type are located in Shionasu and one in Unotsu. There are traditional annual dates for visiting these shrines, but they are now seldom observed, and the shrines receive general use only in cases of illness when any or all of the shrines may be visited by Honjō persons of any *buraku*.

Elementary School:

The elementary school in Shionasu, a sprawling, unpainted, one-story frame building, serves all of Honjō. Its importance in the community is very great, for not only is it the fountain of learning for the children but it is also the scene of many gatherings of older siblings and parents. The frequent school entertainments featuring singing, dancing, and the performance of plays, graduation exercises, and athletic meets are great community mixers, some of them holiday occasions which are virtually community festival days. Men and women participate with gusto in athletic affairs which are basically school events; at track meets there are always relay races, spoon and peanut races, and many other events for adults as well as for schoolchildren. The largest of the annual track meets is a bright spot in the year for parents and children alike.

More effective than the school entertainments and exercises in acquainting the women of different *buraku* with one another is the parent-teachers' association, which has elective officers, and meets several times annually. A similar association, composed almost entirely of women, had long existed in Honjō. In 1947, at the "suggestion" of the prefectural school authorities, in turn acting upon Occupation recommendations, the organization was slightly revised to conform with a uniform plan on a national scale for such organizations. The association was at that time rechristened the P.T.A., pronounced "pee chee ay," sounds which are usually thought of as comprising a single English word. Membership on the parents' side is mostly confined to women and, curiously, includes a number of women who have no children in school.

The branch city office, although large enough for small gatherings such as the meetings of the *sōdai*, is too small for the convening of large groups of people, and the school building is utilized. Prefectural agricultural experts occasionally give lectures at the school, and if there is occasion for a mass meeting or any sort of public speech, the school building or grounds are utilized. Educational films, an innovation since the war, may be viewed by adults as well as by school children. Graduation exercises are important and heavily attended events, amounting to semi-holidays. The school is, in short, the most important single mechanism uniting the people of the community which it serves. (For additional data on schools, see Chap. VI, Infancy and Childhood).

The Shōbōdan:

The *Shōbōdan,* Fire Association, is a *chiku* organization inherited from *mura* days, which now forms a separate fire district under the supervision of the city. Membership is fairly large, up to a dozen or more people in the larger *buraku,* and is formed by appointment. Each *buraku* comprises a division of the *chiku* organization and is presided over by a head who is responsible for the care of fire equipment within the *buraku.* Membership turnover is slow. The *buraku* chief appoints young men to replace older men from time to time and when a man feels that he has served for an adequate period he may pass on his own post to someone else. All members have elaborate billed caps as insignia of membership, which are to be worn when fighting fire and at *Shōbōdan* meetings. Duties demand little time or effort for Takashima men; meetings are rare and fires are infrequent. Official business is usually transmitted to the *chiku* head of the association and through him to *buraku* heads by the medium of the branch city office. In case of fire, members from adjoining *buraku* as well as members within the *buraku* of the fire are charged with providing aid and supervision of fire fighting. In actual practice, all able-bodied members of the community living nearby also pitch in to fight the occasional fire.

The Seinendan:

The Young People's Association has long been a national organization in Japan, and has long existed in Honjō. In pre-war years it was strongly encouraged by the Japanese government and utilized as an organ for promoting nationalism. It is composed of young men and young women who have finished elementary school or have attained an age of about sixteen, and who remain members until the time of their marriage. The *Honjō Seinendan* has existed principally in name only since the end of the war, when government props beneath the youths' associations of the nation collapsed. The organization is presided over by a *chiku* head and every young person belongs, but post-war meetings have been rare and the average young person knows little of the *seinendan* activities beyond the confines of his own *buraku.* The oldest unmarried person serves as head within the *buraku,* and the *buraku* group constitutes a subdivision of the *chiku* organization. In former days there were uniforms for both sexes; meetings and parties were held frequently and regularly, and the group was traditionally charged with providing aid in community affairs. For the average young man of Takashima, membership in the *seinendan* of today consists of one annual drunken gathering (see Chap. V, Ceremonial Calendar, Ninth Month), a traditional affair established long before the formation of the local *seinendan*. For the average girl on Takashima at present, membership amounts to cleaning up the community hall upon occasion, and little else. Aid in collecting contributions for the Red Cross or Community Chest, a post-war innovation, may be solicited from *seinendan* members. The *seinendan,* as it exists in Honjō at the time of this writing, is little more than a reflection of the lingering emphasis on age and is a convenient word to categorize the unmarried youth who have finished elementary school.[8] Certain events at the big annual school track meet are, for instance, limited to members of the *seinendan,* which in this instance at least is as much an age category as the designation of an association.

The Fujinkai:

Like the *seinendan,* women's organizations have long been a part of the Japanese scene. They are everywhere called *fujinkai,*[8] "women's club." During the war years most of them became known under the name of Women's Patriotic Societies, and their efforts were devoted toward war work. The *fujinkai* of Honjō similarly became a patriotic association during the war, and disintegrated at the conclusion of hostilities. Honjō had no women's association until the fall of 1950, when under the impetus of the local elementary school principal, the old organization was revived under the name of Honjō *Fujinkai* with the objective of engaging in activities to contribute to community welfare. Most women rejoined; a constitution was formulated, and officers elected, but activities of the organization had hardly got under way by the time this field work ended in the spring of 1951. Within the *buraku* of Takashima nearly every household is represented by at least one member. A few households, too impoverished to pay the monthly dues of 10 yen, have no representation. Like the *seinendan,* the *fujinkai* is illustrative of the emphasis upon age.

Cooperative Occupational Associations:

Two cooperative occupational associations exist within Honjō, a farmers' cooperative and a fishermen's cooperative. A small number of Honjō persons also belong to freight boat operators' cooperatives, but because few people in the community are engaged in the operation of freight boats, membership is in cooperatives located in other communities.

8. The *seinendan* groups throughout Japan, and perhaps also the *fujinkai*, appear to the author as a survival or outgrowth of ancient customs of age-grading. (See footnote, p. 51). Marital status is also a factor in determining membership, i.e., *seinendan* members are always single and *fujinkai* members are married. There is no counterpart of the *fujinkai* for adult, married males.

Gyogyō Kyōdō Kumiai: The Fishing Cooperative was first organized in 1902 and has since that time undergone a number of reorganizations and changes of name. Membership is of two types, regular and associate. According to regulation, those who engage in fishing more than sixty days per year are regular members; others who fish are associate members. In actuality, the household head of a fishing family is usually the only regular member although other members of the household may engage in fishing quite as often. Members must legally hold one share in the cooperative, and are entitled to purchase up to fifty shares each. Value of shares has been increased from time to time to cope with inflation, but shares pay no dividends and there is no incentive to purchase them. Most members own three shares, purchased years ago, and often inherited from deceased fathers. Although legally possible, shares are not treated as negotiable devices. Transfer by sale is almost never made. The rare new fisherman (i.e., from a new fishing household) can gain admission into the cooperative by purchasing a share by installment payment spread over a period of years. Property owned by the *kumiai* consists of a building and office equipment used for administrative work by a staff of three clerks and a salaried professional supervisor. The building is also the receiving point for fish, and the *kumiai* owns scales, boxes, and other equipment for their handling. In addition, the building is used for meetings of *kumiai* members and officers.

This cooperative is in theory an organization independent of direct prefectural or national rule. In actual practice, recommendations of the prefectural Maritime Products Department are treated as commands, and operating regulations of the cooperative are little more than a copy of those recommended by the prefecture. The *kumiai* is governed by elected councilors who formulate policy and supervisors who serve in an executive capacity. A *kumiai* head and vice-head are chosen by the councilors from among themselves. The position of head of the cooperative is a full-time job, for which a nominal salary is paid. Meetings of officers are held three or four times annually and there is one annual meeting for all members.

The principal activity and function of the cooperative is the sale of fish for its members, for which a fee of 6% is withheld. This fee plus money realized from the sale of shares serve as the operating fund of the *kumiai* with which to pay expenses and salaries and from which to make loans to fishermen. The amount paid to fishermen for fish is the wholesale market price, which fluctuates widely with the season and the supply. Fish are sold by the *kumiai* to merchants. The *kumiai* is also the agency for the issuance of rationed items connected with fishing, reduced in 1950 to gasoline and oil for boats and an extra ration of rice alloted to fishermen. Loans of money, at low interest rates, are also possible to members, but in recent years few have been granted because of the small size of the operating fund. The cooperative further serves as an agency for concerted action in the face of threats to fishing grounds, such as the dumping of harmful waste into fishing waters by pulp factories. All fishing *kumiai* in the prefectures are members of a prefectural fishing cooperative, and the united weight of a number or all *kumiai* is at times effective in protecting the interests of fishermen. As an additional service, various non-rationed materials required in fishing can be purchased through the cooperative.

During the war, this *kumiai* was of vital importance to all fishermen. Many rationed goods, including most materials required for fishing, were available only through this source and all sales of fish were legally required to be made through the fishing *kumiai* of the nation. In 1950 the regulations were changed and fish could be legally sold on the free market. A great deal of dissension soon arose among Honjō fishermen, who felt that the 6% fee was too large and that benefits received from membership did not compensate for the expense to them. During the 1950-51 fishing season most fishermen sold approximately two-thirds of their catches on the open market but, out of a sense of obligation to tradition, sold the remaining one third to the *kumiai*. Many of the officers of the organization resigned in protest against the size of the fee (although they were empowered to change the fee, there was opposition from a few members and from the salaried head of the administrative staff; resignation seemed a better course than forcing the issue without unanimous consent). No one resigned his membership—for one reason because the *kumiai* still remained as the only legal source of supply for gasoline (gasoline above the ration is purchased through the black market, but it is high-priced). Another serious disadvantage in selling fish to the cooperative is that *kumiai* records of sums paid to members are available for inspection by the tax office.

Despite these signs of weakening, the fishing cooperative remains, and will no doubt continue to remain for many years. It has become a tradition, and most fishermen feel that once its policy is ironed out it will again be a useful organ. New officers were elected a few months after the difficulties, and the cooperative is still a going if somewhat limping concern. Most fishermen still feel it a moral obligation to sell part of their catch through the *kumiai*.

Nōgyō Kyōdō Kumiai: The Agricultural Cooperative is organized upon lines similar to that of the fishing cooperative. Like the fishing cooperative, it is theoretically an independent organization but is in reality a satellite of the prefectural agricultural department. The heads of all households in Honjō who own five *se* (one-eighth acre) or more of farm land, paddy or unirrigated, are full members. Other persons of these households who are engaged in agriculture are associate members. A general meeting is held once annually at which a report is made of the past year's operations and plans for the coming year are discussed. Like the fishing cooperative, the agricultural cooperative served during the war as a rationing agency, of fertilizers, insecticides, tools, and other agricultural necessities. All of these are now available on the open market. Government requisition of crops is handled through this cooperative, and liaison between the cooperative and the prefectural government is close. Agricultural experts from time to time give advice on agricultural practices, and seed for crops raised upon government recommendation, such as the chili peppers in 1950, is made available through the agency of this *kumiai*.

To the average farmer, the agricultural *kumiai* is an agency through which crops can be sold, albeit for a fee, a means of getting advice on agricultural matters, and a place where the necessities for farming can be purchased at a somewhat lower price than the open market. Loans are made to members in limited amounts. Most members leave in the organization as savings a small part of the money realized through *kumiai* sales of their farm products, upon which interest at the rate of 2.8% is paid. Shares and savings comprise the major source of the *kumiai* operating fund. Open market sales in recent years have caused the operating fund to dwindle in size and loans have of necessity been decreased. The average farmer feels, however, that the agricultural *kumiai* is a valuable organization.

Kihansen Kumiai: Freight boaters' cooperatives are a wartime growth organized to centralize and expedite shipping and replace loose local organizations of merchants and shippers. Organization and operation are along lines similar to those of the two foregoing cooperatives. These *kumiai* serve to inform members of shipping jobs available, and charge a fee based on gross freight payments as well as a membership fee. Gasoline and an extra rice ration are secured through the *kumiai,* and equipment for boats and work clothing for crew members may also be purchased through its agency. Unlike the fishing and farming cooperatives, which usually serve only one community, *Kihansen Kumiai* may serve several communities for the reason that the operation of freight boats is limited to a relatively few households in each community of the surrounding area. There is no *Kihansen Kumiai* in Honjō; the closest is Ajino, to which two of the Takashima shippers belong. The third Takashima freight boat operator is a member of a cooperative in a port town of Shikoku, from which he has always done the major part of his shipping.

RELATIONS WITH OUTSIDE COMMUNITIES

Relations with areas of Kojima City other than Honjō, with certain long-established exceptions such as occasional shopping, shrine visits, and attendance at school, are as yet very limited. *Buraku* residents participate in good force in both city and national elections, but there is as yet little development of over-all city social cohesion. The geographic separation of the units comprising the city and the existence of the branch city offices are not conducive toward promoting city unity. Ordinary day-to-day wants of Takashima residents are taken care of by the many peddlers who come to Takashima or by going to Shionasu, where there are a number of small shops, a post-office from which one delivery of mail is made daily to all *buraku,* and other facilities and services. For the young people to attend movies, it is necessary to go to Ajino. Shopping for anything but ordinary clothing is done in Ajino or occasionally in Kurashiki, larger but several miles farther away (see Map IV). Ajino also serves as the center for medical care by physicians, and for the services of those who administer moxa professionally. It is also the scene of the occasional visits to houses of prostitution by young men of the *buraku.* On rare occasions trips are made to Okayama City, twenty-three miles away, for shopping and sightseeing. Travel increased after the establishment in 1949 of bus communication through Shionasu, six round trips daily between Kurashiki and Ajino. It was formerly necessary to walk to Ajino and to walk part of the way to Kurashiki. The social and recreational horizon of the *buraku* resident has widened in recent years, but its limits rarely extend as far as Okayama City, and almost never beyond. Although the sphere continues to enlarge, life still revolves principally around the *buraku* and in diminishing extent around the *ōaza* and *chiku.*

SOCIAL DISTINCTIONS AND INTERPERSONAL RELATIONS

Any farmer, shopkeeper or school teacher of Honjō will tell you that fishing communities are traditionally dirty and *ryoshi* (fishermen), if not themselves dirty, are at least a little lazy and unreliable. Fishing is, in the first place, a profession of the lowly. Fishermen are likely to be a little *yaban* and to disregard or treat lightly conventional forms of etiquette. They are *nonki,* "carefree," without much thought for tomorrow and perhaps not too scrupulous in repaying obligations, whether the formalized obligations of returning favor for favor and gift for gift or the repayment of money obligations. But, it is always added, Takashima fishermen are considerably better in these respects than the residents of most fishing communities.

Takashima fishermen concur in the appraisal of occupations. Farming is a more highly honored occupation, even though most fishermen find it distasteful. Keeping a shop is better than farming, and great deference is paid to the teacher, the Buddhist priest, and the few Honjō owners of small-scale home sewing concerns. Takashima fishermen sprung from farmers, as they will sometimes tell you with pride. To have been farmers turned fishermen gives a little prestige, and certainly it is better than to have always been fishermen. Traditional fishermen whose roots as fishermen go back many centuries are far beneath the farmer-fishermen of Takashima.

Such a community of traditional fishermen, a small *buraku* of twenty households treated as outcasts, exists within Honjō. Marriage between people of Hama, the pariah fishing *buraku,* and other residents of Honjō is ordinarily unthinkable. Such marriage are said to be made only when persons are *okane ni mayotta,* "led astray by money." There is no segregation in the schools and children are friendly until they become a little older, when their friendship becomes reserved. Hama people, other persons will tell you, are capable of many base and *yaban* things. They are inveterate operators of the black market, but thrift is unknown to them. Incestuous marriages and such scandalous behavior as *yobai*[9] are not beyond them (in actuality, both are unfounded accusations although there have been a number of first cousin marriages, not uncommon in other communities of Honjō). Hama fisherfolk are, in short, the *ichiban saitei na ryoshi,* "the very lowest of fishermen."

When referring to Hama fishermen or to *Eta,* the traditional pariah class of Japan, it is customary to whisper or speak in hushed tones. There is a great variety of names for *Eta,* and the word *Eta* itself is usually avoided, or, if spoken, it is whispered behind a cupped hand. An *Eta buraku* is a *tokushū* (special) *buraku,* and *Eta* themselves are *shinheimin,* "new commoners," a term referring to the legal establishment of equal rights for *Eta* during Meiji times. The foregoing as well as several other names are euphemisms, but neither they nor any of the various terms of opprobrium meaning *Eta* may be used in direct discourse with a person of this class without giving serious offense. Common opprobrious terms are *yotsu-ashi,* "four legs," and *mitsukoshi,* "passing over three," (i.e., the next number after three is four; thus, "four legs.").[10] Rather than speak the word it is common to hold up four fingers to indicate *yotsu-ashi.*

9. "Night visiting," stealthy visits made during the darkness of night upon unmarried girls by young men. Until recent years this custom, which may once have been widespread, still existed in various communities of Japan, particularly those in the south. Takashima adults have heard of *yobai,* which they regard as a strange and barbarous custom, but no one knows whether or not it ever obtained on the island. There seems to be no evidence that the custom exists in Hama.

10. "Four legs" is said to be derived from the reputed *Eta* custom of eating the flesh of four-legged animals, at a time when good Japanese Buddhists ate no meat.
Kyōto University students have a more sophisticated term for *Eta.* They refer to them as *jūroku-rūto,* "the square root of sixteen," i.e., four, and in conversations among each other also indicate *Eta* by jotting down the symbols $\sqrt{16}$.

There are no *Eta* within Honjō, but many reside in surrounding communities. The Honjō equivalents are the Hama fisherfolk, who are known as *sokobiki*, "trawl net," the term for the type of fishing (traditional) done by Hama fishermen, but which has become an opprobrious designation for the fishermen themselves. Like the word *Eta* and all the synonyms for *Eta* whether euphemisms or terms of opprobrium, the word *sokobiki* must never be used when addressing a fisherman of this class as it constitutes a grievous insult. Hama fishermen are a step above *Eta*, but the step is small and the breach between them and other residents of Honjō is great and unbridgeable. They are not regarded as native to Honjō, having migrated from Shikoku about 1850.[11]

With the exception of the *sokobiki,* who are often referred to as a *chigatta jinshu,* "a different race," social distinctions within Honjō are not rigid. Wealth is an extremely important factor. A Takashima fisher family fortunate enough to amass property and money rises quickly in prestige. Marriages between Takashima fishing households and Honjō farming households are not uncommon, although marriages are more frequently between fishing households. Money, education, and profession are the most important factors in determining social status, and social status fluctuates in fair conformance with household financial fortune. The *sokobiki,* even if he is acknowledged for his intelligence and ability, as in the case of one man who was elected council member by city-wide vote, must however always remain a *sokobiki.*

Within the *buraku* of Takashima where most households are related, long-established, and bear the surname Matsui, the seven non-Matsui households are still regarded as newcomers. Although they participate in all *buraku* affairs such as festivals, meetings, and the *kōrenchū,* their social status in the *buraku* is below that of the Matsui households. There has been only one marriage between Matsui and these non-Matsui households. Persons bearing the name Matsui explain this marriage by saying that the Matsui household from which the bride sprung had fallen into evil days and penury. Otherwise no such marriage would have been arranged, as the groom in question was then only a *dekaseginin*, a migrant worker from another community. The bride, now advanced in years, no longer has any close relatives among living Matsuis, but speaks with pride of the fact that her maiden name was Matsui.

Ordinary relations between the Matsuis and non-Matsuis are good, but social intercourse between them on an individual household basis is limited. Indirect reference to non-Matsuis is usually by surname even

11. Sakurada deals with these groups of migrant fishermen, which appear to have originated in very early times as a low-class occupational group (cf. K. Sakurada, *op. cit.*) or as one of the *be* (guilds) referred to in the early historical accounts of Japan (cf. G. Sansom, *Japan, A Short Cultural History,* rev. ed. [New York: D. Appleton-Century Co., 1943] pp. 37 ff.)

though everyone knows their given names. The breach between the two groups has decreased with the years, and is less pronounced among the young than the old. Relations among themselves of the non-Matsui households are good, and the moderate coolness of the Matsuis toward them serves to some degree as a common bond.

Discussion with *buraku* residents on social relations and social distinctions within the *buraku* usually produces the statements that there are no distinctions or that such distinctions as exist are based upon wealth. Wealth is of great importance. The possession of a fine house, large *hatake* holdings, and many nets gives prestige, but a poor Matsui still looks down to some extent upon a well-to-do non-Matsui. The importance of wealth as a prestige factor is said to have increased in recent years and particularly during the post-war years. One household, well-to-do by *buraku* standards for several generations and now the richest household of the community, holds itself apart and above other households. Many middle-aged adults and most young persons have never been inside the dwelling of this rich household. There have been no deaths within the household for many years and thus no assembling of the *kōrenchū,* the only occasion when it would be necessary to have otherwise unwelcome *buraku* persons within the household. Wealth even in *narikin* (new-rich) form is respected. The one household in the *buraku* which falls within this classification is accorded respect and prestige, mingled with varying degrees of envy.

In a community as small as Takashima where interpersonal contact is frequent, personal qualities are of importance. The habits, reactions, capabilities, and failings of each person are well known to all other persons. Industry, thrift, and intelligence are respected. The unbossy man with whom all relations are smooth is the ideal, but affability to the point of self-effacement is undesirable, particularly in those who must assume positions of leadership. An old saying states, *"Ki ga ii wa baka no uchi,"* (a fool is always good-natured). The proper person must, however, never be pushing, and he must never seem to contradict others or openly express opinions at variance with those of others. He adjusts his actions in accordance with the status of those with whom he has intercourse; elders must be respected and all shades of age and sex distinctions and their attendant behavior patterns are taken into account. Reticence in public in the performance of tasks or actions in which one is experienced and expert is the standard, for failure when witnessed by others is a cruel and long-remembered blow. Transactions of importance such as arranging a marriage should be through the medium of others. Direct action in such matters is untraditional, embarrassing, and so unusual that it results in confusion. Actions or transactions without precedent leave the average person at a loss and are avoided as much as possible.

Education entitles one to prestige, but has not as yet become an important matter on Takashima as most persons within the same age groups have had the same amount of formal education. Illiteracy is, however, considered the *ichiban haji*, "the greatest shame," and efforts are made by the old people who cannot read and write to conceal their illiteracy from strangers and even from the members of other households. Until recent years, no *buraku* resident had received an education beyond elementary school. With the revising of the school system under Occupation directives in 1947, middle school (i.e., six years of elementary school and three years of middle school) became compulsory. In 1950 a young man, the first in Takashima history, was graduated from *kōtōgakkō*, which requires three years of attendance after the completion of middle school. Reactions to this superior education vary between respect and the feeling that the parents of the boy were foolishly extravagant, as expensive general education is felt to be of little value to a fisherman.

Personal frictions and dislikes among *buraku* members always exist, and in the rare case have turned into standing feuds. The current major dissension involves two households, and is said to be the result of jealousy. The present heads of two households in question are said to have been friends during childhood and young manhood, although the household of one was bitterly poor and the other the wealthiest on the island. Through industry, intelligence, and the lucky fact that he was an only child, the fortunes of the poor young man began to improve, and the wealthy young man is said to have become jealous. Relationships became strained between the two and were soon severed. In 1950 the two men, both middle-aged and household heads, were acknowledged enemies. During 1950 the erstwhile poor man was accused by the police of lending money without a license, an illegal practice. Although others in the *buraku* were dubious, there was little doubt in his mind that the difficulty, soon ironed out but disgraceful, was the work of his enemy.

In situations such as the above, or any situation in which there is a possibility of direct discord, the usual course of action is avoidance. Men may once have a disagreement over an issue which involves an exchange of bitter words, but the matter seldom comes up twice. Avoidance does not usually, however, prevent the exchange of greetings. Persons who have differences inevitably encounter each other within the narrow confines of the *buraku* where many of the dwellings almost touch; at such times they usually exchange greetings, but intercourse seldom goes further. It is sometimes convenient to fail to see the other person, a custom in common use to avoid discomfiting others whom one sees or comes upon unexpectedly in any situation which might be embarrassing. Personal disputes must usually be settled by the medium of other, presumably impartial, persons.

Bad inter-personal relations are, however, not allowed to interfere with *buraku* affairs. Foresworn enemies discuss with no trace of rancor the issues at hand during a *buraku* meeting or an assembly of the *kōrenchū*. Beyond the initial situation when tempers and voices may rise briefly, overt expression of dislike or anger toward other persons is not made beyond the confines of one's own household.

Indirect action is also the course taken against petty theft within the *buraku*. Other than petty theft, crime is virtually unknown on Takashima. Visits from the police are rare, and usually only to obtain information on the activities of fishermen or fishing craft of other communities. There are, however, within the *buraku* a few persons known to be thieves. One of them is a grandmother who is said to steal for the love of stealing, who will steal anything, even nightsoil from the vats in the fields, but who never enters other houses to commit her thefts. A young man is feared for his skill at housebreaking and the theft of money. Two or three others also have the reputation of committing occasional thefts, of agricultural tools and small articles.

The method of combating petty theft is to remove the opportunity. Police aid is never called. Implements and easily portable property are inscribed with property marks and are taken home when not in use. The grandmother, who is said to persist in her deeds in face of an awareness that all others know of her activities, is closely watched and thus her thefts in recent years have been confined to a few small articles and occasional buckets of night-soil mixture. Acts of petty theft are also sometimes "not seen." Even in cases where the identity of the thief is known with certainty, neither he nor any member of his household is ordinarily confronted with the crime. No direct action beyond steps to remove further temptation is taken. To counteract the activities of the young man who enters houses and steals money, dwellings are shuttered whenever it is necessary for all members of a household to be absent. In this case, police action might well be requested except that the whole *buraku* stands in fear of the influence or vengeance of the father, the *buraku* rich man, whose word with the police carries great weight.

The physically abnormal have little trouble fitting into the community. The one seriously crippled man is married and leads a seemingly normal if impoverished life, as do the few other persons with minor physical infirmities. The one feeble-minded male is treated with good-humored tolerance, but because he is an outsider and employed as a menial as well as being mentally subnormal, he is not considered a part of the social community.

The nonconformist has greater difficulty than the physically abnormal in adapting himself to the community. Social sanctions for the nonconformist begin with ridicule and may extend to avoidance and dislike. A young woman who uses cosmetics too liberally or a woman who is *o-share* (excessively addicted to showy clothing) are usually quickly brought into line with traditional pattern by the extremely powerful force of ridicule, expressed most frequently by glance and by laughter rather than by speech. Laughter in ridicule, whether the spontaneous laughter produced by unexpected bungling such as when a child performs some task ineptly or the less common derisive laughter, is a dreaded blow which literally makes cheeks scarlet and heads hang in shame.

A city-bred person finds life in the *buraku* difficult. The single case is a city-bred wife, who is ill-adjusted and unhappy and the object of ridicule by her mother-in-law because of her strange city ways.

The most outstanding case of nonconformity is the richest man in the *buraku*. He is aggressive and direct in speech and manner, self-assured, and ready at all times to direct the actions of others both forcefully and volubly. It is his custom to take charge of all *buraku* affairs in which he deigns to participate. For some years he sent his aged mother as household representative to *buraku* affairs, which other persons interpreted as a deliberate indication of his scorn for the rest of the *buraku*. He is above ridicule and, instead, ridicules others. He is, at the same time, acknowledged as the most intelligent, experienced, and capable man in the community in planning *buraku* action or community affairs on a larger scale. In the eyes of this man and his household, the other residents of Takashima, whether or not genetically related, are social inferiors. The opinion of other *buraku* persons of himself and his family means little or nothing to him, and he is inclined to arrogance in his dealings within the *buraku*. The reaction of most other residents toward him and his household is one of solid dislike and avoidance. Without him, however, the *buraku* would be hard put in its dealings with the outside, for his verbal ability is great and his influence strong. He is the atypical but valuable man, one who can make decisions and commands, and as such he fits very badly into the *buraku* social scheme.

CHAPTER V

Religion

INTRODUCTION*

THE religion of Japan is conventionally treated under the two headings of Buddhism and Shinto, but to the average farmer or fisherman the dichotomy is not always strict. A practical rule of thumb seems to be that whatever is not Buddhist is to be classified as Shinto or "native."[1] There is, however, considerable overlap and blending of the two.

Buddhism, to the average Takashima person, means that there is a Buddhist altar *(Butsudan)* in the home in which ancestral tablets are kept and before which offerings of *shikibi,* food, and incense may be made daily or, as is the usual practice, from time to time. Buddhism means that funerals and memorial services will be in accordance with the ritual of Shingon Buddhism, although the ritual is largely meaningless to most persons. It means also that upon death one goes to another world (there are distinctions between heaven and hell, but the ordinary person is never thought of as being destined for hell) and becomes a Buddha (Hotoke-sama)[2] himself. The ancestor or relative turned into a Hotoke-sama must thereafter be worshipped and given offerings out of respect and lest he turn into one of the *gaki,* the wandering host of hungry spirits who have no worshippers and who are capable of malevolence.

Distinctions may be made in many instances between Buddhism and Shinto. Uncleanliness taboos (see Defilement and Taboo, this chapter)

---

1. Many elements of so-called "native" Shinto belief may be traced to China.
2. The suffix *-sama* is honorific in meaning, and like the less formal suffix *-san,* is usually translated as "Mr.," "Mrs.," or "Miss." It is customarily appended to the names of all Shinto deities and is also frequently added to the names of Buddhist figures.

* The term "New Year's" usually refers to a fifteen day period beginning the first day of the first month of the new year. In Japanese usage the term *Shogatsu* (literally, "first month") may, according to context, have several English meanings, including: the month of January; the first day of the first month; the festivities marking the first day of the first month; the first fifteen days of the first month, or the festivities of this fifteen-day period. For lack of a suitable English equivalent, the colloquial term "New Year's" is used here with the thought that its meaning is clear from the context.

119

ordinarily apply only to Shinto supernaturals. Funerals on Takashima are Buddhist, but worship of the dead, usually thought of as Buddhist, contains Shinto elements. The manner of prayer differs between Buddhism and Shinto. For Shinto gods one claps his hands, utters the name of the god, and claps them again — or simply claps his hands, waits a moment, and then claps again. For Buddhist ritual hands are clasped rather than clapped. Offerings are nearly identical except that fish is never to be offered to Hotoke-sama (but may be offered to O-Fudō-sama, a Buddhist figure). The types of shrubs used in ritual may differ. As a general rule any supernatural being called *kami-sama* (although many are popular deities derived from China) is considered to be within the Shinto or "native" realm. As it applies in Takashima, Buddhism is concerned principally with death and the hereafter. Beliefs associated with Shinto deities embrace a very wide field.

There are, however, exceptions to most of these rules and practices, and it is sometimes difficult to tell whether a deity is Buddhist or Shinto. By a process of generalization many Buddhist and Shinto figures have taken on attributes of one another, and all are regarded in a common category as supernatural beings.[3] At *Bon,* the annual Buddhist mass for the dead, the household *kami-sama* also receive offerings, and at New Year's both Buddhist and Shinto deities receive attention. Funeral and memorial services within the house are always held before ancestral tablets taken from their usual place in the *Butsudan* and placed in the *tokonoma* for the occasion. Within the *tokonoma* also hangs a scroll to Amaterasu-ō-mikami, the Shinto sun goddess, which may be allowed to remain there during the services. New Year's prayers, conducted at each household by a Buddhist priest sometime during the New Year's season, are always performed in front of the shelf dedicated to Toshigami-sama, a presumably Shinto deity. Ritual associated with faith-healing prayers to O-Fudō-sama, a Buddhist deity, includes such practices as the blowing of conch shells and the use of Shinto talismans, which are not a part of orthodox Buddhist ceremony. Little distinction can indeed be made between the "Buddhist" faith healing associated with this deity and the rituals of seers and mediums, who are classified as Shinto practitioners. Prayers are made before the statues of the Buddhist Jizō-sama by clapping the hands as for Shinto deities. The Hotoke-sama who enters the bodies of well persons and makes them ill (see Faith-healers and Mediums, this chapter) seems little related to formal Buddhist theology. This belief seems indistinguishable from the spirit entry common in the supernatural beliefs of many primitive peoples of the world.

3. Many Buddhist figures were identified with Shinto deities upon or after the establishment of Buddhism in Japan. The date customarily given for adoption of Buddhism is 552 A.D., but it did not become established among common people until some time later.

The average person is little concerned with theology or distinctions between Buddhism and Shinto, which are the realm of professionals, and he does not examine his beliefs. Religion and religious practices are for traditional occasions, when long-established ritual is followed. Unexpected crises such as serious illness for which medical treatment has proved of little aid, and prayers for help in personal problems (most commonly, the woman who prays for children), are the only occasions in which recourse is otherwise normally made to religious practices. There is no regular attendance at temples or shrines,[4] although there are a few traditionally fixed dates, now seldom observed, for such visits. Temple visits, in particular, have become rare.

Shinto has been classified into three categories: Official, Sect and Popular Shinto. Official Shinto, sanctioned by the Japanese government for nationalistic purposes, ended with the American occupation; that is to say, state support of the many shrines placed under government control ceased. Sect Shinto is still strong in Japan, but with the exception of one young bride who is interested in Tenrikyō Shinto (although nominally at least a Shingon sect Buddhist) there are no sect members in the *buraku*. By this classification Shinto, as known on Takashima, is Popular Shinto only, which includes household and popular gods and the beliefs and ceremonies surrounding them. Vagueness and conflicting opinion are characteristic of all beliefs associated with these deities.

POPULAR BELIEFS AND DEITIES

Supernatural beings classified as figures of Japanese Shinto are said to be many hundreds in number, and beliefs associated with them are correspondingly great in number. Some deities are nationally known, although their importance varies from one locality to another. Many are of only local importance, and the average person is familiar with only a small percentage of the total. Shinto deities dealt with here are those which are well-known or of importance to Takashima residents.

Large quantities of published materials in Japanese on Shinto deities are available for reference. Information contained in the several works examined is, however, sometimes at variance with *buraku* beliefs and is usually in far greater detail than the knowledge of any *buraku* person extends. Little use has been made of these works; what appears in the following pages are principally the beliefs as they exist on Takashima.

Since there is little to distinguish the few Buddhist figures (excluding *the* Buddha) of importance to *buraku* persons from the Shinto figures, and the distinctions are sometimes in doubt, both will be treated together here.

4. It has become customary in English to call Buddhist edifices temples, and Shinto edifices shrines.

Household Gods

Toshigami-sama: In the *shimonoma* of each dwelling is a long wooden shelf dedicated to this supernatural being, whose name is translated literally as "year god." The contents of the shelf are limited to small vases containing tiny pine branches or sprays of leaves, incense in burners, and votary dishes of rice and tea. Toshigami-sama is given offerings at the same time as other Shinto household gods, and he is also the deity before whom the Buddhist priest prays at New Year's. When it is called to the attention of *buraku* residents that the Buddhist priest on this occasion prays before a *kami-sama*, the reaction is usually surprised agreement and the statement that, although such a thought had never occurred to them before, it is indeed strange. This practice is said by the local priest, who identifies Toshigami-sama as none other than Amaterasu-ō-mikami, to be a survival from a period when Shinto and Buddhism were combined *(Shimbutsu konkō jidai)*. The two religions were separated by official edict in early Meiji. Until that time it had long been customary for some shrines, particularly those dedicated to Hachiman, the god of war, and Buddhist temples to be considered as one unit and to be under one priest.

A few *buraku* persons also identify Toshigami-sama with the sun goddess, but most persons know nothing of the nature of this *kami-sama* except that he is thought to be vaguely protective.[5] Some persons, including the Shionasu priest, state that an alternate name is Toshitokujin,[6] and some old persons address this deity in prayer as Toshitokuhasshōjin.

Beliefs vary somewhat from section to section of the country. The people of Sanagi-shima in the Inland Sea, for example, have still different ideas:

> "Toshi-no-kami . . . is believed to be ugly and they therefore (at New Year's) hang a special straw rope decoration with dense hangings (of straw) before his shelf to hide his ugly face."[7]

Amaterasu-ō-mikami: In the *tokonoma* of every household hangs a scroll bearing the ideographs for a formalized version (Tenshō Kōtaijin) of the name of Amaterasu-ō-mikami, the sun goddess, also known as Ise-no-Kōtai Jingū, who is regarded as the most important ancestor of the imperial family. All persons are acquainted with tales of her activities and history as given in the *Kojiki* and *Nihongi*, the semi-historic accounts written in the early eighth century. There are few beliefs concerning this

5. The entry appearing in a Japanese encyclopedia *(Daihyakka Jiten*, 1938), a small portion of which is here translated, makes no mention of the sun goddess:
"She (Toshigami) is the god deified in the beginning of the year, and is also known by the name of Shōgatsu-sama. She is generally considered to be both male and female. The direction from which she comes varies from year to year and it is called *ehō* (lucky direction). There are various theories from ancient times concerning her origin. By the Inyōdō theory she was an empress, the wife of Gotō Tennō, and the mother of eight *shōgun.* . . ."
6. Toshitokujin is also identified as being the "God of Fortune for the year," of Chinese origin. See T. Nakayama, "Japanese New Year," *Travel in Japan*, I, No. 4 (1935-6), pp. 30-35.
7. Translated from Kagawa-ken Minzoku Chōsa-kai, *cp. cit.*

deity which are of importance in daily life. She is a powerful being and one to whom offerings should be made at least at New Year's and during *buraku* festivals. One must be careful not to offend her with uncleanliness (see Defilement and Taboo, this chapter). In day to day living, however, acknowledgment of her presence and power through the hanging of the scroll is adequate.

Ebisu and *Daikoku:* A box-like shelf in the *shimonoma* holds small wooden, ceramic, or metal figurines of these two smiling gods of good fortune. Ebisu-sama is the particular god of fishermen, and Daikoku-sama, the god of wealth, is the special benefactor of tradesmen. Takashima fishermen regard themselves, in a sense, as tradesmen, through their selling of fish. The two *kami-sama* are always placed on a common shelf within the household, together with vases and dishes for offerings of food. The relationship between the two is, however, vague. Both are most frequently thought of as male and unrelated, although some persons regard them as brothers. Offerings to Ebisu-sama traditionally result in large catches of fish. Daikoku-sama brings wealth to the household.

O-Dokū-sama: O-Dokū-sama, the god of the kitchen stove, has a small shelf located on the wall of the *soto-niwa* near the kitchen or close to the stove in the kitchen. Again, there is much vagueness and confusion about this *kami-sama*. A few consider O-Dokū-sama as a fearful being, but to most persons this *kami-sama* is a more or less protective being associated with the stove, and one to whom offerings should be made. He is usually thought of as male, but no one is sure. His shelf, like those of other *kami-sama* within the dwelling, contains a vase for sprigs of pine, *naruten* or *sakaki*, a small vessel for incense, and containers for rice and tea. There is usually no figurine, but in a few households a wooden or earthenware figurine of a cow is placed on this shelf. Some *buraku* persons interpret this as a survival from the days when Takashima was a farming *buraku*, as such figurines are common in farm households where they are known as Ushi-no-kamisama, the god of cows. A few persons also identify O-Dokū-sama with Kōjin-sama, the tutelary god. An old prayer to O-Dokū-sama, now known only to some of the aged, consisted of saying the words *Sambō-daikōjin-sama oyāgami Shodokū-sama* (literally, "Sambō-daikōjin-sama parent Shodokū-sama"), which indicates that O-Dokū is the parent of Kōjin.

Suijin-sama: A small shrine-like structure *(o-zushi)* made of the same clay as the roof tiles is sometimes placed by the well in honor of Suijin-sama, the god of the well. In the few households which have hand pumps, the *o-zushi* is placed in a position close to the pump. A small vase may be placed near the *o-zushi*. Many households have no special object in honor of Suijin, who is now a *kami-sama* of little importance. In the average household, offerings are made to Suijin only at New Year's.

Benjo-no-kamisama: The god of the toilet, in whom young and middle-aged persons seldom believe, is said by some old persons to be blind and to carry a spear in his hand. In order to escape injury it is wise for one to clear his throat before entering the toilet so that the blind *kami-sama* may sheathe his spear. In households where there are old persons, the offering of a little rice is made at New Year's to the god of the toilet, but most persons regard belief in his existence as an amusing superstition.

Inari-sama: Inari, the fox god, is atypical as a household god on Taka-shima. Only three households, all "newcomers" to the *buraku*, have shrine shelves, located in the *soto-niwa*, dedicated to him. These contain a pottery figurine of a fox in addition to the usual vases and votary dishes. Beliefs about Inari are numerous and conflicting. In general, he is thought to represent fertility, in both human beings and in the fields. Women desir-ing children may pray to Inari, but more commonly appeal to the Bud-dhist goddess of mercy, Kannon.

Konjin-sama and the Lunar Calendar: No simple identifying label easily fits Konjin-sama, who, although not regarded as a supernatural being of first magnitude, occupies a position of great importance in the life of *buraku* people. Konjin (not to be confused with Kōjin) is associated with the zodiacal signs *hitsuji-saru* (sheep-monkey) and *ushi-tora* (cow-tiger) and thus the directions southwest and northeast. *Hitsuji-saru* and *ushi-tora* may also serve as alternate names for Konjin. An *o-zushi*, or sometimes only a pile of stones or bricks, is usually placed in his honor near the eaves of dwellings in a northeasterly or southwesterly direction from the *Daikoku-bashira*. In a few houses there is also a shelf dedicated to Konjin located within the dwelling on the southwest wall; in such instances Konjin is usually referred to as Hitsuji-saru. Although this *kami-sama* is important in daily life, offerings are normally made to him only at New Year's and during *buraku* festivals. The few households with a Hitsuji-saru shelf make offerings inside the house to Konjin at any time that such attention is given to the other household gods. The rare household makes daily offer-ings, and some households make offerings twice monthly. Still other households have no regular schedule, and cases of forgetfulness are said to have become increasingly common in recent years. Offerings are normally only a tiny portion of rice, which is usually allowed to remain until it becomes very dry and hard and is then thrown away, and a little tea. The large offerings or offerings of special food made on ceremonial days are soon taken down and consumed by members of the household.

There are a great many beliefs associated with Konjin and con-nected with the zodiac and lunar calendar. Toilets and baths, unclean things, are not to be erected to the southwest or northeast of dwellings for fear of offense to this deity. Konjin is said to revolve about the universe and thus to occupy a different position daily. Some persons think of this moving Konjin, whom they call Mawari-Konjin, "revolving Konjin," as a different *kami-sama*. Before starting out on a trip of any importance, one must consult printed calendar-almanacs to determine the direction in which Mawari-Konjin lies. This direction must be avoided even if it is necessary to postpone travel.[8]

Normal reckoning of time on Takashima is by the lunar calendar.[9] Every household has a Gregorian calendar, usually called *karendā*, on which Gregorian dates, as required by law, are printed in large letters and lunar dates in small letters. This calendar is a necessity as school, city, and national affairs go by Gregorian reckoning. In normal life within the *buraku*, however, dates are by the lunar calendar. When it is necessary to distinguish between Gregorian and lunar dates — and such occasions are very frequent in the present day — it is customary to prefix the statement of the date with the words *shin* and *kyū*, "new," and "old." In addition to the Gregorian calendar, every household has a printed lunar calendar-almanac *(koyomi)*, which is published in the form of a booklet and contains a zodiac, horoscopes, and other astrological information as well as information on the tides and lucky and unlucky days. These calendar-almanacs, which vary in price from thirty yen upwards, may be purchased in any village, town, or city of Japan, and find use among some urban residents as well as country people.

Takashima fishermen say that reckoning by the lunar calendar is a necessity for successful fishing, which depends to a great degree upon knowledge of the moon and tides. Takashima women say that the lunar calendar is a necessity for farming operations, so that they will know when to plant, when to harvest, and when to perform other agricultural tasks. Such statements are, of course, misleading; once adjustment is made, any calendar will serve for such purposes. The lunar calendar is, however, firmly entrenched from centuries of use, and the printed *koyomi* is the source of essential information on the moon and tides not readily available in any other form to *buraku* people. In addition, by use of the calendar-almanac, one can determine which days are auspicious for the building of stoves, houses, toilets, or for any other undertaking, and also determine the location of Mawari-Konjin.

These are real considerations. Fishermen always consult the *koyomi* (called *hi wo miru*, "looking at the day") to select an auspicious day before

---

8. A Japanese reference work *(Daihyakka Jiten, 1938)* contains the following entry on Konjin:
"... this god originated in ... China and was brought to Japan about the end of the Heian Period ... Because he controls war, disturbance, drought, and epidemics, people are afraid to go on a trip, build houses, or begin new works in the direction he lies ... he has seven spirits which do harm in seven different directions ..."
9. For description of the lunar calendar, derived from China in the seventh century and more accurately described as lunar-solar calendar, see E. Papinot, *Historical and Geographical Dictionary of Japan* (Ann Arbor: Overbeck Co., 1948), p. 836 ff.

going out fishing for the first time in the new year and before beginning fishing operations for mackerel in the late spring. Some men may make more frequent reference to the almanac, such as at the beginning of the butterfish season or at any time when catches have been poor for several times in succession. The reason for poor luck may have been that the boats traveled in the direction where Mawari-Konjin lay. The *koyomi* must also be consulted when deciding the date for marriage in order to select a lucky day and, since travel is involved, to determine the location of Konjin. Finding the location of Konjin is called *kuma wo miru*, "looking at the direction" (*kuma* is a word ordinarily used in the *buraku* only in this context).

Exclusive of the location of Konjin, certain days are always unlucky. On *Sanrimbō* one must avoid high places as fire is said to rise on this day and make them dangerous. *Tomobiki* is bad for funerals or memorial services, lest someone else die soon afterwards, for whatever happens on this day is liable to recur. Certain days of the month are unlucky for travel. The seventh and seventeenth are inauspicious days to start out on a journey, and the ninth and twenty-fifth are bad days on which to return. December is a month in which no bells should be rung. This is expressed in an ancient saying, *"Shiwasu-gane tataku na,"* (Don't ring bells in December). Memorial services which should fall during the month of December are usually held before or after December as the ritual of the Buddhist priest includes bell ringing; i.e., the striking of a brass bowl with a padded wooden striker. The last two days of the lunar year are days when one need not look at the day and are called *hi-mizu* (the word for "day," and a negative form of the verb *miru*, "to see," or "to look at"). These are felicitous days, when any sort of activity may be engaged in with good fortune. There are, fortunately, a large number of additional days of varying degrees of auspiciousness throughout the year so that enterprises seldom need be postponed for more than a day or two.[10]

Buraku Gods and Shrines

Of the shrines and religious statues within the *buraku*, some represent Buddhist figures and others Shinto deities, but all are regarded as much the same. Both are treated together here.

Kōjin-sama: Kōjin, whose shrine is located in the pine trees near the top of the major hill on the island, is the tutelary god of the *buraku* and in the course of a *buraku* person's life is perhaps the most important of the *kami-sama*. Kōjin, as the ideographs used in writing his name imply, is a rough and fearsome deity whose sex is unquestionably male. A few people say that he has three heads and two arms. Some persons identify Kōjin with

10. See M. Joya, *op. cit.*, p. 184 ff.

Susa-no-wo-no-mikoto, the rough and mischievous brother of the sun goddess. Others regard Kōjin and O-Dokū as the same deity. Most people have very few ideas about Kōjin (or almost any other deity). According to a Japanese encyclopedia *(Daihyakka Jiten, 1938)*, Kōjin is "a god deified among the Tendai Shingon and Nichiren (Buddhist) sects, worshipped in the kitchen as the god of the stove among common people ... another of his names is Sambō Kōjin ... he came to Japan through the countries of India, China, and Korea. ... It is thought that Kōjin is another form of Shōten or Kōshin's incarnation ... (and hence a deity of Buddhist origin — author's comment)."

Kōjin has powers over almost anything relating to the welfare of *buraku* people, but is most frequently called upon to give aid in cases of illness. Two annual *buraku* festivals are held in his honor and his shrine is traditionally visited at least three times a year. Watches are always maintained at his shrine during the New Year's season. Babies must be introduced to this deity in their fourth month of life, and they visit his shrine again when they reach three years of age.

Entrance to the shrine grounds is through a stone gate *(torii)* and up a flight of stone steps. Within the shrine building is an altar bearing a small wooden shrine structure in which vases for leaves or pine branches, incense and incense burners, candles and candlestick holders are placed. Within this smaller shrine is another, empty, which is the abode of Kōjin, of whom there are said to be no figurines or other depictions. In front of the altar is placed a slotted wooden offertory box. A bell (rung while paying devotions) is suspended by a rope from the lintel of the alcove which forms the altar. Outside the building, an earthenware container for water, a basin, and a strip of cloth tied to a tree to serve as a towel, are provided for ablution before entering the shrine. Except at New Year's and during festivals in Kōjin's honor the water container is empty or contains only a little brown rain water. A miniature wooden shrine *(yashiro)* and an *o-zushi*, both dilapidated, are located in the leveled area beside the shrine, but the *kami-sama* whom they honor are unknown or forgotten, and the tiny shrines are neglected.

Kōjin-sama, although said to be one of the most important of the deities to *buraku* people, is neglected most of the year. Except on the fixed traditional occasions, few visits are made to the shrine, and attendance on traditional occasions has been progressively smaller for some years.

Jizō-sama: Stone statues of Jizō, a Buddhist deity, are of extremely common occurrence throughout Japan. In the *buraku*, there are seven stone statues of Jizō located at the entrance to the cemetery and one near the public meeting hall. Jizō, often thought of as deaf and blind, is regarded as generally protective and the particular guardian of children. He is jolly and benevolent, and the mention of his name evokes affectionate smiles. Jizō has taken on the semblance of a Shinto deity. Offerings are made before his statue by the meeting hall from time to time by nearby households when offerings are made to their household *kami-sama*. There is a private Jizō located behind one of the dwellings, which is treated as a household god. A few old men and women may pray, Shinto fashion, to Jizō, but for the ordinary person contact with him is after a death, when part of the funeral services are held in front of the seven statues at the graveyard. Six of the statues are small figures carved in relief; one is large and carved in the round. All seven are placed in a row with the large Jizō, sometimes referred to as the head Jizō, at one end. The six smaller Jizō are called Rokujizō (six Jizō's) but are undistinguished from other Jizō's in attributes.[11]

Kōbō-Daishi: A miniature shrine (identical with that used for Shinto *kami-sama*) containing two small granite statues of Kōbō-Daishi,[12] the famous deified bonze (774-835 A.D.) who was the traditional founder of Shingon sect Buddhism, occupies a position close to the public meeting hall. Kōbō-Daishi, in ordinary speech called O-Daishi-sama (some people know him only by this name), is of little importance in daily life. In former days, temple visits were made on the anniversary of his death, but for a number of years this deity has received little or no attention from the average person. Such offerings as may appear before his shrine are made by old people of nearby households.

Ebisu-sama: In addition to being a household god, Ebisu is a *buraku* deity, the patron of fishermen. A miniature shrine to him, placed on a solidly built dais of granite and concrete, occupies a prominent position on the beach at the foot of the breakwater. Within the shrine is a partially burned wooden figurine of Ebisu,[13] said to have been salvaged from the holocaust of about 1850 which destroyed all dwellings in the *buraku*. Offerings including lumps of brightly colored coral are made at this shrine by fishermen to implore the aid of Ebisu in securing good catches, and the shrine structure is maintained in good condition. The offerings are inducements only; if the catch of fish is good, Ebisu receives no reward. Payment in advance by means of offerings is the standard procedure in appealing to all deities; the idea of rewards appears seldom to be entertained.

11. In Buddhist theology, but unknown to Takashima people, the six statues symbolize Jizō's "... saving activities in each of the six woeful realms of existence...." (M. Anesaki, *The Religious Life of Japanese People*, [Tokyo: Kokusai Bunka Shinkokai, 1938], plate 12).

12. *Daishi* is a posthumous title given to honored bonzes, first conferred in 866 A.D.

13. Ebisu may in some fishing communities be represented by a large net float, a stone, or various other objects dragged from the bottom of the sea. Sakurada suggests that the household Ebisu and the Ebisu commonly enshrined near piers in Inland Sea fishing communities are different deities (K. Sakurada, *op. cit.*).

Yamagami-sama: Yamagami-sama (mountain god), the *kami-sama* of the major hill on the island, is sometimes referred to, but his identity is hazy and there is no shrine nor edifice in his honor. Occasionally an aged woman may weave a tiny pair of straw sandals and hang them from a bush or the limb of a pine on the hillside as an offering to the Yamagami-sama for the cure of a sick child. Some old persons contend that such offerings are specific devices for the cure of colds among infants or adults. Most persons not advanced in years are, however, ignorant of this custom. For the most part, the god of the mountain hardly exists today.

A certain degree of sanctity is also attached to various areas of the island. The several mounds excavated in past years by amateur archaeologists are regarded with vague feelings of reverence. An *o-zushi* was placed by *buraku* men near one excavation from which a human skeleton was exhumed about forty years ago. This was a shrine before which the excavators could pray, to avoid possible offense to the spirit of the man buried there or whatever *kami-sama* might inhabit or frequent the spot. This *o-zushi*, located in an out-of-the-way place, remains in good condition but is ignored. The passing person may occasionally pluck a small sprig of pine needles as an offering, simply because the *o-zushi* is there, and empty. Most young persons do not know the significance of this little shrine.

Personal shrines are unknown at the present time, although they may have existed in the past. A mound of stones on a rocky point away from the settlements is said to have been erected in honor of Ebisu about a hundred years ago by a *buraku* man, now long dead, as a personal shrine. Near the community hall is a pile of bricks[14] which is said to represent a personal edifice to a *kami-sama* erected more than one hundred years ago by one of the ancestors of a household whose dwelling is nearby. The name and nature of the deity are now unknown, but the pile of bricks is allowed to remain unmolested and the *obaa-san* of the household in question occasionally makes offerings there.

Gods and Beliefs of the Sea

In addition to Ebisu, who is the patron of both fishermen and merchants, two other deities, Funadama-sama and Kompira-sama, are important in the Inland Sea area to those who make their living from the sea.

Funadama-sama: The god of the boats, Funadama-sama, is a deity now only half believed in but who, curiously, receives offerings with unfailing regularity. Whenever rice is cooked on fishing or freight boats a cere-

14. It seems most unlikely that bricks were known or in use on Takashima at that time. Informants agree on this point and suggest that someone may later have replaced stones with bricks.

monial offering is made without fail, and special offerings of *sake*, rice, *mochi*, as well as decorations of ferns, citrus fruit, and *daikon* are made at New Year's. The locus of the Funadama-sama is the approximate center of a fishing or freight boat. Smaller craft such as the boats used in going to and from Shionasu are not considered to be inhabited by this god. The locus within the boat is, however, not considered as sacred to the extent of any restriction upon using that area.[15] As previously noted, consideration is given to the Funadama-sama whenever the bottoms of boats are treated with fire to kill marine worms.

There is no agreement about the nature of this deity,[16] whom some persons regard as having the form of a young woman. Others think the Funadama-sama is a snake god, and still others remain with no convictions or conceptions. The words "snake" and "monkey" are, for reasons unknown, anathema to the Funadama-sama and must never be thought or uttered while in the fishing boats or fishing will yield only empty nets. If a snake (there are a few harmless snakes on the island) should happen to get into a fishing boat, the next fishing trip will be a total failure. No instance of snakes crawling into boats has, however, ever occurred.

Manifestations of the Funadama-sama, which occur two or three times annually at irregular intervals, are famous among fishermen of the Inland Sea. The manifestation consists of a tinkling sound, usually heard only at night and described onomatopoetically by the syllables *"chirin, chirin."* The tinkling moves from place to place within a boat, and when it is audible in one fishing craft it can also be heard in all others within a radius of hundreds of yards and sometimes up to several miles. It is said that if a boat passes a certain promontory in Hyōgo Prefecture the sound will be heard without fail. Some persons state that the tinkling sound follows a returning fisherman from the beach on to his home and there becomes audible to others in the dwelling.

Every man and woman in the *buraku* who habitually goes out in the fishing boats has heard the Funadama-sama, but no one stands in fear of the sound. Supernaturalistic explanations are scorned except by the aged. Nearly all active fishermen of today, although referring to the sounds in the traditional manner as a manifestation of the Funadama-sama, regard them as of unknown but natural origin. The sounds, they say, are strange, but they are most likely produced by some sort of bird or insect — although no bird or insect has ever been seen even on the rare occasions when the Funadama-sama has manifested herself during day-

15. This is in contrast with beliefs of the fishermen of the isolated Island of Tsushima in the Japan Sea, where it is improper to sit or stand on the center post of fishing craft, the home of the Funadama-sama. While visiting this island in the summer of 1950 the author inadvertently sat down on the center post of a fishing boat and was quickly asked to rise lest the *kami-sama* be offended.

16. A Japanese encyclopedia (*Daihyakka Jiten*, 1938) states that the identity of the Funadama-sama is uncertain and presents nine different interpretations.

light hours. Nothing special is done upon occasions when the sounds are audible, and they are not regarded as frightening or awe-inspiring.[17]

The Funadama-sama, although she may be appealed to on the rare occasions when fishing craft are caught in stormy seas, appears to be slowly joining the ranks of the dying gods. Many younger persons, although they still make offerings of rice to this *kami-sama* (in part to appease their parents) and have heard the *"chirin, chirin"* sounds, regard belief in the Funadama-sama as merely an old superstition of their elders.

Kompira-sama: The nationally famous shrine to Kompira located in the town of Kompira on the Island of Shikoku, with its many buildings and thousands of steps, is the scene of an annual pilgrimage by almost all Takashima households. Kotohira is said to be the "proper" name of this deity, but it is seldom heard on Takashima. Kompira is regarded as a patron saint of all seamen, and is the supernatural being appealed to at times of crisis at sea (extremely rare for Takashima fishermen). The annual pilgrimage to Kompira represents one of the major recreation periods for Takashima households.

The trip is made in the winter months during the slack fishing season, and each household goes individually. Bedding and sufficient food, firewood, and water for the two or three day trip are loaded into the household fishing boat together with all members of the household. The trip to the port of Marugame on Shikoku, a distance of about eighteen miles, requires several hours. Upon arrival it is customary to spend the night on the boat in port after adults have gone shopping and younger people have attended movies. A tramcar ride of about one hour on the following day takes the household to Kompira and the shrine, where younger members may at some time or another make the hour-long and arduous trip up the thousands of steps to the topmost shrine building. The usual course is to pay devotions at one of the buildings within ready access, and to obtain a wooden talisman *(o-fuda)* about two and one-half feet long upon which the month, year, and the name Kompira (which may also be read as Kotohira) are inscribed in large ideographs. The whole household is usually back at Marugame, a larger town with more shops than Kompira, by early afternoon for another session of shopping, window-shopping, and attending movies. A second night is usually spent aboard the fishing boat in the harbor before returning to Takashima. The *o-fuda* are carefully transported home and stored in some convenient place. Some forty-odd of these talismans are stacked upon planks secured to the wall above head level in the *kami-noma* of one dwelling.

---

17. One informant describes the manifestations of the Funadama-sama as *"rikutsu igai no rikutsu* (logic beyond logic).''

For a fishing community, beliefs concerning the sea appear rather limited, but seem to be about average for fishing communities of the area. There are a number of ideas concerning prognoses of the weather and the condition of the sea, but these seem largely empirical. It is said that there are a great many beliefs among seamen on large ships, but few of these apply to the small craft of Takashima. In former days sea water was offered to all *kami-sama* at New Year's. A few other customs concerning the sea still exist. While at sea one must not pour soup onto rice (a favorite dish for many) but must reverse the procedure. Certain localities, such as a cluster of tiny, rocky islands in the sea a few miles from Takashima, are said by old men to be populated by *o-bake* (monsters). During the New Year's season one or more boats of some sort (but never, as yet, any from Takashima) will be stranded or wrecked on these rocky islands, owing, old persons say, to the actions of the *o-bake*. In actual fact, such wrecks often do occur during the New Year's season, when the sea is somewhat rougher than during warmer weather, but they also occur at other seasons of the year. A male tiger cat is said to be good luck on a freight boat, as it warns of storms by crawling up the mast.

Protection during stormy weather or other times of danger while at sea may be secured by unfurling a white flag which must be obtained from temples with the blessings of Kannon, the Buddhist god of mercy. Once used, a flag must be put away and a new one obtained. There have, however, been no deaths at sea among *buraku* people for nearly fifty years. Storms in adjacent waters are seldom violent, and, in any case, fishing is not done in rough weather.

Outside Shrines and Their Gods

In addition to the household, *buraku*, and sea gods already described, a number of other deities not enshrined within the *buraku* enter occasionally into the lives of Takashima persons. Within Honjō, and outside of Takashima, are shrines to four *kami-sama*, Tenjin, Yakujin, Shiogama Daimyōjin, and Hachiman. These are all substantial or fairly substantial buildings. There are also a number of small wayside shrines. In Ajino, Shimotsui and other nearby communities are shrines to Inari, O-Dotsū (a snake god), and various other *kami-sama*. Under ordinary circumstances only Hachiman, the god of war, is of importance to the people of Takashima, who regularly contribute to the upkeep of his shrine, the most imposing of the Shinto edifices in Honjō. In former days visits to this shrine were made once or twice a year, but the practice has gone into decline and is now confined chiefly to occasional trips by the *ojii-san* or *obaa-san*.

Tenjin-sama, the deified spirit of the noble Sugawara Michizane (845-903), one of the culture-heroes of Japan, although important to the people of another *buraku* of Honjō, enters the life of Takashima people only to the extent of the observance of one old custom concerning him. It is said that Tenjin-sama is particularly fond of *ume-boshi* (a small variety of plum, pickled), and out of respect for him one must never throw a plum pit into the sea, but must instead bring it back to land before disposing of it.

When contributions are requested by house to house canvass of all households of Honjō, Takashima people give small amounts of money for the maintenance of all Honjō shrines, but they ordinarily never visit these shrines and the *kami-sama* to which the shrines are dedicated are not important to them. An exception is the *daisan* pilgrimage (previously described) when Yakujin-sama (a god of healing, sometimes identified with Gion-sama, who is in turn identified with Susa-no-wo-no-mikoto) and Hachiman-sama are appealed to. Shiogama Daimyōjin-sama, who is said by some Shionasu residents to be a deified noble of long ago and by others to be a *kami-sama* connected with the salt manufacture engaged in at Shionasu in centuries gone by, is a god of no significance to present-day Takashima.

In addition to the annual pilgrimage to Kompira, *buraku* representatives from one household make an annual pilgrimage to the shrine of Kinoyama-sama, a god of epidemic disease, in Tama City, several miles from Takashima. Despite the expenditure of money required in making the trip, the privilege of serving as *buraku* representative (see Chap. IV, *Buraku* Organization) is considered good fortune for the winning household. One *o-fuda* is obtained at this shrine for each household of the *buraku* and delivered upon return.

Occasional pilgrimages are made to other shrines. Pregnant women and those desiring to become pregnant may visit temples to pray before the Buddhist deity Kannon. A Kannon at Konzōji Temple on Shikoku is considered particularly effective in granting children to barren women, but the trip, about forty miles by public conveyance, is considered too long and expensive. The Kannon at a temple en route to Okayama City is regularly visited by someone in the household on behalf of a pregnant woman (see Chap. VI, Sex and Reproduction). Rare trips may be made to noted shrines or temples more distantly located, but these are the treats of the privileged few with sufficient money, and they are as much sightseeing and recreational ventures as religious pilgrimages. When such pilgrimages are made, wooden or glued paper *o-fuda* are always obtained and brought home. The outer walls of dwellings usually bear a number of old glued paper *o-fuda* by the *soto-niwa* entrance.

In case of illness of someone in the household, special charms may be purchased. One type, made of thin wood, bears the name of the shrine and contains a number of ink spots. These charms are to be attached to the *Daikoku-bashira* by means of pounding a nail through the ink spots, driving a nail through a spot upon each occurrence or attack of illness.

RELIGIOUS PRACTITIONERS

Priests

The two Buddhist priests in Honjō are highly respected members of the community and take an active part in community life. Unless one lives in the same *buraku* as a priest, however, contact is usually limited to community meetings, the annual house visits and prayers at New Year's and *Bon*, and to contact upon the occasions of funerals or memorial services. The priests are also in demand as go-betweens in arranging marriages.

There are no Shinto priests *(kannushi)* associated with the shrines in Honjō except the Hachiman shrine, at which a *kannushi* who also presides over shrines in other communities is in part-time attendance. In former years it is said that a priest was in full-time attendance at the Hachiman shrine and that priests also served part or full time at the other three shrines. Dwindling attendance at the shrines, however, is said to have so cut down revenues that the priests were driven to other occupations. Contact with *kannushi* is rare for Takashima householders, usually limited to the infrequent visits to outside shrines with *kannushi* in attendance when talismans are obtained.

Faith-healers and Mediums

Recourse to the services of unorthodox Buddhist practitioners of faith-healing is occasionally made. A faith-healer associated with O-Fudō-sama, a Buddhist deity who is depicted surrounded by flames with a sword in one hand and a rope in the other, began making monthly trips from a neighboring community in 1949 to perform ritual for the cure of a tubercular Takashima man. This priest and his female assistant state that they are independent practitioners who learned their art from other independent practitioners and are connected with no Buddhist temple. In ordinary speech, professionals of this sort are called *kitōsha* (pray-ers), the same term which is applied to faith-healers and mediums associated with Shinto deities. Dress and ritual of these Buddhist *kitōsha* are rich and elaborate.

Preparations for the healing ritual are made in the household of the sick man before the arrival of the two *kitōsha*, who are addressed by the members of the household as *sensei*, a term of respect for teachers and learned persons. A scroll depicting O-Fudō-sama is hung in the *tokonoma*.

In front of it are placed offerings of food ("something from the mountain [fruit], something from the sea [fish], something from the fields [vegetables]"), as well as candles, incense, Shinto *gohei*, and a vase containing sprigs of *sakaki*. A Buddhist *bonten*, a ceremonial object of white paper with ruffled, accordion-like folds, is suspended from the ceiling in front of the *tokonoma* by means of four streamers, one attached at each corner of the main square mass of paper, so that the body of the *bonten* is about three feet from the floor. Beneath the *bonten* are placed a round, shallow earthenware container, a large pile of slim wooden sticks of uniform size and with planed sides (supplied by the *sensei*), and a pile of incense.

Before beginning his ritual the *sensei* builds within the earthenware container a triangular edifice from the sticks, placing a pinch of salt at each corner and filling the hollow formed by the triangle with paper and a mass of incense sticks. Ritual involves chants, prayers, groans, the clapping of hands, the blowing of a conch shell, the rhythmic shaking of *shakujō* (scepter-like rattles of brass or bronze), and the rubbing of prayer beads. From time to time, as instructed by the *sensei*, the assembled household adults join in the simple chants.[18] After a preliminary round of rites, the *sensei* purifies the *tokonoma* by means of dipping a slim wand of plum wood into salt and then into water, tapping the water container twenty-one times, and finally sprinkling the water toward the *tokonoma* with the wand. When this is completed, the triangle of wooden sticks is lighted with a match, and as the flames mount upward the ritual continues. The rising flames cause the *bonten* to dance about perilously and it seems miraculous that the paper does not burst into flame (as far as the Takashima household in question is concerned, the fact that the *bonten* never does catch afire is a convincing performance, indicative that the *sensei* does indeed possess supernatural powers). Ritual continues until the triangle is burned out, and then the whole process is repeated two additional times. The first fire is to the *kami-sama* of heaven *(Ten-no-kami-sama);* the second to O-Fudō-sama, and the third to the various Shinto gods of the household. A few additional sticks, piled on at random, are added at the end for the benefit of the members of the household. There is said never to be any danger of the *bonten* catching afire, as the *sensei* and his assistant, while the sticks are ablaze, clasp their hands in a certain fashion which turns fire into water. When the ritual is over, an hour or more after it began, the house is full of smoke and everyone including the sick man, who occupies the seat of honor next to the male *kitōsha*, is coughing, crying, and sneezing.

18. During a performance witnessed by the author, the younger (but adult) brother of the sick man sat in the room where the rites were conducted and read a magazine most of the time. Other adults gave closer attention to the ritual.

Many persons in the *buraku* deride this sort of religious rite. The household in question is referred to scornfully by these people as *meishin-teki* (superstitious), and the rites themselves regarded as shamefully ignorant superstition.

The services of other Shinto and Shinto-Buddhist professionals are occasionally utilized in times of need. Faith-healers and mediums, both ordinarily called *kitōsha*, are patronized chiefly by old persons. Geomancers *(kasōmi)* are likely to be called in by anyone erecting a new building. Since there are no religious practitioners of any kind within the *buraku*, it is necessary to go to other communities when their services are required. A female *kitōsha* associated with the fox god Inari lives in nearby Unotsu, and there are others in Ajino and Shimotsui. A male *kitōsha* in Shimotsui associated with O-Dotsū, the snake god, is considered skillful.

The usual occasion for calling upon a *kitōsha* is when some member of the household has become unaccountably ill, or when illness does not improve with medical treatment. It is possible at such times that spirit entry may be the cause of illness. The Hotoke-sama (Buddha) of some person who has died an unnatural and unattended death, such as by drowning at sea, and has not had a funeral ceremony or burial is a wandering spirit capable of entering the bodies of the well and causing them to become ill. The term *misaki*[19] (wandering, homeless spirit) is also frequently used synonymously with Hotoke-sama in this connection, although *misaki* has a wider area of meaning and includes wandering spirits in no way connected with Buddhism. Upon being informed of the circumstances, the *kitōsha* makes contact with the other world through the medium of the *kami-sama* with whom he is associated and determines the cause and nature of the death of the person whose spirit has become a *misaki*. At the same time, the *kitōsha* determines any wishes the spirit may have. When these wishes, usually easily granted requests such as making offerings at a shrine, have been complied with, the sick person recovers.

Another device, sometimes recommended by *kitōsha* and sometimes utilized independently without consulting a medium, is the preparation of a *sandōra*,[20] a small, circular boat of rice straw fashioned so that one end of the straws can be united in the center of the miniature craft to represent a sail. The completed craft resembles an overturned mushroom or an opened umbrella with short, thick handle extending into the air. Incense, flowers, a lighted candle, and rice or fruit are placed in the *sandōra*, and the craft is set adrift in the sea to carry the wandering spirit

---

19. *Misaki* are to be distinguished from *gaki*, the spirits of dead Buddhists who become wandering, hungry *gaki* when they have no descendants left on earth to worship and make offerings to them.

20. Known under the name *san-tawara* in other areas of Japan. A similar device, called *sandāra*, is reported as once in use in Akita Prefecture as a means of committing infanticide. Unwanted infants were placed in *sandāra* and allowed to float off down a stream (T. Ōmachi, *op. cit.*, p. 8).

off to his proper home in the other world. The *sandōra* may also be left by the Rokujizō statues in the graveyard, and it is effective to leave it at a crossroads.

Kitōsha also speak with the spirits of deceased relatives of persons who wish to seek their advice in the handling of worrisome problems. Appeal to the other world is made through a particular *kami-sama*. After the *kitōsha* has made contact with the spirit of the dead person (always a certainty), the message from the spirit is transmitted to the waiting client. There is said to be nothing spectacular and no spiritual manifestation involved in this sort of ritual, which consists of prayers and pauses, after which the medium "repeats" to the waiting client the expected message. Although long established in Japan and still relatively common in rural areas, trance is not used by the local *kitōsha*, whose behavior is said at all times to appear normal.[21]

The average young or middle-aged person in the *buraku* regards resort to faith-healers and mediums as baseless superstition, and although they and the *sandōra* are utilized from time to time, it is usually done by or at the instigation of the household *ojii-san* or *obaa-san*.

Geomancers

The lore of the geomancer *(kasōmi)*, based largely upon the Chinese zodiac and astrology, is far too elaborate for comprehension by the average person. It is imperative, however, that a new house, storehouse, toilet, or bath be placed in an auspicious location and that construction begin on an auspicious day, and *kasōmi* are experts in such matters (see Chap. III, Building a House).

Kasōmi may also be consulted upon occasions other than the construction of buildings. If misfortune consistently strikes a household, the *kasōmi* can be of aid. He may recommend that the dwelling or outbuildings be moved or remodeled, or that the well be dug in a new position, and he will furnish lists of auspicious and inauspicious days for any kind of venture or activity. A household which had suffered repeated misfortunes consulted a *kasōmi* in 1946, and received from him a carefully written list of recommendations, which is translated below:

> (Document first lists names of household members and the stars by which they are influenced. Parenthetical items which appear below are the author's.)

> Dig up the toilet, which lies in The Direction of the Hare and place it in The Direction of Junior Brother[22] of the Wood. The chicken pen should also be moved. Auspicious days, Gregorian calendar: February 13, 17, 21, 25, and March 2.

> Purify the area where the toilet was located by burning straw and by using salt.

21. Professionals who communicate with the spiritual world through trance or spirit seizure are most commonly called *ichiko*, and appear to have been established in Japan for many centuries (see M. Jōya, *op cit.*, pp. 163-165).

22. "Elder Brother" and "Junior Brother" are sometimes translated as "Positive" and "Negative."

Place a bamboo pole from which the nodes have been removed (making it into a continuous cylinder) into the ground there and fill in the area with clean earth. Put the toilet receptacle in The Direction of Elder Brother of the Metal at the time the (new) toilet is made. Auspicious days: February 13, 21, 25, and March 4.

Tear down the wall between the main house and the *naya*. Build the *Butsudan* where the *naya* was and have it face toward the south. Auspicious days: March 8, 14, 16, 20, 22, 26. On the same day Dokūjin (O-Dokū-sama) should be moved about six feet to the west.

The front gate, which is in The Direction of Elder Brother of the Fire-Horse, should be moved to The Direction of Dragon-Serpent. Auspicious days: very auspicious, April 9, 10, 13, 17; fairly auspicious, April 11, 22, 29.

The entrance path, which lies in The Direction of the Dragon, should be closed and something should be placed there (to prevent entrance from that direction).

The storage outhouse should be built in The Direction of (illegible). Auspicious days to begin removing the trees and laying stones: April 9, 10, 16, 17. Auspicious days for erecting framework: April 17, 22, 29.

The rear entrance should be made in The Direction of Elder Brother of the Water-Ox from the main house. Auspicious days — also auspicious for putting in windows: April 9, 10, 13, 22. On the day when this construction is begun no one should go to other houses, and so that no one can come to the house from The Direction of Rat-Ox-Tiger, build a fence there.

Move the main dwelling about eighteen feet to the east. Very auspicious days: the Gregorian month of February; the second lunar month.[23] Decide at this time whether the part of the *naya*, three *shaku*, two *sun* (about forty inches), is to be torn down or whether it is to be moved to the south three *shaku*, two *sun*. The large trees in The Direction of Sheep-Monkey should be cut down. Small trees may be planted there or the area may be left as is (after the trees have been cut down). Build a fence to the east of the window of the neighboring house on the west. Auspicious days: March 14, 20, 26.

(Name and address of the *kasōmi*, and a listing of days when he is at home and available for consultation follow.)

The household in question has followed some of these recommendations, but has not as yet followed all advice because of lack of sufficient money for the rebuilding required. There have been no disasters in this household since these preventive measures were taken.

When luck is consistently bad it is sometimes considered advisable to change given names, at which time the advice of a *kasōmi* may be sought (not all *kasōmi* include lore on names among their specialties). Within the *buraku* of Takashima four persons now living have changed names. Official records are not changed, as this requires a court hearing. There are, however, a number of possible readings for ideographs used in writing given names, and it is the practice to adopt another reading of the same ideographs. Thus a boy named Masu-ichi may have his name changed to Sei-ichi, and, since the ideographs are the same, the official record remains correct and unchanged. Of the four cases of name-changing in the *buraku*, three are children whose names were changed by their parents because of prolonged sickness. One woman, who suffered the loss by death of her father and three siblings within a period of only a few

23. All dates except this appear to be by the Gregorian calendar.

years, changed her own name. Adjustment to the new name is quickly made by other persons in the *buraku*. It is noteworthy that the households of the persons who have undergone name changes are regarded as rather more superstitious than the average. Most households, however, call in *kasōmi* for advice when building a house or *naya*.

Fortune-tellers *(ekisha)* may be found in Ajino and all neighboring larger towns. *Buraku* persons may make rare visits to such persons, but they are for the most part avoided.

SPIRITS, GHOSTS, AND DEVILS

Old persons tell tales of ghosts *(yūrei)*, monsters *(o-bake)*, and devils *(oni)*, but little credence is given to them by the average person. A few old persons have seen such creatures, but the statements of young persons are invariably that the oldsters "claim" to have seen these things.

In addition to the *misaki* and *gaki* already described there are, however, other spirits in which some belief is placed. It is said that before one dies his spirit, which resembles a ball of fire with flaming tentacles flickering behind it (in this case the spirit is called *hito-dama*), may be seen leaving the body. The *hito-dama*, which is also likened in shape to the Medusa jellyfish *(kurage)*, shoots from the body of a sick person, whizzes out of the house, and sinks to the ground, where it disappears. If the distance the fireball travels is great, the sick person will live for some time; if it is short, death will come soon. During 1951, the Shionasu niece of a Takashima woman saw her own *hito-dama* leave her body and died the following day.

Another type of fireball, called *kitsunebi* (fox fire) and *hinotama* (fireball), is said usually to be caused by foxes. There have been no foxes in the locality for many years, but reports of witnessing *kitsunebi*, balls of fire which dance or shoot about, in former times and in other regions are not uncommon. Foxes are capable of many sorts of deception and bewitchment, and beliefs concerning them are regarded by the average person as "true superstitions." There is a curious prejudice against a handsome flame-red wild flower of the lily family *(Lycoris radiata)* which blossoms profusely in the fall. It is known by several names which include *higan-bana* (equinox flower) and *kitsune-bana* (fox-flower). Reasons given for the dislike of this flower are that it is common (wild azaleas are also common, and well-liked), that it has an unpleasant odor (it has almost no odor), that it commonly grows in graveyards (true), and, finally, that one of its names is "fox-flower." It is suggestive that the principal reason for the prejudice against this handsome blossom is a heritage from the past based upon the connection of its name with foxes.

Black cats are said to bring good luck, but a double- or split-tailed cat is capable of bewitchment (most household cats in Japan have only stubs of tails, a natural, not induced condition). Little credence is given to these old beliefs concerning cats.

DEFILEMENT AND TABOO

Ideas of ceremonial uncleanliness *(kegare)* and taboo *(imi)* connected with the crises of life seem to have existed in Japan from very ancient times. First mention of them appears in the *Kojiki*, in which reference is made to parturition huts and uncleanliness during childbirth.[24] Death, sexual intercourse, childbirth, and blood associated with the physiological processes of women are traditionally defiling.

On Takashima menstruation is a period of ceremonial pollution, when no contact with the *kami-sama* may be made. Taboos are ordinarily considered to apply only to contact with Shinto or "native" deities, and are said to bear no relation to orthodox Buddhism.[25] Menstruating women may make no offerings to *kami-sama* and may not visit shrines.

When women of the present grandparental generation were young, restrictions during menstrual periods were more rigid than they are today. Women of that time were not allowed to pass in front of statues or wayside shrines of Shinto deities, and if a woman during menses took meals together with her husband, he also became defiled and the taboos were extended to him.

Present-day restrictions in most households apply only to offerings to the Shinto gods and visits to shrines (and thus, of course, prayers to these deities). The household continues to eat together in the usual manner, but it is customary to eat all food prepared by a woman on the last day of her menstrual period before that day is over, even if it is necessary to have an additional snack after the evening meal. On the morning following the end of the menstrual period a new fire is built. A new fire is in actuality now built daily in the normal course of life, but the building of a fire on this day is still referred to as *hi-kaeri*, "changing the fire." Salt may also be sprinkled upon clothing for purification (by the woman concerned only) at the end of the period, and small pinches of salt are sometimes placed on household shrine shelves at the beginning of the menstrual period.

After giving birth to a child a woman enters a thirty-two day period of *kegare* (always spoken of as a thirty-three day period, but restrictions end on the morning of the thirty-third day). Restrictions are the same as

---

24. See G. B. Sansom, *Japan, A Short Cultural History*, rev. ed. (New York: D. Appleton-Century Co., 1943), p. 52 ff. Menstrual and parturitional huts are reported as still existing in a few isolated communities. See E. Norbeck, "Pollution and Taboo in Contemporary Japan," *Southwestern Journal of Anthropology*, VIII, No. 2, 1952.

25. Although Takashima informants usually state that there is no relationship between Buddhism and practices of uncleanliness and taboo, Buddhism appears to have affected these beliefs and practices in at least the matters of food taboos and duration of taboos — and also to have been affected in turn. For additional data see E. Norbeck, *op. cit.*

for menstrual periods, with some additions. Until the fifteenth day a new mother must cover her head when she steps outside the house so that she will not defile the sun with her unclean presence. The washed clothing of both mother and infant, because they are unclean, must be hung in the shade to dry until the fifteenth day after parturition. Before a new mother may resume household cooking, which is usually done on the fifteenth day, she must go through a ceremonial washing of the hands with water. Pollution is thus removed sufficiently so that, although she may not as yet make offerings to the *kami-sama*, a woman may prepare food for the household. During the entire thirty-two day period a woman should not, for fear of offense to the gods, enter or leave the house through the *shimonoma*, where two of the shrine shelves are located. When the period of taboo or abstention ends on the thirty-third day, *hi-kaeri* is done, and clothing is sprinkled with salt.

Death is also defiling and surrounded with taboo. Until about thirty years ago taboo restrictions surrounding death were long and difficult. The whole *buraku* was under a three-day period of defilement and taboo, and unclean periods of relatives of the deceased varied with closeness of relationship from fifty days (ending on the fiftieth day) for children to three days for cousins. At the present time only the household in which a death has occurred and the members of the *kōrenchū* (funeral organization) are considered to be unclean, and the period of pollution lasts only until all funeral ritual has ended, ordinarily three days after death. During this period, members of the household and of the *kōrenchū* must avoid all contact with *kami-sama* and must purify themselves with salt and build new fires in their homes when the funeral period is over. It is necessary to take special measures to avoid defiling the household *kami-sama* by the presence in the dwelling of the deceased and of his polluted relatives and the also polluted *kōrenchū* members. Pieces of paper on which the ideographs for the term *kichū*, "mourning,"[26] have been written must be attached by paste or a tack to each household shrine shelf. A few households observe the custom of removing all statuary and ceremonial paraphernalia from the household shrine shelves during this period as well as putting up the *kichū* papers.

Uncleanliness taboos are usually observed in all households in which there are old people. In many households the practices are now ceasing as soon as the grandparents die, and in all households restrictions have become less rigid whether or not there are old people. One grandmother, piqued by the neglect of taboo restrictions during menstruation by the young women of her household, remarked caustically that life was indeed

26. The word *kichū* is usually translated as "mourning," which obscures the connotations of this term. A literal translation of *ki* is "abstention" or "taboo" (*ki* is another reading of the ideograph used to represent the word *imi*). *Chū* means "in the midst of." *Kichū* can thus be translated as "under taboo."

convenient for the young women of today who apparently are not troubled with menstrual periods. Most women whether young or old, however, still follow the old customs insofar as they concern restrictions against making offerings to *kami-sama* and visiting shrines. The women say they would feel "strange" if they were to make offerings during this period, and they point out that, in any event, these are very simple restrictions which require no effort to observe. Some women seldom make offerings under ordinary circumstances so that the taboos scarcely concern them.

Traditional means of purification for all sorts of defilement are water, salt, and fire. Before entering a shrine one washes his hands in water, as does the new mother before she resumes cooking. Salt is sprinkled upon clothing after attending a funeral, and in some households pinches of salt are placed on the shelves for all *kami-sama* during times of funerals, childbirth, and menstruation which involve household members. Carpenters purify themselves by sprinkling salt on their clothing before they start to build a house.

During their youth it was the custom of the present generation of household heads to sprinkle purificatory salt upon their clothing after visiting houses of prostitution and before re-entering their own homes. Salt is also used by religious practitioners in purificatory rites, and recommended by *kasōmi* (whom *buraku* persons do not ordinarily regard as religious practitioners) for the same purpose. Fire itself is pure and a new fire indicates the end of a period of defilement and the beginning of a new and clean period.

THE CEREMONIAL CALENDAR

A comparison of the ceremonial calendar as observed on Takashima with the national and official holidays shows few points of resemblance. National holidays follow the Gregorian calendar. The Takashima ceremonial calendar follows the standard reckoning of time in the *buraku*, the lunar calendar. National holidays, although generally known to everyone, are given little or no attention except by the few girls who are employed by firms in Ajino and are granted holidays on the days in question. Treatment of the annual round of ceremonial events, except where otherwise noted, will here be made on the basis of the lunar calendar, according to which the new year begins sometime between January 20 and February 19 of the Gregorian calendar.

First Month

The first month is the month of New Year's, one of the most important periods in the annual cycle of events. It is a period when there is no fishing and work in the fields is slack, a month of relative leisure for most households. Preparations for New Year's begin several days before the end of the old year. Glutenous rice and millet must be cooked, pounded in a mortar, and shaped into cakes — a few large ceremonial ones called *kagami-mochi* (mirror cakes) and many small ones. Cakes are frequently tinted pink and blue for this occasion, and although white or colorless *mochi* are said to be traditional for offerings to the gods, the colored cakes are also offered. It is a common practice to place a tier of three cakes, one of each color and graduated in size, in the *tokonoma*. This tier of cakes is considered both an offering to Amaterasu-ō-mikami and a decorative touch for the New Year's season.

Other decorations are also made and placed in traditional spots. *Shimekazari*, made of *daidai* (bitter orange) and *daikon* against a background of wild ferns, are used to decorate the *tokonoma*, all the shrine shelves, the stern ends of fishing boats, and are frequently suspended above the entrances to dwellings. *Shichigosan* may also be hung before the *tokonoma* and used in other places, alone or together with the *shimekazari*. Houses are given a thorough cleaning before the first day of the new year, and everyone bathes in preparation for wearing fine clothes.

Traditionally, one or two small pine trees *(kadomatsu)* are placed in the yard by the entrance. For reasons of economy, fully branching pine boughs are usually substituted. These are frequently supported by a stand made by tying several sticks of firewood around the base of the branch. There is no agreement on the significance of the *kadomatsu*. Some persons say that the pine is symbolic of virility. Others think that the pine, an evergreen, is symbolic of everlasting life. Still others say that it is symbolic of household cohesion, for a pine, although branched, comprises one unit.

All debts should be paid before New Year's, a custom which is said to have gone into decline since the end of the war. Children often bring gifts to their parents at this season which are called *seibo*, "end of the year (gift)." Reciprocal gifts are not given in this case by the parents, as the *seibo* come from members of the household. Persons under obligation *(on)* to others also present *seibo* and thus discharge their *on*. Children are given New Year's spending money, called *o-toshitama*, literally "year's jewels," to do with as they please during the holiday period.

The first day of the new year, *Gantan*, is a rest day for everyone except insofar as women must work in cooking and serving meals. On this day offerings of at least *mochi*, later eaten by household members, and usually other foodstuffs, tea, and *sake*, are made to all the household gods, and someone also always gives attention to the deities of the *buraku*. Incense and fresh sprigs of pine needles or shrubs and occasionally flowers are also included in the offerings. As a rule, no *kami-sama* or Buddhist deity is neglected.

The best food the household can afford is prepared and eaten. Breakfast is traditionally *o-zoni*, a soup in which *mochi* are placed. Toasted *mochi* are eaten in great quantity. *Sake* or *shōchū* are served in drinking households (the majority), and fruit and purchased cakes, seldom eaten with meals, are served as in-between-meal treats. Good or best clothes are donned, and the day is a full one of eating delicious food, drinking (for adult males), rest, and talk.

Sometime during the day a trip is traditionally made to the Kōjin shrine on the hill, which has been cleaned and prepared beforehand for New Year's attendance. This visit is called *hatsu-mairi* (first visit) and must, according to an old saying, precede visits to any other shrines: *"Ujigami-sama e ichiban ni o-mairi shinai to yoso no kami-sama e yukarenai* (It is improper to pray to outside gods unless the tutelary god has been first given respects)."* In actual practice the shrine visit may be omitted. During *Gantan* in 1951 only eleven adults went to the Kōjin shrine, although a few others are said to have gone during the following two days. In prewar days it was customary to make pilgrimages to outside shrines, particularly to the Hachiman shrine in Kayō, but such excursions are now rare.

The second day of the new year is pretty much a repetition of the first. Good food is eaten; good clothes worn, and most persons rest. This day is, for reasons unknown, sometimes called *o-sekku* (there are five traditional *sekku*, festival days, throughout the year; this day is not one of them). Rest continues through the third day, which bears no special name. The first three days of the new year are, however, collectively called *Shōgatsu sanga*, literally, "first month three days."

Mochi with *nanagusa* (seven kinds of herbs) in them are eaten on the seventh day, *Nanokabi*, which is a rest day for most persons. The first *o-zōsui* of the year, a sort of porridge made of rice and various vegetables in which *iriko* (a small dried fish, for flavoring and seldom eaten) and *nanagusa-mochi* are placed, is also eaten on this day. *O-zōsui* is a special dish, greatly liked, about which there is an old expression, *"Nanagusa-zōsui soko ureshii* (literally, *"Zōsui* [made with] *nanagusa* bottom happy")," i.e., the *nanagusa-mochi*, being heavy, sink to the bottom, and when one has drunk most of the liquid these delicious morsels are found. Some of the *o-zōsui* is usually first offered to the household *kami-sama* but it is never placed before the Buddhist ancestral tablets as it contains fish, food of animal origin. *Kadomatsu* are taken down on this day and are later used as fuel.

Beginning after dark on the evening of the eighth day and continuing until dawn of the ninth day, a watch is maintained at the *Kōjin* shrine. This custom, the significance of which is now unknown, is called *O-himatchi*, which may be translated literally as "waiting for the sun."

O-himatchi is a social occasion and one looked forward to by *buraku* children, who prepare firewood some weeks in advance so that it will be dry and burn well, for this and an identical watch called *Ōtsumogori*, held on New Year's Eve. This firewood, although identical with ordinary firewood, is known by the special name *setchigi. Gi* means "tree" or "wood," (hence fuel) but the meaning of *setchi* is uncertain. Some persons venture the opinion that it is a local variation of the term *setsu* (season) and refers to the beginning of one of the ancient seasons of the year.

A fire is built in a firepit in the floor of the shrine building at *O-himatchi*, around which many children and a few adults gather to talk and eat *mochi* toasted over the coals of the fire. Adults on this occasion usually make obeisance to Kōjin-sama upon entering the shrine and place a little money in the offertory; children seldom or never do. *O-himatchi* is a time of fun and excitement for the children, who may on this night stay up later than usual. Most of them, however, fall asleep before midnight and are taken home by adults or sleepy older children. A few adults, sometimes men who are awaiting an opportunity to gamble in privacy, remain until dawn.

The next event of the new year falls on the eleventh day, which is known by the name *Yarebo* (meaning unknown) or *Jūichinichi-no-sekku* (eleventh day *sekku*). A few old persons also call this day *O-taue* (rice planting), a term whose origin is unknown and which appears to bear no relationship to rice planting, which is done in surrounding communities in the Gregorian month of May, nearly three months later. Remnants of a ceremony called *Yarebo* still remain. Until about thirty years ago it was the custom to line up all agricultural tools in the yard at daybreak and decorate them with a *shichigosan*, which was left on the implements until sunset. Sometimes this was done just before the first day of the new year and the decorations were removed on the eleventh day. An adult member of the household went out into the fields sometime during the early morning and repeated the word *Yarebo* several times. This was said to have been both a symbolic cultivation and a gesture of respect toward the soil which served to make the crops for the coming year abundant. The *Yarebo* ceremony in the fields no longer exists today. A number of households still decorate agricultural tools. Some persons rest on this day, but there is no special or traditional food.

Tondo (bonfire) falls on the fourteenth day, when the New Year's decorations are taken down and burned in bonfires on the beach. In former days all households had one communal fire, but today several fires are built throughout the day, around which an indefinite number of households may gather. There are no established rules, and the communal use of bonfires is in large part fortuitous. Some person starts a fire and two, three, or more neighboring households join in. Other fires are built at later times in the day and on other areas of the beach. Communal use depends to some extent upon where one lives, so that persons living in houses at some distance from one another ordinarily use different fires. It also depends to some extent upon personal likes and dislikes.

Each household toasts over the bonfire one of the *kagami-mochi* placed in the *tokonoma* before *Gantan*. When the cake has been toasted, it is taken to the home and ceremonially offered to the *kami-sama*, after which it is divided and a portion eaten by each member of the household. *Tondo* cakes are said to taste bad because they get covered with smoke and ashes, but they are eaten for the sake of custom and because (old people, at least, believe) they give protection from evil and illness. A piece of partially burned *shimekazari*, the straw rope decoration, is sometimes hung over the entrance of dwellings to keep out snakes and evil. Warming oneself in the flames of the *tondo* gives protection against harm and disease during the coming year. The ashes must never be stepped upon nor put to use in the fields as fertilizer; they must instead be left for the tide to wash them away.

Sometime between the first day of the month and *Tondo*, while the New Year's decorations are still up, the Buddhist priest from Shionasu comes to each household to pray. The day may vary from year to year as the priest has many *buraku* to cover, but his visit must be made before the decorations are removed. Prayers, in which the household members join, are said on this occasion before the Toshigami-sama shelf. Food and a little money are always offered to the priest, who, unable to eat some twenty or more times daily during this season, usually declines the food but accepts the money.

A special gruel made of sweet potatoes, red beans, water, and sugar, into which *mochi* are placed is traditionally first eaten in the new year on the fifteenth day *(Jūgonichi-zekku,* "Fifteenth day *zekku")*. Most persons consider this day a holiday.

The first visit to the graveyard of the new year, called *Nembutsu no Kuchiake*, "The First Invocation," is made on the sixteenth day, and offerings are left at graves. This visit is usually made in the early afternoon and should never, according to an old belief, be made after four o'clock for fear of evil consequences.

Traditional activities for the first month end on the sixteenth day but, since this is a slack month, it is frequently the time that visits are made to relatives in other communities or the annual trip to Kompira is made. The first month is the great holiday and rest month of the year.

For about the last fifteen years New Year's by the Gregorian calendar has also been observed. A one-day holiday is taken on January 1, special food eaten, and the household *kami-sama* usually given attention. This is primarily a rest day rather than a religious occasion.

Second Month

The first day of the second month is usually called *Hi-shite Shōgatsu* (thought to mean "one-day New Year's"), and is also known by the more common Japanese name for this day of Koshōgatsu (Little New Year's). Most households eat *mochi* on this day, and some households rest, but there are no other special activities.

O-nihan (a local variation of the Standard Japanese term *nehan*, "nirvana"), which falls on the fifteenth day, is a Buddhist ceremonial day in commemoration of the anniversary of Buddha's death. Visits are traditionally made on this day to the temples at Shionasu or Kayō, where prayers are made to the ancestors. Such persons as now go to the temples are usually women, only one representative from a household, and they offer prayers to their own ancestors. Worship of their husbands' ancestors is thus presumably a responsibility of sisters or other women in the lineage of their husbands. Women who visit the temples usually take with them young children, for whom it is a pleasant day as they are usually taken shopping en route. Offerings given at the temple are usually *mochi*, money, or rice (on this occasion a *shō*, about one-twentieth of a bushel, or more, not just a few grains, as this rice offering represents part of the priest and temple revenue). If it is the first *nihan* since the death of someone in the household, a piece of cloth or an article of clothing in good condition is to be brought to the temple and given to the priest for later sale, but this is a custom now seldom observed. Food at the home may be somewhat special, but for most persons it is a routine day of work with routine food.

The vernal equinox, *O-higan*, normally falls sometime during the second month. This is an official national holiday called, as it is also sometimes called on Takashima, *Shunbun-no-hi*, and formerly known under the name *Shunkikōreisai*. On this day visits are made to the graves of the ancestors. The day is frequently referred to as *Mizu-nagashi-no-hi* (Water-pouring day) because the ceremony called *Mizu-matsuri* (Water mass), the pouring of water on headstones or graves, or into flower vases at graves (as is also done at funerals and memorial services), is performed. Many young daughters who have married and moved away from the *buraku* return at this time to pay their respects to their ancestors at the graveyard and to visit their relatives, and this is a day on which millet cakes, called *higan-dango*, are eaten, after being offered before the ancestral tablets. *O-higan* is for many persons a day of work, interrupted for at least one household representative by a visit to the grave.

Third Month

Hina-zekku,[27] "Doll Festival," also called *Momo-zekku*, "Peach Festival," and often simply *O-Hina-sama*, falls on the third day of the third month. On this day peach blossoms are traditionally offered to Hotoke-sama and to the *kami-sama*, but for lack of the blossoms, this custom is seldom observed on Takashima. *Hina-zekku* is a festival occasion for young girls, who on this day are given dolls. The orthodox set of dolls consists of fifteen characters arranged on a stepped dais, with two dolls representing the imperial court couple *(Dairi-sama)* on top, and includes court ladies, warriors, musicians, and servants, together with miniature furniture, trees, and table-ware.[28] Such a magnificent display is not possible for Takashima children, who may have *Dairi-sama* and one or two other dolls, displayed in the *tokonoma*. Fortunate children may have additional dolls and a little furniture. As new female children are born to the household it is customary to add dolls and furniture and set up one joint display for all.

Many types of dolls, including Western ones, may be used. These are usually presented by the mother's household at *Hina-zekku* in the first year of life of a female child, although additional dolls may also be presented as gifts in subsequent years. The first *Hina-zekku* for a child is the important one. A small feast is then traditionally held for relatives who bring with them the presents for the child, the maternal grandmother presenting the finest doll. *Mochi* is always served.

During years subsequent to the first *Hina-zekku* and until girls reach the age of about seven, it is customary to have special food for the members of the household on this occasion, at least *mochi*. There is no feast for relatives, but the ceremonial dolls, carefully stored most of the year, are brought out and set up for the enjoyment of the girls of the household. Fine dolls are usually housed in glass cases to show them off to good advantage and also to protect them from damage by the children whom they honor.

The twenty-first day is a Shingon Sect ceremonial day commemorating the anniversary of the death of Kōbō-Daishi, and is customarily called simply *O-Daishi-sama*. Temple visits are traditionally made on this day, but few people now do so. Old people remember that until about thirty years ago a custom called *Shichikasho*, "Seven places," was observed on this day, whereby people dressed in beggar's costume and made a pilgrimage to seven temples.

27. *Zekku* and *sekku* are the same. In some cases it is customary to pronounce the word as *zekku* and in other cases *sekku*. The *zekku* pronunciation is usually favored on Takashima.

28. An article in the *Mainichi*, a newspaper of national circulation, of March 1, 1951 reports some 1951 innovations among *Hina-zekku* dolls: a Japanese couple aboard an airplane bound for America; an imperial prince tenderly embracing and kissing a princess (kissing is untraditional in Japan), and a combination composed of a native *sumo* wrestler and a strip-tease artist seated on a dais.

Fourth Month

Shiwasa-nichi, the third day of the fourth month, is a ceremonial day observed by only a few of the aged and is unknown to some of the young people. The significance of this day, on which temple visits were traditionally made, is forgotten, but it is thought that there is some connection with Kōbō-Daishi.

The eighth day, *O-Shakasama-tanjōbi*, the anniversary of Buddha's birth, is at present an occasion of little importance although a few households still make it a holiday. Before the war it was the custom to go to one of the Honjō temples on this day, where offerings were made and *amacha* (literally, "sweet tea"), a beverage made from the leaves of *Hydrangea hortensis*,[29] was received from the priest. The *amacha* was brought home and each member of the household drank a portion, for this beverage, blessed by having been poured over statues of the Buddha, protects against sickness and evil. It was also a pre-war custom to make ink (using *sumi*, India ink in solid form which is mixed with water and used for brush writing) with a little *amacha* and inscribe the ideograph for tea on a piece of white paper. This piece of paper was attached to the outside wall of the house by the entrance with the ideograph upside down, and served to keep snakes and all evil out of the house. Another custom, still observed by a number of households, was to prepare on this day millet cakes and *kashiwa-mochi*, *mochi* wrapped in the leaf of a species of oak (*Quercus dentata*).

The fourth month is a month of heavy labor as the fishing season has begun in earnest, and it is the month when the grain must be harvested and sweet potatoes planted. There is little time for rest.

Fifth Month

The fifth month is again one of heavy work, punctuated by only one ceremonial day, a routine day of labor for the majority. The fifth day of this month is the day of the Boys' Festival, called *Tango-no-sekku*, and also called *Gogatsu-no-sekku* (Fifth Month Festival) and *Shōbu-zekku* (Iris Festival). This day is a counterpart of the festival day for girls of the third month.[30] If a boy has been born to a household during the year there is traditionally a feast in his honor to which relatives are invited. Relatives bring with them presents of paper carp (symbolic of bravery and strength, as they swim against the current in streams), pennants bearing depictions of famous ancient heroes, clothing, and dolls. There is usually, in actual practice, no emphasis in this case on one line of descent in the presentation of gifts; both matrilineal and patrilineal relatives give presents, although the matrilineal line traditionally serves as the donors. Dolls are

---

29. The leaves of this plant were used in Japan for sweetening in ancient times before the introduction of sugar.
30. By the official post-war national holiday calendar this day (May 5th, Gregorian) became Boys' and Girls' Day, and the girls' *Momo-zekku* is omitted.

frequently arranged in the *tokonoma* or on shelves, as is done for girls on their festival day. The types of dolls, however, differ from those given to girls and the number is usually smaller. The most common doll for boys is Kintarō, a fat male child wearing only a small square apron and holding a carp. Kintarō is also sometimes depicted wrestling with a bear. Knights in armor are also common, as are miniature helmets and quivers with arrows. On Takashima the first male child is almost certain to receive one or more dolls; his younger brother may or may not. In any case, the dolls and toy figures, helmets, and arrows are displayed for the enjoyment of all male children.

Special food including *mochi* is made. *Shōbu*, a variety of iris, and *yomogi*, a sage *(Artemesia indica)*,[31] are offered to the *kami-sama*, and sometimes to the Hotoke-sama. *Yomogi* is also used in the preparation of *mochi* on this day. This herb, chopped fine and mixed with the cooked glutenous rice while it is being pounded in the mortar, results in a cake dark green in color and aromatic. Leaves of both *shōbu* and *yomogi* are placed on the roof of the house above the front entrance, often thrown up by the young boys of the household, and are said to keep evil out of the house. The paper carp and pennants are set up on long bamboo poles in the yard where they blow in the breeze until evening or the following morning. If there is a boy in the household, some observance of this day is made all through his childhood, and new paper carp or pennants may be purchased occasionally. The paper carp, some of them six or more feet in length, are usually stored carefully for succeeding years, but they also see use in the fields when the grain is ripening where, inflated by the wind and fluttering, they serve as effective scarecrows.

Sixth Month

The first day of this month, a routine work day, is called *Rokugatsu-hi-shite* (*Rokugatsu* means "sixth month;" *hi-shite* is thought to mean "first day"). An old custom, still observed by some households, calls for fried millet cakes *(kōra-yaki)* to be prepared and eaten together with pickled plums for the morning meal on this day. *Kōra* is the name of a type of cooking vessel in which the cakes are fried in a little cooking oil. There is an old saying, regarded very lightly, concerning the time of day when *kōra-yaki* should be eaten, "*Asahayaku hi ga agaranai uchi ni natsu-itami ga sen* ([If *kōra-yaki* is eaten] early in the morning before the sun rises there will be no summer-illness)."

The ninth and tenth days of this month are the summer festival for Kōjin-sama *(Natsu-no-matsuri)*. Until about twenty years ago this was an

---

31. Moxa is also made from the leaves of this plant.

important *buraku* festival, when everyone rested, made visits to the Kōjin shrine, and had special food. A number of households still make this a holiday and a few persons still pay respects at the shrine, but for many people this is a day of work.

In former years and until about the beginning of the war many *buraku* people attended the Gion (a deity identified with Susa-no-wo-no-mikoto) Festival held in nearby Shimotsui from the seventh to fourteenth days of this month. Attendance was usually confined to a single day, which became a day of shopping and recreation with a visit to the Gion shrine sometime during the course of the day. Today the rare aged person or young people off for a holiday still observe this custom.

Seventh Month

The seventh month is one of the most important ceremonial months of the year as it is the month of *Bon*, which, together with New Year's and the Autumn Festival, comprise the three major events of the year.

Tanabata-zekku (usually translated as "Star Festival"), which falls on the seventh day and precedes *Bon*, is a day of importance only to children. On *Tanabata*, or some days beforehand, children write little poems, names, or wishes on strips of colored paper and attach them to bamboo branches which are set up in the yards. The decorated branches are allowed to remain there until evening and are then thrown into the sea. Older sisters or mothers frequently help the very young children, and the preparation of the *Tanabata* bamboos is now very frequently done at school by children of the lower elementary grades. *Tanabata*, according to a legend borrowed from the Chinese, is the day of the annual meeting of two separated lovers, represented by the stars Altair and Vega.[32] Wishes made on this day are said to come true. *Tanabata* is also said to be a good day to go swimming in the sea, as it is a day when there are no *kappa* (mythical water creatures which lure horses and human beings to death by drowning — usually thought of as inhabiting fresh water), and soap is not needed to cleanse the body. There is an old saying applying to *Tanabata*, "*Shichihen tabete shichihen oyogu* ([It is good to] eat seven times and swim seven times)." No one believes in *kappa* or the effectiveness of soapless bathing, but children are usually allowed to go swimming on *Tanabata*, a privilege not often extended to them.

The thirteenth to fifteenth days are *Bon*,[33] which is usually called by the local term *Bon-i*, the annual Buddhist festival of the dead, an important event throughout all of Japan. Married daughters and sons who have

---

32. The details of this legend are available in a number of English publications. For a good, brief description of *Tanabata* and a recounting of the legend see M. Fujisawa, "Tanabata, the Star Festival," *Travel in Japan*, IV, No. 2 (1928), pp. 4-9.

33. Derived from the Indian term *Ullambana*, which became in Japanese *Urabonye* or *Urabon*, terms still in use.

moved away return to their former homes for this occasion so that *Bon* takes on the aspect of a family reunion. Houses and cemetery plots are cleaned and tidied before *Bon-i* in readiness for the activities to follow. Some persons clean up debts before *Bon-i*, and discharge *on* by the presentation of gifts, which may be called either *chūgen* ("midyear [gift]") or *seibo* (the same term as is used for New Year's gifts, "end of the year [gift]").

On the morning of the thirteenth day a visit is made to household graves to welcome the spirits of the ancestors *(Hotoke-sama no mukae)*, who on this day return to their former homes. Offerings brought to the graves on this day include spherical millet cakes, the significance of which is unknown. Ancestral tablets are taken from the *Butsudan* and placed in the *tokonoma* together with offerings. The evening of the thirteenth day is the beginning of the *Bon-i* fast *(shōjin-gatame)*, which extends until noon of the fifteenth day. During this time no food of animal origin may be eaten. Noodles, in particular the variety called *udon*, are traditional and standard fare during *Bon-i*.

Another visit to the graveyard is frequently made on the morning of the fourteenth day, although its meaning is unknown (the spirits of the dead are now in their former homes and absent from the graves). All outside relatives who are able to come have usually arrived by the fourteenth day. This is the height of the *Bon* season, a day full of conversation and conviviality when good food is eaten and good clothes are worn. Sometime in the evening of this day the household assembles before the ancestral tablets in the *tokonoma* for a reading of Buddhist sutras *(o-kankin)* in honor of the souls now in the dwelling.

Fast is broken at the noon meal on the fifteenth day, when fish may again be served. This is the day for the return of the souls to the other world. Small boats of rice straw *(Hotoke-bune)* about one and one-half feet long are made to convey the souls on their return trip. Candles, incense, rice, and other food offerings which have first been ceremonially offered before the ancestral tablets are placed in the boats, and they are put out to sea with candles lit sometime in the early evening. The preparation and launching of these *Hotoke-bune* is an especially festive occasion for children, who gather about their elders eagerly and like to try to make the boats themselves. A second *o-kankin* is conducted sometime during the late afternoon or evening of this day.

The Buddhist priest theoretically comes to every household to pray sometime before the return of the ancestral souls. Because he has many places to visit within a short interval, however, he may come to Takashima as early as the tenth day of the month. On this occasion prayers are conducted out in the yard before a *mizutana* (literally, "water shelf"), on which ancestral tablets and offerings are placed.[34] The *mizutana*, often called *mizutana-sama*, is a small wooden shelf or stand with a narrow rim on three sides, shaped something like a dust-pan, to which two narrow cylindrical bamboo vases for flowers are attached at the two front corners. The stand is supported by a wooden stake which is thrust into the ground firmly so that the shelf is horizontal with the ground. Among the prayers said is one called *segaki*, on behalf of the *gaki*, those unfortunate souls who have no living descendants to worship them. Offerings of food are also made to the *gaki*.

The sixteenth day of the seventh month is often a rest day for those who have borne the burden of the religious tasks during *Bon-i*. In many households it is common for only one person, often the grandfather, to make all offerings to the Hotoke-sama.[35] Tea and incense may be offered four or five times daily and several offerings of food may be made. Relatives who have not returned home earlier usually leave on this day, and *buraku* life subsides to its normal pace.

In former days dancing was one of the great pleasures of this festival period and continued off and on for a month or more after *Bon-i* ended. Dancing is now occasional or absent, and only half-hearted.

Eighth Month

There are no observances during this month except the diurnal equinox and the remnants of what might once have been another festival day, called *Hassaku* (first day of the eighth month). *Hassaku* festivities consist of preparing and eating millet cakes. The origin and significance of this custom are now unknown.

The diurnal equinox, known in popular terminology by the same name as the vernal equinox, *O-higan* (equinox), usually falls sometime during the eighth month. Like the spring equinox, this is also a national holiday, called *Shūbun-no-hi* (in pre-war years also known under the name *Shūkikōreisai*). Activities are identical with those of the spring equinox, previously described.

Ninth Month

Kiku-zekku, Chrysanthemum Festival, also called *Kugatsu-no-sekku* (Ninth Month Festival), falls on the ninth day, and is one of the traditional *sekku*. To the people of Takashima this is an unimportant event overshadowed by their own great annual Autumn Festival *(Aki-no-matsuri)*, which is held on the ninth and tenth days. This festival, in honor of

34. According to the local Buddhist priest, the custom of holding this service outside in the yard is an indirect result of contact with Christianity during the sixteenth and seventeenth centuries. This service was formerly held inside dwellings, but after the abolishment of Christianity in the seventeenth century it became the custom to conduct it outside in view of neighbors and passers-by as proof that the household religion was Buddhism.

35. Religious service may once have been the primary duties of the aged at a time when clear-cut age classes existed. Sakurada finds religious duties still assigned to persons of the *tairō* (great age) class at Kunezaki Village, Mie Prefecture (K. Sakurada, *op. cit.*).

Kōjin-sama, the *buraku* tutelary god, is one of the great events of the ceremonial year. The festival is said by some persons to commemorate the death of Kōjin, who died on the eighteenth day of this month, and until about twenty-five years ago the festival was held on the eighteenth and nineteenth days of the month. This period by the lunar calendar is, however, always one of low tides, which made it difficult to launch and beach the boats in which relatives were transported to and from the mainland. The date of observance was therefore changed to take advantage of fuller tides.

The Kōjin shrine, cleaned and prepared for devotions, is traditionally visited. All *kami-sama* (and Hotoke-sama) receive offerings. Kōjin, in whose honor the festival is held, is in actuality given scant attention and socializing with visiting relatives is the principal activity. Everyone dresses in good clothing and fine food is served. In some households it is the custom to treat relatives and household members with food of banquet quality during these festive days, and a good deal of *sake* and *shōchū* are consumed.

The Autumn Festival is the occasion for the one fixed annual get-together of all male members of the *buraku* branch of the Young People's Association, i.e., all unmarried young men of the *buraku*. The young men go to the Kōjin shrine sometime in the afternoon of the ninth or tenth day, not to pay devotions but to bring back the *sendairoku*,[36] a ceremonial litter or portable shrine, which is stored there. The young men then decorate the *sendairoku* with red cotton, bamboo branches, and paper lanterns. Red silk curtains are placed on the open sides of the carriage compartment. In the floor of the small carriage is a round hole into which a drum is fitted so that an inch or two of the drum head projects above the floor. The four corners of the carriage bear stylized carvings of bird heads with comma-shaped eyes. When the carriage has been assembled onto its two long carrying poles and all decorations added, the smallest young man in the *buraku* (the carriage is small and there is, moreover, little point in carrying someone who is heavy) crouches or kneels within the carriage with drumsticks in his hands. The other youths shoulder the shrine and carry it about to the accompaniment of their own shouts of "Yossa! Yossa!" (similar to "Heave!" and said whenever lifting heavy objects in unison) and the beating of the drum inside the carriage. Traditionally, the *sendairoku* is transported into the yard of every house in the *buraku* as a signal for the household to give the members of the *Seinendan* a gift of money. In actual practice, several members of the *Seinendan* usually go

---

36. More commonly known throughout Japan by the name *mikoshi*, which is also occasionally used on Takashima. The use of *mikoshi* at village festivals is common throughout much of Japan. The carriage may be empty or contain only a sprig of *sakaki* or *naruten*. In some areas the contents of the carriages are regarded as unknown. It is usually assumed that the *kami-sama* in whose honor the festivities are conducted is inside the carriage, invisible behind the curtains.

from house to house earlier in the day to collect contributions as it is difficult or impossible to transport the long and clumsy *sendairoku* in the
cramped paths between houses and into narrow entryways of yards.
Contributions of money are usually fairly large, and the total is sufficient
to purchase ample *sake* to get all members of the *Seinendan* drunk, the
purpose for which the money is intended. This is the one occasion of the
year when young unmarried men (from about sixteen years of age upward) may, without censure, become thoroughly drunk. It is said also to
be a day when all differences and dislikes between individual members
of the *Seinendan* are forgotten.[37]

Many of the youths are already drunk by the time the *sendairoku* is
assembled, although, traditionally, serious drinking does not begin until
later. It is customary to carry the shrine, weaving and staggering, back
and forth along the main path centering about the community hall for
an interval of perhaps an hour while children and adults watch. Some
young men tie cloths about their heads and a few make up their faces
with cosmetics. It is said that in former days young men commonly
painted their faces upon this occasion, but few now do so. After the
portable shrine has been set down the young men, many of them weaving
from drink and all sweating profusely, convene at someone's house where
they continue drinking until the *sake* purchased is consumed. In former
days most young men became very drunk and very boisterous (but not
quarrelsome). Among the present-day youths there are always a number
who remain sober.

Neither the decorations of the portable shrine nor the ceremony connected with it convey much specific meaning to members of the *Seinendan*
or to most other persons of the *buraku*. If put to it to find an explanation,
they may state that the ceremony is some form of respect for Kōjin-sama.
The portable shrine itself was purchased in Ajino about twenty years ago
to replace another which was worn beyond further use or repair, and it
came to the island replete with the meaningless carvings of bird-heads.
Old people may explain that in their youth the young man inside the carriage impersonated the *kami-sama* and was kept invisible by tightly drawn
curtains. Today curtains are loose and no one is in any doubt as to who is
in the carriage. Few if any young people regard the person inside as im-
personating Kōjin-sama. A few old persons suggest that the ceremony
may be connected with *kami-okuri*, "sending off the god(s)." The tenth
month[38] is traditionally *kaminazuki* or *kannazuki*, a month without *kami-
sama*, who all leave their regular abodes and go to the great shrine of

37. This ceremony may have originated as puberty rites or a combination of puberty rites and a ceremony of induction
into a formalized young men's age group.

38. This "explanation" seems doubtful as the tenth lunar month does not begin until about three weeks after the time
this ceremony is held (about ten days later than the former date for this ceremony).

Izumo during this period. The Takashima *sendairoku* ceremony may, these old persons say, have been a ritual seeing off of *Kōjin-sama*.

Rest, eating, and gossip with relatives comprise the balance of the festivities. Children and young people are usually given spending money at this time, as at *Bon* and New Year's, to attend movies in Ajino or do with as they please. For the average person, the Autumn Festival has little or no religious significance; for young men it is the occasion — for most of them the only such occasion in the year — for a slam-bang drunk.

The Honjō festival in honor of Hachiman, the god of war, falls on October 6 and 7 by Gregorian calendar, normally sometime early in the ninth lunar month. Until about twenty years ago all *buraku* of Honjō participated in a parade of *sendairoku* on one of these two days. Present-day observances are limited to attendance at the Hachiman shrine by a few of the aged and faithful.

Tenth Month

There are no holidays during this month, and the only ceremonial event is the observance of *Inoko*, which is a day of interest chiefly to children. *Inoko* is the name given to the first Day of the Pig *(I-no-hi)* during the tenth month. *Mochi* and *go-mokumeshi*, a dish made of vegetables, fish, and rice, are served in many homes during the evening meal on *Inoko*, but the origin and meaning of the custom are lost in antiquity. Some children still know and sing a traditional *Inoko* song:

> Inoko no konya
> Konya no Inoko
> Iwawanu mono wa
> Oni ume, ja ume
> Tsune ga haeta ko ume
> Daikoku-san to iu hito wa
> Ichi ni tawara wo fumaite
> Ni ni nikkori waratte
> San ni sake wo tsukutte
> Yotsu, yo no naka ei yō ni
> Itsutsu, itsumo no gotoku nari
> Mutsu, mune wo sokusai shi
> Nanatsu, nanigotonai yō ni
> Yattsu, yashiki wo hirometate
> Kokonotsu, koko e kura wo tate
> Tō de dossari osamatta.

> *Inoko* is tonight,
> Tonight is *Inoko*.
> Things not to be said are:
> Give birth to a devil;
> Give birth to a snake;
> Give birth to a child with horns.
> Daikoku-san does the following:
> First, he sits astride the rice bags,

Second, he smiles,
Third, he makes *sake*,
Fourth, he makes the night pleasant,
Fifth is as always,
Sixth, he widens the roof,
Seventh, he sees that no harm comes,
Eighth, he enlarges the residence,
Ninth, he builds a storehouse here.
With ten, having done all this, he sits down astride.

This song is sung during the evening. While singing, children beat the ground rhythmically with a handled switch, made of rice straw and reinforced by placing a withe of bamboo in its center, which is made especially for the occasion.

Eleventh Month

The eleventh month is one of little work and little ceremonial activity. *Himo-otoshi* (literally, "string-dropping") falls on the fifteenth day.[39] Children who have reached the age of three during the year (i.e., those who became three at the last New Year's by the traditional method of computing age whereby one becomes a year older at each New Year's) receive new clothing, the first fine *kimono* for a girl and the first good Western clothes for a boy. On this occasion a girl's *kimono* is her first made with four of the narrow widths in which native-style cloth is sold and it bears no strings or tapes *(himo)* for fastening. Native-style clothing of children is traditionally made from one or three widths of cloth (two widths are said never to be used) until they reach the age of three, when four widths are used. The clothing of adults is made with five widths.

Maternal grandparents traditionally present three-year-olds with sashes *(obi)* to be worn with native clothing and may also make other presents at *Himo-otoshi*. *Obi* are still usually given to both boys and girls although they are useless to the average boy, who now wears Western clothing almost exclusively at the age of three. As is true on all gift occasions for children, articles of good quality are customarily presented for the first child, but as the family grows the quality and price of gifts tend to become poorer and cheaper, and gifts may be omitted altogether when grandchildren have become very numerous.

Food for *Himo-otoshi* is usually special, and includes *mochi* and *sekihan* (rice cooked with red beans). *Mochi* are often put in tiered lacquered boxes on this and other occasions when gifts are received and serve as return gifts. Special foods, as is customary on most ceremonial days, should first be offered to the gods.

All three-year-olds should on this day be taken to the Kōjin shrine, and formerly were also taken to the Hachiman and Yakujin shrines in Honjō.

39. Throughout much of Japan a ceremony called *Shichigosan* for seven, five and three-year-old children is observed on this date.

PLATE 18.—*Priest and female assistant conducting faith-healing prayers to O-Fudōsama.*

PLATE 19.—*Children and adults toasting* mochi *around bonfire inside shrine at* Ōtsumogori.

Winter solstice *(Tōji)* normally falls sometime near the end of the eleventh month. Observances on this day, if there are old people in the household, consist of eating *nankin*, a variety of squash or pumpkin, boiled with other vegetables. The origin and meaning of this custom, again, are unknown.

Twelfth Month

Setchibun, a local dialectical variation of *Setsubun* (also known as *Risshun*), falls at the end of the twelfth month a day or two before the beginning of the new year. *Setchibun* is the traditional date for the last day of winter, although it bears little relation to the actual seasons. No one, for practical purposes, considers winter to have ended until March by Gregorian calendar, normally several weeks after *Setchibun*. This is the day of *mame-maki* (bean sowing), a ceremonial now relegated chiefly to children. Soy beans are roasted over a fire made from *babe*, an evergreen shrub, and after having been offered to the household *kami-sama*, are sprinkled about in the *kaminoma* and in the yard. While sowing the beans one says, *"Oni wa soto; fuku wa uchi* (devils outside; good fortune inside)."* Some persons interpret *fuku*, here translated as "good fortune," to mean the Seven Gods of Good Fortune, among whom Ebisu and Daikoku are included.

The evening of the last day of the twelfth month, New Year's Eve, is the occasion for a watch identical with *O-himatchi* (previously described) but known by the name *Ōtsumogori*. The last day of each month is known as *Tsumogori*, and the last day of the year becomes *"Great Tsumogori."* Tsumogori is a dialectical variation of the word *tsugomori*, which means a watch held on the last day of the month. The custom of maintaining watches of this sort is said to be common in other parts of rural Japan. Ideas of the significance of *Ōtsumogori* differ. Some say that the watch is maintained to protect Kōjin-sama; others say that it is a protection of the *buraku*. Still others say that those who participate in the watch gain the favor of Kōjin-sama during the coming year. A Takashima woman who regards religion rather lightly suggests that this custom was initiated in bygone centuries by Shinto priests as a source of personal revenue through the offerings made to the *kami-sama* in the shrines during the watches. Attendance by children, as at *O-himatchi*, is heavy. Some persons complain that the inside of the shrine is uncomfortably hot from the fire and the proceedings uninteresting.

THE ABANDONED CUSTOMS

In the foregoing pages some attention has been given to customs which are vanishing or have already vanished. There seems to be a great many of these and it is, of course, difficult to obtain data on them since one must rely upon recall memory. A number of customs have died gradual deaths during the lifetimes of middle-aged persons.

Among the abandoned customs not previously dealt with here is *Waka-mizu* (literally, "young water"). Early on the morning of New Year's, before dawn, some adult member of the household arose and drew the first water of the year from the well. This was put to use for cooking during the day. The custom, once observed with the objective of excluding evil from the household in the ensuing year, died out about twenty-five years ago. The stated reason for the abandonment of this custom is a loss of faith in it, "because it was only a superstition." It seemed foolish to arise early and go out into the cold simply to draw the same water which was drawn every other day of the year.

For reasons now forgotten, salt water from the sea was formerly offered at New Year's to the household *kami-sama*. This custom was called *O-shio*, which is also the name for sea water. In accordance with this custom, sea water was dipped from the sea early in the morning on the first day of the new year by means of a small container of bamboo attached to a pole by a piece of cord. Offerings of this water were then made to the household *kami-sama* by dipping a rice-straw or a leaf of the shrub *naruten* into the container and sprinkling the water in front of the household shrines. Once this was done it was also customary to encircle the house, sprinkling the salt water and at the same time reciting the names of shrines or *kami-sama*, any and all that would come to memory, with the meaning of making the offering of salt water to all the *kami-sama* which existed.

A custom called *Kaetsuri*[40] was followed by children until about twenty-five years ago. On the evening of the fourteenth day of the first lunar month children went from house to house in the *buraku* and knocked at the doors, saying:

> Kaetsuri, kaetsuri, kotogoto!
> Mochi wa igandemo ōkii ga ei,
> Kane wa komōtemo kazu ga ei.

> Exchange, exchange, knock, knock!
> No matter that the *mochi* are misshapen as long as they are large,
> No matter that the coins are small if the number is great.

Householders then gave the children money, *mochi*, or other food, and the children gave in return two slices of *daikon* tied together with a straw. The stated reason for the abandonment of this custom is that it was "bad" for children to go to the houses of other people to ask for food or money.

40. The translation of *kaetsuri*, here given as "exchange," is uncertain. This custom was known in other communities of the Kojima Peninsula by the names *Kātsuri* and *Kayutsuri*. The meaning of these terms (all are no doubt variations of the same word) is also uncertain. See T. Katayama, *Setonaikai no Densetsu* (Legends of the Inland Sea) (Kojima City: Kojima Chūgakkō Shuppanbu, 1949).

CHAPTER VI

The Life Cycle

SEX AND REPRODUCTION

OLD MEN of the *buraku* say that in former days greater freedom was allowed and common in sexual matters. Pre-marital intercourse among young people within the *buraku*, while not encouraged, was tacitly accepted as a matter of course. The occasional child born out of wedlock was regarded as no monumental disgrace and love marriages were relatively common. But times have changed. Rules of sex morality for women are strict, and an illegitimate child is a calamity which brings disgrace to the household and near-ruin for the luckless girl. The average young man demands a virginal bride, and in the rare case when a groom fails to regard this as a matter of major importance, his parents will nevertheless demand it. Even the most wayward girl is well aware of the premium placed on chastity and knows that even one slip, if it becomes known, will almost surely prevent her from making a good marriage. Were a girl willing, it would still be extremely difficult for her to commit indiscretions as unmarried girls are under strict surveillance by their parents. The island is small; dwellings are jammed together, and there is no privacy. One cannot remain undetected even in the forest, for he is seen crossing the *hatake* to enter the trees, and once within the screen of pines he encounters women gathering fuel. Darkness is disliked and feared.[1] In any event, no girl can leave her home unnoticed after night has fallen.

A few decades ago, when rules of sexual behavior had first become stringent, parents were even more watchful of their daughters than at present. Many daughters were not allowed to go to *Bon* dances without

---

1. Many persons are said to be afraid of the dark. At the Takashima home where the author and his wife stayed most frequently, it was the practice to leave a bucket just outside the entrance for the use of members of the household who found it necessary to arise during the night. This was admittedly done not as a convenience, but out of fear, to avoid exposure to the unknown horrors which might lie in wait on the way to the toilet (about fifteen steps from the entrance).

the chaperonage of their parents, as gatherings of young people such as these dances were the traditional occasions for sexual license. The modern parents, knowing that their daughters are well informed of moral standards, allow them to go to *buraku* or more public affairs in the company of others of their own sex. An old saying, well-known throughout all of Japan, and used in many contexts, is sometimes quoted in this connection: *"Yo no naka ni osoroshii mono ga yottsu ari: Jishin, kaminari, kaji, oyaji* (In this world there are four fearsome things: earthquakes, thunder, fire and fathers)."

No one expects a young man to enter marriage without some sexual experience. This experience is usually gained during festivals and the New Year's holiday season when adventuresome young men, emboldened by *sake* and conversation, visit houses of prostitution in Ajino. For the average young man of Takashima such experiences are few, but it is said that no young man enters marriage a *dotei* (virgin). It is considered appropriate that instruction in sexual intercourse be given by the experienced groom to the ignorant bride.

So effective have the strictures upon pre-marital intercourse for young women become that there has been no case of illegitimate birth within the *buraku* for twenty years. The only generally known pregnancy among unmarried girls since that time occurred during the summer of 1950, when the problem was solved by an illegal abortion performed by an Ajino physician. The Takashima girl is now almost invariably a virgin at the time of her marriage.

The sex act itself and most matters connected with sex are secret and somewhat shameful. Sexual intercourse is as quiet and secret as it is possible to make it, for there is little privacy within the thin walls of dwellings and small children usually sleep in the same rooms and often the same beds as their parents. There are usually no sexual overtures; the act is an abrupt process, hurried as well as quiet and secret. Discussion of sex is a *hazukashii tokoro* (an occasion for embarrassment) and a subject which is usually avoided. From the statements of the less reticent of *buraku* residents, however, it appears that sexual maladjustment is uncommon. There is no evidence of the *hysteri* as described by Embree,[2] nor does the word convey to Takashima residents the meaning which Embree describes. In Takashima, *hysteri* appears to be the equivalent of the English word "hysteria" from which it is derived, and it involves no necessary connection with sex. Sexual adjustment is said to be better among fisher-folk than among farmers or merchants and their wives for the reason that both men and women of fishing communities are somewhat less inhibited.[3]

2. J. F. Embree, *Suye Mura* (Chicago: The University of Chicago Press, 1939), pp. 175-6.

3. This information comes from a young man born and raised in Honjō, now a laboratory technician in a Mitsubishi hospital, who aspires to become a physician. He is greatly interested in the sex mores of his own and other countries and has read, in English, the Kinsey report (A. C. Kinsey, *Sexual Behavior in the Human Male* [Philadelphia: A. C. Saunders Co., 1948]).

In a community as small as Takashima where all activities of life are pursued within sight or earshot of other people, one must be circumspect in his behavior. Extra-marital intercourse (although traditional for the Japanese husband) is rare and is said to be limited almost entirely to the males of the richest household in the *buraku* who reputedly patronize houses of prostitution regularly. Relations with prostitutes, if they become known, lead to serious discord in the home as wives are resentful. In any case, prostitutes are too expensive for the average man, and although the male spouse controls the family finances, the state of the purse is usually known at all times to the wife so that continued expenditures for such a purpose would not go unnoticed. Adultery, at least among couples within the *buraku*, is extremely rare. In the past fifteen or more years only one incident is generally known to *buraku* adults and that is suspected rather than proved.

Widows on up to middle age occupy a curious position and seem to be traditionally considered fair game for propositions. Widows with young children have almost always returned to their native homes soon after the death of their husbands, which is the expected course unless there is no possibility of other heirs within the household of the erstwhile husband. In the past two decades only two widows under forty, one of whom was born on Takashima and was the heir to all of her husband's property, have remained on the island. In the first few years of their widowhood these two received overtures from a number of the island men, but as both of them rejected all advances, the propositions eventually ceased. Had they accepted, life in the *buraku* would have been extremely difficult for them as they would have become the objects of censure of every woman on the island and also a number of the men.

Contraception is virtually unknown. Infanticide is said to have been a fairly common practice until about fifty years ago but is now unthinkable. In recent years a little information on contraceptive methods and devices has reached a few of the residents of the *buraku* but remains at the rumor stage. Contraception is, however, well known to many of the residents of the larger towns and cities, in which contraceptive devices such as rubber prophylactics and diaphragms, known by names derived from English, are offered for sale in shops. Birth control on Takashima is limited to abortion, performed by a physician, and has become a fairly common although illegal practice in the last decade among women who have already borne a number of children. Some attempt at secrecy is made, but an abortion is usually an open secret among the women of the *buraku*. Attitudes toward abortion are divided. All know that it is dangerous and some women, particularly aged women and new brides for whom abortion is not a pressing personal issue, are strongly opposed. All childbearing women are interested in hearing about contraception.

Pregnancy and childbirth are surrounded with a host of customs, religious practices, and taboos, some of which are ignored and even laughed
at by younger mothers. A pregnant woman must, when cooking, place
water in the pot before she puts in the items to be cooked, for if the reverse
is done she will have a dry delivery. She must never pour foodstuffs such as
rice directly from one bag into another or the child will be born with a caul.
Vegetables with abnormal shapes, such as *daikon* with twin roots, must not
be eaten for fear that the child's body will be misshapen. Squid, crab, and
shrimp should also be avoided for the reason that the child will be malformed to resemble them. The eating of octopus will result in the birth of a
child with no bones. If a pregnant woman witnesses a fire her child will be
born with a red birthmark, and if she sees a funeral procession the child
will bear a white birthmark. Washing of the hands very quickly after seeing
either of these two things is a counter measure which does not prevent the
birthmarks but insures that they will be on the soles of the feet where they
do not matter. Along more practical lines, expectant mothers are cautioned
to avoid stimulants such as tea and pepper, and to eat the bones of small
fish. A few of the younger mothers who have consulted physicians take
calcium tablets, but this is new and not a general practice.

For the first child, most women engage the services of a licensed
Shionasu midwife, and in recent years one or two women have had
physicians in attendance. For subsequent children professional services
are often dispensed with and older female relatives are the only attendants.

The first visit to the midwife is made during the fifth month of pregnancy, at which time the midwife makes an examination. If she finds
anything unusual or pathological she recommends that the patient see a
physician. If the condition appears normal the patient is so informed and
told to pursue her usual course of life but to avoid excessive physical
strain such as the lifting of heavy objects. Little other advice is ordinarily
given. The midwife may be visited once a month thereafter until the time
of confinement or she may not be seen again until the actual time of birth.

The Day of the Dog by the lunar calendar in the fifth month of pregnancy is *obitori-no-hi*, the day on which the abdominal band, a strip of
white cloth about ten feet long, is first donned. This *obi* is either received
by the expectant mother as a gift from the household of her birth or else
is obtained for her by the household of her marriage. The usual practice
is for the mother of the pregnant woman to obtain the *obi* from a temple
near Kurashiki, and the cloth, received with the blessings of Kannon,
insures a safe and easy delivery. Amulets and a bottle of water from a
well near the temple are also obtained at the same time. One of the
amulets, a piece of paper inserted into a partially split section of bamboo
withe serves not only as a protective device but also forecasts the sex of

the child by the number of nodes in the bamboo, one node for a male child and two for a female. Prognoses by this device are said to be accurate in about 50 per cent of the cases. The water from the well is said to remove birth marks if applied soon after the birth of a child. The sex of a child is also said to be determinable by the facial expression of the mother during pregnancy. If the mother's countenance is gentle the child will be a girl; if the expression is stern or "strong" it will be a boy.

Pregnant women usually continue their regular work routines until labor begins. When the first contractions are felt a bed is prepared in the room called the *nando,* and if a midwife has been engaged she is notified. Women lie on bedding *(futon)* until labor pains become quite severe. If labor is attended only by female relatives, a kneeling position with elbows and arms resting on a pile of folded *futon* or on a low table is then assumed for the delivery of the child. This is the traditional position for Takashima women and the invariable position unless a midwife or doctor, who insist upon a supine position, are in attendance. The kneeling position is said to make delivery easier. No drugs are ordinarily taken to temper pain. Cloths sterilized by boiling are used during the delivery, and protective sheeting of cloth or rubber is placed above the *futon.*

Most women are fairly quiet during labor, but there is no stricture against nor censure for the mother who cries out in labor, and some women do. It is considered desirable to be quiet, but no one expects a complete stoic. To aid in passing the placenta, the wooden handle of a water dipper is placed in the mouth of the mother to induce a gagging reaction. The placenta is always buried, but custom in burial place varies somewhat. The usual place in present days is in the ground beneath the floor of the *nando*, where the water used in bathing the mother and newborn child (regarded as ceremonially polluted) is also poured. Boards in the floor of the *nando* are loosened or left loose for this purpose. According to more ancient custom, still followed in some households, the placenta of a male child is buried in the dirt floor just inside the *soto-niwa* and that of a female child at the entrance just outside the *soto-niwa*. This is said to be so that a girl will marry out and leave home and so that a boy, especially an eldest son, will remain in the household.

Special care is given to the umbilicus, although the reason for such care is now unknown. It is preserved in cloth and paper and tucked away in a drawer. Occasionally the umbilicus is kept until death and placed in the coffin together with the body, but it is usually lost long before that time and no further thought is given to it.

Plural birth is greatly disliked, partly for economic reasons, partly because of the physical difficulty in rearing two or more infants at once, and partly because plural births are thought to be unnatural, animal-like, and shameful. Insofar as possible, the birth of twins or triplets is kept secret and the matter is never discussed with members of a household in which such births have occurred. One child may, if possible, be given in adoption, but it is said that few people are willing to adopt a twin or triplet. When arranging a marriage, the fact that a prospective bride or groom is a twin is kept secret if it is possible to do so.

It is said that all children who survive are born during rising or high tide and that children born during low or falling tide will soon die: *"Hikishio ni umareta ko wa jumyō ga amai* (The life span of a child born during low tide will be short)." It is also said that nearly all children are born during rising or high tide.

Upon giving birth, a mother enters a thirty-three day period[4] of rest and ceremonial uncleanliness (see Chap. V, Defilement and Taboo). Until the mother is ready to nurse a child it is given sugar water and an infusion made by steeping one of several purchased herbs in water. The diet of the mother for the first week following birth includes sea bass and *sekihan* (rice with red beans), which are said to aid post-parturitional discharge. Palliative drugs may be taken after parturition but never before. The mother usually remains in bed for at least seven days, and may then rise briefly to do a limited number of tasks. Intermittent rest usually continues for an additional week or longer. During the whole thirty-three day period the mother must eat no persimmons nor even pass beneath a persimmon tree for fear of evil consequences, the nature of which are vague. For reasons of health and to promote lactation, she is to eat no oily food, burdock (the stems of which are eaten as a vegetable), or barley. Most Takashima women also avoid vegetables and all fruit except apples during the first fourteen days following parturition although they are aware that these foods are now recommended by physicians. Partly for practical reasons and partly because of the idea of pollution, no new mother may enter the *o-furo* for seven days following birth.

Traditionally, mothers rest until the thirty-third day. Most women, however, resume household duties on the fifteenth day, but not as yet agricultural work. Special attention is given to children born during unlucky years of their parents (see Chap. VI, The Bad Years). Until about thirty years ago a practice called *inu-no-ko* ("young of a dog," i.e., puppy) was followed whenever it was necessary to take an infant outside the dwelling after dark during the thirty-three day period. Two spots of ink were placed upon the forehead of the infant to deceive devils or monsters, who might harm a human infant, into thinking it a dog. Uncleanliness restrictions are removed on the thirty-third day and the mother may resume her usual full duties in the household and in the *hatake*.

4. As previously noted, the thirty-three day period is actually only thirty-two days. The day of birth is counted as the first day of the period.

CHILDHOOD AND ADOLESCENCE

The birth of a child remains relatively unheralded and there are no special festivities until the naming ceremony, which is held on the seventh day following birth (the day of birth counts as the first day) unless that day happens to be an inauspicious one. Word of the birth is always conveyed to relatives, and the news spreads within the *buraku* quickly. Friends and relatives may bring gifts of apples or candy for the mother and clothing for the child, but there is no general *buraku* participation. For his naming ceremony *(na-tsuke)*, a child is dressed in his best *kimono*, invariably red in color, and placed on *futon* in the *kaminoma*. Several dishes of food of quality better than usual and a bowl of *sekihan* placed on a tray are ceremonially offered to the child — and later consumed by the members of the household. A dish containing a hard beach stone, smooth and round from wave action, is sometimes placed on the tray together with the food so that the child will have the qualities of the stone, strength and firmness.

Names are chosen by various means. They are often those of which the parents, and especially the male parent, are particularly fond. Names of traditional heroes are popular. Sometimes the advice of elders is sought to select propitious names. If there is a question of the choice of several names, they may be written on slips of paper and one of them drawn. The naming ceremony is invariably held for the first child, and usually for the second child, but in recent years there has been a tendency to omit the ceremony for subsequent children. Only members of the household ordinarily participate in the simple ceremony, but there is no secrecy. There is little or nothing to see and other persons are seldom interested. Following old custom for which there is a saying, *"Ubuge wo soranaide kami-sama e maitte wa mottainai* (It is useless to appeal to the *kami-sama* if the hair of a newborn child has not been shaved off)," the heads of infants are usually shaved on the naming day.

The birth of a child is registered in the branch city office in Shionasu a few days after it has been named. In former days, marriages were often not registered until after the birth of the first child, but this practice has become uncommon in recent years. The birth of a child of either sex strongly cements marriage bonds whether or not the marriage has been legally registered before the birth.

A child's first exposure to religious ceremonial is a visit to the Kōjin shrine 110 days after birth for a boy and 120 days after birth for a girl. Anyone may take the child to the shrine but the mother most frequently does so. Kōjin-sama is thus informed of the presence of the new child on earth so that his blessings and protection may be extended to the child. An offering of a few grains of rice and a little money is made, a brief prayer said, and the ceremony is ended.

Toilet training for a child usually commences at the age of about six months, but it may be delayed if the child reaches that age during the cold of the winter months. The mother partially undresses the child and holds it over a receptacle or in a corner of the yard several times throughout the day. After this practice has been continued for a number of weeks children usually begin to understand what is expected of them. Training is fairly complete by about two years of age. There is said to be no punishment for errors except that children old enough to understand are told that they must inform their mothers on such occasions and are sometimes scolded. There is no shaking or physical punishment which might induce the psychological trauma about which much has been made regarding the toilet training of Japanese children.[5]

Weaning is usually done when a child is about two years of age. At this time the mother rubs her nipples with fresh, broken chili peppers. Weaning by this method is said to be dramatically rapid — and might well be traumatic. Children are, however, accustomed to solid food long before weaning time. Rice gruel and tangerine juice are usually the first introductions, at the age of five or six months. Other soft foods are gradually added and the child, sitting on its mother's lap, joins the household at the table for meals by the end of its first year of life. Women's magazines and the advice of physicians have brought about considerable variation in practices of infant care and diet in recent years. The few such magazines as reach the hands of young Takashima mothers are read, and the information they contain, if not the magazines, is passed on to other mothers. Talcum powder, rubber diaper covers, baby oil, and new ideas of diet have come in during recent years from these sources as well as from the occasional advice of midwives. The rare mother with insufficient breast milk uses formulas based on powdered milk and fed to the child by bottle and rubber nipple.

Infancy is a period of indulgence and great attention until a child is succeeded by a new baby. When a second, third or subsequent child is born, the erstwhile baby may be, and feel, neglected. Temper tantrums and jealous attempts to push the new idol off the mother's lap are not uncommon. Takashima mothers do not, however, consider such acts as jealousy; they are natural and, for the most part, expected behavior. If there is a grandmother or older sister, the former baby is turned over to her care and is said usually to adjust quickly and happily with little show of jealousy or resentment over the newcomer.

The first birthday, *tajō (tanjō* or *tanjōbi* in Standard Japanese), is celebrated, but no attention is given to subsequent birthdays during child-

5. See, for example, G. Gorer, "Themes in Japanese Culture," *Transactions of the New York Academy of Science,* Ser. 2, V (1943), pp. 106-124; and W. LaBarre, "Some Observations on Character Structure in the Orient: Japan," *Psychiatry,* VIII (1945), pp. 319-342.

hood. Festivities are usually simple and consist only of the serving to household members of somewhat special food which includes *mochi*. There may also be gifts for the baby, and there is often a gift of cloth from the maternal grandparents.

Whether or not younger children are added to the household, the first years of life for all children continue to be a period of indulgence and spoiling. Children show less respect for their mothers than for their fathers, of whom they may see little during much of the year because of their absence while fishing. Two- and three-year-old children frequently strike their parents (especially the less-strict mother) with their fists. This behavior is to be expected, and is usually laughed at indulgently. Discipline is most commonly in the form of reprimand and, less frequently, by punishment or threats of punishment. Physical punishment, while far from unknown, is usually avoided. Forms of physical punishment include pinching, the application of *moxa*, the pricking of mischievous fingers with a needle, and striking or spanking. Striking or slapping is not in favor. There is an old saying that if a mother strikes a child, the child will strike others. Grandparents are usually extremely indulgent with children. Boys are likely to be more spoiled than girls; the only temper tantrums witnessed by the author were among male children. Children past earliest infancy, and especially those old enough to walk, are frequently turned over for short intervals to the care of older sisters, and occasionally to older brothers, so that mothers may do their work unimpeded. Very young children are carried on the back where their small heads wobble about perilously as their older sisters or brothers play games.

A few simple household tasks are done by children. A common task for older children is the folding and putting away of their own bedding. Young children learn traditional childrens' songs and rhymes from their elders, and, when they are old enough to do so, engage in the various games previously described. The loss of baby teeth assumes the nature of a game. In accordance with ancient custom, a child is told to throw lost upper teeth beneath the raised floor of the house and lower teeth onto or over the roof, meanwhile holding his feet together in a straight line and saying, "Please change my teeth with a rat's teeth," — so that they will be straight and strong.

Boys and girls play together until they reach the age of about ten. According to an old folk-saying, male and female children should be separated at that age, but there is no need for parents to take active measures. The rift between boys and girls begins when they enter school at six years of age. In the *buraku*, girls and boys often play together, but at school boys play with boys and girls with girls, and once the age of ten is reached they seldom play together anywhere.

Quarrels over toys or possessions are common among children of the same household. In such cases, it is the usual practice to tell the elder child to capitulate "because you are older." Physical punishment for quarreling or other misbehavior usually ceases entirely before a child is ten years of age and is replaced by admonition and the much more powerful force of ridicule.

Entering the elementary school at Shionasu at the age of six is an event looked forward to by children. Before becoming enrolled as primary students, most *buraku* children attend public school kindergarten, conducted at the primary school for five-year-olds. The elementary school, established in 1875, has a present attendance of about 350 students in six grades, and a staff of ten teachers, a principal, a nurse, a scribe who prepares forms and writes necessary letters, and a janitress. Teachers with normal school educations are desired, but because the relatively low salaries are unattractive, about half the teachers have only high school *(kōtōgakkō)* educations. The principal is the only college graduate.

Post-war legislation has brought a number of changes to the Japanese school system. Compulsory education, formerly only through the six years of elementary school, has now been extended to cover three additional years of middle school *(chūgakkō)*. Nationalistic teaching and obeisance to the emperor are gone. The number of ideographs used in the written language which children are now taught in elementary schools has been greatly decreased, from an estimated 1,800 to an actual count (as made by the Shionasu school principal in 1951) of 630. The two syllabaries, by which the language may also be written, are used more extensively than formerly by elementary school children, and Romanized writing of Japanese words *(Rōmaji)* is now taught from the third grade on. According to the statements of the Shionasu school principal, the present graduates of elementary schools are unable to read newspapers with the exception of one page (the third page in most newspapers), which contains articles and stories of human interest *(sanmenkiji)* written in a very simple style. Educational film strips, some Japanese-made and some provided by the Occupation, are shown from time to time. "Hot" lunches which include powdered milk are now served at school under the supervision of the school nurse. Monthly fees are charged for these lunches which, like most of the food served in Japan, are much more likely to be cold than hot.

In the words of the Shionasu school principal, the stated aim of the new educational system (instituted in April, 1947) is "to encourage independence and individuality as much as possible." When asked how such encouragement was undertaken, the principal and his staff were at a loss. After considerable hesitation the principal stated that the freedom allowed students from the fourth grade up of choosing one of the subjects in the regular curriculum for additional and more intensive study (*jiyū kenkyū*, "free study") serves to encourage individuality.

The school curriculum includes reading, writing, arithmetic, drawing and painting, simple general science, ethics, and much singing and athletics. The pre-war teaching of ethics (called *shūshin*, "morality") is now taught in changed and non-nationalistic form under the name *shakai* (literally, "society," i.e., social science). *Shakai* also includes history, geography, and civics from a local to a national and international level. There is no longer any great emphasis upon Japanese history. The curriculum of fifth and sixth grade children includes instruction in household matters, "cooking, sewing, dishwashing, the sharpening of knives, and household sanitation."

Discipline is usually no problem, as students have respect for their teachers. Verbal quarrels and physical tussles among boys in the schoolyard during recess are common, but they usually end quickly and it is seldom necessary for teachers to intervene. Students who assume leadership or who dominate other students are called *shidōsha*, "leaders." Some *shidōsha* are "good", whereas others — the bullies of American schools — are "bad". Newly installed swings, slides, seesaws, and sandboxes are very popular during recess periods and also after school.

The school year begins in April, and vacation periods total about seventy-five days throughout the year. The periodic athletic meets and exhibitions of singing, dancing and performance of plays are bright spots throughout the year for both children and their parents. An open-house inspection of the school is held once annually, and is attended by about 60 per cent of the parents, with a strong emphasis on mothers. PTA meetings are scattered throughout the year. Graduation exercises are held at the end of March. There is no question of either promotion or graduation, which are automatic unless a child has for some reason been absent from school much or most of the school year. Tests are given frequently "to determine progress," but they have little or no bearing on whether or not a child will be promoted.

The scholastic standing of children of Honjō fishing households is lower than that of sons and daughters of farmers or merchants. According to members of the Shionasu school staff, this is because fishermen are less serious-minded than farmers or merchants and do not regard education as highly as is general in Japan. Takashima children are said to be very interested in school for the first two or three years, but after that time they are less inclined to study than the average pupil and show keen interest only in games and sports.

The level of education within Takashima *buraku* has always been lower than that of farming *buraku* within Honjō. A fairly large number of Takashima school children from poorer households stop attending school before the legal requirements are fulfilled. No action has as yet been taken in any case by school or other authorities. Present-day Takashima children finish elementary school and perhaps half of them continue through the full three years of middle school. Reasons for stopping school, as given by parents, are economic. The middle school is located in Ajino, three miles away, and transportation, whether by bus or bicycle, is expensive. Over half of the several students now attending middle school walk, but footgear is also expensive. In addition, school supplies and lunches must be paid for. A boy is sometimes needed to help with fishing operations in small households composed principally of women and is for that reason kept out of school.

Few persons ever attain to *kōtōgakkō*, a three-year school which follows middle school. Entrance to *kōtōgakkō* is by competitive examination as there are always more aspirants than the local facilities, in Ajino, will accommodate. It is said that rich men's children with poor standing in the examinations gain admittance easily whereas the bright children of poor households have difficulty in gaining admission. The first *kōtōgakkō* graduate in Takashima history, a young man, finished in 1950. In 1951 another graduate, a girl, was added, and two additional *buraku* students were in attendance. Three of these four young people are from well-to-do families of the *buraku*. Higher education beyond middle school is looked upon by some *buraku* parents and elders as a luxury unnecessary for fishermen. A *kōtōgakkō* education, they argue, does not qualify their children for any occupation, and does not make them better fishermen.

No one in *buraku* history has ever attended a university, and university education is usually beyond imagination. One lone parent, a war widow acclaimed ever since her elementary school days for her intelligence, aspires to a university education for her son, in 1951 a beginning student in *kōtōgakkō*.

Education in matters of sex is seldom or never given to children by their parents. Menstruation, called by a variety of terms including *"Hana ga saku* (The flowers are in bloom),"* is said to come to many young girls as a surprise. Upon informing their mothers on the first occurrence, they are told what to expect in the future and what to do on such occasions. For the most part, the acquiring of knowledge of matters relating to sex is a gradual process beginning in early childhood. Scraps of information and misinformation come from other children. Chance observation in the crowded homes is no doubt also revealing. Adolescents may now receive instruction in school on human physiology, and articles on human reproduction appear from time to time in magazines of national circulation.

Until boys and girls reach the end of their education, life is principally school and play. When schooling is over they begin to help with fishing, farming, and household work. Boys are seldom expected to give aid in agricultural duties, and their work is confined principally to that connected with fishing. If there is a shortage of men in the household, girls may help with fishing as well as with other tasks. The usual age to begin work is fifteen or sixteen, although no young person of that age is experienced or strong enough to assume an adult's share of work.

The brightest spots in the lives of most young persons of the *buraku* are the annual festivals, when they are given spending money, wear their best clothes, eat festival food, and the household is full of visiting relatives. For those who go on to middle school and *kōtōgakkō*, the annual school journeys are rated as even more enjoyable occasions. The custom of making school excursions to scenic and historic spots has been long established in Japan. Although abandoned during the war and during the immediately post-war years, it was resumed by most schools by 1948. Inns customarily have special low rates for students, who are bedded down as many to a room as possible. Elementary school trips are to nearby areas. Middle school students of Ajino in 1950 made a three-day trip to Kyoto and Nara, a distance of about 175 miles from Ajino. Such trips, eagerly awaited and long remembered, are usually the most distant ventures from home in a lifetime.

Beginning with adolescence, the mixing of the sexes is discouraged. Admonition seems never to be necessary, as the "proper" pattern of behavior has become the preferred pattern by the time adolescence is reached. In recent years there has been some mixing on special occasions, such as the playing of ping-pong in the meeting hall on festival days. Dating, practiced to a limited degree among the young people of Ajino and other larger communities nearby, is known to Takashima boys and girls, but it is considered too bold and daring.

Adolescence and young adulthood are trying times for most young men of the *buraku,* periods of discontent and uncertainty. Young persons are never encouraged to accept responsibility but remain under the rule of their fathers until they marry and move away or, if they marry and remain within the household, until the father is ready to retire. It is rare for a young man to want to become a fisherman, and farming usually appeals to him even less. In former days a young man had a period of military service when he was away from home and experienced adventures. Non-wartime military training was usually in areas not very distant from home. It served, however, to remove young men from parental authority and permitted the modest sowing of wild oats. Military service was enjoyed by the average man despite initial hard treatment, and when it was concluded he was usually willing and ready to return home to marry and settle down.

Twenty-two young men of the *buraku,* some of them married and the fathers of children, saw active service in World War II. Of this total, six were killed or died of disease in service. The remaining sixteen returned to their homes in Takashima upon discharge, where nearly all of them soon settled down to *buraku* patterns of living. There was, as a matter of fact, no recourse for them but to return home, as securing food and lodging in a strange community in the immediately post-war years was a difficult problem. According to their own statements none of the young men enjoyed military service and all were happy to return home.

The boy who reaches early maturity today has no service obligations and thus ordinarily has no opportunity to get away from home. He is restless, discontented, and unsure of himself. Above all, he does not want to spend the rest of his life as a fisherman. Some young men accept employment as hands on Inland Sea freight boats, where they may work for two or three years and then return to Takashima to the households of their parents to marry and settle down in the *buraku,* as fishermen. Younger sons are more likely to take up other employment, as carpenters or seamen, and settle down in other communities. Migration to cities is uncommon. No one in the history of the *buraku* has migrated to a foreign country, although a few *buraku* daughters, married out, had gone to Manchuria and Korea. Only one person, an old man who once served as a seaman on an ocean-going vessel, has ever been to America or any of the countries of Europe.

Amusements for unmarried young men, who are dependent upon their fathers for spending money, are comparatively few. Ping-pong at festival times, occasional movies, a little reading, school events as both spectators and graduate participants, and the annual cycle of festival events comprise their major recreation. A few of the bolder young men occasionally go to the public dance halls in Ajino, but knowledge of Western dancing within the *buraku* is as yet principally confined to the young women, who teach each other. In 1950 two young men acquired a guitar, the first instrument of its kind on Takashima, but these young men are considered *nonki,* "carefree", an undesirable quality.

MARRIAGE

The young man of today usually marries at the age of twenty-five or twenty-six, and the young woman at twenty-one or twenty-two. This represents a gradual increase during the past several decades of three or four years in the marriage age. During this period there have been a number of additional changes in marriage customs, the most notable of which is perhaps the decline of unions brought about at the instigation of the principals, i.e., love marriages. Until about forty years ago in-*buraku* marriages based upon mutual attraction are said to have been common. Such unions are now confined principally to those contracted many years ago; there is no instance of love marriages *(renai kekkon)* among persons under forty. The usual marriage today is wholly arranged and between persons who were previously unacquainted or only slightly acquainted. The reasons advanced by *buraku* people for the shift to arranged marriages is that in the past they were uneducated, primitive, and unschooled in the proper methods of contracting marriage.

The services of one or more go-betweens *(baishakunin* or *nakōdo)* have always been utilized, even for *renai kekkon.* There are professional go-betweens in Kojima City but they are disliked by Takashima people, who seek the aid of amateurs in the *buraku* or in other nearby communities. The average person feels it is a humanitarian obligation to serve as *baishakunin* once in his lifetime, but the duties are usually not particularly relished. Some women, however, take great interest in arranging marriages, and once they have managed two or three successful matches their services come into demand. Most Takashima persons have acted as go-between for one marriage by the time they reach advanced middle age. One *buraku* person, a woman in her sixties, and better schooled than the average in social graces, has served as go-between in thirteen unions, nearly all of which are regarded as successful. Her skill is widely known and there are many requests for her services from households in the *buraku* and in nearby communities.

The usual first step in arranging a marriage is for the household of the young person concerned to secure the aid of a go-between. Marriage arrangements may be initiated by the households of either young men or young women; in either case the procedure is the same. In pre-war years young men (i.e., their households) usually hunted brides, but because of a small post-war surplus of marriageable girls the procedure is now often reversed. Go-betweens are now often first approached by the parents of girls and asked to secure husbands for them. In most instances a married couple nominally serves as go-between, but the wife normally assumes most of the duties. Whether or not the male spouse of a go-between couple actively aids during the arrangements, he takes precedence over his wife during the wedding feast. In a few cases both households concerned engage go-betweens so that negotiations are between two sets of *baishakunin.*

Once the duties have been assumed, the go-between (usually only the female) begins looking about for a suitable spouse, often making contact with households suggested by the parents who engaged her. Arrangements usually require four, five, or more months to complete, during which time the go-betweens may have investigated and approached several households. The ideal bride is a large, strong, and healthy virgin with no record of insanity, leprosy (rare in the Kojima area), or tuberculosis[6] in her lineage. It is considered desirable that bride and groom be of approximately the same social and economic level. For Takashima men, daughters of either farmers or fishermen are acceptable.

When a likely prospective bride has been located, the *baishakunin* makes a "secret" investigation of the girl and her relatives, checking with neighbors and friends on the characters, reputations, and financial statuses of the household and related households of the girl concerned. If the groom's household shows interest at this preliminary stage, the parents of the prospective bride are approached. If they in turn are interested, an intensive investigation is made on both sides. A conscientious go-between learns as much as she can about a prospective spouse which would be of interest to the household she is representing. Because go-betweens are amateurs who assume their tasks with primarily philanthropic motives, they seldom attempt serious deception or exaggerate virtues of their clients to an unreasonable degree. Subterfuge on a minor scale is, however, common among clever and skilled *baishakunin*. For a small and delicate girl, who might seem ill-suited for the heavy agricultural tasks expected of a bride, the introduction to a prospective groom and his household may be made in a small room or against some other background which will serve to make her appear larger and stronger.

Snapshots or photographs are sometimes given to the go-between in preliminary stages to show to the party of the other side. Beauty of a young woman counts to some extent, and a pretty girl who fulfills all other qualifications of a bride has no difficulty in securing a husband. Other qualities, however, override mere beauty, although a conspicuously ugly girl does not usually make an advantageous marriage. The wishes of the young man and young woman are said always to be considered, and if either voices objections to a prospective spouse the matter is dropped forthwith. Young persons are said never to be forced into marriage. The actual situation appears to be a compromise between the wishes of young persons and those of their parents.

If both sides are interested and the preliminary *kikiawase* (investigation) is satisfactory, a *miai* (meeting) is arranged at the home of the bride or the go-between, or at some public place such as a shrine, and the young people are introduced to each other. If, after this meeting, the young couple and their parents are still interested, arrangements con-

6. This seems to be a requirement for bride or groom in all of Japan. With the high incidence of tuberculosis in most areas, one wonders how marriages are ever arranged. The explanation seems to be simply that ideal and actual circumstances differ.

tinue with further investigation by persons other than the go-between. Members of the respective households or other persons related to the households recheck the reports of the go-between. If they are satisfied with their findings, the go-between is instructed to go ahead with arrangements for the *yuinō,* an engagement gift of money. In a number of cases, the official go-between is not called upon until after the *miai,* or, if the young persons are acquainted, until after tentative agreement has been reached between the two households through the medium of some non-official go-between. In such cases it is customary for the groom's family to select the *baishakunin.*

Once negotiations have gotten to the point of discussion of the amount of the *yuinō* (during 1949-51, usually about 15,000 yen) there are seldom any direct contacts between the households concerned even if they have been on friendly terms for years. The two households are often acquainted, and the marriage of distant relatives is not uncommon. The marriage of relatives has the point in its favor that no investigation is necessary and both sides know what to expect. Of the many marriages within the *buraku* of nominally related persons, the relationship in nearly all cases is distant and sometimes so tenuous that it can no longer be traced. Inbreeding is feared because it is said that the offspring of such unions are deaf and dumb or mentally deficient. There have been, however, occasional marriages of first cousins, a practice said to have been more common in the past.

The *yuinō* is presented to the household of the bride in formal fashion, in three sums of money, each separately wrapped in white paper lined with red and tied in a traditional knot with special cord *(mizuhiki)* colored red and white or gold and silver, felicitous colors. One sum of money is traditionally for clothing for the bride on her wedding day, and the other two for fish and *sake* for the feast at the time of the bride's departure from her home. The *yuinō* also includes two *noshi,* pieces of red and white paper folded in a roughly triangular shape which are customarily attached to gifts,[7] a pair of folding fans, and a *furoshiki* which bears the picture of a *tai* (sea bream), also a felicitous symbol. The *yuinō* is presented upon a small, pedestaled wooden stand or tray *(sambō)* over which a red silk cloth, often tasseled and elaborately embroidered, is placed. The silk cover is returned to the groom's household, but the *sambō* usually remains in the household of the bride. Upon receipt of the engagement gift items, the head of the household of the bride-to-be prepares a formal receipt written in the form of a letter in which each item is listed. This letter is concluded with wishes for the health and welfare of the donor household.

7. *Noshi* are symbolic of a gift of fish. In former times a *noshi* consisted of a strip of dried abalone folded in red and white paper. Many modern *noshi* are made entirely of paper, and the wrapping paper used by shops and department stores often bears a printed picture of a *noshi.*

The *yuinō* must always be presented on an auspicious day and the letter acknowledging receipt bears the month and the word *kichijitsu,* "lucky day," as the date line. A *mizuhiki* is always tied about the letter of receipt. *Mizuhiki* used in connection with weddings are frequently in the shape of butterflies, another auspicious symbol. The household of the bride customarily sends a small gift of a *furoshiki,* dried bonito, or occasionally a small amount of money,[8] together with the letter of receipt.

Weddings are almost always held during the winter months for the stated reason that the heat of the summer causes the heavy makeup of a bride to run and smear from perspiration. Final decision on the date of the wedding, which usually takes place several weeks after the presentation of the *yuinō,* is made by mutual agreement on both sides. In case of conflict, the wishes of the household of the groom carry the greatest weight. The day chosen must be auspicious. Since travel is involved, attention must also be given to the location of Konjin-sama in choosing the date.

The interval between presentation of the *yuinō* and the wedding ceremony is one of heightened activity for both households. Word of the forthcoming marriage, kept as secret as possible during preliminary negotiations, is spread about quickly and relatives living in other communities are notified. The bride is busy with her trousseau, which may have been started two, three, or more years earlier, and with the purchase and preparation of the items which comprise her dowry. The well-equipped bride brings with her to her new household a large wooden wardrobe with a compartment for the hanging of Western clothing on clothes hangers, in which her Western-style clothes are placed; a second wardrobe or chest-of-drawers for Japanese clothes, which are folded; a wooden chest containing bedding adequate for two; a miniature dresser with mirror containing cosmetics; a *geta* box containing both Japanese and Western style footgear; sewing equipment; a washbowl and towels; a clothes rack, and miscellaneous personal items. Even the poorest bride brings with her at least a chest of bedding, a wardrobe containing clothing, and a *geta* box.

The household of the groom is also busy with preparations. Formal native-style clothing is purchased or made for the groom, and the house is put into good shape for the wedding party and to welcome the new bride. Preparations for the wedding feast begin in the house of the groom a day or two before the wedding. The house bustles with relatives who have come to aid in the preparations and to participate in the wedding and feast. Gifts of food, goods, or money, all bearing *mizuhiki* and special gift wrappings, are brought by these relatives and presented to the house-

---

8. There is a good deal of variation in the details of *yuinō* practices from area to area in Japan. In some localities, the household of the bride returns a fixed percentage of the sum received from the groom's household. See I. Kurata, "Rural Marriage Customs in Japan," *Contemporary Japan,* X, No. 3 (March, 1941).

hold. Relatives who do not arrive until the time of the wedding present their gifts at that time.

On the morning of the wedding day (or the night before if the bride is from a community somewhat distant), the bride and all adult females included in the wedding party have their faces, including the forehead, lobes of ears, throats and necks, shaved by a professional barber. A professional dresser (called *kamii-san*, "hairdresser") takes care of the dressing of the bride, and later serves as her attendant throughout the journey to the groom's house and during the wedding ceremony. The dresser brings with her a large kit of cosmetics which are used in lavish quantities on the bride in a make-up process which requires two hours for completion. When the make-up is applied to the satisfaction of the dresser and other females of the household, a wig of the traditional wedding hair-style *(Bunkin-taka-shimada)* is placed over the permanent-waved hair of the bride, and the elaborate silk bridal clothes are donned. Until about ten years ago the bride's own hair was dressed in the traditional wedding style, which requires long and straight hair. After the wedding ceremony was over and before the bride of ten years ago joined the wedding banquet party she changed the style of her hair-dress slightly and simply to indicate changed status to that of a married woman. It is impossible to transform the short, permanented hair of the young women of today into the towering bridal coiffure and wigs are used, to which the various traditional hair ornaments are added. Wigs are usually removed after the ceremony is over and before the bride joins the banquet party.

A piece of white or red and white silk cloth, the *tsuno-kakushi*, "horn-hider," — all women traditionally have horns which may be seen when they become jealous — is placed atop the coiffure. To complete her outfit the bride carries a tiny brocade purse[9] with a tasseled, silken cord and places a fan in her wide brocade waistband. Most brides have two wedding outfits, one to wear while traveling to the house of the groom, which serves as a "best" outfit after marriage, and a more elaborate costume which is the bridal outfit. The bridal outfit is never worn again by the bride although it is occasionally used by other brides or the material is later utilized for other purposes. The bride from a wealthy household has additional costumes into which she changes at intervals during the wedding banquet.

At an appointed time, but almost invariably one or two hours late,[10] a party from the household of the groom arrives at the bride's home to take her with them to the groom's home for the wedding ceremony. The

9. In former days the bride carried a glass or crystal ball, a pin, and a mirror in this purse, but it has been the practice for many years simply to stuff the purse with paper.

10. Hours of appointment are usually regarded only as approximations. Most persons are one or more hours late for appointments, and gatherings such as community meetings are invariably one or more hours late in convening.

PLATES 22, 23, 24.—*Two brides, photographed in ordinary clothes and in wedding-day attire with wigs.*

composition of this party varies, and may include uncles and aunts of the groom rather than his parents, but it always includes the groom and the go-between couple. After the groom's party has arrived at the bride's house and an exchange of formal greetings has taken place, a feast *(kadode-no-enkai,* "departure feast"), usually modest in proportion, is held at the bride's house. The bride may or may not participate in this feast, and she is often still occupied with dressing. When the feast is over and the bride is ready to leave, she emerges from her home directly from the *kaminoma* (see Chap. III, *The Dwelling*), descending to the yard from the elevated floor by means of a plank or extemporized steps. The bride's embroidered sandals and tight clothing — and particularly the traditional deportment of a bride — do not allow her to take large steps nor to do anything so undignified as to jump. She emerges from the house hardly recognizable beneath the thick coatings of cosmetics, walking with short and measured steps, and looking like a somewhat animated doll. Her expression is serious, for it would be a dreadful breach of etiquette to smile on this occasion, and her eyes are downcast. As the bride leaves the house, some adult member of her household builds a small fire of rice straw *(kadobi)* in the yard, as is done at funerals (see Chap. VI, Death).

The procession of a bride and her party from her home to the waiting boat or from a boat to the home of her groom is of great interest to all in the *buraku,* who line up to watch her pass. It was the custom until about thirty years ago to attempt to make a departing *buraku* bride laugh. A common stratagem was for young men to pass wind loudly, which is said to have produced hearty laughter among the bystanders but in no instance ever caused a bride to change expression. Young men also formerly threw handfuls of sand at the bride, so that she would bring to her new home some of the soil of her native place in the folds of her garments.[11] Taxis are hired to transport brides and grooms traveling on the mainland, and trucks are engaged a day or two before the wedding to transport the dowry of the bride.

After arrival at the groom's home and another formal exchange of greetings, the bride retires to change into her wedding dress. When she has finished, the wedding ceremony is ready to begin. All shutters and sliding panels from the front of the house are removed so that neighbors and friends who gather in the yard may have an unobstructed view of the ceremony, which is conducted within the *kaminoma* and *shimonoma,* made into one large room by the removal of the sliding panels between them. The wedding party is seated in order of prestige according to a seating arrangement decided upon by the go-between couple, who

11. This custom, as reported for Takami Island in the Inland Sea, is an expression of anger at a girl's marrying out and leaving the community (Kagawa-ken Minzoku Chōsa-kai, *op. cit.*). See also T. Omachi, *op. cit.*, who interprets similar actions as evidence of anger by young men of the community.

occupy the seats of greatest honor. Most frequently the parties from the
two households are seated in separate lines extending around the room
from the pillar of the *tokonoma*, where the go-between couple sits. Bride
and bridegroom, separated by one or two persons, sit with their backs
against the sliding partitions of the adjoining *nando* or *naka-e* and thus are
in full view of the onlookers assembled outside.

When all guests are seated, the male go-between makes a simple
address wishing the union and both households well and apologizing for
the ineptness of himself and his wife in their capacities as *baishakunin*. The
father of the groom then speaks briefly, thanking the go-betweens and
saying flattering things about the bride and her family. After the father
of the bride has returned the compliments and added his thanks to the
go-between, a ceremonial round of drinks is taken. Upon the instruction
of the female go-between, one of the serving girls (younger sisters or relatives of the groom) brings forth a *noshi* on a tray, places it carefully on the
tatami in front of the go-between, and then returns it to its place in the
tokonoma. A set of ceremonial drinking cups *(sakazuki)*, in a graduated tier
of three, is then also placed before the female go-between. Two sets of
sakazuki, one larger than the other, are sometimes used. The larger is
referred to as the "male", and the smaller as the "female". A tray containing tiny pieces of dried fish and pickled plums is placed beside the
bride's dresser by the serving girls after being presented before the female
go-between.

After this ritual has been concluded the ceremonial *sake* is ready to
be mixed and served. A tray holding two *sake* containers, shaped like tea-
pots and often decorated with metal butterflies, are placed before the go-
between, who pours *sake* from one into the other to symbolize the mixing
of blood. This concluded, she gives the tier of ceremonial *sake* cups to the
waitresses together with a container of *sake*. The first drink is served to the
male *baishakunin*, the second to his wife. The groom's father and the
bride's father are served next. It is then customary to go around the room
from the left of the go-between couple until all persons assembled, including the bride and groom, have been served. The order may vary and the
bride and groom may precede certain other persons.

The drinking of *sake* at a wedding ceremony is formalized. The serving girls first present the tray with its tier of cups before the person to be
served, and bows are exchanged. The person about to drink then lifts the
tray and cups with both hands, puts them down, picks up the smallest
cup, and holds it forth for the pouring of a few drops of *sake*. When the
sake (only a few drops) has been carefully poured into the cup, drinking
is accomplished in three sips, and afterwards the edge of the cup is wiped
carefully with a piece of white paper which every person carries in the

fold of his *kimono* or in the breast pocket of a Western suit. An exchange of bows between the serving girls and the person served ends the individual ceremony.

As each person is served the bride's dresser deftly moves two tiny pieces of dried fish or plum from one side of the tray in front of her to the other to symbolize feasting. This is done because the ceremony as described is an abbreviated form. For a full, traditional ceremony, guests are served elaborate food in between the ceremonial *sake* drinking, a procedure which takes many hours, and both sets of *sakazuki* are used. Only the abbreviated ceremony is followed on Takashima, and the dresser's manipulation of the symbolic banquet food serves as a ceremonial substitute for feasting during the round of drinks.

During this ceremony, which requires about one hour for completion, the friends and neighbors assembled outside watch with great interest, push and crowd for a better view of the proceedings, and are often so noisy that the speeches delivered within are hardly audible to other members of the wedding party. Young men make jokes and attempt to make the bride laugh. Although a few other persons in the wedding party may smile, the bride remains ever serious and carefully maintains the proper sitting posture. When the last ceremonial cup of *sake* has been served, the crowd assembled outside leaves, as the banquet which follows is for the members of the wedding party only.

At this time the bride, groom, and female go-between arise and leave the party. In the seclusion of the *nando* the female go-between officiates in the *sansankudo*, "three, three, nine times", a ceremonial drinking of *sake* confined to these three persons. Rounds of a few drops of *sake* are drunk, first by the go-between, then the groom, and last by the bride, from each of the three graduated *sake* cups (three rounds, making a total of nine cups served). With this, the marriage is sealed.

The wedding banquet has in the meantime begun, and the groom, go-between, and bride (who often doffs her wig after the *sansankudo*) join the party, which continues with heavy feasting, drinking, and revelry from this time, late afternoon, until midnight or later. The bride, who usually retires after a few hours, must be quiet and demure, but the groom may join in the singing and merriment.

Ceremony does not end with the wedding. The *sato-gaeri*, the bride's first visit to her native home after marriage, is traditionally made on the third day following the wedding but is often postponed for several weeks. The *sato-gaeri* consists of a social visit of a few hours by the bride accompanied by her husband and, in most instances, her new parents-in-law. There is also a semi-formal visit made upon the go-between couple by the bride and groom within a short time after the marriage. The date of this visit, at which a light repast is served, is usually set by the go-betweens. Go-betweens are commonly referred to as *nakōdo-oya*, "go-between parents," by the couple whom they have united and remain persons of importance in the life of the couple. It is customary for a man and wife to remain in friendly contact with their go-betweens during the remainder of their lives and to participate in their funerals.

A ceremonial gift exchange between the parents of the bride and groom follows the wedding. It extends over a period of three years and involves the exchange of gifts at *Bon* and New Year's, a total of six exchanges. Gifts are usually modest, cloth or *mochi*, and in recent years the custom has often been discontinued before its full cycle of three years.

Another and less common type of marriage ceremony called *naishūgen*, "private ceremony," is restricted for the most part to very poor households. It consists of a simple private ceremonial exchange of *sake* between the bride and groom, who are then considered to be married. These marriages are arranged by go-betweens in the same manner as the ordinary union, and some weeks or months after the *naishūgen* a simple wedding ceremony and banquet of the traditional kind is usually held. This type of marriage is not officially registered until after the regular ceremony, and although such marriages may (rarely) be dissolved before the normal ceremony is held, they are not looked upon as trial marriages. The *naishūgen* is, rather, a matter of convenience. During 1950 a young *buraku* man with no close relatives except an aged grandmother with whom he lived married a girl from a neighboring community by *naishūgen* in September. The normal ceremony was held the following February. The autumn months are a period of heavy agricultural activity so that a marriage ceremony of the usual sort can be held then only with difficulty. The *naishūgen* was performed at that time so that the bride could help the aged grandmother with agricultural work, in particular so that she could help in the heavy work of harvesting sweet potatoes and planting grain in October and November. The marriage had been arranged through a go-between, but it was improper for the girl to stay in the dwelling of her future groom without being married, i.e., without the performance of the *naishūgen* or a regular marriage ceremony.

A variation of the standard type of marriage is the adoptive marriage, in which the groom *(yōshi)*[12] assumes the surname of his bride and becomes a legally adopted member of her household. Entering a *yōshi* marriage is distasteful to most men. An old saying expresses this attitude: *"Konuka sangō attara, iri-mukō ni yuku na* (As long as you have three *gō* [about a pint] of rice bran, don't become an adopted husband)." The amount of

---

12. This term is sometimes also applied to adopted male children; the female counterpart is *yōjo*. A more common term on Takashima for adopted children of either sex is *moraigo*, "received child."

the *yuinō* in a *yōshi* marriage is greater than for the usual type of marriage, and the arrangements are carried out much as if the young man were the bride. The groom brings a dowry with him of chests, clothing, and bedding equipment; the bride goes to fetch the groom, and the wedding ceremony is at the bride's home. The groom then resides in the home of the bride and becomes, in effect and by law, a son of the bride's parents. Cases of oldest sons becoming *yōshi* are rare, as they have in the past usually been the heirs to their fathers' property. The incentive to make a *yōshi* marriage is the property which the groom will eventually inherit, and, in the case of a penniless young man, such property may be a very attractive inducement. Despite the feeling against such marriages, they are common.

Economically, a wedding entails a tremendous expenditure of funds, especially for the bride's household. It is customary to have as resplendent a ceremony and banquet as the household can afford, as a fine affair reflects prestige. An average wedding will usually require the expenditure of about a half-year's earnings or more for each household, and saving for the occasion must begin long in advance. The *yuinō*, once no doubt a form of compensation for the economic loss to the household of the bride, is now considered little more than a token as the bride's clothing and dowry represent the expenditure of many times the total of the engagement gift.

Marriage ceremonies of persons who have been previously married are on a much simpler scale. A widow, widower, or divorced person usually marries someone else who has been previously married, and the field of choice is considerably restricted. Go-betweens state that second marriages are usually easily arranged because both principals know that prospective spouses are limited and they are therefore more easily satisfied. A widow with children usually experiences difficulty in getting a second mate and must usually accept a man below par in marital qualifications. A widower, even if he has children, usually has little difficulty. For the most part, second marriages quickly follow the dissolving of an old union by death or divorce.

THE BAD YEARS

Certain years of a person's life span are both critical and unlucky years *(yakudoshi)*.[13] Great attention is normally paid to these years and measures are taken to prevent calamity. Long trips and important undertakings are avoided because they are likely to end in misfortune. The twenty-fifth, forty-second, and sixtieth years of life are generally considered the *yakudoshi* for men, and the nineteenth and thirty-third years

13. Belief in *yakudoshi* is not restricted to people of the rural areas of Japan, but is found everywhere in Japan. Included among the believers in *yakudoshi* are many highly educated and sophisticated persons.

the *yakudoshi* for women. Many persons also regard the twenty-ninth year as a *yakudoshi* for both men and women, and some persons regard the twenty-fifth year as a bad year for women as well as for men. All computation of age for *yakudoshi* is by the old Japanese system whereby a person is one year of age at birth and becomes a year older upon the passage of each New Year's.

Ages twenty-five and twenty-nine are particularly bad years for marriage. Twenty-five is worse than twenty-nine, and marriage is avoided by Takashima males during their twenty-fifth year. If one marries at twenty-nine, a protective charm *(mamori)* is worn during the wedding ceremony and until the thirtieth year is reached. Special prayers and offerings are made at New Year's for household members entering a *yakudoshi*, and additional prayers and offerings may be made at other times during the year. Some persons state that the year of bad luck does not begin at New Year's but covers a period beginning six months before the New Year when one enters a *yakudoshi*, and ending six months after that time.

Great attention is not paid to all *yakudoshi* by every household. The twenty-fifth year and the sixtieth years are usually regarded as bad and special precautions are taken during them. The thirty-third year is by far the worst year of life for women, and the forty-second the worst year of life for men. These are years which are particularly dangerous and in which every precaution should be taken. Special prayers and offerings are sure to be made.

The danger of calamity inherent in these years of life extends even to children born during them. A female child born to a woman during her thirty-third year is a child of misfortune and must be ceremonially cast away, as must a male child born during a man's forty-second year. A child of sex opposite to that of its father or mother born during these years is under no ill omen and requires no special attention. The ceremonial discarding of a child consists of wrapping it carefully in clothing soon after birth ("so that it will not catch cold") and handing it, by prearrangement, to an unrelated neighbor or to the midwife at the edge of the yard or in the nearby *hatake*. The infant is handed back at once to the member of the household who has brought it out and, the ill luck now broken, it is brought back into the house.

A recent (1949) publication written by a Japanese offers the following explanation of *yakudoshi:*

> "The idea of "yakudoshi" originally developed from the fact that those ages mark the times when men and women undergo particular mental and physical changes, and when many of them will experience notable changes in their social position. For instance, in the case of men, 25 would be the time when they reach manhood, and so the time is very important and critical. Then at 42, they would reach the height of development, and

at 60 their decline begins. For women, 19 is the age when they attain womanhood, and at 33 they are at their full bloom."

". . . "Yakudoshi" warns the people that they are at their critical stage, and has saved many persons from falling into unlucky failures."[14]

In contrast with the unlucky years, a lesser number of years of life are regarded as felicitous. The eighty-eighth year of life is very lucky. Few persons, of course, reach this age, but for the few who do, special offerings are made to the *kami-sama*, special food prepared, and gifts are presented. The ages of sixty-one (the traditional age of retirement) and seventy-seven are also thought to be lucky but usually involve no special ceremonial.

The year of birth of a man or woman according to the lunar calendar also governs his future life to some extent. Women born during the Year of the Sheep or the Year of the Horse and men born during the Year of the Tiger are unlucky, and it is said sometimes to be difficult to arrange marriages for them.

MATURITY AND OLD AGE

After marriage both bride and groom are removed from the class of *seinen* (youths) and become adult members of the community. The next major event in life is the birth of children, eagerly awaited by household elders as well as by the young couple. As quickly as she is able — many modern brides know little about cooking — the bride takes over the preparation of household meals. She has, in addition, many other household tasks, which include giving aid in agricultural work. The good bride goes through this process of adjustment and assumption of duties meekly and dutifully and asserts herself very little until she is a matron with children.

With the taking on of years and the assumption of responsibilities the erstwhile young men, formerly diffident and unsure of themselves, become more or less assured adults whose opinions and actions are of importance in *buraku* and community affairs. Within the women's sphere the same situation applies. The bride has become the mother, a person of some stature in the household and in the community. Age alone gives prestige. The bearing of children, although eagerly desired, is not an absolute requirement for a status of maturity in the *buraku* and community. There are always a number of barren women who, although not envied by other women, are as a rule not looked down upon or considered inferior to women who have borne children.

There are no beliefs or practices associated with menopause, and it is not considered to be a difficult or dangerous period for women. The age of forty-two is, however, considered the climacteric for men (see The Bad

14. M. Jōya, *op. cit.*, p. 75.

Years, this chapter). After having become parents the next important step for a man and woman is the attainment of grandparenthood. Grandfathers and grandmothers are in a different age category and in a somewhat different behavior category. As men and women grow old they are allowed considerable freedom of speech and behavior which would be unbecoming at a younger age. For many men and women this is a prerogative little exercised, but some persons, particularly old men, are at times given to bawdy jokes and frank speech which is laughed at indulgently by others.

When a man feels that his powers are failing and his duties as household head become difficult or troublesome for him, he and his wife "retire." Such retirement is always voluntary and usually desired. There is no established year of life for retirement — the traditional retirement age of sixty-one is almost always passed unheeded — and no pressure is ordinarily placed upon a man to retire. Upon retirement, usually in the late sixties, a man and his wife sleep in detached quarters where they will be less annoyed by noisy grandchildren. Both now assume the role of helpers to the new household head and his wife in the performance of household tasks. Grandmothers physically unable to do heavy work often serve as nursemaids for their grandchildren. Until the time of death or physical incapacity old persons continue to do such work as they are able, and they usually receive indulgent treatment from the younger members of their households.

DEATH

The death of an old person, long forseen, is not an occasion of great sadness for most members of the household, but it is the occasion for an elaborate funeral. The more descendants one has — and consequently the more worshippers of the spirit after death — the more elaborate is the funeral. Funerals for children and for a young married woman are usually simple, but for a grandfather or grandmother they are as elaborate as the household can afford. Males are, in general, accorded preferential treatment in funerals. There is usually relatively little to distinguish the funerals of grandmothers from those of grandfathers, but the funeral of a mature but young son is usually more elaborate than that for a daughter. The funeral of a young married son is always more elaborate than that of a young bride, a newcomer into the household. Memorial masses held in years subsequent to death usually continue over a longer period for males.

After the *kōrenchū* (funeral organization, previously described) has assembled and gone into action, the body is washed and prepared for burial by adult members of the household. The services of professional

PLATE 20.—*New Year's decorations before the shelf dedicated to Ebisu and Daikoku.*

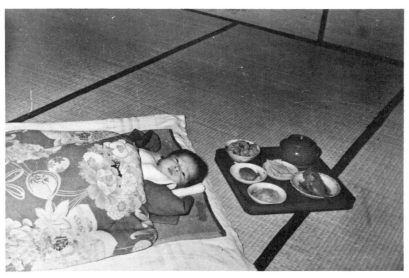

PLATE 21.—*Ceremonial offering of food to child on its naming day. Dish directly above child's head contains a round, smooth stone.*

undertakers are never utilized except in cases of death from contagious disease, when the body is cremated. The bereaved family and *kōrenchū* members are now under a three-day restriction against the eating of fish or meat and against contact with the *kami-sama*. Mourning papers are placed on all shrine shelves (see Chap. V, Defilement and Taboo). After the body has been washed with warm water and dressed in good clothing, a shroud of white cotton is placed over the top of the clothing, and the body is placed in the coffin in a flexed position with knees drawn up under the chin. Some households still follow the traditional but gradually vanishing custom of shaving the head of older adults who have died. Various possessions of the deceased are placed in the coffin with the body, a doll in the coffin of a child, a pipe or razor for a man, and a pair of scissors for a woman. A small cloth bag containing a little money, bits of favorite food of the deceased, and tobacco if the deceased smoked, is fastened about the neck by means of a string. These items are for use during the trip to the other world.

After the body has been placed in the coffin, a ceremony called *Matsugo-no-mizu* "The last water," is performed by close relatives. A few drops of water are placed on a leaf of *shikibi* and brought to the lips of the deceased by every adult member of the family in order of seniority. The lid of the coffin is then nailed down. It is important that the coffin, while in the house, be placed in the *kaminoma* at a central point against the sliding panels leading to the *nando* in such a position that the body faces to the north. An offering consisting of tea and a bowl of rice on a tray is then placed before the coffin. The chopsticks (normally laid flat on a food tray) of the deceased are placed in a vertical position in the bowl of rice on this occasion. A stick of burning incense must also be placed in a container on the tray to serve as "guide-post" for the spirit of the deceased in its journey. A curtain of striped black and white cotton, about three feet in width, is hung from the ceiling by the *tokonoma* and extended around the greater part of three walls of the room.

Funerals are usually held in the early afternoon of the day following death, or as soon thereafter as the *kōrenchū* has finished all the necessary tasks. Relatives and members of the *kōrenchū* assemble in front of the coffin and participate in prayer led by the Buddhist priest. When the prayers are over, a procedure which takes about thirty minutes, the coffin is removed from the house directly from the *kaminoma* and the funeral procession to the graveyard begins. At this time a male member of the *kōrenchū* builds a small fire of straw in the yard (as is done when a daughter leaves the home as a bride),[15] and breaks a dish from the household of the

15. Chamberlain interprets the funeral *kadobi* (fire) as a form of purification. He also considers the fire built at the time a bride leaves her home to marry out as identical in purpose — the daughter is considered dead to the household of her procreation. B. H. Chamberlain, *Things Japanese* (London: John Murray, 1898).

deceased. This is said to prevent further misfortunes; i.e., by having three calamitous things, a death, a fire, and the breaking of something occur at the same time, they are said to be unlikely to happen again in the near future. As the pallbearers and coffin leave the yard, a *kōrenchū* member sweeps with a broom the ground over which the coffin has been carried. This practice is said by some persons to remove pollution incurred from the dead body. Others say that it is to erase the footsteps of the members of the funeral procession so that the spirit of the deceased cannot find its way back to its former abode. A spirit of this sort can do harm, and, even if harmless, it is always uncomfortable to have about.

There is an established order of precedence for persons and objects in the funeral procession, and there are traditional rules as to who may fill the positions. These matters are only poorly known to the ordinary person and it is customary to prepare beforehand a listing of the positions and of the names of persons filling them so that the procession may be organized without undue confusion at the final moments. The significance of most of the large number of items of funeral paraphernalia is unknown to the average *buraku* resident; they are traditional and proper things, and people are content to be ignorant of their meaning. For a full funeral there are twenty or more positions or offices in the funeral procession involving upwards of forty persons. Some positions are to be held only by relatives; others are for non-relatives. Sex and closeness of relationships to the deceased govern the selection of persons for the positions which relatives may fill. Most of these offices or positions entail the transporting of funeral equipment, which includes ceremonial pennants; lanterns of two types; baskets of paper flowers (held in higher esteem for funerals than natural blossoms); candlestick holders and candles; incense burners with incense; an arrangement of living flowers; trays of dry rice; a brass container of tea; a cylindrical bamboo container of water; a temporary ancestral tablet made of wood; and a small object shaped like a miniature shrine in which the ancestral tablet is placed. Also included are the stick and hat of the deceased if a male, and an article of clothing of the deceased, silk, and in good condition.

Friends and distant relatives who are not members of the funeral party proper follow the procession to the foot of the graveyard where a stone bench and a stone table stand in front of the lines of Jizō statues. At this place a second ceremony called *Kokubetsu-shiki,* "Farewell ceremony," is conducted, which consists of prayer led by the priest. The coffin is then taken to the grave and lowered. Relatives begin filling in the grave, each, in order of seniority and relationship to the deceased, covering the casket with one shovelful of soil. When all relatives are through with their symbolic filling in of the grave, the pallbearers, who are members of the *kōrenchū* and unrelated to the deceased, complete the task. The silken garment of the deceased brought along in the funeral procession is given to the priest, who sells it at some later time, presumably for the benefit of the temple. The hat and cane are left beside the grave, as are flowers and incense. The temporary ancestral tablet must, however, be returned to the home and placed in the *Butsudan*. When a permanent tablet is received, the temporary one is brought to the graveyard and left behind the statue of the "head" Jizō. Various of the ceremonial pennants are thrown into the sea, but most of them are returned to the temple from which they were borrowed.

There are no further activities until the afternoon or evening of the day following the funeral when relatives, the *kōrenchū* members, and the priest assemble for the reading of Buddhist sutras *(o-kankin)* at the household of the deceased in front of the ancestral tablet. *Kōrenchū* members may make presents of money or other gifts at this time if they have not done so previously. Relatives and friends who are not members of the *kōrenchū* usually make their presentations earlier. Funeral gifts are theoretically for the purchase of incense for the deceased and are so named. Money is the traditional gift, wrapped in paper with a black and white *mizuhiki*. Flowers are also given, and in recent years circular funeral wreaths of paper leaves and paper flowers have come to be used. Peach and plum blossoms may never be used on this occasion. Foodstuffs and firewood are acceptable gifts and are sometimes presented by *kōrenchū* members.

During the *o-kankin* both priest and one or more *kōrenchū* members read sutras. *Buraku* residents who can read with fine, sonorous voices are in demand to lead the chanting, in which all others present join. After the reading of the sutras, a simple feast is served to the priest and to the *kōrenchū* members.

A service, *Dan-age*, "Raising the altar," in which only the priest, the members of the household and other close relatives of the deceased participate, is held on the third day. A stepped dais *(dan)* for holding the ancestral tablet, incense, and food offerings is earlier placed in the *tokonoma*. Prayers, led by the priest, are said in front of the *dan*. As at the memorial services held later for the deceased, it is customary to have among the items of food offered at this time one large and two small uncolored *mochi* called *kugi-uke mochi*, "nail-receiving *mochi*." It is said that devils try to pound nails into the head and knees of the deceased on his trip to the other world and these cakes, the large one placed on the head of the deceased and the two small cakes on his knees, render the nails harmless. When the *Dan-age* ceremony is over, fasting also ends, and the priest and household have a fairly elaborate meal at which fish is again eaten. It is customary at this time to place a screen in front of the ancestral tablet in the *tokonoma* so that the Hotoke-sama will not be offended by the sight of persons eating fish. The altar is removed or dismantled after the ceremony and feast are ended.

Until recent years women wore their hair in a special style during funeral periods. Water used by the household during the funeral period was ladled with a backhand motion, the reverse of the normal practice. The reversal of normal habits still applies in certain customs associated with funerals. The sash of the dead person must be tied with a granny knot instead of the standard square knot used during life. The folds of the *kimono* of the deceased must also be placed over one another in the reverse of the usual order. A custom called *yobi-ikashi*, "calling to life," was followed until about forty years ago in an attempt to avert death. When someone seemed on the verge of death, all members of the household old enough to do so climbed onto the roof where each called out the given name of the dying person, at the same time pulling out a piece of straw from the thatch of the roof or loosening a roof-tile. *Yobi-ikashi* was practiced only for persons who had not as yet lived out their normal span of years; no attempt was made to call old persons back to life.

After the funeral, the household of the deceased and the members of the *kōrenchū* purify themselves with salt and build new fires in their dwellings. There is no fear of the body of the deceased during the washing and dressing and usually none until several days after death, when some persons get the unnatural feeling that the spirit of the deceased is near them and they grow to fear the spirit. No one thinks of the spirits of infants or children, however, as being fearful.

For a period of seven days after interment a male member of the household of the deceased visits the grave each morning and pours water onto the grave *(Mizu-matsuri)* or onto the gravestone if one has already been erected. The water must be poured from a small cylindrical bamboo vessel used only for this ceremonial, which is usually performed at all grave visits and is thought in some vague way to indicate reverence or respect for the spirit of the deceased.

A person does not entirely leave the household upon death, for his spirit must be worshipped and receive offerings. During most of the year this is done before the ancestral tablets in the *Butsudan*. There are, in addition, many traditional memorial services *(tsuizen kuyō)*. The first of these is held on either the thirty-fifth or the forty-ninth day after death, at which time the Buddhist priest leads the household in prayers for the deceased. These prayers are conducted in front of the ancestral tablet placed on an altar in the *tokonoma*. Close relatives who live in other communities also attend the ceremony, and partake of a modest feast afterwards.

Subsequent memorial services are traditionally held on the first, third, seventh, thirteenth, seventeenth, twenty-fifth, thirty-third, and fiftieth anniversaries of death. In actuality, such services seldom extend beyond the seventh or thirteenth anniversaries, although a few households may continue on to the year of the seventeenth anniversary. Memorial services for infants are usually limited to the first anniversary, and those for young children or a young bride seldom go beyond the services for the third year. To avoid the expenses for food and the payment of fees to the priest, poor people may pray at the temple on anniversaries and no home memorial service is held.

Memorial services are often happy rather than sad affairs. After the prayers and a visit to the grave there is always a feast for the priest and assembled relatives, and it is an occasion for pleasant association with relatives whom one does not often see. Such memorial services, and also the funerals of aged persons, are sometimes referred to as *Mago-ko-no-Shōgatsu*, "Grandchildren's New Year's," because they are occasions of excitement and pleasure for children. This is by no means to say that funerals are uniformly happy occasions for all. With the foregoing exceptions there is no formal mourning for the deceased, but there is in many cases deep and heartfelt mourning among members of the household for someone who has died. Such emotions are a private matter and are not displayed to the community. The shedding of tears at funerals is considered permissible for men as well as women. Noisy sobbing or outcries are, however, outside the accepted pattern of behavior.

A fine funeral and a fine headstone bearing the name in life and the posthumous Buddhist rank of the deceased are desired by everyone. Headstones are usually not purchased until some months or years after a person's death and, if a household is very impoverished, a simple pile of beach stones may serve instead. Occasionally a man purchases his own headstone before his death. In such cases the stone is placed in the graveyard over the plot of ground to be used, but it is encased with boards or straw mats until the time of the death and funeral. Small structures made of wood or metal and resembling houses are sometimes placed over graves.[16] These structures, called simple *ie*, "house," and also rarely *tamaya*, "soul house," are said to be placed over the graves when the deceased was especially cherished and loved. Their stated purpose is simply to shelter the body from the elements.

16. These structures may represent a survival of old practices associated with pollution from death. In former times in Japan a bereaved, and polluted, household lived in isolation during periods of death-pollution. Sometimes the household observed pollution taboos by living a secluded life in a hut built near the grave. Cf. T. Ōmachi, *op. cit.*

CHAPTER VII

The Impact of Westernization

IN THE description of *buraku* life given in the foregoing pages an attempt has been made to call attention to changes which have come about within the memory of presently living persons. Changes in way of life on a national scale — due largely to contact with the West — have been given little attention and no systematic treatment here. The great changes which began in the second half of the nineteenth century, including the abolishment of feudalism, the beginning of compulsory education for all, the industrialization of Japan, and the introduction of a vast number of Western inventions and ideas, have had far-reaching effect. A recounting of the many devices and ideas taken over from the West is readily available in any of a number of published accounts and will not be attempted here.[1]

Introduction of machines into a country or official adoption of foreign ideas does not, of course, mean that such machines or ideas necessarily become established among all classes of people. Neither does it mean that establishment, if it is made, occurs at the same time and produces the same effect among urban and rural dwellers. For acculturative change to take place there must, of course, be contact either direct or indirect with a foreign culture. In the case of Japan, contact with the West has usually been first through port cities and other urban centers. From these centers innovations have spread gradually to smaller centers of population and to rural areas. The rate of advance or adoption of foreign objects and ideas has by no means been uniform. To many Japanese urbanites the customs described in these pages are to a good measure strange and unknown, because they disappeared from urban areas many

1. See, for example, E. H. Norman, *Japan's Emergence as a Modern State* (New York: Institute of Pacific Relations, 1940) and G. B. Sansom, *The Western World and Japan* (New York: Alfred A. Knopf, 1951).

years ago. Among rural areas of Japan there is also variation in the degree of modernization and, in general, the more isolated areas cling in greater degree to the old ways of life. Differences which exist between such an extreme area of isolation as the Island of Tsushima in the Japan Sea and the relatively non-isolated Takashima appear to the author to be less extreme, however, than the breach that exists between average urban and rural ways.

Within rural Japan the basic patterns of life are everywhere much the same, with local variations. A comparison of the foregoing description of Takashima with life as depicted by Embree in Suye Mura, an isolated village several hundred miles from Takashima, reveals a strong basic similarity, although Suye appears to have been considerably less Western-ized.[2] Since the basic culture of rural areas is everywhere much alike, it seems reasonable to assume that the effects of Westernization will also be similar. Takashima seems neither conspicuously advanced nor retarded culturally in comparison with other rural communities of Japan. In all likelihood, what is true of Takashima has been, is now, or will be true in large measure of other rural communities.

In order to attempt to appraise the degree and effect of acculturative change in any culture it is necessary to know the conditions which obtained prior to contact with other cultures and the changes which have taken place subsequent to the time of first contact. Specifically, a detailed picture is required of conditions in immediately pre-Meiji times in Japan, before the opening of the country to the invasion of ideas and objects from the Western world. Unfortunately, such a picture must in some part be assumed. The many Japanese historical accounts and other writings of pre-Meiji times are concerned principally with court activities. They do, however, give occasional glimpses of the life of the ordinary man, and the cumulative total of these writings together with the study of modern archaeologists, historians, and other observers provide adequate data to furnish fairly clear ideas of the major outlines of the culture of former days. Deletion of historically known additions derived from foreign cul-tures also aids us in determining the conditions of pre-Meiji culture.

The basic pattern of life appears to be extremely old. An examina-tion of Sansom's description of the prehistoric indigenous religion of Japan, for example, will reveal many elements still to be found on Takashima.[3] The rural community of pre-Meiji times was a closely knit, largely self-sufficient unit with strong traditions of communal activity. It was based on a rice economy and under the firm control of a feudal lord with whom the

2. J. F. Embree, *Suye Mura* (Chicago: University of Chicago Press, 1939). Japanese anthropologists and sociologists regard Suye Mura, even at the time (1935-36) of which Embree writes, as a village retarded beyond the average for Japan. The war and other influences are said, however, to have brought many changes toward modernization in Suye Mura.

3. G. B. Sansom, *Japan, A Short Cultural History*, rev. ed. (New York: D. Appleton-Century Co., 1943), Chap. III, "The Indigenous Cult."

average person had no contact except for the payment to his agents of taxes, in rice. Social classes, based principally upon birth, were rigid throughout Japan at that time, although elevation to warrior or noble rank was occasionally effected by wealthy urban merchants through the payment of money, which was beginning to be of importance. As Sansom points out, an embryo capitalist system and the faint beginnings of industrialization existed before Meiji,[4] but their effect on rural communities of the time was doubtless very slight. Religious beliefs centered about a vast number of unsystematized gods, some of them clearly of Chinese origin; a body of popular belief, "simple ritualism based on an animistic creed and tinctured with magic,"[5] and the beliefs of Buddhism. Many of the details of ordinary life such as diet, dress, treatment of disease, and marriage customs are also known.

Rather than proceed here with a partially hypothetical description of the cultural conditions of that time, many details of which have already found statement herein, the changes themselves will be given attention. As a matter of convenience, a resumé of changes apparent in some of the major aspects of life — in part a repetition of material scattered throughout the foregoing pages — will be given in brief form here. It is to be borne in mind that the following is a description and listing of changes. The author does not necessarily wish to imply here that all changes are the result of contact with the West; this is a matter which will be dealt with later.

Techniques of Gaining a Livelihood:

The great change in fishing has been the addition of motorized fishing craft and the abandonment of the use of sails. This is a change of considerable consequence, giving increased mobility and greater efficiency. A motored boat can also quickly take one to shore when storms arise and take fishermen home when there is no wind to belly sails. Fishermen are no longer at the mercy of the tides and winds of the sea or of the gods of the sea. Fishing techniques themselves as used on Takashima seem little influenced by contact with the Western world.

Agriculture is little changed from ancient times. Crops have changed to some degree by the addition of Western plants, and commercial fertilizers and insecticides are used to a limited extent. Technical advice from trained agricultural experts is available through the Agricultural Cooperative, but it is often little heeded by Takashima persons for lack of funds and because farming is on a very small scale. Fertilizing methods might well change if it were economically possible to use commercial fertilizers extensively. Farm implements are the traditional Japanese, suited

4. G. B. Sansom, *The Western World and Japan* (New York: Alfred A. Knopf, 1951), p. 499.
5. G. B. Sansom, *Japan, A Short Cultural History,* rev. ed. (New York: D. Appleton-Century Co., 1943), p. 55.

for small-scale farming, but they are now usually all machine-made. Home milling of grain is a dwindling practice; instead, *buraku* people take their barley, millet, and wheat to a commercial mill. Plots of land are too small to warrant the use and expense of modern machinery. Even under optimum conditions there is likely to be little change in agriculture, because it is essentially garden plot farming and not the primary means of gaining a livelihood.

Housing and Household Equipment:

Houses are of native style with the addition in relatively recent years of considerable glass replacing paper in shutters and of a few glass windows. Although there is little or no change in architecture, building materials now include bricks (ordinarily used only for cooking stoves and bathhouse fireplaces) and cement. Few persons in the *buraku* have ever seen a dwelling of Western style (except in the movies), and it is almost inconceivable that any fisherman would desire a house of Western style. In any case, the cost of the much more solidly constructed Western house would be tremendously great. Even the thought of the Japanese farmer or fisherman owning a home of Western style seems fantastic.

Household equipment includes many items of Western origin. Random inventories of household and personal possessions revealed a large number of common items of Western origin, inspiration, or provenience. In many cases the origin is indicated by the use of English names for the objects. A list of the more common items follows:

> Barometers and compasses
> Batteries and light bulbs
> Bicycles
> Books printed and bound in Western style
> Carpenter's tools (drills, bits, nails, screws and screwdrivers)
> Clothes irons
> Clothing of many sorts
> Cosmetics (Western style)
> Flashlights
> Gregorian calendars
> Kerosene lamps
> Kitchenware of aluminum and aluminum alloy, including utensils of Western
>   origin such as frying pans
> Magazines, newspapers, comic books
> Medical supplies, including ammonia, Vaseline, gauze, mercurochrome
> Pencils, fountain pens, ink, notebooks
> Phonographs
> Photo albums and photographs
> Rubber goods, including toys of Western style and ice bags
> Pocketknives
> Sewing machines and sewing equipment, including thread on spools, hooks
>   and eyes, snaps and buttons
> Suitcases
> Tableware, including spoons, cups, saucers, glasses

Thermometers
Tin cans and can openers (few)
Toothbrushes (Western style)
Towels ("Turkish")
Wall clocks and wrist watches

With detailed consideration of boat equipment, school supplies, garden flowers, and medications, to mention but a few categories, the list of articles acquired from the West swells. A total summation of all articles of Western derivation to be found in the *buraku* would be extremely lengthy and very tedious reading. It is perhaps not wildly inaccurate to state that most of the small conveniences and devices common to American households of a low income bracket about forty years ago for which there were no native Japanese counterparts can be found on Takashima today. In some instances foreign articles have replaced Japanese counterparts, and among adopted items are a few, such as ballpoint pens, DDT insecticides, and nylon-like plastics, which are relatively new in America or Europe.

Diet:

The daily diet is still basically Japanese. The new vegetables and fruits of Western origin (i.e., those which have come in since the beginning of Meiji) are unimportant in the routine diet. Among confections there are a number of Western origin, including ice cream, soft drinks, caramels and many other candies. Refined sugar has become a staple although the quantity used is not great (it is still rationed). Bread and various cakes of Western origin are known but little used — they cost money. Coffee and beer are known but can hardly be regarded as ordinary items of diet. Imported foods and Western foods commercially prepared in Japan, even if known, are far too expensive for *buraku* purses.

Dress:

Dress and hair-styles are overwhelmingly Western among children and younger adults on up to middle age. It appears likely that the clothing thirty or forty years from now will be almost totally Western, if with a native flavor, for persons of all ages. Curly hair, once disliked, is a beauty prerequisite (in the form of permanent waves) for the young women of today. Nakedness or partial nakedness, which appear to have been common among peasants in pre-Meiji times and during early Meiji,[6] are now more and more regarded as embarrassing if not shameful.

Sex Mores:

There has been a noteworthy change in attitudes toward sex. In former days some sexual license was extended to the young, and local

6. Many references to the nakedness of common people may be found in early accounts by Westerners. See, for example, E. Kaempfer, *History of Japan* (orig. ed., London: Published for the translator, 1727; republished, New York: The Macmillan Co., 1906) or I. L. Bird, *Unbeaten Tracks in Japan* (London: John Murray, 1881).

festivals were the traditional occasions for such license. Sexual expression within approved channels appears formerly to have been regarded as natural behavior. Sexual intercourse is today rather shameful, and a girl must remain a virgin until her marriage. Obscenity (i.e., markedly vulgar references to sex or sexual intercourse) in song and dance are uncommon and "uncivilized."[7]

Entertainment:

Entertainment and recreation have in the past been closely tied with religion for at least the rural population of Japan, and this situation also obtains to a considerable extent today. Visits to shrines and participation in local festivals and feasts were formerly the chief forms of entertainment. Events of the traditional ceremonial calendar have, however, progressively dwindled in number, and secular entertainment of Western inspiration is of mounting importance. The young people of today are fond of ping-pong, baseball (although opportunities to play baseball are limited for lack of an appropriate place on Takashima), and movies. Festivals and shrine pilgrimages are still important as entertainment, but at least to the young they are principally days of pleasant rest or travel and movie days. Activities of the elementary school and in particular the track meets are important events of entertainment which found no place in the old ceremonial calendar.

Education:

The Japanese public school system, initiated during early Meiji, was based upon that of the West (France). The educational system which finally became established in Japan, however, differs in many respects from that of France or any other Western country. There are many characteristics which appear to be wholly Japanese developments or adaptations. No attempt will be made here to describe or recount the history of the national education system. Attention will instead be given briefly to public school education as it applies to Takashima.

With rare exception, persons over seventy in Takashima cannot read or write. The level of education in the *buraku* has, however, risen steadily in the past five or six decades. As a result of the post-war regulation making nine years of school compulsory instead of the former six, the level of education has also risen perceptibly since the end of the war and will no doubt continue to rise. This is extremely important from the point of view of Westernization and modernization as the public schools are perhaps the most important single means for the dissemination of new and foreign ideas.

7. For a description of relations among the unmarried young in backward areas of rural Japan see T. Ōmachi, *op. cit.* See also J. F. Embree, *op. cit.,* for references to obscene dancing and singing.

Foreign Words:

The vocabularies of even old persons who cannot read or write contain many words derived from English. Over a period of two months the author jotted down such foreign words as he heard used in casual conversation by Takashima adults, and found the total to be approximately 150 (see Table 5). The English vocabularies of middle school and *kōtōgakkō* students are considerably larger. The rare foreign terms of non-English origin noted during this period are principally words introduced by the Portuguese in the sixteenth century. Most foreign words are thought by their users in the *buraku* to be of native origin.

The Crises of Life:

Practices associated with birth, marriage, and death, although still following traditional custom in major outline, have undergone considerable change. Midwives must receive technical training and they pass on some of their knowledge to their patients; new ideas on pre-natal, postnatal, and infant care are creeping in, and the taboos associated with menstruation, childbirth, and death are vanishing.

Wedding customs on Takashima have followed an interesting course, swinging away from love marriages to wholly arranged marriages (the result of education in the "proper" course of action, informants state). Some of the young people of today, although willing to abide by the wishes of their parents in this matter, express themselves as favoring unions based on love, which all of them know as the marriage practice of America. Grooms may marry in Western clothes; brides must wear wigs over their permanent waves, and wedding parties travel by taxi.

Funerals still follow ancient Buddhist ritual with little apparent change, but funeral taboos have become less strict. Old customs associated with death such as the "calling to life" have been abandoned.

Crises occasioned by illness are now largely met with the aid of physicians and modern medicine. Faith in magico-religious remedies has suffered a great decline.

Economy and Social Structure:

Perhaps the most significant and important change which has occurred in *buraku* life since the beginning of Meiji is the adoption of a money economy. This transition has brought with it a number of other changes and its effect seems particularly evident in altered social relationships. Because the changes evident in social structure seem in many instances to result from a changed economy, both are dealt with together here.

Takashima, although never a rice-growing community, in former times used rice as a medium of exchange, trading dry farm produce for

TABLE 5

Foreign Words in the Adult Vocabulary

(Noted over a period of two months)

English Word	Japanese Adaptation	Remarks
album	arubamu	Photograph album
all right	ārai	Used to signify "all clear" in such cases as passing another boat at close quarters.
ammonia	āmonya	
apple	appuru	
apron	ēpuron	Woman's apron of cloth
back	bakku	The backing-up of an auto, bicycle, or other vehicle
balance	baransu	A sum of money
baseball	bēsubōru	Many baseball terms, such as "strike," are also known.
band	bando	A belt or waistband
battery	batterī	
biscuit	bisketto	
black	burakku	
bloomers	burūma	
blouse	burausu	Woman's blouse
bolt	bōruto	
boy	bōi	
brown	buraun	
brush	burāshi	
bucket	baketsu	
bus	basu	
cake	kēki	
calendar	karendā	Gregorian calendar
canna	kana	
caramel	kyarameru	Caramel candy
cardigan	kadēgan	
case	kēsu	Container; e.g., cigarette case
cat	katto	
cellophane	serofan	
chalk	chyākki	Chalk as is used in schools
chewing gum	chūing(u)gāmu	
chocolate	chyakoretto	
Christmas	Kurisumasu	
cider	saida	Used for a type of softdrink. Does not mean apple cider.
coffee	kōhī	
coat	kōto	A coat of Western style

TABLE 5—*(Continued)*

Foreign Words in the Adult Vocabulary

English Word	Japanese Adaptation	Remarks
collar	kara	The collar of Western clothes
compass	kampasu	
cosmos	kosumosu	The flower
coupon	kūpon	
course	kōsu	
cowboy	kauboi	
cream	kurīmu	Cold cream
cuffs	kāfusu	
cup	koppu	Usually means a small water-glass
dahlia	dāria	
dance	dansu	Western-style dancing
DDT	dīdīchī	
diamond	daiomondo	
dry cell	duraiseru	
dry cleaning	duraikurīningu	
east	isuto	
feet	fīto	Linear measure
flapper	furappa	The "flapper" of the American 1920's
fork	fōku	Table fork
fruit	furūto	
fry	furai	
frying pan	furaipan	
gauze	gaze	Gauze bandage
game	gēmu	
girl	gāru	
glider	guraida	Glider plane
grease	gurīsu	Grease for vehicles and other mechanical devices
green	gurīnu	
handle	handoru	A carpenter's drill
headlight	hedoraito	
high school	haisukūru	
hysteria	histeri	
ice candy	aisukyandi	Shavings of ice on which a sweet syrup is poured
ice cream	aisukurīmu	
inch	inchi	
ink	inki	
jumper	jāmpa	A woman's jumper dress (Western)
kilometer	kiro	
knife	naifu	
knot	natto	

TABLE 5—*(Continued)*

Foreign Words in the Adult Vocabulary

English Word	Japanese Adaptation	Remarks
lemon	remon	
lighter	raita	Cigarette lighter
milk	miruku	
motor	mōta	
meter	mētoru	Linear measure
mile	mairu	
modern	modān	
modern boy	mobo	A contraction of *modān* and *bōi*
modern girl	moga	A contraction of *modān* and *garu*
Naphthalin	nafutarin	
necktie	nekkutai	
north	nōsu	
note	nōtto	Notebook
nylon	nairon	
one-piece	uanupīsu	A one-piece dress of Western style
orange	orenji	Citrus fruit
overcoat	ōba	
pants	pantsu	
pen	pen	
penicillin	penishirin	
permanent wave	pāma or pāmanento	
picnic	pikunikku	
pink	pinki	The color pink
platform	puratofōmu	Railroad station platform
platinum	purāchinamu	
plug	purāgu	
pocket	poketto	
pomade	pomādo	
program	purōguramu	
propeller	puropera	Propeller of an airplane
puff	pāfu	Powder-puff
pump	pāmpu	
puncture	panku	A punctured tire
race	rēsu	Foot-race or boat-race
radio	rajio	
raincoat	rēn(u)kōto	Western-style raincoat
record	rekōdo	Phonograph record
rice curry	raisukāri	
rope	rōpu	
route	rūto	
salad	sarada	
Santa Claus	Santa Kurāsu	
sauce	sōsu	
scoop	skōpu	A shovel

TABLE 5—*(Continued)*

Foreign Words in the Adult Vocabulary

English Word	Japanese Adaptation	Remarks
serge	sāji	
set	setto	An ensemble
shirt	shatsu	Shirt or undershirt
skirt	sukātsu	Woman's skirt of Western style
soda	sōda	Soft-drink
south	sausu	
sox	sakkusu	
spoon	supūn	
spring	supuringgu	Mechanical spring
suit	sūto	A suit of Western-style clothing
stop	sutappu	Used in directing movement of boats, bicycles, and other vehicles
stainless	sutēnresu	Stainless steel
sweater	suēta	
tack	takku	Metal tack
tape	tēpu	
test	tesuto	School tests
tie	tai	Necktie
tire	taiya	
trump	tsurampu	A trump card
top	toppu	Used in the expression *"toppu o kiru,"* (literally, "to cut the top"). A person who "cuts the top" is one who is the first or the most outstanding in some activity.
towel	tauru	Turkish towel
two-piece	tsūpīsu	A two-piece dress of Western style
vitamin	bītamin	
yard	yaru	Linear measure
west	uesto	
whiskey	uisukī	
white	uaitto	

TABLE 5—*(Continued)*

Japanese Words of Portuguese Origin
(Introduced in the 16th Century)

Japanese Adaptation	Remarks
pan	Bread
botan	Button
meriyasu	A type of knitted underwear
furasoko	Flask
juban	A kind of undershirt
kasuteira	A kind of sponge cake (said to be derived from Castile or Castella)
karuta	Playing cards

In writing the Japanese versions of foreign words, English letters have been used to represent and approximate the Japanese sounds. Some explanation is, however, necessary:

a has the sound of *a* in *father*
i has the sound of *i* in *ravine* or the *ee* in *seed*
u has the sound of *u* in *rule* or the *oo* in *school*
e has the sound of *ey* in *whey* (somewhat shortened)
o has the sound of *o* in *cold*

The diacritical mark "-" placed over vowels indicates that the sound should be drawn out or lengthened.

Note: No attempt was made to determine whether all of these words are known to every adult person. The author is confident, however, that most of them are known to the average adult. This listing by no means exhausts the foreign vocabulary of the ordinary person, whose English vocabulary probably embraces about three hundred words and expressions. Words of the metric system (meter and kilometer) in the foregoing list may have come through the French.

* * *

rice. When the conversion from a farming to a predominantly fishing economy occurred about seventy years ago, some bartering of fish for rice is said still to have been done. It has been impossible to determine the exact date when virtually full reliance upon money as a means of exchange (the condition which exists at the present day) came about. Money had long been in use at the time the *buraku* changed from farming to fishing, but it did not become the sole means of exchange until a later but undetermined date.

Money is the prime topic of conversation for most men.[8] It has ceased to be merely a medium by which to get necessary or coveted goods to enable persons to live or to contribute to their well-being; it is coveted for itself as a symbol of the things which it can buy and for the social prestige it brings.

8. Some men were poor informants for the reason that it was difficult to get them off the topic of money. Their thoughts appeared to revolve constantly around the cost of material obje cts, and the amount of money possessed by other (and richer) individuals.

A noticeable trend in *buraku* social structure which seems closely allied with the adoption of a money economy is a tendency toward individualism. Everywhere, with the rise of money economy, cooperation has dwindled and individualism begun.[9] The *buraku*, while still forming with the household the two basic social units, is no longer the tightly knit structure of former years. Many communal activities — the pounding of *mochi*, construction of houses, the common use of the New Year's bonfire, all-*buraku* participation in wedding and housebuilding feasts — have become or are becoming the activities of individual households. The effect of the war is a consideration not to be ruled out entirely in this connection. Extravagances such as large feasts were officially discouraged during the early years of Japan's war, and foodstuffs were lacking during the later war years and early post-war years. Communal banquets are of course impossible without food. Foodstuffs in sufficient quantity to allow feasts had, however, been available through legal channels and the open blackmarket for about two years at the time this field study ended, but the old customs, already dying in pre-war years, were not resumed. Full *buraku* participation in shrine watches and *Bon* dances are a thing of the past — although this is perhaps as much the result of a decline in religious faith as an indication of an increase in individualism.

A publication entitled *The Japanese Village in Transition* prepared under the auspices of the Occupation and dealing with thirteen Japanese villages located in various parts of Japan also reports a decrease in communal activity:

> "The post-Surrender trend toward a decrease in size of the mutual aid group is in all probability the result of the increase in the family labor supply brought about by the influx of civilian and military repatriates, as well as of the increased use of livestock and farm machinery. . . . Food shortages and inflation also appear to have had some effect, because providing the food for the many workers who gathered for mutual aid, which was a traditional obligation, is extremely difficult under current economic conditions. . . . The size of the groups participating in weddings and funerals decreased considerably in all the villages in recent years. Villagers attributed this directly to food shortages and to the high cost of entertaining guests. Attendance at weddings in most villages is now restricted to close relatives and friends. In the few villages where the neighborhood group is still invited, the size of the group has decreased."[10]

The period of time covered by this study is 1947 and 1948. Since then food shortages and inflation have ceased to be a serious problem — at least for Takashima people. It appears unquestionably true that the deprivations of the war and early post-war years were an important factor in the decline of communal activity. It also seems clear for Takashima, however, that the decline began long before the war. Most significant is the fact that some communal activities which were abandoned

9. See, in this connection, R. Redfield, *The Folk Culture of Yucatan* (Chicago: University of Chicago Press, 1948).

10. A. F. Raper, *et. al.*, *The Japanese Village in Transition* (Tokyo: General Headquarters, Supreme Commander for the Allied Powers, Natural Resources Section, Report No. 136, 1950), p. 198.

during the war because of food shortages have not, now that there is adequate food, been resumed.

The foregoing is not to say that communal and cooperative activity
no longer exist; they do exist and the feeling of *buraku* unity is still strong.
The custom of reciprocity for favors received or labor performed on one's
behalf is firmly entrenched and felt to be a moral obligation. Most activities of daily life are, however, on an individual household basis. The rare
occurrence of communal or reciprocal labor is in part due to the fact that
most types of fishing done by Takashima fishermen are better suited for
the joint work of only a few persons, i.e., a single household. Cooperative
labor, essential for the irrigation of rice in farming communities of Japan,
is simply not necessary on Takahima for carrying out fishing operations.
Ruling out, then, consideration of communal labor in fishing, which
seems never to have been the custom on Takashima, one is still confronted
with a picture of a considerable decline in other cooperative activity.
Money appears again to be a factor here. There is little incentive to
exchange labor with other households unless reciprocity is foreseen in the
near future. If a man helps another build a house, he thereby forfeits the
earnings of good, solid cash which might be gained from fishing or other
labor during the time devoted to this work.

Closely allied with the adoption of a money economy is the development of specialization in labor. There are, to be sure, few specialists in the
buraku except fishermen, but there are many in surrounding communities.
The development of specialization as it applies to Takashima lies in the
very development of fishing to the exclusion of other trades or skills. The
buraku fisherman can no longer, for example, build a house or a boat. He
must rely upon the services of other specialists for these and many other
things. With industrialization have come not only a money economy but
also increased urbanization. In the histories of the nations of the world
urbanization has led to or has been otherwise closely linked with specialization in occupation.[11] Industrialization is virtually synonymous with
specialization. The effects of the industrialization of Japan have reached
far out into its rural areas. To give but one example, Takashima fishermen rely upon motored boats, but no *buraku* man can build a motor and
few men can make anything except minor repairs when a motor breaks
down. And why should a man spend hours fashioning a clumsy implement at home when the money earned during this time at a regular occupation in which he is skilled will pay for a better specialist-made or
machine-made implement?

Within the *buraku* of Takashima the greatest factor in determining
social status is money. In Japan as a whole the traditional hierarchy of

11. See, for example, V. G. Childe, *What Happened in History* (Harmondsworth, Middlesex: Penguin books, 1950),
for an account of urbanization-specialization in the history of early civilizations of the world.

lords, warriors, farmers, and merchants changed long ago (and changed to a considerable extent before the beginning of Meiji) to classes based largely upon wealth. There are still lingering traces of the old national social hierarchy evidenced in the deference with which *buraku* persons refer — there is no contact — to households of noble lineage (one of course also still defers to anyone above him in the present social hierarchy). A strong survival from ancient times is the attitude toward Eta and other pariah groups such as the traditional fishermen of Hama *buraku*, who remain as social outcasts.[12] Within the *buraku* of Takashima there are said to have been few social distinctions in the past. The exact circumstances which existed before Meiji are impossible to determine. One can surmise, however, that in a community such as the pre-Meiji Takashima, where all persons were peasants and genetically related, emphasis in the social hierarchy was placed upon such factors as age and relationship to the founding households as well as upon wealth. It is clear today that the emphasis is primarily upon wealth.

Household ties remain strong, but show signs of weakening. It is still too early to note any effect upon the pattern of relationship between children and parents, particularly between father and eldest son, as the result of the post-war regulations on inheritance. Industrialization has drawn few Takashima persons to cities but it has resulted in a number of young men leaving home to accept employment as seamen on freighters operating in the Inland Sea. The weakening of ties in the extended household is more clearly evident. The number of persons of the extended household group who actually come together for traditional occasions such as funerals, memorial services, and marriages, has decreased markedly in the past few decades, and increasingly little reliance is placed on any occasion upon relatives who are outside the immediate household. *The Japanese Village in Transition* has the following to say on this subject:

"The mutual aid activities and solidarity of the extended family have been in a process of change for many years. This process, which is in the direction of lessening the importance of the extended family, has been accelerated since the Surrender. . . ."

"Prior to the war, members of the extended family in all of the villages were obligated to go to the assistance of any member in financial difficulties, and they were expected to consult the head of the family about the selection of brides for their sons. At present, neither of these practices is followed in about half of the villages. Also, in most of the villages, the head family no longer acts as go-between in the selection of spouses for members of its branch families. To an increasing extent, go-betweens are non-relatives. . . ."

"In summary, it can be said that the gradual deterioration of the extended family system, which began in the mid-Taisho era (about 1920) was considerably accelerated by post-Surrender conditions and by the land reform program. . . ."[13]

12. The history of the *Eta* since Meiji times is in some ways similar to that of the negro in the United States. The *Eta* were extended equal legal rights at about the same time that slavery was abolished in America. In folk thought *Eta* persons represent a different race. During 1950 a paper on the *Eta* to be delivered by a Japanese sociologist at a sociological convention in Osaka was cancelled because of pressure from *Eta* groups of that city.
13. A. L. Raper, *et. al., op. cit.,* p. 210.

This publication also reports that only members of the immediate household and close relatives come together for weddings, funerals, and memorial services.[14] The breakdown of the extended household seems equally evident on Takashima, although the land reform program of the Occupation has had virtually no effect.

There is little evidence of change in the position of women. Post-war legislation has extended a number of legal rights and privileges to women which they did not previously have. Among these are the right to own property independently of their husbands, the right to share the husband's or father's inheritance, the right of initiating action for divorce, and the extension of the franchise. The effect of these innovations is not as yet evident on Takashima. Women participate in fairly good force in elections, and few men object to the extension of the franchise to them. Many women feel, however, that they are not as yet sufficiently educated to be able to vote intelligently. Most women think it appropriate that the household property should go to the eldest son, who will follow tradition and assume the responsibility for taking care of his father's dependents. By and large, the position of women (as markedly inferior to men) remains unchanged. An indication of future change lies, however, in the relationships between young spouses. The young wife of today may walk beside, not behind her husband. (Traditionally, women walk a few paces behind their husbands, but this is not always done. Narrow paths and passageways often force persons to go single-file. In such cases, and when entering buildings, a man — even a modern young man — precedes his wife.) Young couples also have begun to appear together publicly at social affairs.[15] Schoolgirls are said to be less meek and retiring than the schoolgirls of pre-war years. There is said now to be little difficulty between brides and mothers-in-law of the *buraku*, which might be interpreted as a weakening of the authority of the mother-in-law.[16]

Another social trend evident is the tendency toward the formation of larger political units. This is a national tendency which began during Meiji with the reduction of the number of villages by consolidating them. Takashima, in pre-Meiji times a part of the small village of Shionasu, became during Meiji a part of the larger village of Honjō, which through the schools and other common institutions achieved some degree of village unity. Takashima is now one of the parts of a city and, although life has as yet been little altered by this change, at least the germs of a feeling of city unity exist among *buraku* residents. Attendance of Takashima chil-

14. *Ibid.,* p. 198 ff. The author has used the term "extended household" for the social unit which this publication calls "extended family."
15. This is in contrast with a statement appearing in *The Japanese Village in Transition:* "Joint participation of men and women in nonfamilial social functions is unheard of." (A. F. Raper, *et al., op. cit.,* p. 217).
16. The report cited above suggested that the authority of the mother-in-law is declining in the villages covered by the study *(Ibid.,* p. 219).

dren at middle school and *kōtōgakkō* in Ajino, now just getting under way, will no doubt serve in future years as an important integrating mechanism for Takashima as well as for all other *buraku* of the city.

The *buraku* is no longer isolated. The formation of larger political units has served increasingly to make small units a part of the whole. Today, thanks to newspapers, radios, buses, and trains, even geographically isolated communities are part of a national unit. The strong central government of Japan during pre-war and war years, while strictly controlling political and individual activity, did much to promote unification through its program of nationalism. This program was aimed at reaching even the most remote rural communities, and in order to carry the program out it was necessary to establish an efficient network of communication for the dissemination of government-promoted ideology. After the surrender and the collapse of the Japanese government,[17] the lines of communication remained, and in the Kojima area they have been strengthened in post-war years by increased public transportation facilities. This network of communication, of which schools are an important part, serves effectively to integrate the village and the *buraku* into the national whole. Everywhere, as the level of education has risen through the public school system, the horizon of the rural man's world has grown more distant. Newspapers and magazines reach a growing body of readers and serve as effective organs for the dissemination of ideas, including many foreign ideas. The *buraku*, in short, is gradually becoming a part of the nation and of the world.

The return of servicemen appears to have had little effect on Takashima. Because of the shortage of able-bodied males during the war, a number of women who did not otherwise do so were forced to serve as crew members on fishing boats. The returning servicemen relieved these women of their fishing duties. In other respects, these men seem to have had little effect. None of the military repatriates was ever in direct contact with American or European troops. Few foreign objects and (as far as the author was able to determine) no foreign ideas of any consequence came back with them. Upon their return most men appear to have settled down quickly to *buraku* patterns of living without effecting any noticeable changes in the patterns. The one change observed is in marriage customs: because there is still a small over-balance of females in the area, marriage arrangements are now initiated more frequently than in the past by the households of marriageable girls.

17. The previously government-bolstered young people's associations and women's patriotic associations, in the Kojima area at least, appear to have collapsed since the end of the war. It is perhaps more accurate to state that they have lost their nationalism and have reverted to something of their former status as basically age-group associations. This is in strong contrast with *The Japanese Village in Transition*, which states that these associations are very active in the thirteen villages reported upon. Honjō may be atypical in this respect. This study, however, also implies that these organizations are Occupation inspired and never existed in the communities in question until after the end of the war, a situation which seems improbable (A. F. Raper, *et al., op. cit.,* p. 232 ff.).

Religion:

It is a temptation to state baldly that *buraku* people are less religious than in the past. Such a statement demands that the criteria for judgment be stated. It appears to the author that a valid criterion by which to judge whether or not the people of a given culture are religious is the degree to which they adhere to the religious ideals of their own culture. In Takashima there has been a marked decline in religious observances. Shrine and temple attendance has decreased. *The Japanese Village in Transition* also reports a general decline in religious observances among the thirteen villages upon which it reports, and further finds that there are few religious practitioners in the villages:

> "... Five of the villages reported that they have not had resident priests [Shinto] for at least a decade, and a few villages had not had a resident priest for as long as 40 years. ... All of the younger Shinto priests have full-time jobs in addition to their priestly duties. ..."
>
> "Before the war the Buddhist clergy had been able to manage on their salaries; after the Surrender, however, more than one-half have been compelled to do outside work as well. ..."
>
> "The total number of Shinto festivals observed has declined, primarily because ultra-nationalist ceremonies (such as Empire Day and the Emperor's Birthday) have been prohibited by law. The festivals which remain, however, have become increasingly elaborate and exuberant in a number of villages. ... Buddhist festivals, however, have decreased both in number and elaborateness. ... In addition, the observance of death anniversaries has become less elaborate and fewer individuals participate. ... Because of the need to economize, fewer anniversaries are celebrated."[18]

The foregoing statements agree in general with conditions which existed in 1950 and 1951 in Takashima and Honjō, but vary in some points. (It is to be borne in mind that the SCAP report covers the years 1947-48.) There has been no resident Shinto priest in Honjō for many years. The author does not know whether or not the two Honjō Buddhist priests took outside work after the surrender of Japan; judging from their present appearance of relative affluence, they did not. There is no evidence that the remaining festivals in Honjō have become more elaborate (although they are of course more elaborate than those of the late war and early post-war years). Finally, there was, during 1950-51, little more need to economize than had existed before the war.

Religious ritual has become largely meaningless. This in itself I do not wish to interpret wholly as an indication of a decline in religious faith. There is ample evidence in the history of world religions of ancient ritual, while preserved in form, becoming meaningless in changed or modern context. It is possible, however, that the religious *feeling* may remain — but this is a subject I am unable to deal with further.

18. A. F. Raper, *et al.*, *op. cit.*, pp. 224-225.

More significant is the decreased reliance upon religion and the greater dependence upon empirical action, scientific findings, and naturalistic explanations at time of crises such as illness and in explanation of the unknown. Taboos, like many other religious practices, are now observed in many households only out of respect for aged members who believe in them. When the old people die, the practices cease. During the lifetime of even middle-aged persons a large number of religious customs have been abandoned. The challenge may be presented that some of the instances of relinquishment of customs may be a result of the *buraku* change from a farming to a fishing economy. There is little doubt that the change in economy brought about some changes in religion. No *buraku* person can remember a time when the present gods and beliefs associated with the sea were absent from the religious complex. It seems reasonable, however, to state that these beliefs were added at some time after the settling of Takashima; agriculturists do not ordinarily concern themselves with gods of the sea. In this matter, a comparison with the religious beliefs of Honjō farming *buraku* is worthy of note. The essential difference is that Honjō farmers give no attention to the sea gods; in other respects religious beliefs and practices are almost identical. Honjō farmers have by and large abandoned the same customs and relinquished the same beliefs as Takashima fishermen.

The decline in religious faith began long before World War II. There followed a sharp but brief increase in observance of religious practices during the war years. After the end of the war there seems to have been first a sharp decline and then a brief and small renascence which turned into a gradual but steadily continuing decline. Explanations offered by *buraku* people for the decline in religious observances are usually two in number. One is that defeat in the war caused people to lose faith in the gods to whom they prayed for the welfare of their sons and their country. This is an explanation I do not wish to brush lightly aside. Defeat in the war may well have been the jolt which speeded up a process already under way. When, however, it is pointed out to these same *buraku* persons that by their own statements the decline began long before the war, the reply is that in many ways religion is no longer needed, as modern knowledge has explained much which was at one time thought to be of supernatural origin, and modern medicine has proved more effective than appeals to the gods. Sometimes the explanation advanced by *buraku* people is expressed in these words: As culture *(bunka)* advances, "superstitions" naturally disappear.

Excluding the aged, there is now among most persons a curious state of half-belief. Many of the practices observed are referred to in embarrassed fashion as "superstitions" by the very people who practice them.

But it is possible that there may be something to the old beliefs and it is better to be on the safe side. When something does go wrong there is always the uneasy feeling that neglect of some traditional practice is the cause.

———————

The foregoing, then, constitute some of the major changes observable in the *buraku* since Meiji times. They may be summed up as the adoption of a money economy with attendant emphasis upon individuality and a decrease in communal activity; social status based largely on wealth; a decrease in the size and importance of the extended household; a tendency toward ever-larger community structure; the end of isolation and self-sufficiency for the *buraku* or small community; the adoption of a great many foreign inventions and ideas and a decline in religious faith.

The periods when these changes came about seem fairly clear in major outline and appear to tie in strongly with educational attainments of *buraku* people. Compulsory education officially began in Japan in 1872 and the elementary school in Shionasu was established shortly thereafter. Few persons and, particularly, few females of Takashima began attending school, however, until about twenty years later. Changes appear to have been gradual until about 1920, when a period of accelerated transition began which lasted until shortly before the opening of World War II. This is the period when motorized fishing craft became general, and when many of the other objects of Western inspiration became common. There is a marked dichotomy between the aged and younger persons in attitudes, particularly toward religion, and in customs followed. This is a breach which seems greater than might normally be expected. It appears likely that the cumulative effect of public schooling and the many innovations that came into Japan beginning in Meiji times first started to be strongly felt in the *buraku* about the time the present generation of household heads (the first to receive public school education) matured, around 1920. The young have had increased exposure to Western ideas.

Some impetus in the rate of speed of adoption of Western articles of personal or household use seems attributable to the influence of Japanese emigrants to Hawaii and the continental United States, many of whom were drawn from the Inland Sea area. No individuals from Takashima were among the emigrants, but surrounding communities are said to have been well represented. Large numbers of these emigrants returned to Japan after a number of years, bringing with them new ideas and new products. The Inland Sea area is said to have adopted many Western ways earlier than other rural sections of Japan as a direct result of these returning emigrants, many of whom returned from America about 1906.

American missionary activity in an area of the Inland Sea not far from Takashima covering a period of about twenty years and ending before the outbreak of the war is said also to have been effective in the spread of Western objects and ideas.[19] There was at no time, however, any direct contact between the people of Takashima and the missionaries in question.

Acculturative change reached something of a plateau, if not a recession, during the war years. A period of intense change began again after the end of World War II and the beginning of the American occupation. Foreign goods, esteemed in pre-war days, have reached new heights of prestige. Goods and mechanical devices patterned after American models are abundant and eagerly received (if one has the money).

Receptivity to elements of foreign culture, now almost wholly American-derived, varies with age. The young are the most eagerly and the least critically receptive. Such opposition and antagonism as exists is found principally among the aged, who, while passive toward many Western objects and ideas, do not change their old habits.

Referring to cultural receptivity with regard to all of Japan one is impressed with the eagerness with which the Japanese have in the past and are now accepting foreign things. It is not the intention here to state that foreign objects and ideas which have been accepted retain their original form. The actual circumstances are far from it. Most foreign-derived ideology and many material objects have received adaptations which are distinctly Japanese. The suggestion has been offered that an already long-established tradition of acceptance of things foreign is what has made the Japanese from Meiji times on so eager to receive foreign culture. A ready objection can be found to this "explanation" of Japanese cultural receptivity; it appears to be merely a statement of historical fact rather than an explanation of causes. For many centuries (particularly the period from the sixth to the ninth centuries A.D.) Japan eagerly received elements of Chinese and other Asiatic mainland cultures. Although officially soon repressed, Christianity and other items of Western culture as they came to the Japanese through the Portuguese, Spanish, and Dutch beginning in the sixteenth century, were also well received. Sansom offers a suggestion in this matter:

> "It may not be out of place here to speculate in very general terms why Japanese culture offered less resistance to new ideas than Chinese or Indian culture. The problem is not easy to understand. . . . Perhaps a clue may be found in the fact that Japanese culture, especially in its political features, contained a number of anachronistic and even irrational elements. In so far as it was based upon the assumptions of early Shinto, a primitive theocratic creed, modified by Buddhism and overlaid by feudal thought, it was riddled with contradictions and had not the strength and coherence of such great systems as Confucianism and Hinduism. In fact it might be argued that the Japanese never worked

19. Based upon conversations with Tsuneichi Miyamoto, Japanese social scientist and specialist in the study of Inland Sea communities.

out a satisfactory and stable system of political life, but were always experimenting. This is a view that their disturbed and changeful domestic history tends to confirm; and it is significant that when, under the Tokugawa, they arrived at some degree of stability, it was achieved by disregarding indigenous precedents and calling in the aid of Confucian teaching."[20]

On the *buraku* level, one is also impressed with the ready acceptance of the foreign objects which reach the people.[21] There would no doubt be a great many additional objects of Western inspiration among Takashima people but for one very good reason — the purchasing power of the fisherman is too low to allow it. Foreign ideas, as they come to Takashima, have usually been so filtered in transit that they are often not recognizable to *buraku* people as being of foreign origin.

The "American Way," as it comes to Takashima young people via magazines, newspapers, movies, and a variety of other means, is usually admired and considered fashionable (if sometimes strange), and in cities it is the current rage. Americanism is everywhere in evidence in urban centers in dress and entertainment, where the attitude seems to be that "if it's American it's good." For Japan as a whole, the present is a period similar to what has been called "the period of intoxication"[22] in the 1870's and 1880's, when in the cities of Japan foreign things were in extreme vogue and affectation of foreign ways was carried out to what was later regarded as ridiculous extremes. As also existed during that period, there are unfavorable or antagonistic reactions today. As expressed in the *buraku*, however, they are mild. Some persons feel that the acceptance of things American is far too uncritical and that "bad things" such as night clubs, dance halls, and whiskey find more ready acceptance than unspecified good things. The attitudes toward the new inheritance laws and the franchise for women have already been stated. A few persons state that some young men (but none of the young men of Takashima) think that *minshu-shugi* (democracy) means that all persons are equal and that, consequently, they have no social obligations to anyone. A case at point is the *anchan* (a contraction of *ani*, "elder brother," and the familiar suffix -*chan*), a post-war phenomenon. *Anchan* are found only in larger towns or cities, but everyone is familiar with the term, which is one of opprobrium. *Anchan* are young men from the lower classes with little education and are perhaps roughly comparable with the zoot-suiters of America. An *anchan* is an inconsiderate rough. He uncritically

20. G. B. Sansom, *The Western World and Japan* (New York: Alfred A. Knopf, 1951), p. 314.
21. Shortly after the author's field work on Takashima had begun it became the custom in a number of households to serve coffee (powdered) in Western-style tea cups to the author, his wife, and to household elders. Wearing apparel and other small possessions of the author and his wife were at all times much admired, and received with joy when presented as gifts. Such Western foods (meats, canned fruits, candies and other confections) as were introduced through the author and his wife were usually eagerly accepted and liked, although many persons thought they seemed too rich for a steady diet.
   The author does not mean to imply in the foregoing that these little items are of any consequence, but wishes only to illustrate the willingness with which *buraku* people accepted these small foreign objects and ideas.
22. For a description of this period and of the reactions to it, see G. B. Sansom, *The Western World and Japan* (New York: Alfred A. Knopf, 1951), p. 387 ff.

accepts anything which he thinks to be American. His hallmark is a brightly colored aloha shirt, and he is addicted to permanent waves and the use of strong-smelling pomades and perfumes.

The institution of American-sponsored ideas of such things as education, the public welfare system, the Community Chest, government and law appear to be meekly accepted and, as a whole, approved. They are, however, still new and their effects are as yet hardly discernible in the *buraku*.

The question now arises whether all changes referred to in the foregoing pages are foreign-derived or whether some of them are indigenous developments which would have come about if Japan had gone on its own way, unexposed or little exposed to other cultures of the world. Many of the innovations and changes mentioned herein are clearly the result of contact with the West. Machines and industrialization reached Japan from Europe and America. But would the inventions embodied in these machines and the industrialization of Japan have come about on an indigenous basis? Were it possible that Japan could have gone on completely isolated from the rest of the world — a condition almost impossible to imagine unless the rest of the world were also unmechanized and unindustrialized — the inventions would perhaps eventually have come about anyway. The history of simultaneous and near-simultaneous inventions in the world is impressive. The record of independent inventions in the history of Japanese culture is, however, impressive only because of its minuteness. Kroeber states, "Japan's inventions have been few, and mostly concern manners of doing things rather than strictly original devices. Two exceptions, outright mechanical devices, are gadgetlike rather than fundamental: the folding fan and the revolving theatrical stage."[23] These inventions are hardly of sufficient stature in themselves to do much toward stimulating an industrial revolution. To ponder on the question of how many centuries or millenia it might have taken a Japan, unfertilized by contact with other cultures, alone and unaided, to have reached the state of scientific advance of present-day Japan is useless conjecture.

Leaving such speculations aside, then, what we have before us is that the industrialization and scientific knowledge of Japan are from the West. With industrialization comes a total reliance on money economy, urbanization, and greatly facilitated channels of communication. One thing builds upon and affects the other. Industrial urbanization itself means that an increasing number of people become increasingly exposed to knowledge and ideas which accompany industrialization. Foreign contact in which only material objects and scientific knowledge are passed on or exchanged seems inconceivable, and such is certainly not the

23. A. L. Kroeber, *Anthropology*, rev. ed. (New York: Harcourt, Brace and Co., 1948), p. 745.

case in Japan's history. It is difficult to appraise the extent to which the changes evident in social structure in Japan are linked with Western contact, but they are intimately connected with industrialization and thus with Westernization.

It appears to the author that there is no aspect in the life of the people of Takashima in which Westernization is not evident in some form, either directly or indirectly. The impact of that Westernization varies from a powerful force which has brought about great changes in some matters of living to a relatively pale and weak influence in other aspects. It does not appear that material culture has been more strongly affected than non-material culture. A superficial view of Takashima might easily indicate that items of material culture such as clothing have changed more drastically since Tokugawa times than, let us say, religion (which is certainly not the religion of the West). A closer look, however, will reveal that religion has been profoundly affected.

Religion and clothing are in some respects different universes and difficult if not impossible to compare and equate. There is no convenient yardstick for measuring degree of change in items of different universes for purposes of comparison. The very division of the things which comprise culture into the categories "material" and "non-material" has created something of a false or non-existent problem. It is by no means necessary of course to think of acculturation in terms of material and non-material cultural aspects. These are for some purposes very useful terms. If, however, the objective of anthropological research is an attempt to understand culture as a whole, then thinking of the things which go to make up culture discretely as material and non-material may lead us astray to false problems. The material and the non-material are so intimately connected that it is difficult for many purposes to consider them separately. Suffice it to say here that "non-material" aspects of Takashima culture such as religion and social structure have been profoundly affected by Westernization — this is a matter to be dealt with again later.

Discussion of Westernization leads to the subject of acculturation. The term acculturation is usually defined as an aspect of culture change or as a type of culture change.[24] A great body of acculturation studies have been made, but few generalizations have as yet emerged from them. What has almost invariably emerged has been descriptive history of contact and change.[25] The studies are of interest and of value, but *as acculturation studies* they have contributed little toward gaining an understanding of culture as a whole.

24. A definition presented by a committee of the Social Science Research Council in 1935 states: "Acculturation comprehends those phenomena which result when groups of individuals having different cultures come into continuous first-hand contact, with subsequent changes in the original cultural patterns of either or both groups." A number of objections have been voiced to this definition. See M. J. Herskovits, *Man and His Works* (New York: Alfred A. Knopf, 1949), p. 523 ff.

25. For an account of American acculturation studies and the conclusions they present, see M. J. Herskovits, *op. cit.* See also M. J. Herskovits, *Acculturation* (New York: J. J. Augustin, 1948).

If the objective of an acculturation study is an attempt to arrive at an understanding of the culture process as a whole (as opposed to specific historic problems between the cultures of two peoples), then it seems that the approach must be through the study of culture as a whole.[26] It seems reasonable to state that no important part of the culture of a people can undergo serious change without correlated changes in other spheres of culture. The individual elements which comprise the total culture of a people are so intimately related that one major aspect cannot be strongly affected without other aspects being also affected. A study of the effect of change in one part of culture upon other parts would seem more productive, more revealing of the dynamics of culture than treatment of acculturation as merely a phase or type of culture change. (One here gets into terminological difficulties; such a whole-culture study, by the generally accepted definitions of acculturation, is not a study of acculturation but may perhaps be called a study of culture dynamics.)

In the case of Japan, there have been profound cultural changes within less than a century. Japan's industrial revolution is without doubt one of the most rapid and smashing chains of events in the history of any culture of the world. Profound changes have also come about (and been observed) in the cultures of other peoples. It is in this connection that the data presented in acculturation studies is of potentially great value. Comparative study of the changes and interactions of part against part in these whole cultures seems necessary if one desires an understanding of culture as a whole.

Attempts to analyze the effects of change in one part of culture upon other parts and the order of precedence of change are difficult for one research area alone. This study remains the study of a single small area; large-scale comparative work is beyond its scope. It is interesting to note, however, that in the case of Takashima, religion has undergone a marked change in the past several decades. Had the native Japanese culture evolved of itself with no contact with the West there would undoubtedly have been changes — a totally static condition seems most improbable — but, judging from the history of Japan during the period when it was closed to foreign contact, the changes would probably have been slight. The changes in religion, as well as those in social structure, appear largely due to Western influence. If the thesis is acceptable — and there seems to be a very good deal of evidence in world history in support of it — that with the advance in culture there is a concomitant decline in religious faith and practice (these are the words of Takashima fishermen only slightly altered), then it appears that the changes in Takashima religion are the result of Western influence.

26. See, in this connection, M. J. Herskovits, *Man and His Works*, p. 534 ff., for the argument advanced by various scholars in the matter of the whole-culture approach to acculturation studies.

The ultimate basis for change appears clearly to be technological advance: the inventions, machines, and scientific knowledge of the West. Attendant upon technological advance have come urbanization, money, and machines, and consequent changes in human relations. The human relations are what we commonly label political and social structure, categories which, for the purpose of attempting to arrive at principles of cultural change, appear too broad, loose, or ill-defined for effective utilization as tools in conceptualizing. Within the category of human relations a considerable latitude of form appears compatible with what, for lack of a better expression, may be called bound form in other categories of culture. The political and social structure of industrialized America have hardly been the same as those of industrialized Japan. Technology (in this case let us call it machine technology) may, in other words, be the same and social structure differ. There are indications, such as the tendency toward the formation of larger social units (and this is a world tendency), that technological evolution or advance limits the form of social structure, but the boundaries, the types of form possible are anything but clear.

The case of religion seems much clearer in the respect that it becomes less vital as scientific knowledge (technology) advances. The form of religion which undergoes change (i.e., the types of religion we classify as monotheism, polytheism, pantheism, etc.) seems inconsequential.

The major changes in Japan since the beginning of Meiji seem to this writer the direct or indirect result of Westernization. *From the viewpoint of understanding cultural change or evolution, however, the fact that the changes are largely Western inspired is less important than an analysis of the changes themselves.* The force of change in one cultural aspect upon other aspects, as in the cases of religion and social structure as they apply to Takashima, appears quite as strong as the force of direct contact through objects, devices and scientific knowledge, and even more significant.

The culture of Japan is very old, and for a fairly long period of time Japan shut itself off from contact with the rest of the world. History has shown that old cultures are likely to become "crystallized" in pattern and slow to change without cross-fertilization from other cultures. Such crystallization had occurred in Japan; the basic pattern of living appears to have survived for well over a millenium. Serious change in this pattern came with contact with the West beginning in late Tokugawa and early Meiji times and is continuing at what appears at present to be a greatly accelerated pace. Despite culture crystallization Japan has also had a very long history of successful selective absorption and adaptation of foreign culture from the Asiatic mainland and, in the past eighty or ninety years, from Europe and America (as well as absorbing and adapting a trickle of European culture beginning during the sixteenth century and continuing until the opening of Japan). In most cases absorbed items have received an adaptation which is peculiarly Japanese. It will be of particular interest to observe this process in coming years.

APPENDIX
Glossary

baishakunin: Go-between.

benjo: Toilet.

Bon: Annual Buddhist festival in honor of the spirits of departed ancestors. The local term *Bon-i* is more frequently used on Takashima.

Bon-i: See *Bon.*

buraku: Small face-to-face living community, a subdivision of a village.

Butsudan: Buddhist altar.

chiku: A word usually translated as "area." As used here, the term for the major subdivisions of Kojima City.

Daikoku-bashira: The so-called central pillar of a house, near which the god shelf to Daikoku is placed.

daikon: A type of large white radish, a staple in the diet.

dango: Millet cakes.

furoshiki: Squares of cloth in which small objects are wrapped for convenience in carrying.

geta: A type of wooden footgear.

gochisō: A feast or treat.

hachimaki: Narrow bands of cloth tied about the head.

hanare (beya): A sleeping room separated from the main dwelling.

hatake: Dry farm plots.

hibachi: Movable charcoal brazier, used chiefly for heating.

hotoke: Buddha. In most instances as used herein *hotoke* means the soul of someone who has died (and become a Buddha).

imi: Taboo or abstention.

kado: Yard and/or gateway. In Standard Japanese *kado* means a gate or door, and the word *niwa* conveys the meaning of *kado* as it is customarily used on Takashima.

kaminoma: The best room of a dwelling, sometimes also called by the Standard Japanese term *zashiki.*

kami-sama: Generic term for Shinto deities.

kasōmi: Geomancer.

kegare: Ceremonial pollution.

kitōsha: Professional pray-ers. Embraces seers, mediums, faith-healers.

kōkaidō: Community hall.

kōrenchū: Communal funeral organization composed of one member of each household, which functions at the time of death of someone in the *buraku.*

kōseki: Official records of births, marriages, adoptions, divorces, and deaths.

koyomi: Lunar almanac-calendar.

kumiai: Cooperative association.

matsuri: Festival.

mizuhiki: Colored cords used in wrapping gifts.

mochi: Cakes made of glutenous rice, which is cooked, pounded in a mortar, and shaped into cakes. This term is also often applied to cakes made with other grains; in such instances, it is usually prefixed with the name of the grain, such as *awa-mochi,* "millet cakes."

mura: Village.

nando: One of the rooms of a dwelling, and the room used for childbirth.

naruten: Shrub *(Nandia domesticus Thumbergia)* used in Shinto ritual.

223

naya: An outbuilding.

niwa: Dirt or concrete-floored entrance room of a dwelling. This is the term used in Standard Japanese to mean "yard." See *kado.*

noshi: Strip of abalone wrapped in red and white paper attached to gifts and symbolic of gifts.

o-: Honorific prefix appended before many words.

ōaza: A subdivision of a village. As used herein, a subdivision of Kojima City.

obaa-san: Grandmother.

o-furo: Bath or bathroom.

ojii-san: Grandfather.

on: A moral obligation in the sense of a debt of gratitude.

o-zushi: A miniature shrine.

sake: Rice wine.

-sama: An honorific suffix often translated as Mr., Mrs., or Miss.

sasaki (sakaki): Shrub *(Cleyera japonica)* used in religious ritual.

seinendan: Young people's association.

sekihan: Rice cooked with red beans.

sendairoku: Portable Shinto shrine.

shichigosan: A Shinto talisman.

shikibi: A shrub, the Chinese star anise *(Illicium religiosum),* used in Buddhist ritual.

shōchū: Alcoholic drink, stronger and cheaper than *sake.*

sōdai: Buraku official.

soto-niwa: See *niwa. Niwa* is usually partitioned into a *soto-niwa* and *oku-niwa,* "outer" and "inner" *niwa.*

tatami: Grass floor mats.

tokonoma: A recessed ornamental alcove in the *kaminoma.*

yaban: Uncivilized.

yakudoshi: Unlucky year of life.

yōshi: An adopted husband or an adopted male child.

yuinō: Engagement gift to a bride or to an adopted husband.

Bibliography

Anesaki, Masaharu. *History of Japanese Religion*. London: Kegan Paul, Trench, Trubner & Co., Ltd., 1930.

————————— *The Religious Life of the Japanese People*. Tokyo: Kokusai Bunka Shinkokai, 1938.

Aston, W. G. *Shinto: The Way of the Gods*. London: Longmans, Green & Co., 1905.

Benedict, Ruth. *The Chrysanthemum and the Sword*. Boston: Houghton Mifflin Co., 1946.

Bird, I. L. *Unbeaten Tracks in Japan*. 2 vols. London: John Murray, 1881.

Chamberlain, B. H. *Things Japanese*. London: John Murray, 1898.

Daihyakka Jiten (an encyclopedia). Tokyo: Heibonsha, 1938. (In Japanese.)

Dixon, J. M. "Etiquette in Japan," *Transactions of the Asiatic Society of Japan*, XIII, No. 1 (1935).

Embree, John F. *Suye Mura*. Chicago: The University of Chicago Press, 1939.

Florenz, Karl. "Ancient Japanese Rituals, Part IV," *Transactions of the Asiatic Society of Japan*, XXVII, Part I (1900), 1-112.

Fujisawa, M. "Tanabata, The Star Festival." *Travel in Japan*, IV, No. 2 (1938), 4-9.

Glossary of Japanese Fisheries Terms. Tokyo: General Headquarters, SCAP, Natural Resources Section, Report No. 63, 1946.

Gorer, Geoffrey. "Themes in Japanese Culture," *Transactions of the New York Academy of Science*, X (2d ser., 1943), 106-124.

Herskovits, M. J. *Acculturation*. New York: J. J. Augustin, 1938.

————————— *Man and His Works*. New York: Alfred A. Knopf, Inc., 1948.

Hulse, F. S. "Physical Types Among the Japanese, *"Papers of the Peabody Museum of American Archaeology and Ethnology*, XX, Harvard University (1943), 122-133.

Japanese Fishing Gear. Tokyo: General Headquarters, SCAP, Natural Resources Section, Report No. 71, 1947.

Jones, Thomas Elsa. "Mountain Folk of Japan: A Study in Method." Unpublished Ph.D. dissertation, Columbia University, 1926.

Jōya, Mock. *Japanese Customs and Manners*. Tokyo: The Sakurai Shoten, 1949.

Kaempfer, Engelbert. *History of Japan*. Orig. ed. 2 vols. London: Published for the translator, 1727. New York: Macmillan Co., 1906.

Kagawa-ken Minzoku Chōsa-kai. *Takami, Sanagi-shima Minzoku Chōsa Hōkoku* (Ethnographic Report on Takami and Sanagi Islands). Takamatsu: Kagawa-ken Kyōiku Iinkai, 1950. (In Japanese.)

Katayama, Takashi. *Setonaikai no Densetsu* (Legends of the Inland Sea). Kojima City: Kojima Chūgakkō Shuppanbu, 1949. (In Japanese.)

Kroeber, A. L. *Anthropology*. Rev. ed. New York: Harcourt, Brace and Co., 1948.

Kurata, Ichiro. "Rural Marriage Customs in Japan," *Contemporary Japan*, X, No. 3 (March, 1941).

La Barre, Weston. "Some Observations on Character Structure in the Orient: The Japanese," *Psychiatry*, VIII (1945), 319-342.

Miyamoto, Keitarō. "Gyoson Nenjū Gyōji (The Ceremonial Calendar of a Fishing Village)," *Ryo* (December, 1948), 48-56. (In Japanese.)

Miyamoto, Tsuneichi. *Yakushima Minzokushi* (Ethnography of Yakushima). Tokyo: Attic Museum, 1943. (In Japanese.)

Murdock, George Peter. *Social Structure*. New York: Macmillan Co., 1949.

Nakayama, Taro. "Japanese New Year," *Travel in Japan*, I, No. 4 (1935-36), 30-35.

Nishikiori, Hideo. *Tōgō-mura*. New York: Institute of Pacific Relations, 1945.

Nitobe, Inazo. *Japanese Traits and Foreign Influences*. London: Kegan Paul, Trench & Co., Ltd., 1927.

Norbeck, Edward. "Age-grading in Japan." *American Anthropologist*, Vol. 55, No. 3, 1953, 373-384.

BIBLIOGRAPHY—*(Continued)*

.... *Japanese Folk Music.* New York: Ethnic Folkways Records Co., 1952. LP disc and descriptive account.

.... "Pollution and Taboo in Contemporary Japan." *Southwestern Journal of Anthropology,* VIII, No. 2, 1952, 269-285.

Norman, E. Herbert. *Japan's Emergence as a Modern State.* New York: Institute of Pacific Relations, 1940.

Ōmachi, Tokuzō. *Ceremonial Practices in Japan.* ("Cultural Nippon" Pamphlet Series, XLIII). Tokyo: Nippon Bunka Chuo Renmei, 1942.

Papinot, E. *Historical and Geographical Dictionary of Japan.* Ann Arbor, Michigan: Overbeck Company, 1948. Yokohama: Kelly and Walsh, 1910.

Raper, A. F. *et al. The Japanese Village in Transition.* Tokyo: General Headquarters, SCAP, Natural Resources Section, Report No. 136, 1950.

Redfield, Robert. *The Folk Culture of Yucatan.* Chicago: The University of Chicago Press, 1948.

Rein, J. J. *Japan.* 2 vols. New York: A. C. Armstrong & Son, 1888-89.

Reischauer, Edwin O. *The United States and Japan.* Cambridge: Harvard University Press, 1950.

Sakurada, Katsunori. "Gyoson no Ie ni tsuite (On the Fishing Village Household)," *Minzokugaku Kenkyu,* XII, No. 2 (1947), 41-46. (In Japanese.)

.... "Gyōgyo to Meishin (Fishing and Superstitions)," *Gyoson,* (June, 1948). (In Japanese.)

.... *Gyonin* (Fishermen). Tokyo: Rokuninsha, 1942. (In Japanese.)

Sansom, G. B. *Japan, A Short Cultural History.* Rev. ed. New York: D. Appleton-Century Company, Inc., 1943.

.... *The Western World and Japan.* New York: Alfred A. Knopf, 1951.

Scott, J. W. Robertson. *The Foundations of Japan.* London: John Murray, 1922.

Segawa, Kiyoko. "Dōrei Shūzoku ni tsuite (On Age-class Customs)," *Minzokugaku Kenkyū,* XII, No. 2 (1947), 46-52. (In Japanese.)

Shinmura, Izuru. *Western Influences on Japanese History and Culture in Earlier Periods (1540-1860).* Tokyo: Kokusai Bunka Shinkokai, 1936.

Steinilber-Oberlin, Emile. *The Buddhist Sects of Japan.* Translated by Marc Loge. London: George Allen & Unwin, Ltd., 1938.

White, Leslie A. *The Science of Culture.* New York: Farrar, Straus, 1949.

Yanaga, Chitoshi. *Japan Since Perry.* New York: McGraw-Hill, 1949.

Yanagida, Kunio (ed.). *Kaison Seikatsu no Kenkyū* (A Study of Fishing Village Life). Tokyo: Nihon Minzoku Gakkai, 1949. (In Japanese.)

.... (ed.). *Nihon Minzokugaku Jiten* (Ethnographic Dictionary of Japan). Tokyo: Tōkyodō, 1951. (In Japanese.)

Abandoned customs, 159-60, 213; *see also* Ceremonial calendar
Abortion, 162-63
Acculturation: Chap. VII; receptivity to, 215-16
Acupuncture, 82
Adolescence, 167-74
Adoption: 10, 53-54, 166; adoptive husbands, 10, 53-54, 184-85; *junyōshi*, 53-54
Adultery, 163
Age, distinctions and emphasis on, 51, 54, 77, 98, 108, 115, 155, 187-88
Age-grading, 51, 108
Agriculture: 28-38, 110-11, 197-98; crops, 30-38, 197-98; fertilizing, 34-35, 197; implements, 32, 197-98
Aki-no-matsuri. *see* Festivals, Autumn
Alcoholic drinks, 71-72; *see also Sake, Shōchū,* Beer
Almanac. *see* Calendar, lunar
Amacha, 149
Ama-en, 57
Amaterasu-ō-mikami, 62, 120, 122-23, 143
Ami-moto, 18
Ancestral tablets, 120, 144, 153, 191-93
Anchan, 216-17
Archaeology, 5, 129
Arts and crafts, 67-68
Associations: Farmers' Cooperative, 30, 46, 108, 110-11, 197; Fire Association, 107; Fishermen's Cooperative, 13, 21, 25, 42, 46, 108-10; Freight Boat Operators' Cooperative, 39, 108, 111; Funeral organization, 96, 103-4, 115, 141, 188-94; PTA, 106, 171; Women's Association, 91, 108, 211; Young People's Association, 107-8, 154-56, 211
Baishakunin, 175-77, 182
Barrenness, 52, 133, 187
Baths, 60, 124-25, 137, 166
Beauty, standards of, 74, 78-79, 176
Bedding, 62-63
Beer, 71, 199
Benjo, 60, 61, 124
Benjo-no-kamisama, 124
Birth. *see* Childbirth
Birth rate, 52
Birthdays, 168-69, 186
Boats: fishing, 19-20; 130-31, 197, 208; god of boats, *see* Deities, Funadama-sama; freighters, 41, 174; launching ceremony, 20; maintenance, 20; passenger boats, 2; school boat, 39; *see also Hotoke-bune*
Bon: 39, 71, 89, 91, 101, 120, 151-53, 156, 161, 184; dances, *see* Dances; gifts, 184
Bon-i. see Bon

Bonten, 135
Boys' Festival, 149-50
Brides, 50-51; *see also* Marriage
Buddhism, Chap. V; sects of, 105, 127-28
Budget, 43-47
Bullies, at school, 171
Bunke, 48-49
Buraku: Chap. IV; cooperative activities, 100, 102-4, 144-46, 207-8, 214; deities, 126-29; officials, 96-100; political organization, 96-100; property, 100-2; relations with city, 104-6; relations with outside communities, 8, 112
Burial. *see* Funerals
Butsudan, 62, 119, 120, 138, 152, 192, 193
Calendar: ceremonial, 142-60, 200; Gregorian, 125, 142; lunar, 64, 124-26, 142, 164
Chiku, 95
Childbirth, 165-66, 186
Child training, 168-74
Chinese zodiac, 64
Chō, 95
Chūgakkō. see Schools
Chūgen, 152
Climate, 4-5
Contraception, 163
Cooking, 69-70
Cooperative activities, Chap. IV, 18, 38, 63-67, 85, 98-104, 106-11, 144-46, 154-55, 159, 176-79, 182, 188-94, 207-9
Cosmetics, 78, 118, 155, 178-79, 181
Crises of life, Chap. VI, 140-42, 201
Daidokoro, 58, 70-71
Daikoku-bashira, 64, 124, 134
Daikoku-sama, 64, 123, 156-57, 159
Dairi-sama, 148
Daisan, 133
Dan-age, 192
Dancing: traditional, 88, 91-92, 101, 153, 161, 171, 207; Western, 85-86, 174
Dating, 173
Death, 79, 103, 188-94
Deities: Chap. V; of the sea, 129-32; Amaterasu-ō-mikami, 62, 120, 122-23, 143; Benjo-no-kamisama, 124; Ebisu-sama, 2, 123, 128, 129, 159; Daikoku-sama, 64, 123, 156-57, 159; Funadama-sama, 20-21, 129-31; Gion, 151; Hachiman, 106, 132-33, 144, 156, 157; Hotoke-sama, 119, 120, 148, 150, 152-54, 193; Inari-sama, 124, 132; Jijin-sama, 65; Jizō-sama, 86, 120, 127-28, 191, 192; Kannon, 124, 132, 133, 164; Kinoyama-sama, 133; Kōbō-Daishi, 128, 148, 149; Kōjin-sama, 59, 123, 126-27, 144, 145, 150-51, 154-57, 159, 167; Kompira-

sama, 129, 131; Konjin-sama, 64, 124-26, 178; Mawari-Konjin, 125; O-Daishi-sama, *see* Kōbō-Daishi; O-Dokū-sama, 123, 127, 138; O-Dotsū-sama, 132, 136; O-Fudō-sama, 120, 134; Rokujizō, 128, 137, 192; Seven Gods of Good Fortune, 159; Shiogama-Daimyōjin-sama, 132-33; Suijin-sama, 123; Tenjin-sama, 132-33; Toshigami-sama, 122, 146; Yakujin-sama, 132-33, 157; Yamagami-sama, 129
Devils, 139, 166
Diet, 26, 44-45, 68-73, 199
Disease: 79-83, 103; magico-religious treatment of, 82-83, 120, 127, 129, 134-37, 146, 149, 201, 213; *see also* Chap. V
Divorce, 51-52, 184-85, 210
Dolls, 83, 148-50
Doll Festival, 148
Domestic animals, 40, 49, 139-40
Dowry, 178, 185
Dress: 45, 57, 67, 73-79, 157, 178-79, 199, 201, 218; bridal, 179
Drinking. *see* Beer, *Sake*, *Shōchū*; ceremonial drinking, 182-83
Dwellings: 49, 55-67, 198; construction, 63-67; furnishings, 62, 198-99
Ebisu-sama, 2, 123, 128, 129, 159
Economy, Chap. II, 201-2, 206, 214
Education: 116, 170-73, 200, 214; educational attainments, 116, 171-72
Electricity, 11
Emigration, 174, 209, 214
Engagement. *see* Marriage; gifts, 177-78, 185
English vocabulary, 201-6
Equinoxes, 147,153
Eta, 113-14
Entertainment, 66, 83-92, 106, 173-74; 200; *see also* Games, Dancing, Movies, Festivals, Gambling
Festivals: 50, 127, 173; Autumn, 151, 153-56; *Bon*, see *Bon*; Star, 151; *see also* Ceremonial calendar
Fire Association. *see* Associations
Faith-healing, 83, 120, 134-37
Family, Chap. III
Farming. *see* Agriculture
Fear of darkness, 161
Feasts: 71-72, 87-88; boat launching, 20; decline of, 207; funeral, 192-93; house-building, 63-66; wedding, 179-82; *see also* Ceremonial calendar
Fertilizer, 34-35, 111, 197
Fireballs, 139
Fire-fighting, 99-102, 107
Fish: commercial species, 13; for home consumption, 13

Fishing: 12-28; boats, 19-20; changes in, 197; licenses, 21, 23, 25; size of catches, 25; techniques, 12-28; waters, 21-22
Flowers, 61-62, 139, 191, 192
Flower arranging, 62, 68
Foods. *see* Diet; special foods, *see* Ceremonial calendar
Footgear, 74
Forests, 28-29, 100-1, 104
Fortune-tellers, 139
Fox fire, 139
Foxes, 139; *see also* Deities, Inari-sama
Fujinkai. *see* Associations, Women's Association
Funadama-sama, 20-21, 129-31
Funatade, 20-21
Funeral organization. *see* Associations
Funerals, 50, 77, 85, 119-20, 188-94, 201; see also *Kōrenchū*, Taboos
Furoshiki, 88, 177, 178
Futon, 63, 165
Gaki, 119, 153
Gambling, 51, 86-87, 145
Games, 4, 83-84, 169, 200; *see also* Ceremonial calendar, Dolls, Entertainment
Gantan, 143, 146
Geisha, 53, 87, 89, 92
Genealogy, residents of Takashima, 10-11
Geomancy, 61, 64-65, 136-39, 142
Ghosts, 139-40
Gift(s): 88, 104, 143, 148, 149, 151-52, 154, 157, 169; *Bon*, 184; engagement, 177, 185; exchange, 88, 103, 112, 177, 184; funeral, 192; wedding, 87, 184; see also *Chūgen*, *Seibo*, *Yuinō*, Ceremonial calendar
Gion, 133, 151
Go-between, 115-16, 134, 182-85; see also *Baishakunin*
Gods. *see* Deities
Gogatsu-no-sekku, 149
Gohei, 65
Gyogyō Kyōdō Kumiai. *see* Associations, Fishermen's Cooperative
Hachimaki, 74
Hachiman, 106, 132-33, 144, 156, 157
Hairdress, 78-79, 193; *see also* Permanent waves, Wigs
Hanare, 60
Hari, 82
Hassaku, 153
Headstones, 194
Heating devices, 5, 62-3
Hibachi, 63
Higanbana, 139
Hi-kaeri, 140-42
Himo-otoshi, 157
Hina-zekku, 148

Hinotama, 139
Hi-shite Shōgatsu, 147
History of Takashima, 4, 9
Hito-dama, 139
Hobbies, 86
Holidays, 142-60
Honke, 48-49
Hospitals, 82
Hotoke-bune, 152
Hotoke-sama, 119, 120, 148, 150, 152, 153, 154, 193
House names, 55
Household: Chap. III; composition, 48-51; equipment, *see* Dwellings; extended, 50, 209-10; gods, 62, 122-26, 128; head of, 49-50, 98-99, 173, 187-88; weakening of, 50, 209-10, 214
Hysteria, 162 ·
Ideal personality, 115
Hysteri, 162
Illegitimate children, 161-62
Illiteracy, 50, 116, 200
Imi, 140-42
Inari-sama, 124, 132
Inbreeding, 113, 177
Incomes, 25, 30, 41-47
Individualism, 102, 207-8, 214
Industrialization, 197, 208, 209, 217, 219-20
Infanticide, 136, 163
Inheritance, 28, 48, 49, 185, 210
Inoculations, 82
Inoko, 156-57
Insanity, 80, 176
Insecticides, 35, 197
Insurance policies, 46
Interpersonal relations, 112-18
Inventions, Japanese, 217
Ippontsuri, 16
Jijin-sama, 65
Jimmu, 5
Jizō-sama, 86, 120, 127-28, 191, 192
Jungyoson, 12
Junyōshi, 53

Kado, 58
Kadomatsu, 143
Kadode-no-enkai, 181
Kadobi, 181, 190-91
Kaetsuri, 160
Kamii-san, 179
Kaminoma, 57, 58, 62, 87, 131, 167, 181, 190
Kami-okuri, 155-56
Kami-sama. see Deities
Kannon, 124, 132, 133, 164
Kappa, 151
Kasōmi. see Geomancy
Kegare, 140-42

Kichijitsu, 178
Kichū, 141
Kikiawase, 176
Kiku-zekku, 153
Kinoyama-sama, 133
Kinship terms, 54, 55
Kintarō, 150
Kitchen, 58
Kitchenware, 69
Kitōsha, 120, 134-37
Kitsune-bana, 139
Koaza, 93
Kōbō-Daishi, 128, 148, 149
Kōjin-sama, 59, 123, 126-27, 144, 145, 150-51, 154-57, 167
Kokubetsu-shiki, 191
Kompira, 133, 146
Kompira-sama, 129, 131
Konjin-sama, 64, 124-26, 178
Konro, 19, 69
Kōra, 150
Kōrenchū. See Associations, Funeral organization
Kōseki, 104
Kotatsu, 63
Kōtōgakkō. see Schools
Koyomi. see Calendar, lunar
Ku, 104
Kudo, 58, 69, 71
Kugatsu-no-sekku, 153
Kugi-uke mochi, 192
Kumiai. see Associations
Kyōdai, 54
Labor: division of, 4, 17, 30, 41, 67-68; specialization in, 12-13, 208
Land: cultivated, 28-30; holdings, 29; reform, 30, 210; rental, 29
Laundry, 77-78
Life cycle, Chap. VI
Loans, 41, 46, 110, 111
Luck, breaking ill-luck, 137-39
Lucky and unlucky days: 137-38, 167, 178; years, 166, 185-87; *see also* Calendar, lunar

Magic: Chap. V; exuvial, 165; *see also* Disease, Talismans
Mago-ko-no-Shōgatsu, 194
Male dominance, 47, 49, 51, 53, 65, 66, 98, 163, 175, 188, 210
Mame-maki, 159
Mamori, 186
Matsugo-no-mizu, 190
Marriage: 50, 126, 166, 174-86; changes in customs, 174-75, 201, 211; expenses, 185; love marriages, 175, 201; trial marriage, 184
Maturity, 187-88

Mawari-Konjin, 125
Meals, 69-70
Medications, 81-82
Mediums, 120, 134-37
Memorial services, 119, 126, 188, 193-94,
212; *see also* Ceremonial calendar
Menopause, 187
Menstruation, 140-42, 172; *see also* Taboos
Miai, 176, 177
Midwives, 164, 165, 168, 186, 201
Military service, 173, 211
Mi-ma-nagare, 67
Misaki, 136
Missionaries, 215
Mizuhiki, 177, 178, 192
Mizu-matsuri, 147, 193
Mizutana, 152-53
Momo-zekku, 148
Mompei, 74
Money, attitudes toward, 26, 41, 114-15,
206, 208-9, 214
Money economy, 201, 206-8, 213-14, 217
Mother-in-law, 50, 118, 210
Mourning, 141, 190, 194
Mogusa. *see* Moxa
Moxa, 81-82, 169
Movies, 85, 107, 131, 170, 174, 198, 200
Muneage, 65
Mura, 93

Naishūgen, 184
Naka-e, 58, 62, 182
Nakōdo, 175
Nakōdo-oya, 184
Name changing, 138-39
Names, personal, 9-10, 54-55
Naming ceremony, 167
Nando, 58, 62, 165, 182, 190
Naniwa-bushi, 84-85
Na-tsuke, 167
Naya, 60, 138, 139
Nehan. see *O-nihan*
Nembutsu no kuchiake, 146
Nets, 12-24, 60, 101
New Year's festivities, 142-47
New-rich, 115
Night-crawling, 113
Night watch, at shrine, 144-45, 159
Niwa. see *Oku-niwa, Soto-niwa*
Nōgyō Kyōdō Kumiai. *see* Associations, Agri-
cultural Cooperative
Noshi, 177, 182

Ōaza, 93
O-bake, 132, 139
Obitori-no-hi, 164
Obscenity, 84, 88-89, 188, 200
O-Daishi-sama. *see* Kōbō-Daishi
O-Dokū-sama, 123, 127, 138

O-Dotsū-sama, 132
O-fuda, 131, 133
O-Fudō-sama, 120, 134
O-furo, see Baths
O-higan, 147, 153
O-himatchi, 144-45, 159
O-kankin, 152, 192
O-kazu, 68-69
O-kyū, 81-82
Oku-niwa, 58
Old age, 187-88
On, 103, 143, 152, 208
O-nihan, 147
Orientation of buildings, 57; *see also*
Geomancy
Ornaments, personal, 78-79, 179
O-Shakasama-tanjōbi, 149
O-shio, 160
O-toshitama, 143
Ōtsumogori, 145, 159
O-zushi, 123, 127, 129

Peach Festival, 148
Permanent waves, 78-79, 179, 199, 217
Physical type, 10
Physicians, 82, 83, 104, 112, 162-66, 168
Pilgrimages, 85, 99, 102, 103, 131, 133-34,
148; *see also* Ceremonial calendar
Placenta, 165
Plants used in ritual, 38
Plural births, 165-66
Pollution, ceremonial, 140-42; *see also*
Taboos
Political organization, Chap. IV
Prayer, manner of, 120
Precipitation, 4-5
Pregnancy, 133, 164-65; *see also* Taboos
Priests, 103, 105-6, 120, 134, 146, 152, 190-
94, 212
Prostitutes, 53, 92, 112, 162-63
Proverbs, 50, 115, 126, 144, 150, 151, 162,
166, 167, 184
PTA, 106, 171
Puberty rites, 155
Purification, ceremonial, 137, 140-42, 193;
see also Pollution, Taboos

Quarrels, 50-51, 99, 116-17, 170, 171

Reading matter, 86
Recreation. *see* Entertainment
Religion: Chap. V; changes in, 197, 212-14,
219-20, *see also* Abandoned customs; religious ceremonial: boat launching, 20;
consecrating ground, 64-65; housebuilding, 64-66, 137; ridgepole-raising, 65;
see also Deities, Disease, Funerals, Priests,
Shrines, Taboos, Talismans, Temples
Renai kekkon, 175

Retirement, 60, 77, 188
Rodents, 36, 80
Rokugatsu-hi-shite, 150
Rokujizō, 128, 137, 192
Rōmaji, 170
Rural Japan in pre-Meiji times, 196-97
Sakazuki, 182-83
Sake, 44, 65, 66, 71, 72, 86, 87, 99, 130, 143, 144, 154, 155, 157, 162, 177, 182, 183, 184
Sandōra, 136-37
Sanrimbō, 126
Sansankudo, 183
Sato-gaeri, 183
Savings, 46, 110, 111
Schools: 106, 116, 170-73, 200, 211; curriculum, 171
Seibo, 143, 151
Seinendan. see Associations, Young People's Association
Sekku, 144, 146, 148, 149, 153
Sendairoku, 154-56
Servants, 49
Setchibun, 159
Setsubun, 159
Seven Gods of Good Fortune, 159
Sex: 161-63; adultery, 163; education, 172; mores, 161-63, 199-200; pre-marital intercourse, 161; *see also* Prostitutes
Shi, 95
Shichigosan, 65, 143, 145
Shichikasho, 148
Shimekazari, 146
Shimonoma, 57, 62, 87, 181
Shinsui-shiki, 20
Shinto: Chap. V; sects, 121
Shiogama Daimyōjin-sama, 132-33
Shiwasa-nichi, 149
Shōbōdan, 107
Shōbu, 150
Shōbu-zekku, 149
Shōchū, 44, 71, 72, 86, 87, 99, 144, 154
Shōgakkō. see Schools
Shōjin-gatame, 152
Shrines, 62, 85, 101, 103, 105-6, 121, 126-34, 140, 142-60, 212
Shūbun-no-hi, 153
Shunbun-no-hi, 147
Sickness. *see* Disease
Sibling relations, 51, 168
Social: classes, 113-14, 197, 208-9; sanctions, 116-18, 163, 169-70; status, 12, 67, 112-18, 185, 208-9, Chaps. III, IV; structure, Chaps. III, IV; structure, changes in, 201, 207-11, 218-20
Soko-biki, 113-14
Son, 93

Songs, 88-92, 169, 171
Soto-niwa, 57, 58, 60, 62, 123, 124, 133, 165
Soul house, 194
Specialists, 39-40; *see also* Labor, specialization in
Speech, 10
Spirits: 136, 191, 193; spirit entry, 120, 136, 153
Standard of living, 11, 45
Suijin-sama, 123
Sun Goddess. *see* Amaterasu-ō-mikami
Susa-no-wo-no-mikoto, 127, 133, 151
Suye Mura, 162, 196, 200
Taboos, during pregnancy, 164-65
Taboos, uncleanliness: 119-20, 140-42; changes in, 201, 213; childbirth, 140-42, 165-66; death, 140-42, 190-94; menstrual, 140-42
Tai, 72, 88, 177
Tajō, 168-69
Talismans, 62, 65, 83, 103, 120, 131-34, 164, 186
Tamaya, 194
Tanabata, 151
Tango-no-sekku, 149-50
Tatami, 57, 58, 60, 67, 87, 182
Taxes, 41-43, 104
Temples, 105-6, 121, 133, 142-60
Tenjin-sama, 132-33
Terms of address, 54-55
Theft, 117
Toilet, 60, 61, 124
Toilet training, 168
Tōji, 159
Tokonoma, 62, 87, 120, 134, 135, 143, 150, 152, 182, 190, 192, 193
Tomobiki, 126
Tondo, 145-46
Torii, 127
Toshigami-sama, 122, 146
Trousseau, 178
Tsuizen-kuyo, 193
Tsuno-kakushi, 179
Tsushima, 130, 196
Twins, 165-66
Vaccinations, 82
Vermin, 80
Village, Chap. IV.
Vital statistics, 5-6
Uchi, 49, 55
Umbilicus, 165
Urban-rural contrasts, 195-96
Urbanization, Chaps. I, VII
Waka-mizu, 160
Wealth. *see* Money
Weaning, 168

Weaving, 18, 24, 32, 40, 41, 68
Wedding: ceremony, 181; dress, 76, 181;
    see also Marriage
Weeping, 165, 194
Wells: 61, 100, 101; god of, 123; *Waka-mizu*, 160
Westernization, ix, Chap. VII
Widowers, 12, 185
Widows, 12, 14, 163, 185
Wigs, 78, 179, 183, 201
Winter solstice, 159
Women, position of, 210; *see also* Male dom-
    inance, Social status, Sibling relations
Women's Association. *see* Associations

Yaban, 53, 88, 112, 113
Yagō, 55
Yakudoshi, 185-87; *see also* Lucky and un-
    lucky years
Yakujin-sama, 132-33, 157
Yamagami-sama, 129
Yard, 58, 61-62
Yarebo, 145
Yashiki-dori, 64-65
Yashiro, 127
Yobai, 113
Yobi-ikashi, 193
Yōfuku, 73
Yomogi, 150
Yōshi, 184, 185
Young People's Association. *see* Associa-
    tions
Yuinō, 177-78, 185
Yutampo, 63

Zabuton, 62
Zekku, see *Sekku*

A NOTE ABOUT THE MECHANICAL
MAKE-UP OF THIS BOOK

Takashima has been set up in Baskerville type on the Intertype Fotosetter, and is believed to be the largest hard-cover book printed in this manner by a university press.

The Fotosetter has accomplished a revolution in the graphic arts industry, since this new typesetting machine eliminates the casting of lead slugs, producing, instead, film. It is thus possible to wed directly the Intertype Fotosetter with offset printing (photo-lithography). The reader will note the resultant sharpness and clearness of each type character.

Typesetting for *Takashima* was performed by the Twin Typographers of Salt Lake City. From the negatives, the Sun Lithographing and Printing Company, also of Salt Lake City, has made plates and printed the book on ATF offset presses. Bindery work is that of the Deseret News Press.

The University of Utah Press is proud thus to take its place among the pioneers of the printing industry of tomorrow.

TAKASHIMA URBANIZED

TAKASHIMA URBANIZED

By EDWARD NORBECK

University of Utah Press

Salt Lake City

1978

Table of Contents

I.   INTRODUCTION   241

First Impressions   241

The City of Kurashiki   250

Takashima: Ecologic, Economic, and
Educational Changes   257

Demography   274

II. THE COURSE OF URBAN LIFE:
CHANGES AND ADJUSTMENTS   282

Daily Life   282

Family and Kin   296

The Community and the Outside World   305

Religion   320

Problems of Adjustment   328

III. CONTINUITIES AND DISCONTINUITIES   335

The Social Realm   335

The Future   347

GLOSSARY   349

BIBLIOGRAPHY   352

INDEX   355

List of Illustrations

1. Takashima in Late 1974, with a Wooded Eminence
   in the Background   240

2. View from Takashima over the Landfill to the Former Shore   244

3. The Highway Entering Modern Takashima   244

4. The Shipyard, from the Takashima Hill on a Smoky Day   246

5, 6. The Young Have Grown Tall: A Woman with Her Two Grandsons;
   A Mother and Her Teenage Daughter   248

7, 8. Tourist Haunts in Kurashiki: The Fine Arts Museum and the
   River Walk   251

9. Abandoned Kitchen Gardens and the Remains of the Pine Forest   258

10. The Community's Eldest Resident, Age Ninety-seven   278

11. A Modern Kitchen, Including a Butane Stove and an
    Automatic Rice Steamer   286

12. A Young Couple and Their Children, in Everyday Clothes   289

13. A Household of Four Generations, Now Uncommon.
    14. The Senior Generation: Takashima Women
    and Visiting Friends and Relatives   299

15. The Dying God of Fishermen, His Protective Shrine Destroyed
    and not Repaired   321

16. The Aged Preserve Tradition: A Woman Performs a Home Rite
    Honoring Her Ancestors   321

17. A Retired Man in Traditional Work Clothes,
    Helping To Build a Garage   332

List of Tables

1. Types of Employment, January 1975   264

2. Sex and Age Distribution, January 1975   276

3. Common-Interest Associations in Takashima, 1950–51 and 1975   310

4. Semiassociations in Takashima, 1975   318

1. *Takashima in late 1974, with a wooded eminence in the background.*

CHAPTER I

Introduction

FIRST IMPRESSIONS

Takashima had remained sharply etched in my memory for over twenty years as a picturesque hamlet nestled on a beautiful island in a tranquil sea, a place of quiet, peace, and unhurried country life. The houses, miniature farm plots, and the pine forest on the island were arranged as if composed by an artist, and in the distance similar islands stretched off to the horizon. Here and there the surface of the sea was dotted with small watercraft, principally fishing boats, and these too looked calm, unhurried, and as if they were a proper part of the composition of serenity and beauty.

I had maintained contact with the people of Takashima during the twenty-three years since I left the community after studying it for eleven months, and I had later made two brief visits to the hamlet, the last ten years earlier. No great changes were evident at the times of these calls, but I knew from correspondence with Takashima people and Japanese scholars that drastic changes had later occurred, that Takashima was no longer an island, and that the hamlet of Takashima was now part of the heavily industrialized city of Kurashiki.

My feelings were regret. I wanted the past to continue, even though I knew that for most of the people of Takashima it had meant terrible poverty and attendant suffering. From letters, photographs, and published writings, I knew also that industrialization had ruined the beauty of Takashima and its setting. But I was not prepared for actuality, which seemed to me an act of heedless aesthetic atrocity.

After making arrangements with Takashima people by letter and telephone for my first visit in late June 1974, I traveled to the community by car from central Kurashiki, where I had just found living quarters. Following a heavily traveled main highway of the city, I missed the mark on my first attempt. Takashima and its surroundings had changed so greatly that, failing to recognize them, I drove about a mile past the community. Stopping in hilly, unoccupied terrain that I recognized as lying beyond Takashima, I asked about the proper route at a roadside shop. When I reached the exit to the side road that my instructions stated now led to Takashima, I stopped the car to verify the route by eye.

The vista was appalling. Before me stretched a maze of industrial plants, all gray and looking grimly functional. A haze of smoke filled the air and extended to the horizon in all directions, behind me to the tops of the hills of the Kojima Peninsula and before me far past Takashima over the waters of the Inland Sea. Only the nearest of Takashima's neighboring islands were visible, dimly, in the haze. After some moments of inspection, I recognized Takashima as a hilly eminence rising from a sea of industrial plants where once a genuine sea had existed. The large pine trees had disappeared, altering the outline of the former island, and the small pines that remained stood in ragged, small patches or in isolation amidst low vegetation, the red-brown needles of many of the trees announcing sickness or coming death. A long procession of large tankers and freighters was visible in the sea at both ends of Takashima, sailing in nearly single file in opposing directions in what I later learned was the deep-draft channel to Mizushima harbor, the new industrial port of Kurashiki about a mile from Takashima. In the road by which I had stopped to inspect the scene, twin streams of cars, trucks, buses, motorcycles, and a few bicycles similarly proceeded in opposing directions. Behind Takashima, a volume of dense smoke drifted into the air, issuing from the waste stacks of a steel mill covering hundreds of acres of a fill projecting into the sea to form a miniature peninsula. Everywhere were signs of industry, in both senses of the word, and everywhere the panorama gave the dismal feeling that important things had been lost. Nothing seemed the same.

Reflecting that most of the world had also changed greatly in the past two decades, I knew that I must be prepared for equally great changes in other matters, things that the eye could not so easily note or even note at all. My investigations in the ensuing months did indeed reveal such changes, but they also brought to light many survivals or continuities, matters in which fundamental attitudes, values, and behavior continued as before, often altered in outward form or visible practice so that the old was sometimes not quickly recognizable.

A chronicle of the changes might appropriately begin with a more complete account of the way in which the visitor reaches modern Takashima and what one sees upon first entering the community. In its new status as part of a city dependent upon efficiently operated industries, the community must be easy to reach. Today one travels there by means of the kinds of transport characteristic of industrialized communities of affluent nations. The most common way to reach Takashima, which lies a dozen miles from the center of the city, is by private car. Another means of travel is an elaborate system of municipal buses, equipped with cooling and heating facilities, that pass the Takashima station at intervals of about fifteen minutes during the working day and early evening. Because Takashima has a small population and lies to one side of the main line of municipal travel, bus passengers bound for the community must walk about one-fourth mile from the Takashima bus stop. Most of the people of Takashima travel by private car. A few people, generally young, use motorbikes. Bicycles are ordinarily used only to travel short distances.

The route of travel from the bus stop to the community is technologically one of the finest stretches of public road in the city, a smooth four-lane highway divided by a traffic island bearing plantings of unhealthy young camphor trees, a species said to be resistant to the effects of polluted air. On both sides of the highway are additional alignments of small camphor trees, many of which, like those in the traffic island, are sick or dead. Paralleling the road on both sides and extending into the distance is a maze of industrial plants and parking lots for the automobiles of their employees. Chemical plants of various kinds are the most common among the establishments aligned beside the highway, but many other kinds of industries are also represented in more distant locations stretching beyond the limits of vision.

The entrance to Takashima is now marked on the left by an impressive municipal fire station, housing two new fire trucks which the firefighters maintain in spotless condition, and on the right by the many facilities of a shipbuilding plant. A few restaurants and restaurant-inns, small, flimsy structures operated by Takashima residents, flank the narrow main road along the former shore.

On the slopes immediately above the entrance are three large ferroconcrete buildings of modern, functional architectural style, boxlike structures that serve as the administrative offices of the shipbuilding concern and its affiliated smaller firms and as a hostelry for quartering crew members of ships arriving at the yard for repairs. Atop the hill stands a tall, new lighthouse, erected in late 1974, which warns ships of the presence of land and serves as a station to record the passage of all ships in the busy Mizushima ship channel lying just offshore.

All that first strikes the eye looks uncharmingly businesslike, a scene that has many counterparts elsewhere in Japan and shows no characteristics that are obviously Japanese except the script in the signs identifying the names of the industrial firms. The largest of these signs bears the

2. *View from Takashima over the landfill to the former shore.*

3. *The highway entering modern Takashima.*

name of the shipbuilding firm, Sanoyasu, which appears in Roman letters rather than in Japanese script. Painted in large, bright red letters on the towering steel goliath or derrick-crane frame of the shipyard, the sign stands high in the air and is legible from a distance of a mile or more on days when the pall of industrial smoke is not dense. Since Sanoyasu now owns part of Takashima and its yard extends immediately from one end of the former island, more than anything else the prominent sign has come to identify the community.

As one proceeds into the residential community, the scene changes to become unmistakably Japanese. The dwellings and their grounds and outbuildings are distinctively so. Nearly all the old houses of 1950–51 remain in use and various similar dwellings have since been erected. Some of the old houses have been renovated and the new dwellings are "modern," but modernization consists principally of changes to beautify and make more convenient the entrance rooms, kitchens, dining facilities, and baths, changes that are invisible from the exteriors of the houses, and the newer dwellings resemble the old in general architectural style. All except one of the few thatched roofs still existing in 1951 have disappeared. Difficult and expensive to maintain and considered a fire hazard, they have been succeeded by roofs of ceramic tile, the older roofs gray and the new sometimes of brilliant blue.

The most noticeable changes are reflections of economic prosperity — the presence near the houses of parked cars, many of which are unsheltered for lack of space to build carports or garages, and an appearance of sprightliness from plantings of shrubs and garden flowers that few people could formerly afford. In the summer and fall of 1974, many entranceways to houses blazed with the multiple colors of well-tended chrysanthemums and other flowers. Dogs and cats are more abundant and are obviously better fed than in former times. The arrangements of the closely spaced houses and outbuildings continue to be haphazard, and passage to nearly all dwellings continues to be by means of narrow paths. The tiny hamlet meeting hall remains in unaltered shabbiness, as does the shrine on the hill to Kojima, the tutelary god of the community. The communal cemetery appears scarcely larger than formerly and otherwise unchanged.

A stroll away from the settlement into the kitchen gardens, into the pine forest, and along the remaining shore of the former island reveals many changes. Vegetable plots lying near the dwellings are well cultivated, but most of the more distant plots are no longer used and, in accord with the length of time since they were last cultivated, vary from being plots of wild grasses to jungles of wild vines and shrubs. A familiar odor, less powerful and prevalent than in former times, announces that

4. *The shipyard, from the Takashima hill on a smoky day.*

night soil is still used as a fertilizer by at least some households. The pine forest of former times is also a jungle of vines and shrubs, among which a few young pines survive poorly, often with withered, rust-colored needles, and the skeletons of large pines protrude starkly, denuded of bark. Once maintained like a well-kept park by the daily activities of scouring the ground for fallen branches, twigs, and needles to be used as fuel in heating and cooking, the old forest is now impassable by foot and dangerous because of the presence of poison sumac and thorny shrubs.

The remaining shoreline has become similarly altered. The once clear water is murky and full of floating and sunken debris, and the shore is littered. Because the landfill on the mainland side of the island rendered the old Takashima pier useless, the prefecture had constructed on the remaining shore a small concrete harbor for Takashima boats. Well-maintained by the prefecture, it now shelters a few small, decaying boats, little used today and never used for commercial fishing. Unless the sea is freed of pollutants so that it becomes suitable for pleasure craft, the value and future of the harbor seem questionable. The Mizushima ship channel, several hundred yards from the remaining shore, is full of ships and other watercraft day and night.

My first impression of the people of Takashima in 1974 was that time had stood still. They at least seemed as before. To be sure, all whom I knew had gotten visibly older and there were additional children and brides in the community. But the many old friends and acquaintances whom I met were easily recognizable and seemed to have borne the passage of time well and in good health. Better clothed and seemingly better nourished than formerly, they appeared otherwise to be little changed.

Once my eyes turned from the adults, whom I knew, to the children, all of whom were strangers to me, another change was obvious. Teenagers often towered above their parents, and the children in general were larger and more robust than those of a generation earlier. Bodily proportions had also changed toward relatively longer and often slimmer legs. These changes are national trends of the years after World War II, reflecting improved conditions of nutrition and, in the change of the ratio between lengths of legs and torsos, a change in custom that has only indirect relation to nutrition. Japanese researchers on bodily growth have for many years explained the change in bodily proportions as a result of a great decline in the custom of sitting on the floor with folded legs, a practice that is held to inhibit growth of the legs by restricting circulation of the blood to them. This interpretation was accepted by the Japanese public years ago, and it is common for young women to be reluctant or unwilling to sit in the traditional posture.

5, 6. *The young have grown tall: a woman with her two grandsons;
a mother and her teenage daughter.*

Inevitably, my first conversations with old Takashima friends at this time included remarks about the changes that had occurred since I had first studied the community and, on my part, regretful statements about the loss of the natural beauty of the surroundings, remarks which, in Japanese fashion, I expressed obliquely. This opinion met with polite concurrence, but the expressions of regret were tempered. It was soon clear that the people felt little dissatisfaction with their present conditions of life. Rather, they saw changed times as bringing mostly good things. Almost no one wanted to return to conditions of the past. Some people were scarcely conscious of the ugliness of their present surroundings, and others thought that some loss of what is desirable was inevitable if regrettable.

Later investigations, more systematically conducted and derived from a combination of interviews, observations, and documents, generally verified my first impressions, and they allowed me to understand the prevailing view of Takashima people that today, and probably tomorrow, are infinitely preferable to the past. Later investigations also allowed me to form ideas of the factors involved in easing the change to urban life, a transition that came about swiftly and with little obvious social disturbance. To understand the process of transition, knowledge is required about many circumstances, including economic, ecologic, and demographic conditions, matters that are discussed in the following pages of this study.

In 1951, Takashima had for three years officially been a part of the small city of Kojima, with a population at that time of about 80,000 people. But the center of the city was over the hills and far away, several miles from Takashima, and the city was an aggregate of administrative convenience composed principally of dispersed small communities separated from each other by farmland or hills and united by no convenient system of transportation. As described in my original study, life on Takashima was accordingly rural, although it was not a life of detachment from the main lines of change of the Japanese nation. What happened elsewhere in the country was at least known to the residents of Takashima, by means of newspapers and ubiquitous radios, and all political and economic matters important to the nation as a whole were in some way shared.

The great industrial growth of Japan was quickly felt on Takashima, even though most of its wage earners continued to support their families and themselves by fishing and to live essentially rural lives. Technological developments in Japan notably extended to techniques of fishing, and the innovations that were locally applicable quickly reached Takashima by means of the national network of fishermen's cooperative associations.

Fishing became more efficient, and, as the economic development of the nation progressed, the price of fish rose. By the 1960s, Takashima fishermen regarded themselves as being financially favored as compared with their former circumstances. This development, added to their lack of training in other occupations and the knowledge that their low levels of formal education made opportunities for other employment very poor, fostered continuation of work as fishermen. Although most men worried about the long-range economic future, today and tomorrow seemed to them financially secure enough. Only a few men, generally young and equipped with the advantage of high school educations, sought other employment, beginning in the early 1960s. This was usually in nearby Kurashiki and sometimes in Osaka, about 150 miles away. No one traveled far.

The abandonment of fishing and the adoption of industrial employment was late and generally involuntary, a shift that for most men and women took place in the 1970s, principally within a period of two years. A combination of economic, political, and ecologic changes, national and local, then forced the change to urban life. Fishing was no longer possible and the growing industrialization of the region had put an end to rural life. These changes offered no sensible course of action except to adjust as best one could.

THE CITY OF KURASHIKI

One important development that affected Takashima represents a continuation of a national trend since the late nineteenth century toward forming ever-larger communities by amalgamation, a tendency that only recently has declined as cities grew to be so huge, sprawling, and congested that they became difficult places in which to live and conduct commercial and industrial enterprises. In 1951, the city of Kurashiki was known to the nation principally as a quaint, old city of some regional importance since feudal times and as a small "cultural" center known for its pottery and other folk crafts and three small museums specializing in archaeology, folk art, and a fine collection of oil paintings by French impressionists and other famed European artists. Before the 1960s, large industry in Kurashiki consisted principally of the production of textiles, which provided the wealth for the establishment of the museums.

Better favored than neighboring Kojima in its location and the amount of land potentially available for industrial and other urban uses, Kurashiki began to expand greatly in the 1950s, and by 1970 its Mizushima area had become the fifth largest industrial complex in the nation. With the encouragement and aid of the national government, a large

7, 8. *Tourist haunts in Kurashiki: the fine arts museum and the river walk.*

area of seaside swamp and adjacent shallow sea was reclaimed by drain-ing and filling to serve as the site for the new industries of Mizushima; a deep ship channel was dredged in the shallow Inland Sea; the port of Mizushima was constructed as the terminus of the channel, and munici-pal leaders energetically encouraged large industrial concerns of the nation to establish manufacturing plants on the reclaimed land.

The filling of the sea between Takashima and the mainland, a project which took several years, was a part of the program of reclama-tion, and Takashima lies within and near the northern boundary of Mizushima. On the reclaimed land south of Takashima, the earliest to be ready for occupancy, construction of industrial plants began in the 1960s.

As a part of the program of development, the city of Kurashiki con-tinued at an accelerated pace to annex villages and towns. The largest addition took place in 1967, when the entire city of Kojima, including the community of Takashima, was annexed. Modern Kurashiki repre-sents the amalgamation during the past century of nearly 200 once inde-pendent communities, principally villages and small towns. In 1975, the city covered an area of about 300 square kilometers, had a population of about 400,000 people, and showed all signs of continuing to grow in population if not in area of land.

Like other recently developed or expanded industrial cities of Japan, much of modern Kurashiki appears to be rural. Parts of former rice fields have become the sites of private houses, apartments, and large company *danchi*, the apartments and dormitories maintained by indus-trial firms to provide residences for their employees. Office buildings and the buildings of many other kinds of urban enterprises and facilities also stand on former agricultural lands. Spacing of buildings is uneven so that high rise apartments might lie near hospitals or other large build-ings but be separated from them by some acres of cultivated rice lands sprinkled with old farmhouses and new dwellings. Company *danchi* often lie nestled against unoccupied, forested low hills that are unsuited for construction of buildings except at great expense, and these expanses of green vegetation contribute to the rural atmosphere.

New industry is concentrated in Mizushima, a vast conglomerate of oil refineries, chemical and petrochemical plants, cement factories, an automobile factory, one of the largest steel plants in the world and many small firms producing iron and steel products, the Sanoyasu shipbuilding yard, and various other kinds of industrial establishments including firms producing machinery, auto parts, and food. Many older firms that pro-duce textiles and clothing lie within the boundaries of the former city of Kojima and in old Kurashiki.

A network of modern and heavily used highways unites the parts of the sprawling city, and its main arteries are the scenes of traffic jams during the morning and evening rush hours. An expensively constructed highway passing in the unoccupied, scenic hills of the narrow Kojima Peninsula is principally a show piece and tourist attraction that affords a view of the Inland Sea. Officially named by the English term "Skyline Drive," this highway is sometimes jocularly called *Kusai* Line, "Foul-Smelling Line," because of pollutants from Mizushima that are visible everywhere from the road and sometimes detectable by smell.

A major national railroad line serves Kurashiki and connects with the superexpress line in Okayama City, a few miles away. Public transportation within Kurashiki is chiefly by municipal buses. Together with its neighboring city of Okayama, which had a population in 1975 of about 500,000 people, and various small peripheral communities, Kurashiki lies in a commercially thriving area with about one million residents.

Like various other cities of Japan, Kurashiki has not converted entirely to modern industry. A serious attempt has been made to preserve some of the old and the aesthetically pleasing. In part as a conscious result of these efforts, one of Kurashiki's modern economic enterprises is tourism. Daily the trains bring to the city hundreds of tourists, principally Japanese but including a growing number of foreigners, attracted by the picturesque architecture of dwellings erected in feudal times in the heart of old Kurashiki, by the museums, and by the products of folk artists, who are not simple country bumpkins but well-trained professional artists and artisans specializing in the branch of aesthetics that Japanese call folk art. Pottery is the most noted product, and the famous Bizen ware produced near Kurashiki may cost staggering sums. A subtle combination of sophistication and calculated crudeness, Bizen pottery runs the range from folk art to high art. The scenic beauty of the Inland Sea, now marred by industry but still beautiful as viewed from the finger of hills of the Kojima Peninsula, is an added attraction. Well-maintained and popular tourist facilities are available there on the side of the peninsula away from the sight of Mizushima, and streams of tourists gaze at the sea from a park constructed atop the scenically famous hill called *Washūzan*, "Eagle Mountain."

In the process of its rapid growth, Kurashiki drew about one-third of its residents from parts of the nation other than its home prefecture of Okayama. Skilled technicians and specialists necessary for industry and commerce came from Osaka, Tokyo, and other large cities with elaborate training centers. Skilled and unskilled laborers were drawn from many parts of the nation, wherever circumstances made them available.

Incorporation of the newcomers caused no serious social disturbances beyond a temporary increase in the rate of minor crimes during the peak of construction of the industrial plants of Mizushima, when many laborers from other cities were in Kurashiki temporarily.

One minority group of the city consists of about 3,000 members of the outcast group called *burakumin* (in unabbreviated form, *tokushu burakumin*, "people of the special hamlets"). This term is one of the many euphemisms for *eta*, an opprobrious word that has seldom been used in Japan for some decades but which survives in scholarly writings in English. As in the past, most *burakumin* live in certain areas of the city and thus continue to be socially segregated. A smaller number of Koreans form a second minority group, most of whom live in one part of the city. Despite the enactment of national legislation similar to the statutes known in the United States by the name Equal Opportunity, both minority groups appear to suffer from continued discrimination; they have less education, poorer employment, smaller incomes, poorer health, and higher rates of crime than exist among members of the majority group. But the number of these minority group members is small, and they do not represent a serious social problem in the city as a whole. Most majority group members have no witting contact with *burakumin*, who are indistinguishable physically from other Japanese, and few people have or wish to have contact with the Koreans. Only a double handful of Europeans and Americans are long-time or permanent residents of Kurashiki.

Lying near the periphery of Mizushima and in the area which was the last to be reclaimed, Takashima was drawn into urban life later than most parts of the city of Kurashiki. The reclaimed land adjoining Kurashiki, which consists of sand and gravelly material dredged from the sea in the process of constructing the ship channel and which lacks humus or organic matter suitable for the growth of plants, was ready for occupancy in the late 1960s. The first industrial plant in this newly reclaimed area near Takashima was erected in 1969, and, by late 1973, eight additional plants had been erected in this northern extension of the area of reclaimed land, making a solid assembly of hundreds of industrial plants extending along the seashore for several miles to the south of Takashima and about a half-mile to the north.

Unplanned, but frightening, changes were happening during this interval to the entire city, and these strongly affected Takashima and its neighboring hamlets of fishermen. Like other industrial cities of the nation, Kurashiki had not foreseen the devastating effects of the growth of industry upon the physical environment.

The first ominous indications appeared in the mid 1960s in an area of the sea some miles from Takashima. Fishermen's nets then drew in live, but foul-smelling, fish, a term that came to be rendered in Japanese by a single word, *ishūgyo*. Their strange condition was attributed to industrial wastes of one kind or another. In the next few years, reports of such catches became increasingly common, and the afflicted area drew nearer to Takashima and to the waters in which Takashima residents had fishing rights. Catches dwindled in size for Takashima fishermen, a circumstance that seemed only partly attributable to intensive fishing with improved equipment and techniques, and the catches sometimes included fish with strangely malformed spines. Accounts through national news media of environmental pollution in other cities had by this time become abundant. Reports of such events in certain cities where environmental pollution was particularly bad, such as Minamata, Kyushu, and Kawasaki, near Tokyo, informed everyone in the nation of the evils of industrial effluents, and the names of these cities became synonymous with pollution. A disease caused by mercury became known as the "Minamata disease," and a similarly serious ailment, a pathological condition of the bones popularly called the "ouch-ouch disease," *itai-itai-byō*, became identified as the result of absorption by the human body of cadmium. Translating an English expression, the Japanese news media called the badly afflicted victims of these ailments "human vegetables," a term which quickly became current among the general population.

By the late 1960s, environmental pollution, particularly that caused by industrial wastes, rose forcibly to national consciousness as constituting a crisis. Remedial action became a national cause espoused by fishing and farming cooperatives, civic groups, and political leaders. The term *kōgai*, literally "public damage," came into general use to mean damage, suffering, or injury to the inanimate physical environment and to living things, including human beings, as a result of environmental pollution. Dependent upon context, in modern usage this term now often means environmental pollution without specific reference to the harm it causes. Much news coverage was devoted to the striking cases of injury to human beings, such as the victims of the Minamata disease, and legislation intended to control the harmful activities of industrial concerns soon followed. Throughout the nation, invalids whose ailments were judged to be the result of *kōgai* became known as "official invalids," *nintei kanja*, the cost of their medical care to be borne by the government.

Later in becoming heavily industrialized and less seriously afflicted than various other cities in at least the extent of damage in the form of sickness among its citizens, Kurashiki and its environs did not become nationally known as one of the country's critical areas. The damage was nevertheless severe and readily visible. As in other affected regions, the citizens clamored for remedial action, and civic administrators took up the cause. One course of action was the encouragement of local news media to give reports of damage caused by industrial wastes; these reports reached their height in the early 1970s. Ensuing legislation included statutes controlling the height of smokestacks, imposing penalties for improper disposal of harmful wastes, and providing that compensatory payments be made for damages incurred by industrial activities.

Despite the short period of time that Kurashiki had been heavily industrialized, these remedial steps were too small and came too late to bring a return to the conditions of the past. By 1973, an area of many miles of the adjacent sea was contaminated beyond any hope of a quick recovery, and fishing in these waters was entirely abandoned. As the result of publicity concerning pollution of the area, many people had before this time become reluctant or unwilling to consume fish from local waters. The air above Mizushima was heavy with sulphurous smoke that spread in varying density to all other areas of the city, affecting the vegetation on even the most remote hills of Kojima Peninsula, the scenic backwoods of the city. Most striking was the effect upon the pine trees that had formerly grown luxuriantly everywhere on the many low hills in the city. Dead and dying pines were visible everywhere. The ultimate cause of their death was clearly insects, and even the fairly distant, uninhabited mountainous regions of the prefecture, where the air seemed free of pollutants, suffered the loss of some pine trees. But the loss in Kurashiki was much more severe and was usually interpreted as resulting from sulphur in the air. Weakened by the fumes, the pines are said to succumb easily to the attacks of beetles.

The year 1973 appeared to represent the height of pollution in Kurashiki. In 1974, the air seemed less dense with smoke and seldom noticeably bad in odor, and the intentional dumping of industrial wastes appeared to have stopped. Attitudes among both civic officials and other citizens toward publicizing the conditions of *kōgai* changed drastically, principally on economic grounds. Everyone agreed that a national reputation of being a troubled spot, a center of *kōgai*, was harmful to the future development of the city. Helpful action should henceforth certainly be taken, but it should be done quietly. In any case, the conditions of pollution appeared to have improved, and most people thought optimistically that improvement would continue. An event occurring in mid December of 1974, which received international publicity, gave no support to this optimism. An accidental, but giant, spill of crude petroleum from storage tanks of the Mitsubishi Corporation refinery in Mizushima severely damaged a large area of the Inland Sea and led to compensatory payments by the corporation to fishermen; in January 1975, these payments were reported to have reached 1 million dollars. A smaller spill occurred a few weeks later, in early 1975. In late January 1975, the waters on the shores of Takashima, which lies about one-fourth mile from the site of the oil spills, were reported still to be black from the floating oil.

TAKASHIMA: ECOLOGIC, ECONOMIC, AND EDUCATIONAL CHANGES

Lying within the Mizushima industrial area and on the sea, Takashima suffered heavily from pollution of both air and water. Serious worry about the future began in about 1965, before the industrial area had grown to include the community. By 1969, conditions of the air and sea around Takashima had become noticeably bad, and they continued to worsen in the succeeding few years. By the early 1970s, the returns from fishing had become poor and the air was often rank from the fumes emitted by the nearby steel plant. Increased incomes had already led to the abandonment of some of the vegetable plots, and the changed air and light now led to the abandonment of additional areas.

Nothing seemed to grow properly and some plants simply died. In most places in the community, bamboo would not grow at all; tangerines produced thick, warty skins; plums, peaches, and watermelon plants would not set fruit; many other plants appeared so sickly that people were reluctant to eat them. The pine trees began to die, and other noxious plants sprang up in the forest and in the abandoned kitchen gardens. Only undesirable vegetation seemed to flourish. Poison sumac, formerly a rare plant on Takashima, suddenly appeared in abundance and it was joined by a rank growth of *kuzu* vines, a troublesome weed, and a new plant which no one could identify by name. A sizeable shrub bearing many painfully sharp thorns, this unfamiliar plant was an appropriate companion for the sumac, and some people referred to it with rueful humor as "part of the *kōgai*." [1]

Ecologic change was not limited to the effects of harmful industrial effluents. Filling the sea to join Takashima with the mainland brought an unexpected change in climate, making the island noticeably cooler in the winter and spring so that the date of maturation of vegetables and fruit came one to two weeks later than in former times.

---

[1] This plant was identified by a trained agronomist at Okayama University as the species *Aralia elata seen*, a plant which he described as being fairly common in various other regions of Japan.

9. *Abandoned kitchen gardens and the remains of the pine forest.*

On the shore, in the sea, and in the air above Takashima, similar events occurred. The several species of clams in the beach sand and gravel disappeared, presumably by death, as did the edible crabs. In any case, no one would now care to eat shellfish from such contaminated water. Offshore fish became scarce, and even the thought was abandoned of catching goby and octopi from the beach for domestic consumption. Now and then, small fish with weirdly curved spines were visible in the water and the sight of them made some people shudder. Most of the birds disappeared, leaving only a diminished number of hardy doves, sparrows, and crows. Even the kites, the fierce predators that had once been the scourge of the community's kittens and small puppies, fled to more hospitable regions.

Pollution of the air brought one small compensation, the disappearance of the large and formerly abundant mosquitoes which announced their presence by making the sound "bun bun," and a reduction in the number of mosquitoes of another species, small and silent, which formerly had also been common. The number of cicadas was also thought to have shrunk, and this was looked upon as a misfortune. For centuries, cicadas have been regarded with affection in Japan, and they have often been the subjects of literary allusion. Catching cicadas and keeping them in cages is an ancient practice of children, often aided by adults. The thirteen species of Japanese cicadas bear well-known, popular names, and some people take pride in identifying them by the sounds they make. Listening to the songs of cicadas as one species succeeds another from summer to fall is a traditional Japanese pleasure.

For a time, human health appeared to be impaired by the environmental pollution. The air was foul and some people complained of respiratory problems. Whether or not polluted air was the cause was uncertain, but a number of men and women felt ill enough to seek medical aid and the judgments of designated physicians as to whether or not they were official invalids because of air pollution. Commercial fishing was dwindling to a stop.

Crisis seemed imminent, and the people of Takashima responded by joint action conducted through the fishermen's cooperative and a newly formed voluntary association with aims of meeting the problems of environmental pollution. Separately, and together with similar groups from other communities, representatives of these associations talked with city officials and with directors of industrial plants; they were given courteous hearings everywhere. Alarmed by the mounting evidence of serious pollution, the city officials attempted to investigate conditions in all parts of Kurashiki. Takashima and two other communities, all once independent hamlets or villages, were judged to be especially afflicted.

In 1972, the city sponsored a sociological survey of these communities conducted under the leadership of two sociologists from Tokyo. This investigation reported what was already well known, that pollution was indeed severe, that the residents of the communities were serious worried about prospects for the future, that the means of livelihood of many people was endangered, and that the health of everyone appeared to be in peril. Physical examinations were conducted without charge on a voluntary basis, and a few people were designated as official invalids, troubled principally with respiratory ailments called asthma.

For a time, relocation at government expense of the people of all three communities was considered. This proposal was met with interest by some Takashima people, until it seemed apparent that the governmental contribution to relocation was ungenerous and would result in less desirable housing than that they would leave behind. In the meantime, statutes governing the emission of industrial wastes had been enacted and environmental conditions seemed to improve somewhat. The turning point was late 1973 and early 1974. The air was generally smoky at Takashima in 1974, but less so than formerly, and the bad odors of previous years had disappeared. In 1974, the kitchen gardens seemed generally healthy. Many fine watermelons were produced; the tangerines bore good fruit; one sizeable clump of bamboo appeared to be growing well; and garden flowers grew vigorously. By mid summer 1974, the kites had returned; the ragged outlines of their outspread wings as they glided against the background of the sky once again became a familiar sight. In the summer and fall, the cicadas sang lustily. Hope for the future also came from occasional articles in the local newspapers about the survival or return of species of flora and fauna, such as the reported return in 1974 of helmet crabs to an island in nearby Kojima Bay from which they had disappeared many years earlier.

In 1974, the municipal administration judged that only the community of Matsue, lying in the heart of the Mizushima area three or four miles from Takashima, was damaged beyond any hope of recovery. All its residents were to be moved elsewhere in 1975. For residents of the other two communities, relocation became optional. No Takashima residents chose to move.

Governmental action came too late to save the sea. In the late 1960s and early 1970s, several instances of damage to fishing from industrial effluents occurred, and the local fishermen's association was aggressively successful in seeking financial compensation. A small payment was made for the loss of Takashima fishing waters as a result of the landfill, and later payments, all relatively small, were made as severe instances of pollution from industrial wastes occurred. In 1973, the fishing waters of

Takashima and neighboring communities were judged to be irredeemably polluted, and commercial fishing in them stopped completely. The fishermen's cooperative then waged its last and most successful campaign for compensation. In early 1974, each full-time fisherman was awarded a sum of approximately $47,000 as compensation for the permanent loss of his source of livelihood. Now functionless, the cooperative association, which included fishermen from several adjacent communities, officially disbanded on March 31, 1974.

The compensatory payment seemed huge, a sum that, if invested, would yield a tidy annual income, although not enough to support a family of four or five persons beyond the level of poverty. Unfortunately, most of the wage earners of Takashima did not qualify for the payment. Some women had been regular members of familial fishing crews, but only males were members of the fishermen's cooperative qualifying for payment of compensation. Moreover, as conditions of environmental pollution had worsened and alarm over the future had heightened, Takashima fishermen, especially the younger men, had gradually found other employment. In 1973, only thirteen men, the youngest just past forty years of age and the oldest seventy-four, were still officially full-time fishermen. If worst came to worst, these families could survive by using the compensation, and at least their young members, male and female, could find employment if they had not already done so. But the families of Takashima were now generally small, and many had only one male wage earner. Dependence upon offspring offered no security. Daughters were expected to move elsewhere when they married, and, throughout the nation, sons, even eldest sons, also often left their natal homes when they became mature.

The employment policies of industrial firms were also worrisome. Local industrial establishments were mostly branches of great corporations with plants in many different localities of the nation, and they followed national policies of employment. In industrial firms throughout the nation, a premium was placed on youth, and most male wage earners of Takashima were no longer young. Twenty-two heads of households were between the ages of forty and sixty, too old to be highly valued by industrial concerns which nationally classified men and women of ages nineteen to twenty-seven as "young" and those of twenty-eight years and above as "mature." These firms were reluctant to take into employment people whose ages exceeded early "maturity." As all Takashima people knew by this time, large firms seldom engaged as regular employees men and women over the age of thirty-five, and the policy of nearly all firms was that all employees below the level of the topmost executives be retired at age fifty-five. To become a *honsaiyōin* or *honko*, a regular employee assured of "lifetime" employment and entitled to all fringe benefits including a pension upon retirement, one needed to be young and to have at least a high school education. *Honko* were ordinarily trained for their work by the firms employing them in programs of training that covered periods of months or even years, during which the trainees were often not very productive economically until they had mastered the skills required for their work.

People over thirty-five and those over age fifty-five who had been retired from employment ordinarily could find employment only with small firms offering low wages and few or no fringe benefits, employment that usually gave little promise of stability. They might also, at low rates of pay, become *rinjiko*, "temporary employees," of large firms. Few of the remaining Takashima fishermen had learned any skills except fishing; their education generally ranged between six and nine years, and they were all well past thirty-five years of age.

For many Takashima families, the years 1972 and 1973 were a time of great worry over the future. Unemployed fishermen earnestly sought other employment, and, in the view of some of the seekers and their wives, they were miraculously successful by early 1974. The most helpful life line was extended by the shipbuilding firm, which needed a supply of labor, preferably local labor. No very lengthy period of training and no great technical skill or knowledge were required for the positions this firm offered, which were principally as metal workers and welders. The firm established its yard in a way calculated to win the goodwill of local people, particularly the residents of Takashima, from whom an area of pine and garden land was purchased for the erection of offices and temporary quarters for crew members of ships. Representatives of Sanoyasu had much earlier carefully explained the plans for establishment of the shipyard to the people of Takashima and, as a token of goodwill, had distributed to all households souvenirs that consisted of a plastic representation of a ship's wheel to which a mirror and a thermometer were attached. Another act of the firm, although doubtless prompted by practical motives of protecting the shipbuilding facilities from damage by ships straying from their course in bad weather, was locally interpreted as a magnanimous deed. A lighthouse 100 meters high was built atop the highest point on Takashima by the firm, which then "gave" the lighthouse to the prefecture, with the provision that its operation and maintenance were to be prefectural responsibilities. The representatives also took care to make known that none of the activities of the firm would contribute to environmental pollution and that steps would be taken to ensure no encroachment upon the community by employees of the yard. These procedures reached their objective, and the goodwill they produced was later enhanced by other actions of the firm. Construction of the necessary facilities of the shipyard was completed in late 1973, and the firm began to construct its first ship in January 1974.

Bending its policies of employment, Sanoyasu engaged four Taka-shima men well past the dividing line of thirty-five years of age as trainees eligible for promotion to the status of *honko* upon satisfactory comple-tion of about six months of training as welders, as metal workers, or as pipefitters, in whatever capacities their responses to training showed them to be best suited. Six young Takashima men who had not been full-time fishermen were similarly engaged. Two Takashima women past forty years of age were employed as *rinjiko*, with expectations of continued employment, their work consisting of handling food in the firm's dining rooms and performing janitorial duties.

Through its eight small subsidiary firms, Sanoyasu provided employ-ment for thirty-one additional Takashima people, some of whom re-signed from other recently acquired employment to take these positions. Such subsidiary firms are called *shita-uke* companies, a name usually translated into English as "subcontractors" but which has connotations different from those of the English term. Companies known as *shita-uke*, literally "receivers from below," are small firms that provide to large firms, under terms of contract, certain services and skills which the large firms do not or cannot provide by themselves. No large corporation of Japan is known as *shita-uke*, a somewhat demeaning term which con-notes small size, fleeting existence, extemporaneity in procedures and policies, and, generally, undesirability as an employer. The Sanoyasu subcontractors specialize in painting and in various kinds of specialized metal work, and employment by them is regarded as much inferior to employment by Sanoyasu.

Other Takashima men and women found employment here and there in other nearby industrial plants or by their subcontractors. Most people past the magic age of thirty-five were obliged to become *rinjiko* or to work for subcontractors, which in effect also usually made them *rinjiko*. By July 1974, all able-bodied males of the community were employed except one, a man in his forties who had never held regular employment beyond some fleeting and questionable business enterprises of his own devising. His last venture of operating a pinball parlor having failed, he neither had nor sought employment, and he and his family were said to subsist on the earnings of his wife and on occasional wind-falls that came to him from gambling.

For the community as a whole, employment that brought returns in cash went far beyond the limits of former times. For the first time, employment was readily available for women, and almost all able-bodied

adult females except aged grandmothers became wage earners. Only
three women under fifty years of age did not seek employment. Two
were homemakers in well-to-do families and one was a semi-invalid.
Many women over fifty took part- or full-time employment. In the community of 200 adults and children, 78 persons, 50 males and 28 females,
had full-time employment, and 26 additional people, 20 females of varying age and 6 males over sixty years of age, were in part-time employ.
No employment could be called rural.

The largest category of employers were manufacturing and construction firms, engaging fifty-three of the seventy-eight full-time workers as
skilled, semiskilled, and unskilled laborers. (See Table 1.) Males gen-

TABLE 1

TYPES OF EMPLOYMENT, JANUARY 1975

	Male	Female	Total
FULL-TIME			
Skilled and unskilled workers, in industrial or construction firms	38	15	53*
White-collar, industrial firms, city or other governmental offices, shop clerk	5	6	11
Blue-collar, civic, or prefectural institutions	3		3
Lodging house and/or restaurant operators and workers		4	4
Independent carpenters (husband and wife)	1	1	2
Ship's crew member	1		1
Box factory operators (husband and wife)	1	1	2
Gas station attendant		1	1
Domestic servant	1		1
	50	28	78
PART-TIME			
Machine sewing at home, Western clothing		13	13
Hand sewing at home, Japanese clothing		1	1
Workers in local inns and restaurants	2	3	5
Unskilled laborers (local box factory, 2; large industry, 1)		3	3
Boat work using own boats, communications, emergency aid, etc.	3		3
Entrepreneur	1		1
	6	20	26
TOTAL PART- AND FULL-TIME	56	48	104

* In January 1975, five males were rated as skilled workers; several others were
expected to receive this classification soon, upon completion of their on-the-job
training. No females held skilled ratings.

erally had more desirable employment than females. Only part-time employment was available to men or women of sixty years of age or older. Women of middle age generally could find employment only as food handlers or janitors. Young people of either sex with high-school educations were able to find employment in clerical and in other white-collar positions. Young men could easily enter employment as trainees for positions as skilled laborers in large industrial firms.

Other employment included a small number of blue-collar jobs outside industry as well as self-employment, the operating of small restaurants and restaurant-inns in Takashima that are patronized chiefly by outsiders employed by small *shita-uke* firms, carpentry (a husband and wife), and the operating of a small paper box factory as a family enterprise, a venture which foresight had led the male head of the household concerned to initiate ten years earlier. Only one person, a middle-aged man who had married a Takashima girl and moved into the community, held a professional position. Trained in civil engineering, he was employed as an administrator in a municipal office supervising the operation of a harbor in Kojima used by fishing and sport craft and was the only white-collar worker in a position of any eminence. One man, age fifty-nine, who is mentally subnormal, continued to work for Takashima's richest family as a menial of all outside work, a position he had held since he was first brought to Takashima about thirty years earlier. As in the past, discussion with Takashima people about conditions in the community ordinarily continued to omit him from consideration. No other family had domestic help, and no other person had domestic employment, circumstances that also applied in 1950–51.

The male head of the richest family in 1950–51 retained his status of wealth and power. Seventy years of age in 1974, he was officially identified until 1973 as a fisherman and did in fact engage in or direct familial operations of fishing. He had also engaged at that time in other activities concerning finance which were unknown or little known to the rest of the community, and, in 1974, he continued to do so. For lack of a better term, he is described as an entrepreneur. (See Table 1.)

As the preceding statistical information suggests, a fairly important part of familial earnings came from part-time work, principally by women. Thirteen women, most of whom could not take full-time employment because of their roles as mothers of small children, did machine sewing of Western clothing in their homes for commercial firms. Professionally trained by instructors who came to their homes, these women did work of professional quality. Their earnings in 1974 were estimated to average $150 monthly and to represent one-fourth to one-third of the income of the average family. One woman sewed Japanese clothing by

hand under similar arrangements. Three aging men, all formerly fishermen, worked part-time for municipal and prefectural maritime agencies
when their boats and their services were needed to place and to move
buoys and to handle numerous small emergencies that arose in connection with water traffic in adjacent reaches of the sea. A handful of men
and women worked part-time in other occupations. (See Table 1.)

Economically productive labor that does not produce wages has been
a traditional part of Takashima life and, although less important than
formerly, continues today. The greatest source of such uncalculated income in 1951 and the only source of importance in 1974 was cultivation
of kitchen gardens. Most of the cultivators are "retired" grandmothers
and grandfathers. No aged person who has retained vigor is idle. Two
of the most industrious gardeners, a man and a woman, were over eighty
years of age, and even the sixty-six-year-old grandmother of the community's richest family was active as a kitchen gardener. Although plots
under cultivation are small even by Japanese standards of professional
farming, the mild climate allows cultivation of multiple and varied crops,
and the annual value of the produce of the larger plots was estimated by
informants to be several hundred dollars. Over the years since 1951, the
sale of crops for cash has dwindled to insignificance, and today almost
all garden produce is consumed at home.

Some attempt was made to gather precise information on individual
and familial incomes but was abandoned as being difficult and of doubtful value. During 1974, both occupations and incomes were changing
rapidly, and national trends of inflation seemed to assure that industrial
wages would continue to rise so rapidly that any compilation of statistics
on them would quickly become outdated. In 1950–51, the well-do-do
families of Takashima and a few of the very poorest families had been
secretive about their incomes. In 1974, for a variety of reasons that included the possibility of bringing to light invidious comparisons with the
circumstances of neighbors, a larger number of people were reluctant or
unwilling to give complete accounts of household finances. Most families which had received the final fishermen's compensation were still
pondering how they might best use it and did not as yet know what
returns of annual income these funds might bring if invested.

The gathering of data on incomes was rendered still more complex
by the custom of paying bonuses, a practice which all large firms follow.
Generally paid to all employees twice annually, in mid summer and at
the end of the year, the sums vary greatly from firm to firm and year to
year, dependent principally upon the financial conditions of the industries concerned.

Information on industrial wages and earnings if not for total incomes was readily given by Takashima informants, however, and information on wage scales was also available from officers of industrial firms. Many Takashima people were quite willing to estimate the incomes, from whatever sources, of their neighbors. It was thus possible to make estimates of incomes that are thought to be fairly accurate.

In September 1974, the monthly wages of male workers, temporary and permanent, employed by Sanoyasu shipbuilding firm, ranged from 82,000 to 170,000 yen (approximately $290 to $600) and for most full-time employees of middle age were about 130,000 yen ($425). Men receiving the highest rates in this range were supervisors or foremen. Bonuses for the year, which were lower than those paid by many other concerns, totaled 61,000 yen (about $215) for each person, whether a temporary or a regular employee.

Fringe benefits for all Sanoyasu employees consisted of low-cost health insurance for employees and members of their families, as required by law, and a modest welfare program providing compensation for illness and injury. For regular employees only, a retirement payment was given in one sum when employees reached age fifty-five. Officials of the company were reluctant to state the amount of this payment, saying that they hoped it would soon be changed. The amount was said to be a few thousand dollars and thus was unexceptional among Japanese firms, which seldom have generous retirement programs. Also available to regular employees was the privilege of living in the company *danchi*, about three miles from Takashima. Although the rental fees, ranging from about $65 to $80 monthly, were low, the apartments were tiny and, in the opinion of Takashima people, inconveniently distant. Since Takashima people already had much roomier and, in general, superior housing, none moved to the *danchi*. Young single men could live for very small sums in the company lodging house provided especially for them as a part of the *danchi*. Like other *danchi* throughout the nation, the Sanoyasu facilities were a necessary business expense operated by the firm at a substantial loss. In 1974, single men paid only $42 monthly, for which they received use of a private room, two meals daily, and the privilege of using various facilities for sports and other forms of recreation. Only one young Takashima man, age nineteen, elected to live in the company dormitory.

Other fringe benefits included voluntary participation in recreational clubs concerned with sports and aesthetics, which the firm encourages and supports financially. Regular employees of some years' tenure had the privilege of occasionally using for rest and recreation the facilities of a "mountain cottage" and a "sea cottage" maintained by the company in other prefectures for these purposes. Regular employees were auto-matically members of the company labor union, which had an influential voice in matters related to conditions of employment, including deter-mination of the amounts of annual bonuses, and employee welfare in general.

Estimates by Takashima people of the monthly income necessary for them to meet minimally all expenses for a home-owning family of four composed of two parents and two children were generally 100,000 to 120,000 yen ($355 to $415). Monthly incomes of the average family with two wage earners probably exceeded $600, a figure below the national average but nevertheless fully adequate to meet normal expenses of residents of a provincial city who owned their homes. Estimates of expenses for living quarters consisted only of a small amount for main-tenance of the houses and taxes and a larger, but highly variable, amount for utilities.[2]

As these data suggest, at the beginning of 1975, it was clear that the financial crisis which seemed earlier to threaten Takashima had been averted. The average family felt no want, could afford some luxuries, and could easily save some money for the future. Incomes were in fact both absolutely and relatively at their greatest height in the community's history. Inflation was also at its greatest height, but the rise in familial earnings had nevertheless elevated most families to positions of relative affluence.

By early 1975, most of the Takashima trainees at Sanoyasu had become regular employees, and the remainder were expected to achieve this status soon. Sanoyasu had turned out to be a good place of employ-ment. Classified in Japan as a medium-sized industry, the firm had two yards employing approximately 4,500 people, about half of them at Takashima, and appeared to offer good promise of occupational sta-bility. The convenient location of the Takashima yard, a few minutes' walk from the homes of Takashima people, eliminated all problems of commuting. The firm had erected a high chain-link fence at the bound-ary of its land in Takashima, a boundary marker which was so respected by its employees that no problems ever arose of trespassing onto property of Takashima people. In September 1974, the firm launched its first ship constructed in the Takashima yard (officially designated as Mizushima yard), an 86,000 ton tanker destined for delivery to Norway, and con-struction of a second vessel was well under way. All Takashima residents

---

[2] A press account of May 31, 1975, reported average monthly earnings during 1974 of $712 for Japanese workers, most of whom live in very large cities where they must rent living quarters and where wages and the cost of living are higher than in smaller cities.

were invited to the launching ceremony, which included a guided tour by bus of the yard and the serving of soft drinks.

October saw the arrival of the first foreign ship to put into the yard for repairs, a service which Sanoyasu also provides. The crew members of the ship, an English freighter, were housed in the Sanoyasu hostelry in Takashima for several days, during which their presence made no noticeable difference in the tenor of community life. A few old people had expressed mild concern over problems that might arise if foreigners were quartered there, but this concern was essentially disinterested speculation about what the visitors would find to do in a community such as Takashima which provided no opportunities for recreation.

Discussing this subject with me, one man of seventy-five years recalled laughingly an event of his childhood, the first arrival on Takashima of foreigners. A ship operated by a Baptist missionary had anchored offshore, and some of its passengers had rowed to shore in a boat. All Takashima people fearfully took refuge in their houses until the strangers disappeared. In 1975, no one was fearful, and no one was even very interested. A few of the foreign seamen appeared peacefully in the small Takashima restaurants to drink beer, ordering and paying for it by the use of extemporaneous sign language. As the aged Takashima woman operating one of the restaurants observed, this procedure was unnecessary since any Japanese understands the word "beer" and since the Japanese numeration of commerce had been chiefly that of foreigners (that is, Western numerals) during her entire lifetime. She needed only to write a check and any foreigner would understand it. Two European women, presumably wives of the officers of the visiting ship, were seen by a few people while the women were taking a stroll along Takashima's narrow main road. Some Takashima people, absent from their homes during the day because of their employment, never knew of the presence of the foreigners, who were quartered a few hundred feet from the nearest houses.

To most residents of the community, conditions in late 1974 looked very good. Anyone could see that the garden crops and flowers now grew well, and the sickness and death of the camphor trees along the highway was interpreted with probable realism as the result of lack of care and the poor soil in which they were planted, which consisted mostly of sandy material of the landfill. To most people the highway leading to Takashima along which the trees had been planted was in fact *subarashii*, "splendid," an admirable and aesthetically pleasing example of modern technological knowledge and skill. The cars, motorcycles, refrigerators, gas stoves, telephones, heating and cooling devices, and color television sets which increased incomes had allowed them to buy were still comforting luxuries and had not yet become commonplace necessities.

Conditions of health were generally excellent, and medical attention was readily available and generally uncostly. Life spans had lengthened and the number of healthy, aged men and women had grown. Chronic sickness was uncommon. A few of the middle-aged and aged had mild or serious ailments, of course, but only two persons had chronic sicknesses, respiratory ailments, that were now officially declared to be instances of public damage, and many people doubted the validity of their classification as official invalids. Only a very few Takashima people now thought it useful or necessary to undergo the periodic physical examinations conducted at municipal expense at the nearby elementary school to determine the extent of illness caused by environmental pollution.

For nearly everyone, the disturbing feelings of economic insecurity of the preceding years had vanished. It was no longer necessary to face the uncertainty of life in a strange, new community, as had once seemed necessary, and conditions of the present were far better than they had ever been in the past. Families receiving the last compensatory payment of $47,000 were regarded as rich, and for some time they were incredulous of their good fortune. None had really expected to receive such a magnificent sum, free of taxes, or ever in their lifetimes to accumulate such a fortune in cash.

Conditions of the dimming past were now regarded as unendurable hardship. Who today would want to do such things as gather firewood in the forest, use kerosene lamps, cultivate by hand tools the steep and poor soil of most of the abandoned kitched gardens, eat despised barley mixed with rice, draw water from wells, and suffer unnecessarily from illnesses for lack of money and facilities for medical treatment? Children and adolescents had no knowledge of these matters except dimly by hearsay and looked upon them as unimaginable circumstances of a remote and primitive past. For children and adolescents in particular, the future looked especially promising. Finances would allow college educations — and thereby secure futures — for them. Several young men and women had already gone off to college.

Of course, everyone agreed that modern conditions of life had a fast pace and left little free time for adults, since almost all except the very aged were employed. They could remember that their former work had seasonally allowed much leisure and the pleasure of unhurried association with relatives and friends. Now their association with their nearest neighbors might for weeks and months at a time consist only of hurried expressions of greeting when circumstances momentarily brought them together. And, of course, some people were conscious of the lost beauty and the gained ugliness in their physical surroundings. But the ugliness and pain of past poverty could not be matched by any of the drawbacks of modern times. These were the prevailing views. Only here and there among the aged were other opinions held, and these were rarely expressed.

Even the aged who were nostalgic for the conditions of life of their youth saw only good in the great changes in formal education which the years had brought. In 1950–51, the children of Takashima seldom exceeded the nine years of schooling required by law. They were described by their teachers as being poorer students and less interested in learning than farm children. The value placed upon education by their parents was said generally to be less than the mode for the nation, a statement that seemed accurate. At the time, to Takashima people a high-school education represented advanced learning, and only a few had reached this impressive height. Elsewhere in Japan, however, the view that education is the golden key to success was already well established, and evidence of its truth seemed to lay before the eyes of anyone interested enough to look.

As the years passed after World War II, the premium placed upon advanced education rapidly grew to heights that probably have no counterpart elsewhere in the world. Parents planned the educational careers of their children years in advance, seeking to enroll them from the beginning in the finest private or public schools that familial finances and the scholastic abilities of their children would allow. The golden plums that lay ahead for the most fortunate children were admission to any one of a few universities of towering national prestige, of which Tokyo University stood as supreme, in a position of national eminence for which no counterpart exists among universities in the United States. A graduate of Tokyo University, Hitotsubashi University in Tokyo, or Kyoto University was said to be almost assured of future economic success. Certain great industrial firms were held to employ only graduates of these and a few other noted institutions.

Provided one's child were bright, the path to admission to a select university began with kindergarten. Admission to a kindergarten of fine repute served as a springboard for admission to a noted elementary school, which in turn successively paved the way through fine junior and senior high schools and on to a prestigious university. By the late 1950s, the competition for admission had become intense, and newspapers carried accounts of mothers taking their places in queues at the doors of business offices of private kindergartens as much as two days before the announced hour when applications for admission would first be accepted.

In the 1960s, the striving for education grew even more feverish, although compulsory education continued to be nine years, as it is today. Facilities for providing advanced education expanded correspondingly but always lagged behind demand, making competition for admission to favored schools all the more intense. By the early 1960s, every city of the nation had many *yobikō*, cram schools operated by private entrepreneurs which "prepared" high school graduates for university training; that is, the schools gave instruction in how to pass university entrance examinations. Admission to the finest universities, such as Tokyo University and other public universities supported by national funds, was uncompromisingly democratic, depending upon one's performance in the tests. Wealth had no bearing upon admission, although financial support while in attendance was generally left to the student.

The period in the spring when examinations were given had become a time of annual crisis for much of the nation. The tests became known as "examination hell," and the occasional suicides among unsuccessful aspirants unfailingly received attention by the news media. A romantic, well-known term from feudal times was revived, half-humorously, to label the unfortunates who failed the entrance examinations but continued to aspire to enter a university. *Ronin*, formerly samurai who had lost their feudal lord by his death or by his flight into hiding after defeat in feudal strife, were now young people who had lost the university of their choice, and their number was said to be many tens of thousands. Among families of the humblest educational and economic backgrounds, the purchase at Shinto shrines of talismans inscribed with prayers for success in the examinations became popular. Television, radio, and newspapers carried accounts of the number of admissions to the great national universities, and local radio stations gave the names as well as the numbers of those admitted to local institutions.

Like all other Japanese citizens, the people of Takashima were well aware of these developments in education, and, as their financial circumstances improved, they too saw more and more value in formal education. By the mid 1960s, graduation from high school had generally come to be regarded as necessary or even routine for a child of either sex, but university educations seemed beyond reach or unnecessary. The end of fishing and the accompanying worries about gaining a livelihood taught the entire community a hard lesson about the value of education. Anyone could now see that education was necessary in modern Japan and that college degrees were required to provide substantial security.

Eiichi, one of Takashima's first high-school graduates, often publicly expressed his views on the matter. In his early forties in 1974, he had become worried over the future a decade earlier and had abandond fishing for employment as a trainee in one of the chemical firms of Mizushima, where he now held a well-paid position as a skilled worker operating control devices for various chemical processes. Eiichi had quickly learned that his occupational horizon was limited, and he told his friends and neighbors why: Only people with college educations could ever rise to positions of importance. He predicted that young people who lacked high-school educations would, in fact, soon find it difficult even to find desirable employment in industry, and in 1974 his prediction seemed to be coming true. In that year, a time of inflation and economic recession, a major textile firm announced that it would no longer employ young people who had not finished high school. General national attitudes had by this time come to look with suspicion upon young people who lacked high-school training as being either mentally or morally deficient.

In 1974, the educational circumstances for Takashima people looked favorable, nationally and locally. The number of colleges and universities in Japan had grown to over 400, the second greatest number among nations of the world. Many were prefectural institutions with low tuition fees and the very best, the national universities, also were not costly. In the number of high-school graduates going on to college, Japan also held the second position internationally, and females were not denied or even discouraged from admission. In 1974, the number of female college students in the nation was only a fraction of 1 percent below that of males.

In 1974, five young people of Takashima, all males, were attending universities, and almost any person in the community of high-school age or older could quickly recite their names. Nearly two decades earlier, the first Takashima youth had entered college, in a noted national university, but no others had followed him until 1970. None of the later students had won admission to a renowned university, but none had expected or really aspired to do so. Most families with sons and daughters in high school were making plans to send them to college, and three high-school graduates of 1974, two males and one female, were enrolled in cram schools in Okayama City in preparation for taking entrance examinations in the winter of 1975. Three young men who had recently finished high school and who, with the approval of their parents, had decided against further education were generally looked upon as being unfortunately shortsighted.

In 1975, the average number of years of formal education of Takashima residents beyond high-school age was about eight. The figure was perhaps two years below the rapidly changing average of the nation, where the proportion of high-school graduates who enter universities continues to grow annually and in 1975 was over one-third. The low number of years of schooling of Takashima people reflects in part its disproportionately large number of aged people. All normal males of whatever age are literate. Two women in their eighties and the mentally subnormal man of fifty-nine have had no formal education. Only the middle-aged engineer who married a Takashima high-school graduate has a college degree. In general, years of education correlate with age and sex. From all indications, the average figure will rise rapidly in the future and, among people of comparable age, will vary little by sex.

DEMOGRAPHY

The trend of population movement from rural to urban areas characteristic of industrial nations has long applied in Japan and is well recorded. Heightening after the end of World War II, it has resulted in a dense concentration of well over one-half of the nation's population in what is called the Tokaido Megalopolis, a narrow corridor extending somewhat over 300 miles from the Tokyo to the Osaka-Kobe areas. Smaller concentrations exist regionally outside this area, especially in the extreme south of the main island of Honshu and in adjacent northern Kyushu. This trend of urban concentration has been so striking and so well recorded that it masks another lesser trend, the survival of rural communities like Takashima that have become enveloped by spreading cities. Although no longer rural, under certain conditions these communities may retain for fairly long, if not indefinite, periods some of the qualities of rural life and some degree of corporate unity, a subject that will later be discussed.

Another demographic trend in Japan of which everyone has become aware is small and recent, and it is popularly thought to oppose the old, general pattern of movement from country to city. Called by the English term "U-turn" (*yew-tahn*), this trend refers to the return to one's natal community in the country after a period of living in an urban center.

Demographic circumstances of Takashima during the past two decades include both of the lesser trends described above. If the shift from rural to urban living is interpreted to include rural communities that have become urbanized, the history of Takashima also exemplifies this great national trend. The city came to Takashima, as it did to many other rural communities. So far, it has left Takashima essentially intact demographically. Some emigrants also returned to Takashima.

Despite great cultural changes since 1951, however, the composition of Takashima's population in 1974 differed little from the pattern that had existed for some decades before 1951. Outflow and inflow followed with little deviation the patterns of previous decades in the twentieth century and probably of the late nineteenth century, patterns that have sometimes been described as "traditional" in Japan. Excluding the loss by death since 1951 of thirty-six persons, outflow consisted principally of young women, thirty-five of whom left the community at the time of their marriages. Four entire families, totaling twenty-seven persons, and fifteen young single men also left. All except two of the single men were younger sons who, under the custom of primogeniture which was generally followed, could not be economically incorporated into the community. In the past also, most younger sons had left the community because it could not provide support for them as adults. Only one *chōnan*, "eldest son," is said to have left the community permanently.[3] The first person born and raised in Takashima to attend college was awarded a degree in law in the early 1960s. This man lives in Osaka and is employed as a patent attorney, an occupation which had no place in Takashima or in Kurashiki at the time his university training in Osaka ended.

Inflow consisted principally of children born in the community and brides coming from other communities. Since 1951, seventy-three children were born to parents that resided on Takashima, and nearly all are alive today. Most were born in Takashima and live there today. Twenty-three brides came from other communities. Seven adult males who married Takashima women, four of whom are adoptive husbands, came from other communities. Only two families of outsiders, totaling seven people, entered the community. Renting small houses of poor quality, these newcomers and their families are industrial workers who are assumed by Takashima people to be temporary residents. Other additions to the community since 1951 are composed of relatives of Takashima people, including aged parents of Takashima wives, and returnees and their children who were born elsewhere. For several years, a few males, single or unaccompanied by their families, have from time to time resided temporarily in the Takashima inns, built to meet this need. These are men employed by subcontractors of Sanoyasu and other nearby firms who serve briefly in specialized occupations, and they have been omitted from the statistics on the population of Takashima.

In 1951, the population totaled 188 persons, and was equally divided by sex. In 1974, permanent residents numbered 200, of whom 107 were

---

[3] The head of one of the emigrant families is an eldest son, but since he had reached middle age at the time he and his family moved, Takashima informants usually fail to regard him as an emigrant. In their view, the category of *chōnan* who have left the community refers to eldest sons who leave while young and unmarried.

male and 93 female, a proportion that departs from the national mode of somewhat more females than males. As a small community, Takashima might of course be expected to deviate from national demographic modes. The rate of growth of the population also deviates in being lower than the national rate of increase, a circumstance that is accountable in large part by the exodus already noted of four families, one of which had thirteen members.

The disproportionately large number of males in 1974 is puzzling and unexplainable, especially since it reflects principally a disproportionate number of males among those under twenty years of age. (See Table 2.) Some unevenness in male-female ratios in certain age groups (which, following Japanese statistical practices have been divided into ten-year units) is attributable to customs of marriage, since husbands are usually a few to several years older than their wives. The age of marriage for girls, however, continues to be well past nineteen years. Sex ratios by age group are sometimes markedly, and generally unexplainably, irregular. For example, compare the figures in the ten to nineteen age category with the sex ratio of people sixty years of age and older, according to Table 2.

The proportion of aged people in the community reflects the national trend toward an increase in this age group, but far exceeds the national ratio.[4] The number of Takashima people of ages sixty to sixty-nine in

TABLE 2

SEX AND AGE DISTRIBUTION, JANUARY 1975

Age Category	Male	Female	Total
0–9 years	10	6	16
10–19	28	18	46
20–29*	14	12	26
30–39	8	15	23
40–49	19	14	33
50–59	13	9	22
60–69	8	10	18
70–79	5	6	11
80–89	2	1	3
90–99	—	2	2
	107	93	200

* 138 persons are age twenty or older.

[4] Persons sixty years and older comprise 17 percent of the community population; persons sixty-five years and older comprise 13.5 percent. In 1973, only 7.5 percent of the people in the nation were sixty-five years and older.

1974 is much greater than it was in 1951,[5] but the number over seventy years does not represent a great increase over the number in 1951. Takashima informants hold that the climate, diet, and way of life of fishing communities encouraged hardiness and longevity and that the community has "always" included men and women of great age. A proportion of aged people higher than the national average seems to be common in rural settlements of Japan, however, and it is likely also common in communities such as Takashima that have recently become urbanized, a subject on which no statistical information is available. In 1974, the oldest residents of Takashima were two women, aged ninety-seven and ninety-one, and the oldest male was eighty-two. Many people took pride in the great age of its oldest resident and expressed the hope that she would reach at least 100 years.

The proportions of people in the lowest age categories are erratic and puzzling, showing a large growth followed by a large decline. When these variations were called to the attention of Takashima people, they evoked speculation and one recurrent and emphatic opinion regarding the causes. The large number of children from ten to nineteen years was called Takashima's *bēbi būmu*, "baby boom" and was surmised to be the result of improved economic conditions while fishing was still the main occupation. The small number of children under ten years of age was usually described with assurance as the result of planning, aided by general knowledge of techniques of contraception. Some people held that the economic worries of the preceding decade were the primary factor holding down the birthrate. Several people laughingly expressed the view that in very recent years everyone had been too busy to have children.

The average size of the Takashima family has followed a long-established national trend toward reduction. In 1951, the average number of persons per family in Takashima was 5.7; in 1974 it was 3.9, a figure somewhat greater than the national average (estimated to be about 3.4 in 1974). Factors fostering the reduction in Takashima appear to be those applying to the nation as a whole: family planning; widespread practices of contraception; a conception of the ideal family as consisting of two parents, one son, and one daughter — a view that appears to have become general since shortly after the end of World War II; and improved economic conditions that operated in a way unrelated to fertility to reduce the size of households, that is, the number of people living under a single roof. As economic circumstances brightened, the number of roofs increased.

[5] There were seventeen people in this age group in 1974 as compared with six in 1951.

10. *The community's eldest resident, age ninety-seven.*

In twenty-one years, the number of dwellings and, correspondingly, of family units in Takashima increased greatly, from thirty-three to fifty-one, whereas the population increased by only twelve persons. This tendency reflects the long-established national trend toward an increase in the number of nuclear families and a decrease in the number of extended families. As soon as Takashima people were economically able to do so, they followed the national trend. Most of the added dwellings on Takashima were constructed in the late 1950s and early 1960s, when earnings from fishing rose, and these generally became the homes of married sons of living Takashima parents. As later discussion (Chapter II) will illustrate more clearly, the general sentiment had grown to favor small nuclear families as the residential group. Young men and, perhaps particularly, young wives strongly prefer to live separately from their parents or parents-in-law. A young man who is *oya-tsuki* (literally "parents-attached" or "parents-stuck") often has difficulty in finding a bride. Few modern girls wish to face the prospects of years of life with parents-in-law, a period that may extend to three or four decades. Aged couples, widows, and widowers in Takashima have sometimes also preferred to live alone. In 1974, five aged widows with children in the community lived in separate quarters, all except one of which were complete houses of normal size. This separate residence was said to be a matter of choice by the widows. Partly for reasons of sentiment and partly because of the availability of dwelling sites, these homes are near those of the children of the widows. One aged widower, a U-turnee with relatives but no children in the community, lived alone. Nine aged widows and three widowers lived with their children; of these, several were senile or otherwise infirm and unable to care for themselves adequately.

Several features of the composition of the population of Takashima and the changes occurring in it since 1951 warrant special note. The increase of nuclear families and of the number of domiciles implies the existence of many changes of other kinds that will be discussed later. A demographic feature of which Takashima people were not fully aware is the great decrease in the number of very young children, eighteen under ten years of age in 1974 and forty-two in 1951. This decrease accords fairly well, however, with the trend of the nation as a whole. Since its height in the late 1940s, the national birthrate had dropped about 50 percent by 1974. What this circumstance implies for the future is uncertain, but it suggests that continuity of family lines will be broken for lack of stay-at-home male offspring, unless the traditions of adopting husbands for daughters or of adopting male children are followed.

Another demographic feature, which is set aside for later discussion, is the large and growing number of aged men and, particularly, women, a matter of which the people of Takashima and the entire nation are well aware and regard as a serious social problem.

Returnees to Takashima also need special mention, since their circumstances do not accord very well with the popular national interpretation that return to one's nation village is a response to the trying pace of modern urban life, a nostalgic return to rural simplicity. Eight persons, six females and two males, made the U-turn to Takashima, of whom all except one had left the community after 1951. The motivating factors stated earlier might apply in part to a few of these people, but those who made the U-turn appear generally to have done so as a matter of convenience or necessity. The most likely candidate for the label of nostalgic refugee from urban life was an aged war widow born and raised on Takashima who had married a Takashima man and lived in the community until after his death, which occurred when she had reached middle age. She then worked for years in Osaka to support her son while he attended Osaka University. Her return to Takashima was willing, moved by nostalgia for relatives, old friends, and rural life, and by still other considerations. In Takashima, she owned agricultural land and a home better than anything she could afford in Osaka. Other returnees include a young widow with two children who returned after the death of her husband to open a restaurant that she operates with the aid of relatives; a young woman whose marriage was unsuccessful; and two outmarrying women who had lived in nearby communities and had moved back to Takashima with their husbands because living quarters were available for them there.

Elsewhere in the nation, the phenomenon called the U-turn is also doubtless often conditioned by similar economic motives. Few people of modern Japan are willing to sell land and houses unless forced to do so, and many people are eager to buy. Rural people are well aware that economic developments since World War II have had the curious result of giving them living quarters — their old country homes — that are much roomier and, with only a little renovation, otherwise superior to the cramped domiciles of most urban residents. Through the news media, rural people have all heard much about the trying life in the great urban housing developments of the nation, some of which shelter hundreds of thousands of people in single aggregates of tiresomely uniform and tiny apartments. Moreover, the old home town is often no longer rural but, like Takashima, is instead a suburb with some of the advantages of rural life but where the facilities of the city are readily available.

The demographic continuity of Takashima along lines of the past which we have described is also noteworthy as an example of a national phenomenon which, if not common, is probably far from rare. Several conditions favored continuity, one of which is spatial. Takashima is now a residential island, separated from other communities by large expanses of industrial plants and the sea. Within the community, land available for house lots is very limited and its owners are reluctant to sell. Takashima landowners have seen the value of land rise astronomically, and, like most other citizens of their nation, they regard land as precious. Few opportunities therefore exist for outsiders to join the community, unless the steep forest land is expensively converted for use as the site of a *danchi* or private apartments, a possibility which the polluted air and disagreeable scenery discourage. The availability nearby of industrial employment and the ownership of homes better than can be afforded elsewhere have also favored survival of Takashima as a community. So also have bonds of kinship and the communal ownership of property, matters that will later be discussed in greater detail.

Continuity in a demographic sense does not necessarily coincide with continuity of social relationships, however. The circumstances discussed above all have bearing on social solidarity, and the question now arises as to what extent Takashima continues to be a socially unified community. The foregoing pages strongly suggest that social relationships in Takashima have changed in accord with other changes in the way of life, a subject that will be considered in the following chapters. For the time being, it may be said that, although changed and changing in this respect, Takashima continues to exist as a social community.

CHAPTER II

The Course of Urban Life:
Changes and Adjustments

DAILY LIFE

The activities of the ordinary day for nearly all the adults of Taka-shima under age sixty-five differ little in general outline from those of their suburban counterparts in the United States and in many other industrialized nations. The day is one of rising early, eating a hurried breakfast, going to one's place of employment, working, eating lunch in the facilities provided by employers, and returning promptly to one's home when working hours end. For many Takashima men, this is a time to bathe, to drink a glass or two of Coca Cola, a Fanta soft drink, or beer, a beverage which long ago displaced *sake* as the nation's most popular for pleasurable consumption, and to watch television before and after the evening meal. As time has passed since the 1950s, the national work week has shortened, and in 1975 somewhat over one-half of the industrial firms had a five-day week. Most Takashima people work five and one-half days, but men who are employed by small subcontractors of the large industrial firms may work every day with only a few days of leisure at Obon and New Year's.

For women in industrial employment the routine day is similar, but they have the added tasks of the preparation of meals and other domestic work, and they seldom drink beer, which is generally regarded as mascu-line behavior. After washing dishes in the evening and taking a late bath, women often join their husbands and other family members in watching television. As in the past, the mother is usually the last person of the household to use the common bath water.

This daily routine is admitted to be uncharming and to leave little time free for pleasurable association with kin and friends, but it does give the warm feeling of financial security and of promising improved condi-tions of life in the future for their children as well as for themselves and such aged relatives as may depend upon the wage earners.

Domestic tasks are much lighter than in the past and require far less time. Thanks to household appliances and facilities and the new kinds of foods in the shops, the preparation of meals has become comparatively simple. Most men and women still take pleasure in the household conveniences which recent times have brought to them, and the prospect of purchasing additional things that lighten work and provide comfort or pleasures makes the daily routine of employment less onerous and even pleasurable. Many middle-aged women enjoy the social contacts and the change of pace from domestic work that employment affords them.

Shopping must be squeezed in as best one can, using the aid of children and grandparents when necessary. Working homemakers do most of their shopping in the early evening and, of course, on Sunday, the busiest shopping day of the week everywhere in Japan, when the mercantile establishments of the nation make their greatest sales. Only a few commodities, such as tobacco, matches, sugar, salt, soy sauce, beer, and soft drinks, are available in Takashima shops, but the closest well-stocked stores are only minutes away by car, motorbike or bicycle, and a fish peddler's truck visits the community daily.

The first "modern" convenience to reach Takashima was electricity, in the 1950s, decades later than in most of the nation because of the high cost of bringing it to a small island community. The 1960s saw the general addition of television sets, automatic rice steamers that allowed even the most inexperienced cook to produce rice pleasing to the palate, refrigerators, piped water, butane *gasu rēnji*, "gas ranges" usually consisting of two burners and a tiny broiler and always lacking an oven, miniature butane water heaters for kitchen use, bathtubs equipped with butane heating units, small electric washing machines, and a variable host of small electrical appliances, such as clothes irons, electric fans for summer cooling, and food blenders. The inefficient charcoal heating devices disappeared in the early 1960s, replaced by small electric heaters used only in the brief season of cold weather.

The 1970s brought telephones, a much used convenience regarded by every family as indispensable, and, for some families, color television sets, electrical aircoolers, and, the greatest acquisition of all, automobiles. In early 1975, about one-half of the households, except those composed only of aged people, owned cars, recently purchased and painstakingly maintained in spotless condition and fine running order, and many families planned to buy cars in the near future.

Construction of new houses, generally for use by young adult sons and their families, held first priority in the use of money and began in the late 1950s. Construction was the work of outside professionals. No able-bodied Takashima man could build a house, and the building of dwellings as a communal undertaking had come to an end decades earlier. The newly built homes were generally much like the newer of the existing structures, which had been erected before World War II.

Still greater affluence, which began for most families in 1974, saw the beginning of the extensive remodeling of homes of the financially most highly favored families. Less fortunate people made lesser improvements. Entrance halls were made more attractive by floors of terrazzo or of concrete in which attractive polished stones were embedded. The appearance of toilets was improved by the installation of porcelain fittings to replace the wooden splashboard and aperture in the wooden floor, which were now regarded as old-fashioned and primitive. To the regret of everyone, the civic administration did not install either piped gas or a sewage system for the houses of the community for the stated reason that their haphazard and congested placement made such installation too costly or impossible without razing, moving, or reconstructing some houses. Only one flush toilet was installed, in a small, newly constructed restaurant-inn built on the edge of the landfill, where it was possible to make connection with the sewage system serving the facilities of the nearby industrial plants. For families which did not wish to use human wastes as fertilizer in their kitchen gardens, however, the city provided the mode of disposal still prevailing in even the nation's largest cities. Vacuum trucks with long hoses make weekly visits, announcing their presence by playing a recording of tinkling music.

The most highly desired kind of remodeling of houses, in 1974 still a dream of the future for most families, was expansion to give more room and reconstruction of the kitchen — the wish of every homemaker. Traditionally looked upon as separate from the house proper, the kitchen had usually adjoined the entrance room and had a floor of concrete or, in poor homes, of packed earth, lying at a lower level than the raised rooms of the house proper. Dining was ordinarily done on an elevated platform extending from a living-sleeping room into the kitchen, where the diners sat on the floor around a low table.

Modern times changed views of the nature of a kitchen and brought sharply to consciousness the inconvenience of the traditional cooking and eating arrangements. A kitchen today should be part of the house proper, attractive in appearance and convenient for use. For aesthetic and hygienic reasons, it should be sparklingly clean. For convenience and comfort, it should have a stainless steel sink and drainboard, a water heater, a smooth, easily cleaned floor of vinyl tile, and convenient cabinets on the walls for storage. It should also have a dining table and chairs of Western style as well as space for the already owned refrigerator and clothes washing machine, which were now placed wherever circumstances would allow. For many women, having such a kitchen is another of the modern inducements to work and earn money.

The daily round of the young stay-at-home homemaker with small children is only somewhat different from that of women who leave their homes daily for work. The young wife is at least as busy as they, since she generally does professional sewing at home, attempting to work out routines for domestic chores that allow her a few uninterrupted hours daily for work at her sewing machine. Much of her time is given to the care of the children, a matter which she feels that she cannot shirk or even abbreviate greatly. Perhaps more than other women, she makes use of prepared and semiprepared foods and other modern timesavers. The young wife is, in fact, usually so busy that it was not possible in the time available for field research to gather detailed information on practices of child care, such as feeding, weaning, and toilet training.

Some of the circumstances of the care of children could, however, be learned. Infants are ordinarily breast-fed, and mothers follow the instructions of their pediatricians with regard to the health of their children, calling for their professional aid wherever a child is ailing. Great variation appears to exist in customs of weaning, the exercise of sanctions for behavior, and other aspects of the care and socialization of children. It is certain that one ancient set of attitudes and customs has not changed. Parents generally regard their children as precious and give them as much attention as time will allow. Childhood is still a golden period of indulgence, and the bonds between children and parents are close, especially with the mother.

The working day of the young of school age is one of preparation for roles as economically productive adults, and, as such, it follows the customary pattern of other advanced nations. Attending school is their work, and, although girls may help their mothers with cooking and other chores at home, little practical aid in domestic matters is expected of either girls or boys. In order that they may mature as normal adults, so most parents think, children should be allowed time for pleasure, and their work at school is a load amply heavy to teach them to be responsible human beings.

So far, this chronicle of daily behavior constitutes a routine account of the activities of people in many other nations. For Takashima residents too old or regarded as too infirm for employment, however, the pattern varies. The able-bodied work, and they take pride in doing so. Those who live with their children help with household tasks, especially with the care of infants and young children. They and the aged who live alone are economically productive in another way that produces no money but can readily be seen as providing monetary gain. They are the

11. *A modern kitchen, including a butane stove and an automatic rice steamer.*

farmers of the community, cultivating plots of diminished size as compared with the past; they raise vegetables and fruits for domestic use by traditional techniques of cultivation to which the only innovations are the addition of a few chemical fertilizers and insecticides. The most energetic of these farmers include a woman of eighty-four years and a man of eighty-two. In this matter, the division of labor by sex has changed. In former times, only women were ordinarily the cultivators, and the roles of men were limited to help in turning the ground and in harvesting crops. The change has been an accident of default; no other gainful work is available to these aged men who formerly performed tasks connected with fishing, and healthy men usually feel that being useful to others is a moral obligation.

Crops that the grandmothers and grandfathers raise have changed in keeping with modern times. Several of the traditional plants are still cultivated, especially *daikon*, the white radish used for pickles, but the general trend has been toward kinds of produce that were once regarded as luxuries, plants to which a social as well as a gustatory value is attached. Cultivation of most plants with low social status has stopped or decreased. An unregretted and early abandonment was the cultivation of barley, which was formerly the main crop of winter. Despite their humble status and ready availability at moderate prices in the shops, sweet potatoes are often liked and are raised in smaller quantity than formerly. Other common plants are tomatoes, cucumbers, peas, onions, eggplant, and peanuts. All of these were also raised in the past, often for market. Today they are almost entirely for home consumption and are new, improved varieties. Increasingly, the kitchen gardens are planted to luxurious watermelons, strawberries, figs, and citrus fruits. Cultivation of the half-dozen tiny pieces of paddy rice land in nearby Shionasu owned by Takashima people, plots which vary in size today from one-tenth to one-half acre, was abandoned in the 1960s as representing a time-consuming, economic loss. Ownership of the land is, however, even more important than formerly, since it may readily be sold at high prices to serve as the sites of houses or commercial buildings.

As the preceding paragraphs have often either stated or implied, many of the routine domestic activities of former times have ended, for lack of time, because they had become unnecessary, or, like the weaving and repair of nets, because they had become useless. Any time-consuming, but unnecessary, economic activity has generally been abandoned. The raising of chickens ended in the 1960s. Droppings were then no longer needed as fertilizer, and fresh, clean eggs of better quality had become cheaply available in the markets. As a source of meat, the chickens had been useless, since no one wished to eat members of the family flock and they had uneconomically been allowed to die of old age.

Takashima wage earners of today are specialists in a nation composed of specialists, and for services outside their spheres of competence they rely upon the appropriate specialists. No handicrafts of any kind exist, although some women knit and sew garments for other members of the family and for themselves. Various of the utilitarian objects of the past, such as kerosene lamps and octopus pots attractively encrusted with oyster shells, have become marketable curiosities. The lone manually operated rice thresher in the community, a curiosity in 1951, has become a valuable antique.

One ancient household facility, the water well, has partially survived. Several of the wells in the community are still used for drawing drinking water because the piped city water is thought to have an unpleasant taste from the chlorine it contains. Fear of disease from contamination of the well water prohibits a growing number of people from drinking it, and use of the wells will probably come to end within a few years. One informant explained the circumstances by saying that even one incident of sickness would quickly put an end to use of the wells voluntarily and also by order of municipal authorities if their water were even suspected to be the cause of the illness. In former times, the wells were social centers where women exchanged pleasantries and gossip. This role is said jokingly, but with some truth, to be performed today by two small restaurants in the community which serve a little food and much beer, and where some of the men of the community gather for "well-side gossip."

Traditional clothes are expensive, inconvenient, and unsuited for modern life. Except among old women, everyday clothing is customarily ready-made and Western or international in features of style. Middle-aged women often wear kimonos on festive occasions, mostly, they say, because this attire is more becoming to them than modern garb. Footgear is mostly Western, but still includes traditional sandals and wooden clogs, ordinarily for home use only. The lone traditional garment that has generally survived among males is the *yukata*, a full-length garment of cotton that is worn in the home, especially in the evening after bathing. Styles generally follow international trends of change but tend to be conservative; for example, the use of miniskirts by women and abbreviated shorts by men has never been popular in Japan and is unthinkable in Takashima. In 1974, pants suits were favored by some Takashima women of about thirty to forty-five years of age, and some adolescent boys liked blue jeans.

The use of cosmetics by Takashima women is also conservative, although they use many more than in the past. Such embellishments as

12. *A young couple and their children, in everyday clothes.*

false eyelashes and heavy makeup for the eyes are well-enough known but are avoided because they are regarded as the symbols of "professional" women. Among young and youngish females, straight or only lightly waved hair has long been the standard; only quite mature women have tight permanent waves and wear their hair in the curls nestling against the head that were fashionable for middle-aged women about fifteen or twenty years ago. Certain international styles of male hairdress failed to become established on Takashima and had little currency in other parts of Japan. Beards were never favored and, for most men, were possible only in token form. Although long hair had long been a symbol of identity of some artists and other professional aesthetes of Japan, the general male public did not adopt the style after it became current in Western nations. Both dress and bodily adornment may be described in brief summary as another of the trends toward internationality. In clothing, many differences, often subtle, of color, cut, and design exist that are Japanese elements. In their ordinary street dress, however, young and middle-aged people of Takashima and elsewhere in Japan would not appear unusual in most cities of the world.

As elsewhere in the world in the past two or three decades, the diet of the people of Takashima has changed greatly. Consumption of meat and foods that were formerly luxuries, such as fresh fruits, has increased. Although fisherfolk, the people of Takashima in the past had ordinarily sold all saleable fish, consuming only damaged fish and unmarketable species and relying principally for animal protein upon clams dug on the beaches of the island. Today even the consumption of fish is greater than in the past. Fruits and green vegetables are available the year around, and many new foods have been added. Everyone is familiar with such once-foreign foods as spaghetti, Jello, sandwiches, and fresh salads with Western dressings, of which thousand island is popular. Many households use fresh or instant coffee in small quantity, generally as a gesture of hospitality for guests regarded as city people, although Japanese tea remains the standard nonalcoholic drink with meals and for refreshment at other times. Bread and other baked goods made with wheat have become increasingly common, and such products of good to excellent quality are readily available in the markets.

Many of the added foods are of Western derivation, but Japan has added its own indigenous products to the list of innovations in such forms as dried, instant noodle soups of traditional kinds and quick-frozen whole tangerines. Other frozen and dried foods are available in the shops, in small supply and variety as compared with the circumstances in the United States, but most of these foods are regarded by Takashima people as expensive, unnecessary luxuries. Fresh fish and most other seafoods from local waters are very expensive and, for consumption on all except special occasions, frozen seafoods are the standard — imported or transported by Japanese fishing vessels from many parts of the world. Most fresh shellfish, such as shrimp, crabs, rock lobster, and abalone, have risen to prices beyond the reach of Takashima people. Fresh beef commands astronomical prices and is purchased only occasionally, in small quantity and sliced very thin, for the preparation of *sukiyaki* on gala occasions. As elsewhere in most of Japan, lamb and mutton are unavailable and are known only as meats that some foreigners eat.

The popular and least expensive meats are pork and chicken, now identical with the market chicken of the United States and said to be of American stock. Together with the less expensive seafoods and inexpensive eggs, chicken and pork are the principal modern sources of animal protein.

Everyone is acquainted with scientific ideas of nutrition, a field of science in which Japan has held international importance for many years, and conscious attempts are made to have nutritionally balanced diets that include fruits, almost always eaten raw, and raw and cooked vegetables. Flavorsome bananas from Taiwan and southeast Asian countries are always available, cheap, and popular, and fresh Japanese tangerines may be purchased at moderate prices during much of the year. The list of fruits, vegetables, and other foods consumed by Takashima people has become international, and only a relatively small number of items, including loquats, taro root, burdock, white radish, soy bean curd, and glutenous rice cakes, are distinctive of Japan and the Far East. Although lavish as compared with the past, expenditures for food by Takashima people are conservative by national standards. A few traditional luxuries are nevertheless looked upon as necessities for meals during the holiday seasons of Obon and New Year's. Most householders think it necessary to purchase for Obon at least a little *matsutake*, the fragrant mushroom which cannot be cultivated and is gathered in the mountain forests of the nation. In 1974, *matsutake* cost about $10 per pound in Kurashiki, and some proprietors of lands in the mountains of the prefecture on which the mushrooms grew allowed people to gather them upon payment of high fees.

People with adventuresome palates and adequate money to allow such adventure may experiment with many imported foods, such as Taiwan pineapple, Tasmanian kiwi fruit, European cheeses and wines, and many of the luxurious prepared foods of the United States and Europe. Experimentation of this kind is generally slow and cautious, but every year sees a growing acquaintance with new foreign or foreign-derived foods as well as with Japanese innovations in convenience foods.

Young people experiment with hamburgers and milkshakes in the restaurant of the largest department store in downtown Kurashiki, and a trip to Kobe or Osaka allows them similar adventures in eating at McDonald's, A & W, Colonel Sanders, and Dunkin' Donuts.

It is inappropriate, however, to regard the changes in diet of Takashima and Japan in general as being principally the result of Western influence. Nations of the Western world have also seen many changes in diet during the past few decades, including the adoption of foreign foods. Industrialized nations may all be said to have international diets, and, in the growing use of convenience foods and chemically produced nutrients, all may also be described as experimenting with a diet entirely unknown to humanity in the past. In the international roster of cuisines of the great and scientifically advanced nations of the world, perhaps Japan's stands out as being the most distinctive. Japan has certainly added to its foods many foreign items, but, as in politics, industry, and other spheres of life, the addition has meant adaptation. The result today is a diet that in its constituent elements has grown more and more like that of the West but a cuisine that is still distinctively Japanese. Even introduced beer and the native *sake* have been adjusted to each other, and, although their roles overlap, they are not identical. Beer is the most common alcoholic beverage for secular occasions and holds higher social status than it does in the West. *Sake* carries a connotation of tradition and has not been displaced for use on ritual occasions, such as the vow of marriage and ceremonial offerings to supernatural beings. Rice continues to be the center of any substantial meal, and, in matters of flavor and modes of serving, even Western-derived dishes that are commonly eaten are Japanese.

As the number of aged men and women in Takashima suggests, conditions of health are very good, a matter which mature people look upon as one of the boons of modern times. Medicine in Japan was socialized many years ago. National Health Insurance, which includes basic dental care, is available at modest cost to everyone, either through one's company of employment or, if self-employed or unemployed, through a governmental agency with widely distributed branch offices. For those of seventy and more years, medical care is without cost. Except for some incidence of tuberculosis, infectious and contagious diseases had never been a serious problem in Takashima. Lesser ailments such as dental problems, mild but painful forms of arthritis, and, especially, chilblains among women who used cold water for domestic tasks in the winter months and an infection of the eyes that reached epidemic proportions during the summer months had, however, been ever-present woes for which no effective treatment was available. Chronic invalids with debilitating ailments, other than those incidental to old age, were few in the past and are few today. Several people are senile or suffer from arthritis, but nearly all of the few seriously ill people have respiratory ailments or afflictions of heart and the circulatory system. One informant described the conditions of health by saying, "Our sicknesses are now modern." One ailing woman in her sixties has been ordered by her doctor to cease eating pork, one of her favorite foods, because of a dangerously high cholesterol level. One aged woman and one aged man have respiratory ailments diagnosed as "asthma" and, as previously noted, officially declared to be the result of polluted air. One aged man, the grandfather of a very poor household with a long history of tuberculosis among its members, has been bedridden for years with that disease. Refusing to go to a hospital, he is cared for at home, a circumstance of which the rest of the community strongly disapproves as working a hardship on the members of his family and constituting a menace to the health of others.

Children undergo periodic, routine physical examinations at school, and the first suggestion of the presence of infectious or contagious disease among them or among adults brings emergency action from official sources. Physicians and hospitals are available within a few minutes by car, and local physicians are usually willing to make house calls. The hospitals have been modernized to provide all necessary services for their patients. It is no longer necessary or possible for patients to be accompanied to the hospital by a family member to prepare their food and to take care of other ordinary needs, and patients no longer bring with them bedding, cooking utensils, dishes, and food. When emergency medical care is needed, the nearby fire station has a vehicle for transporting the afflicted person. Therapeutic techniques and medications are similarly modern and follow the instructions of trained medical personnel. Such traditional techniques of therapy as moxibustion and acupuncture find no use among Takashima people today despite the recent experimental use of acupuncture in Western nations.

Entertainment has also become principally modern, although much that is traditional remains. Traditionally popular diversions, such as the game of *go*, flower arranging, the viewing of cherry blossoms, and Japanese wrestling, show no signs of demise. Pre-eminent among the present forms of recreation, however, is the watching of television programs, a pastime of people of all ages and, especially among children, in part a displacement of old amusements. Viewing television is often a joint familial undertaking in Takashima, and it has become the principal form of recreation of the aged, who are partial to Japanese domestic dramas and comical performances. As compared with television in the United States, the entire range of Japanese programs is conservative, avoiding displays of strong violence and frankly sexual themes and leaning much more to instruction in useful foreign languages and to other educational programs.

For young men, a popular new form of recreation is bowling. For everyone, local sightseeing by car is a new pleasure. Vacation trips of sightseeing by car, train, or bus are another new luxury, for which the English term "vacation" is often used. Aged people who can afford to do so make "pilgrimages" to temples and shrines, near or far in accord with their pocketbooks. Younger people usually simply go sightseeing, to the great cities of Osaka and Tokyo or to famous scenic places.

Many sports, games, and other recreational activities are additional instances of international commonality, yet the leisure activities of the people of Takashima and of the Japanese in general constitute a combination that is uniquely Japanese. As elsewhere in the world, the Japanese activities reflect ideas and ideals that are evident in other aspects of the nation's culture. Team sports and games are favored over the individually competitive. Contact sports, such as football, that seem to display hostility as well as individual competitiveness have no popularity. *Sumo*, Japanese wrestling, involves only momentary physical contact and, moreover, is a spectator sport. Physical contact between the sexes in public has traditionally been disfavored, and, although young men and women now may walk arm in arm, Western dancing that brings partners into bodily contact has never become common. Among Takashima males, the most popular participant sports are bowling and baseball, both of which are national favorites. During their lunch periods at work, Takashima men and their workmates often play baseball, a sport that became popular throughout Japan several decades ago.

Asceticism is another theme that is evident in Japanese forms of aesthetics such as painting and poetry and also in other behavior. Thrift, sobriety, and the avoidance of excesses of any kind are long-established ideals. Among the residents of Takashima, where conditions of the past did not allow much aesthetic freedom or opportunity, the value placed on asceticism is strongly evident today in the hobby of flower arranging, in which most women have recently had or are now receiving professional instruction in the classic, sparse styles.

The range of other recreational activities of Takashima people is large and mostly shared by other large nations. Some people read. The range of literature extends from comic books to classics and translations of foreign writings. In 1974, a translation of *Jonathan Livingston Seagull* was popular nationally and reached Takashima. Other people drink beer and chat with friends, play cards, swim, do needlework, listen to high-fidelity music, raise tropical fish or canaries, and follow a host of other hobbies, some of them idiosyncratic. One middle-aged man collects driftwood, shaping and polishing it to make attractive ornaments. Some former fishermen have turned their old occupation into a hobby, using their otherwise idle boats to fish for pleasure in distant and supposedly uncontaminated waters. But everyone agrees that the flavor of the fish has changed for the worse, and many people are fearful of eating them.

The great hobby of men and women of middle age or older — the raising of ornamental shrubs and flowering plants — is a national development of recent years. Piano playing, a pastime that has swept the nation in recent years and continues to mount in popularity, has not yet reached Takashima, but everyone knows of the national trend, and aspirations to own a piano, a prestigious symbol, have been expressed as wishes for the future.

Most of the many festival occasions of the past hold no importance today as times of recreation except among some of the aged, who may then make festive trips to nearby temples and shrines. Obon and New Year's are exceptional and are the great annual periods of rest and pleasure, times when relatives see each other and times for joyous celebration with unrelated friends as well as with relatives. Trains continue to be packed to capacity at these seasons, and a festive air of holiday is evident everywhere. New Year's is the great season of rest and revelry for Takashima and all of Japan, when most of the commercial activities of the busy nation come to a halt for a few days and are fully resumed only after the passage of many days. At Obon and New Year's, all recreational activities that the seasons and other circumstances will allow are possible. For most young women, however, it is only at New Year's that fine traditional clothing is worn, and, for many men, it is only at New Year's that they drink alcohol to the point of getting drunk. Even on these two annual occasions of familial gathering, a trend of change is evident that applies also at all other times. Increasingly, the participants in recreational activities tend to be unrelated persons and people who are not members of the community of Takashima.

Among the foreign influences on Takashima culture discussed in the account of 1950–51 was the use of foreign words, which consisted principally of English terms. In common with the rest of Japan, the speech of Takashima people includes a greatly increased number of English words. As a language, modern Japanese is in fact appropriately described as consisting in its vocabulary of three major elements: native Japanese terms, many thousands of words derived in antiquity from Chinese, and, in modern times, an increment of English and English-derived words that grows annually. For the average person today, English items of vocabulary number several thousand, but they are often unrecognizable by native speakers of English because of the Japanese manner of rendering them phonetically and because they are often otherwise modified, especially by abbreviation. The transition to industrial life brought hundreds of new English words to Takashima people, although their linguistic derivation is often unknown to their speakers. Men employed in the chemical industry use terms such as "polymer," "monomer," "catalysis," and "polyethylene." Most of the words referring to automobiles are similarly English or derived from English, usually from the vocabulary of the United States, but the automobile is to some degree linguistically a hybrid. Many words, such as "motor," "trunk," and "gasoline," appear to be derived from American English, but what is known in the United States as a "hood," a phonetic combination that is difficult for the Japanese to pronounce, is called "bonnet" (*bonneto*), the term used in England. The characteristic term for "full tank" (of gasoline), also used to instruct service station attendants to fill the tank, is *mantan*, an abbreviated hybrid of Chinese and English. The element *man* means "full" or "to fill," and the element *tan* is derived from the English word "tank," which Japanese render in two syllables as *tanku*. *Mantan* came quickly to be adapted by Takashima children to mean a full stomach.

English words have sometimes displaced their Japanese equivalents; for example, "milk" (*miruku*) has for many years been customarily used in place of the ancient Chinese-derived term *gyūnyū*, and "vacation" is commonly used in place of the native *kyūka*. Other English words that are cumbersome to render in Japanese phonemes are abbreviated and thereby have become what must be regarded as distinctively Japanese terms. Two long-established examples are *genesuto*, an abbreviation of *generaru sutoraiki*, "general strike," and *demo*, "demonstration," as by a labor union. Takashima people sometimes say *koresto* instead of the lengthier *korestororu*, "cholesterol." Although words that are known to be foreign, especially those with Japanese equivalents, are occasionally used as affectations presumed by their speakers to give prestige, people are generally little concerned with the provenance of their vocabularies. A useful word is simply a useful word, and no obvious feelings of opposition to the employment of foreign terms exists. As is characteristic of the addition of foreign words to any language, the foreign elements of speech have become Japanese; that is, the grammar of the Japanese language has been unaffected by them.

FAMILY AND KIN

Changes in national and local ways of life had already affected kin groups and kin relationships on Takashima by 1950–51. The history of these trends of change for the nation reaches back at least to the nineteenth century, to the time of the ending of Japan's self-imposed isolation from the rest of the world and the beginning of its industrialization and modernization. As a small rural community distant from any city of substantial size, Takashima lagged behind urban centers in changing, but had nevertheless already been affected. The overall trends of change may be summarized briefly in the statement that kinship dwindled in importance and kin groups became smaller. Everywhere the family has shrunk in size and changed in composition and in the relationships of its members. Large kin groups of any kind that operate as corporate units became uncommon years ago throughout the nation, and the nuclear family composed of only parents and their children has been the predominant form of the family for decades. Except for a brief time after World War II when residents of the devastated cities were forced temporarily to take up life with country kin, the nuclear family saw its greatest increase after World War II and continues to increase today.

As earlier demographic information attests, Takashima was late in strongly conforming with the national average, which was increasingly based upon urban populations as the cities of Japan swelled after the war. Even today the families of Takashima embrace a larger number of members than the national average. Poverty fostered the survival of the extended family on Takashima until the late 1950s. Increased incomes then allowed the construction of added dwellings which, in turn, meant the fission of extended families.

In early 1975, ten of the fifty-one Takashima households were extended families which included one or both parents of the male head of the household or, in two instances, of the wife of the household head. Other households were composed of aged single persons, couples of varying age but mostly old who had no children or did not live with their children, and, principally, nuclear families. Among the ten extended families, two families of means included three generations of spouses (*sandai fūfu*), a circumstance which was a source of pride to the eldest couples of these households. Two of the ten families included persons other than grandparents and spouses and their children. These were two young women of about twenty-five years, a sister of a household head and a sister of the wife of a household head. Although older than the average woman at the time of marriage, neither had yet married, and their residence in the homes was expected to come to an end at any time.

Relationships of kin are sometimes complex or unusual because of customs of adoption. One household headed by a man who had been adopted in childhood and whose father had died now includes the still vigorous foster mother of the household head and his senile natural father. Another household includes a grandfather adopted in childhood whose natural mother is alive and a member of another household as well as a man of middle age who was adopted by the grandfather and his wife as the husband of their lone child, a daughter adopted in childhood. In addition, this household embraces a third generation of three natural offspring of the adopted daughter and her husband and also the husband of the eldest daughter of this couple.

Most of the parents of household heads who live with their offspring are well past middle age. If the family has been at any time financially able to construct a special room for them, they sleep and spend most of their waking time in these *hanare-beya*, "separated rooms." After the deaths of these aged men and women, the number of extended families will decline still further.

The possession of considerable wealth sometimes appears to hold extended families together, making them in some degree exceptions to the general trend toward small families. However, the three instances of this kind in Takashima reflect attitudes and practices on the parts of their male heads which are not those prevailing in the nation and also other special circumstances. In two cases, the household heads are old men, of ages seventy-one and seventy-five in 1975, who continue to serve as heads of their households. Both are forceful, physically vigorous men who have long exercised strong control over familial wealth and the behavior of members of their households and who are said to be unwilling to relinquish their positions of authority. The male heir apparent in one household is a *yōshi*, a son adopted at the time of his marriage to the daughter of the household head, also an adopted child. Relations between the aged household head and his now middle-aged daughter are close, but relations between the head and his son-in-law (who is also legally a son) have always been strained. An official city record lists the son-in-law as household head, but this does not represent the circumstances within the family in question or the opinion of the community. The future successor to headship of the second exceptional household is generally regarded as a ne'er-do-well, and relations between him and his father are said to be poor.

A third household is composed of a household head of advanced middle age and his wife, who have had no children, and, according to municipal records, a youngest brother, his wife, and their two children, who live in a separate house still legally owned by the eldest brother. Another younger brother lives independently in the community with his wife and children. The three brothers had lost their parents by death when the eldest brother was a young adult and his much younger brothers were small children. The eldest brother then assumed the role

13. *A household of four generations, now uncommon.* 14. *The senior generation: Takashima women and visiting friends and relatives.*

of surrogate father, a status which he continues to hold. Relations among the three brothers are close and without strife. The youngest brother is said, however, to be excessively fond of alcohol and to exercise poor judgment in other ways. Retention of the headship of the household by the eldest brother and of legal ownership of the house occupied by the youngest brother is generally assumed by other community members to reflect paternalistic supervision caused by the weaknesses of character of the youngest brother.

Young adult men and women who have not yet married usually continue to live with their parents, to whom they may or may not give part of their earnings. The old custom of pooling familial earnings has followed a partial course of change. Some families do so, and, in others, young men and women place their earnings or savings in separate bank accounts.

As in the past, most Takashima families bear the surname Matsui and are in some manner relatives. But the relationships are now often very remote and these are generally unknown in their specific details to the young, who have little interest in learning them. The aged still speak of three lines of Matsuis, now admittedly blurred by some intermarriages, but only a few of the aged are able to trace all the relationships. Among the several households composed of old-time residents who are not Matsuis, the process of fission to form nuclear families has also occurred.

Within the residential family, relationships continue to be intimate if otherwise changed. Intimacy is thinned, however, by growing contacts with people outside the family, and changed roles of kin accompanied by changed conceptions of the right and proper behavior among kin have tempered the nature of the whole realm of kinship. Fathers are less commanding, mothers less meekly submissive, children less bound by ideals of filial piety, and mothers-in-law — the mothers of married sons — have ceased to hold strong control over their sons' wives. No mother-in-law wishes to gain a reputation in this respect as being a traditional tyrant and thus bring upon herself the demeaning charge of being "left behind the times" and "feudal." In any case, the number of new or recent brides who live with their husbands' parents has become small.

Eldest sons long ago lost their thrones, in some measure acceding them to younger brothers and even to sisters. Eldest sons are still often expected to remain at home and, when the time comes, to care for their aged parents. Younger sons may go elsewhere, where economic opportunities are better and where they are unencumbered by the responsibility of caring for aged parents. A "bride famine" for eldest sons began in the nation in the late 1950s and has been especially acute in farming families, where younger sons and even daughters were for some years often given better educations than eldest sons, who, as future farmers, were then thought to need no education beyond that of high school. Although statistical information on this subject is not available, the present trend among the dwindling number of farm families and generally throughout the nation appears to be toward equal educations for all sons and daughters. The bride famine nevertheless applies to any young man faced with the care of his parents, unless the onus is conditioned by some compensation, such as great wealth.

The nuclear family as a residential group has, for many years, been the ideal of most of the young people of the nation, and aged parents have come to share this view. In the congested, large cities, the lack of housing beyond tiny apartments has given further support to this attitude. Both the traditional and the new views and customs exist in Takashima, but the great number of Takashima dwellings alone points to participation in the national trend of change.

The relative statuses of males and females in Takashima have clearly changed, but measurement of the degree of change is impressionistic. Takashima women have a long history of recognized economic productivity as fishers, a circumstance which enhanced their positions so that the difference in social statuses between men and women in former times was smaller than in most communities of the nation. Farm wives were not ordinarily looked upon as being economically productive. In the nation today, official records of gainful employment show that women compose about 40 percent of the labor force and that about 80 percent of adult women are employed. Today it is possible for a Japanese woman to provide for herself economically without dependence upon males or upon any relatives. Nearly all Takashima women work, and their cash incomes are readily measurable — and carefully measured.

In most homes of the community, the appliances and improvements of recent years have come from the added earnings of women. This economic weight alone has probably done much to reduce the breach between female and male statuses. Every adolescent and adult, male or female, is aware of the national movement toward sexual equality, which is given much publicity by the news media. A women's liberation movement is nationally active, although generally moderate in its activities as compared with the movement in the United States. One of its lesser manifestations is a national voluntary association known by the abbreviated name *Chupiren*, which concerns itself with the activities described in a translation of its name, "Federation for Women's Liberation Demanding the Free Use of the Pill and Opposing the Law Against Abortion." In 1974, female employees of a radio broadcasting company successfully took legal action against their employers on the charge of discrimination by following the policy of retiring them at thirty years of age, and other similar court actions are common enough. Also in 1974, the Japanese Association of University Women, established in 1946, was host to the eighteenth annual conference of the International Federation of University Women, an event given much publicity in which 918 delegates from 40 nations participated. Politicians have long been respectful of the *Shufuren*, a national organization of homemakers that expresses its views firmly on matters of social welfare and many other things. Peaceable demonstrations by tens of thousands of obviously respectable homemakers are impressive, and the association represents many votes.

Despite these changes toward a leveling of the statuses of the sexes, the position of men appears to be much above that of women in ideal if not always in fact. In fact, the adult sex roles evident in Takashima seem characterized more by differing than by being markedly unequal in prestige or authority. Few Takashima women are said to chafe about dominance by their husbands; none regard themselves as strong adherents of the women's liberation movement, and most are the undisputed authorities in many matters concerning the home and children. As in the past, the wives are often the guardians of familial funds and the keepers of financial records. As elsewhere in Japanese society and probably in much of the rest of the world, the breach between them and their husbands declines as the marriage continues and they become mothers, and, in the final decades of their marriages, they are sometimes the dominant spouses, exercising authority in ways that are usually pleasing or acceptable to their husbands.

Ties with relatives outside the immediate family have grown noticeably thinner in Takashima. New houses built for sons and their families still tend to be called *bunke*, "branch houses," but they are in no sense economically or otherwise branches of the traditional kind, which had essentially ceased to exist by 1950–51. They are instead independent families between which emotional ties exist. Only in case of dire necessity, however, should one family ask another for any substantial financial or other aid. Many young men and women have so little contact with relatives older than themselves in other households of the community that they do not know their given names and, often, the precise nature of their relationships to them. Relatives outside the family roof are thus generally undemanding today, and most people think it is good to have relatives of this kind. Weddings and funerals unfailingly bring a convocation of many relatives, a matter of the emotions that involves no important economic considerations.

Tradition and modernity coexist in practices of marriage. The tendency toward *renai kekkon,* "love marriages," has grown, but the traditional marriage arranged by a go-between is still common. Coexistence of the two modes of arranging marriages appears to fit the times. Young men and women have many more opportunities today to meet potential spouses, and parental approval of marriages arranged by the principals is generally routine, although tradition then takes over and a nominal go-between handles all arrangements. For young people who lack the opportunity to meet potential mates or who are socially inept in matters of courting, the go-between is still available.

Brides continue to be drawn from nearby communities, and in-community marriages are uncommon. The two instances of such marriages since 1950–51 are unusual in a number of ways. The second son of the richest family in the community chose as his bride a remotely related young woman from one of the community's poorest families, and even his status-conscious and domineering father did not stand in the way of the marriage. The second union was between a brother and a sister, both adopted and genetically unrelated. This marriage is said to have been planned by the foster parents at the time of the adoptions on the grounds that such a union would insure amity in the entire family, reasoning which most other members of the community looked upon as being strange. Of thirty-eight marriages upon which information about the manner of marriage was gathered, thirteen were unions of love and twenty-five were arranged by go-betweens. The couples in question ranged in age from the early twenties to the late sixties, and most of the marriages of love were among the young.

The age of marriage is unchanged. Women generally marry while in their early twenties and men at about age twenty-five. Brides are usually a few years younger than their husbands, but as in former times, the marriage of a man to a woman a few years older than herself is not regarded as strange. Divorce is still strongly disfavored unless conditions of the marriage are deplorable. None has occurred since 1950–51, although two Takashima women who married and left the community later divorced their husbands. Several men of the community are *yōshi,* "adoptive husbands," but no young man has entered this kind of marriage, which, from ancient times, has been looked upon as a last resort. Young men can now provide for themselves without entering such unions, and maintaining continuity of male lines of descent has ceased to be a matter of great importance.

Many features of modern weddings differ from customs of the past. A gift of money (*yuinō*) is still given to the parents of the bride by the parents of the groom in ceremonial fashion; the amount is now about

$75 to $150 and is looked upon as being an inconsequential sum, merely a token of goodwill. Weddings and the wedding feasts that follow are customarily held in commercial wedding halls in Okayama City rather than in the homes. As in the past, the weddings are secular events that do not include the services of priests unless, as rarely happens, the wedding is conducted in the marriage hall of a Shinto shrine. Guests are more numerous than formerly and include a growing number of nonkin, friends from school days or from the places of employment of the bride and groom. Food and drink are provided by the firm operating the wedding hall and include Western dishes of buffet style as well as beer. Brides of recent years have generally favored white wedding gowns of Western style, which are both "modern" and much less expensive than traditional wedding clothing. Expenses for the wedding, formerly the responsibility of the bride's family, are now usually divided equally between the families of the bride and the groom. The traditional items of the trousseau of the bride have been replaced by modern equivalents and often include refrigerators, washing machines, cooking stoves, rice steamers, and sets of dishes. Uncommonly, automobiles have been parental wedding gifts. The ceremony is now customarily followed by a honeymoon trip to visit one of the famous scenic spots of Japan or to see the sights of Tokyo or Kyoto.

Married couples want and expect to have children, when the time is right, a few years after their marriage. Until this time, the bride continues to work and the couple saves money that will allow them comfortably to have two children, a boy and a girl. Adoption of children is less common than formerly, probably because the ideal family is now small and because male successors are no longer regarded as truly necessary, but, as in the past, no special feelings oppose or stigmatize such adoptions.

Except in a generalized way having to do with the number of children in the community, sexual relations were not a subject of inquiry for the reason that most informants were reluctant quickly to give personal information on this topic, and interviews with many people were brief, sandwiched into their busy round of daily activities. Birth control was a matter about which many people were willing to talk, however. From informants' statements and also from the demographic data previously presented, it is evident that techniques of birth control are well established and that births are carefully planned. Intrauterine devices and the pill are both prohibited by Japanese law as being injurious to the health. Several middle-aged women of Takashima are said to have had legal abortions in earlier years when as many as a million such surgical operations were performed annually in the nation. Legislation then made this mode of birth control illegal, except under certain conditions of health of the mother. Contraceptive devices used in Takashima seem to be principally rubber prophylactics used by males. Absolute fidelity is expected of both husband and wife, but casual and occasional remissness on the part of the husband after some years of marriage is not usually regarded as an offense serious enough to lead to divorce.

THE COMMUNITY AND THE OUTSIDE WORLD

Community solidarity has followed the general course of kinship, thinning but retaining some strength. In this respect, Takashima differs from many communities of the nation, where "community" often means a residential aggregation which seldom or never acts as a corporate unit. Several circumstances, some which have been previously noted in passing, foster this survival of communality. One of these conditions is the isolation of Takashima, today a residential island surrounded by industrial plants and the sea — a community which is unlikely to see the incorporation of outsiders because of its lack of space for additional dwellings and its undesirability as a residential site. Kinship and long-established ties with nonkin in the community also help to maintain a feeling of unity, even though contacts are less frequent and, except with close kin, less intimate than formerly.

As a suburb of a city of substantial size, Takashima is unusual in retaining ownership of some communal property, an additional factor which helps to bind its members. A few wells and a small plot of land formerly in forest are communally owned; their value today consists principally of future promise as pieces of real estate. Although not owned by Takashima residents, the small harbor erected and maintained by prefectural funds is for the common use of Takashima people. Forecasts by informants of its future use see it as a place for pleasure craft, once the sea is cleared of pollutants. The communal meeting hall and the shrine of the tutelary god as well as the land on which they stand are also common property to which emotional and materialistic values are attached. Most important is the communal cemetery. Maintenance of the meeting hall, shrine, and cemetery are still joint undertakings. Tasks connected with maintenance are assigned to families and individuals in rotation at an annual meeting of representatives of all households, and no one shirks his or her responsibilities. Funds required for such maintenance are derived from common levies, decided at the annual meeting.

Matsuis still associate principally in the community with other Matsuis, among whom they draw many fine distinctions of status based upon familial and personal circumstances. Relations with non-Matsuis, as in former times, are less common and generally conditioned by an attitude on the part of the Matsuis that they are superior. Individual traits and the course of economic fortunes have conditioned these attitudes, however, so that some Matsuis are generally held in low regard and some non-Matsuis have risen in status.

The busy lives of most people still leave time for the spreading of news and for gossip about events that are regarded as important, such as purchases of cars, places and conditions of employment, births, deaths, marriages, and the entry of young people into college. News of unseemly and scandalous behavior continues to spread quickly. The community kleptomaniac, a healthy woman now well into her eighties, has not abandoned her habit, and her activities are the subject of mild and tolerant gossip. As in the past, what she is able to steal seldom has much value, and she is otherwise a respected member of the community. Gossip about the philandering of two aged, but vigorous, men of the community who are said to have mistresses in other communities is much less tolerant. One is said to have taken as a mistress a distant relative born and raised on Takashima who married unfortunately and was divorced. The other, a rich man, is said to have had a long succession of secret mistresses.

Personal foibles of other kinds and desirable traits of personality or character are also well known. All adults of the community are known to each other by such traits as being stingy, generous, hot-tempered, agreeable, industrious, lazy, and the like. Cordiality continues to prevail, and even serious misdeeds do not ordinarily put an end to civil relations. A few adults are known to be "enemies," but their feelings of animosity are seldom given expression in any way that is generally disruptive to the community.

Modes of address in some degree reflect changed communal and kin relations. Most people continue to use the kin terms "aunt," "uncle," "grandmother," and "grandfather" for unrelated people and for distant kin of appropriate ages who do not hold those statuses of kinship, but change seems evident in the choice of alternative suffixes for these terms and for personal names. The use of the suffix *-chan*, a term that connotes intimacy, appears to be less common than formerly. The richest and most powerful man in the community, as in the past generally respected but disliked, is never addressed as "grandfather" by anyone except junior members of his household; he is instead referred to and often addressed by most people of forty or more years of age by his given name to which the more formal suffix *-san* is added. Some people avoid using any term of address for him. As in the past, surnames are seldom used in address, since most people have the same surname, and long acquaintance with non-Matsuis makes the use of surnames seem strange in addressing them.

The two families of outsiders in the community are truly outsiders in whom the old-time residents have little interest. Both families are renters and are therefore assumed to be temporary residents; both are ordinary, poor families headed by ordinary industrial workers. Moreover, both are strangers to whom no special obligations are owed. For these reasons, in most social contexts, they are not regarded as community members. One family, composed of a childless couple of middle age from a distant province, took up residence in Takashima in 1973. In 1974, about eighteen months later, most people except immediate neighbors had never met this couple, both of whom are employed in industry, and did not know their surname. The other family consists of a young couple from remote Okinawa and their three small children, who moved to Takashima in early 1974. In late 1974, the only Takashima people whom this family had met were one of the two elected community heads and the owner of the house which they rented. Few other community members even knew the family surname or showed any interest in learning it.

In one respect, however, both families of the outsiders are included in the community. Both qualify as members of the still existing *burakukai*, "community association," and are invited to attend the one scheduled annual meeting and any special meetings that might be called. Membership in this association of all households in the community, each having an equal voice in all decisions, is looked upon as an important, democratic tradition, although, as later discussion will bring out, functions of the association are today much less important than in the past. Lack of representation today would not affect in any important way the lives of members of any household.

Much of the preceding account of community relations may be restated in brief summary. Many of the roles once performed by a large group of cooperating kin and by unrelated community members are no longer needed, desired, or even possible. Even association with many community members for purposes of recreation or entertainment is impossible because of the demands of daily lives. Social orbits have grown very greatly for the young and for people who are in employment, and the individual social networks of these people are highly variable in the identity of the people they include. These words are to say that, more and more as time has passed, individual social worlds have grown past the boundaries of the community. Places of employment are various, and, since the years of formal education of the young bring them into a variety of social contexts, the associates of even the children may differ greatly by the time they are adolescent. At ages four and five, some Takashima children attend a nearby kindergarten, which is not compulsory; all attend a single elementary school and a single junior high school. High schools attended by Takashima children in 1974–75 totaled six, in different parts of the city, one of which was a private school for girls; all others were public. Specialization in employment brings different human associates for even men and women employed by the same industrial concern, and individual interests and traits of personality operate similarly.

In relations with members of outside communities, ancient attitudes and prejudices have not entirely disappeared. The *sokobiki*, who reside in a section of nearby Shionasu, are still regarded as near outcasts. Social relations with them are cordial, involving no readily obvious expressions of contempt, but they are confined only to necessary contact, such as meetings of the P.T.A. of the elementary school. Intermarriage with them continues to be unthinkable, even though the economic positions of some *sokobiki* families have risen.

None of the foregoing statements means to imply that atomization or isolation from emotionally rewarding association with other people has occurred. As in the past, Takashima people are joiners who become affiliated with social groups of various kinds. These groups of nonkin or common-interest associations are of special interest because they represent both continuity and change. It is largely through membership in common-interest associations that community solidarity is fostered and also largely through them that ties are formed with people outside the community.

As in former times, the associations have varying goals, and, following a scheme of classification current in the social sciences, they may be distinguished on this basis as being primarily instrumental, expressive, or as combining both kinds of goals in approximately equal degree. Goals of instrumental associations are practical matters, such as civic improvement, social reform, or the performance of tasks requiring cooperative effort. Expressive associations center upon emotional or affective activities, such as sports and other forms of recreation and aesthetic and religious activities.

Associations were abundant on Takashima in 1950–51 and were one of the principal means by which social unity of the community was established and maintained. Consciously egalitarian in their operation, they are democratic forms of social organization which coexist in a compatible and complementary way with hierarchic lines of order that exist in the family and in many other sectors of daily lives. Associations are vigorously alive in Takashima today, and they have been notably plastic in adjusting to changes in the conditions of life of the community and the nation. Viewed broadly as a form of social organization, the associations have not changed; viewed individually, they have undergone extensive change that includes the extinction of certain associations and the creation of others.

The study of voluntary associations, age-graded societies, clubs, and other types of common-interest associations has a long history in anthropology, but it has never been an outstanding focus of either field research or formulations of theory. These circumstances also apply to studies of Japanese society, which have given such great emphasis to hierarchy and kinship as the main themes of social organization that associations have often been overlooked. Associations are ancient in Japan. They have long coexisted with kin groups and social alignments based upon hierarchy in complementary ways that make it difficult to judge the relative importance of any one of these principles of organization. All have been and continue to be important. A trend of change has long been evident, however, toward growing importance of associations that has accompanied declines in the scope and functions of kinship and the firmness of hierarchy as Japan has become increasingly industrialized.

Studies of common-interest associations have been notably weak in considering such trends of change, perhaps in part because little observation has been made of associations over a substantial period of time. A list of the associations of Takashima shows many changes. (See Table 3.)

The first of the four associations existing in 1951 that have since disappeared was the Young People's Association, an ancient group. In principle concerned with both community affairs and recreational activities, it had long been weak in 1951. Young men and women entered this group at age sixteen and remained members until their marriage. In times dimmed by antiquity, the youths' group seems to have performed communal tasks requiring joint labor, but no such tasks which were not otherwise assigned had existed for many years. In 1951, the single joint activity of the youths' group consisted of a rite of initiation, conducted annually for males only who became sixteen years of age during the year. No counterpart existed for females. In 1951, the only other activities of members of this association consisted of extemporaneous games of table tennis in the community hall, using equipment purchased for that purpose by the Hamlet Association. One of the reasons given by informants for the demise of the association was the nature of its annual rite of initiation which traditionally allowed or required that the initiates and all other male members of the group participate in a feast at which they drank rice wine to the point of intoxication. This custom, disfavored in 1950–51, later met with increasing disfavor by parents who had ceased to think that age sixteen was an appropriate time for drunkenness.

TABLE 3

COMMON-INTEREST ASSOCIATIONS IN TAKASHIMA

Existing in 1950–51	Type	Status in 1975
*Hamlet Association (*Burakukai*) (General community affairs; e.g., maintenance of roads, wells, shrine, and relations with outside communities; conduct of communal festivals)	IE	Active but weakened
*Women's Association (*Fujinkai*) Community affairs and social club)	IE	Disbanded in 1973
*Young People's Association (*Seinendan*) (Community affairs and recreational activities)	IE	Disbanded about 1955
*Funeral Association (*Kōrenchū*) (Provides aid for bereaved families at times of death)	I	Active but weakened; now two smaller associations
*Fire Prevention Association (*Shōbōdan*) (Fire prevention and fire fighting)	I	Moribund
*Pilgrimage Association (*Daisan*) (Makes pilgrimages to shrines at times of critical illness of any community member. Not regarded as an association by Takashima people.)	I	Moribund
Buddhist Parish Association (*Danka*)	IE	Weak, as in 1951
P.T.A. (*Pee-Chee-Ay*)	I	Active; functions somewhat changed
Fishermen's Cooperative Association (*Gyogyō Kyōdō Kumiai*)	I	Disbanded in 1974
Farmers' Cooperative Association (*Nōgyō Kyōdō Kumiai*)	I	Active but weakened
Freight Boat Operators' Association (*Kihansen Kumiai*)	I	No local members
Ward Hamlet-Representatives' Association (*Ku-Sōdaikai*) (Community affairs of the ward; composed of heads of hamlet associations)	I	Active but weakened

Added Since 1951 and Existing in 1974:	Type	Current Status
*Takashima Special Association for Meeting Problems of Public Damage (*Takashima-chiku Kōgai Taisaku Tokubetsu Kyōgikai*) (Concerned with environmental pollution, illness, and other problems caused by industrial effluents)	I	Nominal existence
*Old People's Club (*Rōjinkai*)	E	Weakly active

Added Since 1951 and Existing in 1974:	Type	Current Status
*Flower arranging group (no name) (Informal organization not regarded as an association by its members)	E	Active
Labor Unions (*Rōdōkumiai*) (Various company unions)	E	Active
Recreational associations in industrial firms *kurabbu*; i.e., clubs) (Sports and aesthetics)	I	Active
Sōka-Gakkai (a lay Buddhist sect)	IE	Weakly represented in Takashima

I — primarily instrumental.
E — primarily expressive.
IE — instrumental and expressive.
* Associations with varying degrees of autonomous existence on Takashima, although they may be affiliated with larger regional or national associations.

A broader view of the reasons for the disbanding of this association concerns national changes in culture which lengthened the period of social immaturity of societal members and, at the same time, directed the functions of the association into other channels. In the Japan of 1955, the approximate year of the collapse of the Young People's Association, the age of attaining social adulthood had generally been variably lengthened far beyond sixteen years by the demands of education and employment. As in the United States, the age of social maturity in the sense of economic independence varied greatly according to social class and years of formal education, a circumstance that was rendered still more complex by incongruence and variations in the ages at which marriage was legally possible and at which the legal right was given to drive cars, buy alcohol, and own property. In Takashima, these conditions also existed, and the old roles of the association could not be performed. Communal enterprises suitable for the young no longer existed, and young people had long ago found recreational activities that did not limit them to association with youths of their own small communities.

The Women's Association was also an instrumental and expressive association with deep roots, and the reasons for its dissolution in Takashima are essentially the same as for the youths' group. Long before it was disbanded, the Women's Association had ceased to be a satisfactory organ for recreation. Such communal responsibilities as it retained in 1951 consisted of service or auxiliary roles under the Hamlet Association, especially in connection with communal festivals, and these were then almost extinct. Communal women's associations continue to exist in many communities of Japan, but it seems safe to state that they are often weak and generally have no vital instrumental goals. The disappearance of the Takashima group appears to have been expedited by the fact that nearly all Takashima women are daytime wage earners and nighttime wives, mothers, and homemakers who have little time, as well as little inclination, to participate in group activities which they no longer regard as necessary or rewarding.

The once important fishermen's and freight boat operators' associations disappeared simply because the occupations disappeared. Essentially identical associations continue to have vigorous life in communities where the occupations they represent are important, and fishermen's cooperatives are particularly forceful nationally in combatting environmental pollution that endangers their occupation. For similar economic reasons, the farmers' cooperative association became weak, although it remains important in communities where agriculture continues to have importance. Membership in the farmers' cooperative had been valuable to Takashima people because of its multiple functions as a credit and savings association, a medium for the purchase of farming necessities as well as for the sale of cash crops, and a means of keeping abreast with developments in agronomy. For those who continue to do kitchen farming, membership in the agricultural cooperative is maintained, but it is not regarded as important, and banks are generally the main institution of domestic finance.

Two associations, the Hamlet Association and the Funeral Association, remain alive but have weakened. Formerly the most important of the autonomous community associations, the Hamlet Association continues to include all households, each of which is represented at association meetings by one person, usually the male head. Ideally, each family, whether composed of one or of many persons, has equal voice in community affairs governed by the association. Traditional functions of the association were communal affairs of every kind that were not administered by governmental agencies, including the use and maintenance of communal property, the construction and maintenance of roads and paths, and the conduct of once numerous communal festivals. Most of these roles have been assumed by the municipal government, have disappeared entirely for other reasons, or have no existence as communal undertakings. Communal wells were displaced by piped city water. The small patch of communal forest atop the hill behind the dwellings is essentially valueless today. Communal vats for treating fishing nets became useless and were discarded. Communal festivals centered on devotional rites for the tutelary god of the hamlet ground to a slow stop in the late 1950s, according to informants, for lack of interest and lack of belief in the guardian spirit. Maintenance of roads, preservation of peace, and similar functions of the past are now all responsibilities of the city.

A general meeting of the Hamlet Association is still held at New Year's, and other meetings, formerly held monthly, are now called two or three times during the year, as the occasions demand. Becoming *chō*, "head," of the Hamlet Association, a position acquired by a process beginning with the recommendation of a suitable male and later approval by all members, was once an honor. Today leadership is generally avoided or assumed reluctantly and is divided among two people, who are called *sōdai*, "counsellors." Leaders are eventually found, however, and the association retains certain functions. The most important of these is the maintenance of the communal graveyard, the shrine of the local tutelary god, and the communal meeting hall. These tasks are performed with the aid of all households of the community acting in rotation, each serving for a fixed period, usually one year. The shrine, formerly used for various annual ceremonies, now sees no use except for occasional visits by grandmothers accompanied by small children. Most middle-aged and young adults have not visited it for years. Partly in deference to the older members of the community, however, maintenance of the shrine is regarded as a moral responsibility.

The hamlet counsellors' roles also include the maintenance of liaison with neighboring communities, which is done by means of their membership in a ward association composed of the heads of hamlet associations. Meetings of the Ward Hamlet-Representatives' Association have for some years generally been limited to one held at New Year's. Like its smaller counterpart—the Hamlet Association—this association suffered the loss of various functions to bureaus and agencies of the municipal, prefectural, and national governments, and it has little importance today. Serving in former times as a voice of the people in a chain of communicative liaison with higher authority, it is today redundant or unnecessary, and the future will probably see its disbanding.

Like the Hamlet Association, the Funeral Association of Takashima represents one of the oldest and most prevalent types of cooperative associations in Japan. Similarly also, modern times have weakened this group by making various of its traditional functions unnecessary. Traditionally, the *Kōrenchū* provided emotional support for bereaved families at times of death. It also gave practical aid by preparing food for ordinary consumption of the bereaved family and for the wake and later funeral feast, giving notification in person of the death to the parish priest and to relatives of the deceased living in other communities, and filling many other roles in connection with the funeral and the disposal of the body of the deceased. Today, the telephone and the automobile make notification of death a simple matter; commercially prepared foods and catering companies remove much of the former labor from food preparation, and disposal of the body is wholly a task for professionals.

A gradual weakening of communal ties has also made participation by all households seem unnecessary. Moreover, lack of space in the homes to accommodate the increased number of household representatives and the high cost of food for such a large number of people at wakes and funeral feasts have also made full participation undesirable. The increase in the number of households had made a single funeral association unnecessarily large, and, for this reason, two groups were established in about 1969 that represent geographical divisions of the community. Ideally, a representative of every household still attends the funeral proper to pay respects to the deceased, but only members of the same funeral association now participate in the prefuneral wake and stand ready to aid the family of the deceased. For the most part, relatives of the deceased can today handle the tasks connected with the death, and, beyond certain traditional roles in the funeral ceremony that must be filled by nonrelatives, little neighborly aid is needed.

The Buddhist Parish Association, of which Takashima constitutes a subdivision, is seldom regarded by its members as an association. Ideally, all members of the parish participate jointly in a series of traditional calendrical rites conducted at the temple, a short distance from Takashima but, in fact, no joint meetings or any other kind of face-to-face contact of many or all parish members have been required or even expected for a great many years. Almost all Takashima residents continue to be members of the ancient Shingon Sect of Buddhism, and one adult male serves as the community representative and liaison agent in parish affairs. Most of the people of Takashima have rarely visited their temple for more than twenty years even on its traditional festival days, but funerals and later commemorative services for deceased relatives continue to be conducted in their homes by the local priest, and some degree of parish in-group feeling exists. The incumbent priest annually makes two routine and traditional visits to each household to perform ceremonies.

Of the associations existing in 1951, only the P.T.A. can be described as retaining its vigor; this association appears even to have gained in importance. In 1951, the P.T.A. meant only the association of parents and teachers of the nearby elementary school which all Takashima children attended. Children of that time who had finished elementary school commuted by schoolboat and by bus to the nearest junior high school, some miles distant on the main island, too distant for active participation by their parents in its P.T.A. At the time, only two or three young people attended high schools, which were also similarly distant. Rising levels of education and improved means of transportation, including private automobiles, have fostered greater participation in various P.T.A.'s. Today, Takashima parents are active participants in the P.T.A. of the elementary and junior high schools which their children attend. A Takashima father was vice-president of the P.T.A. of the junior high school in 1974. P.T.A.'s appear to have only token existence in the six high schools attended by Takashima children. Functions of the P.T.A.'s are much like those of their counterparts in the United States, from which their name is derived, but, as later discussion will bring out, their auxiliary functions differ in ways that reflect old customs of Japan.

Among the associations added since 1951, three may be called Takashima associations, that is, associations confined to Takashima or groups in which the Takashima membership constitutes a recognizable, organized subdivision of a larger organization. All three of these are voluntary associations. One of these, the Takashima Special Association for Meeting Problems of Public Damage, is a truly voluntary association with wholly instrumental goals. The Takashima organization, which at its height was composed of representatives of about one-fifth of the households of the community with able-bodied male heads, was formed independently in Takashima in 1971. A ward organization of the same sort had arisen a few years earlier and some Takashima people had been members. Feeling that their problems were distinctive and could best be handled by themselves, Takashima residents withdrew from membership in the ward association, which was composed mostly of residential settlements that did little or no fishing, and formed their own group. Activities consisted of a number of discussion meetings and the contacting of city officials and heads of industrial plants to call attention to the polluted condition of the air and the sea about Takashima.

Similar societies already existed or were established in surrounding communities and in other industrial cities of the nation. All were active in lodging complaints. Following a national trend, the city administration then actively took up their cause, passing various ordinances that attempted to control industrial wastes. By 1974, when it appeared to be fairly clear that environmental pollution in and around Takashima had diminished somewhat and would continue to diminish in the future, the Takashima association became inactive. Its functions now assumed by municipal and other governmental agencies, the association last met in November 1973 and made no plans at that time for future meetings.

The Old People's Club is a wholly expressive organization founded paternalistically in the mid 1960s by the city administration, which provides the small funds it uses. All people sixty years of age and older qualify as members. Takashima members compose a subdivision, with two liaison officers, of a larger ward association that is united with other ward associations under a municipal administrative office. Activities consist of one pleasure trip annually by bus, an event in which about one-half of the Takashima elders participate. No activities limited to Takashima residents are conducted.

The flower arranging group bears no formal name, and, as noted in Table 3, it is not recognized by its members as an association. About twenty women, all married and ranging in age from the twenties to the sixties, meet twice monthly in the community hall for professional instruction in flower arranging, for which each participant pays a fee. The emergence of this group, which occurred in 1972, is described as the "spontaneous" result of a conversation among some of the Takashima women. Except for the guidance of the instructor, such leadership as exists in this organization is extemporaneous and informal. To the resentment of some of the younger women, the group is said to be somewhat dominated by its older members, a circumstance that, according to tradition, should not exist in any common-interest association.

Important additions among the expressive associations are the various *kurabbu*, "clubs," sponsored by large industrial concerns of the area. The clubs existing among the employees of the shipbuilding firm which employs many of the adults of Takashima are representative. In 1974, these consisted of groups centered on baseball, rugby, tennis, table tennis, yachting, flower arranging, and the tea ceremony. These clubs are a prominent national phenomenon. Firms larger than the shipbuilding company, which is classed as a medium-sized company, ordinarily have a much larger variety of such associations. New clubs are willingly formed by the firms in response to requests from employees.

Labor unions have great and growing national importance in Japan but, for nearly all Takashima wage earners, they are as yet unimportant because membership in them is not yet common and is generally very recent. Labor unions in Japan are characteristically "industry-based," that is, company unions that exist only in large or fairly large industrial concerns and service organizations. These are loosely united nationally in complex federations based upon the type of employment. Ordinarily, only *honko* or *honsaiyōin* of firms qualify for membership, and, once an employee successfully passes a trial period of variable length and becomes a permanent employee, membership in the company labor union is automatic. In early 1975, about one-sixth of Takashima wage earners in full-time employment were engaged by large concerns as *honko*, but, with rare exception, their status as permanent employees and union members was very recently acquired. As a result, the role of the labor unions has as yet made little impression on the consciousness of Takashima informants, although all are aware that the unions concern themselves with the welfare of their members, that they operate very much like other familiar associations, and that they hold great importance nationally.

One new religious organization was added to the Takashima roster of associations in 1964, when five adults and two children, composing two families, joined the lay Buddhist sect *Sōka Gakkai* after the community had been subjected to a campaign of intensive proselytization. Other community members strongly disfavor *Sōka Gakkai*, a sect which first rose to national prominence in the 1950s, because they, in common with most of the population of Japan, regard it as a militant organization seeking to control the nation politically as well as in all other ways. No formal subdivision of the sect exists in Takashima. Weekly meetings of members, a standard practice of *Sōka Gakkai*, are held at one or another of the homes of the few members in the ward in which Takashima is included. Takashima members of *Sōka Gakkai* are well aware of the opposition to their sect and tend to be apologetic about their membership in it. Curiously, they fulfill their traditional roles in helping to maintain the community Shinto shrine, a practice opposed by *Sōka Gakkai*, which holds itself to be a religiously exclusive faith, tolerating no other religious beliefs or acts.

Other cooperative groups which bear names ordinarily translated as "associations" also exist, but these are better described as service groups, or committees. (See Table 4.)

The first three of these semiassociations appear to have existed before 1951, but the precise date of their emergence is difficult to trace because they have never been regarded by Takashima people as active associations in the same sense as others that are listed, and they do not involve joint face-to-face relationships. The first four are all service organizations sponsored by the municipal government, and counterparts of them exist throughout the nation under governmental sponsorship. Membership in these service groups is limited to one or a few representatives, who may be residents of Takashima or residents of other subcommunities of the ward which embraces Takashima. These organizations are worthy of note because their activities represent a transfer of functions from older associations in which many people actively participated. The care of health, for example, at various times in the past has been a concern of the Hamlet Association, the Ward Hamlet-Representatives' Association, the Women's Association, and the P.T.A. Of these, the P.T.A. still concerns itself with health, but only of schoolchildren, of course. As

TABLE 4

SEMIASSOCIATIONS IN TAKASHIMA, 1975

Name	Type	Current Status
Service Organizations		
Loving Care Association (*Ai-iku-Iinkai*) (Concerned with health, particularly of pregnant women and small children)	I	Active
Tax Savings Association (*Nōzei Chochiku Kumiai*) (Collects taxes of various kinds)	I	Active
Self-Rule Associaiton (*Jichikai*) (Provides notification of municipal affairs and conducts Red Cross Drives)	I	Active
Kurashiki City Traffic Accident Mutual Aid Association (*Kurashiki-shi Kōtsū Saigai Kyōsai Kumiai*) (Provides city-sponsored group insurance)	I	Active
Semiassociations Subsumed Under P.T.A.		
Councillors' Association (*Hyōgi-inkai*)	I	Active
Insurance Association (*Hoken Kumiai*)	I	Active

I — Primarily instrumental.

previously noted, health relating to environmental pollution was very recently a concern of still another association until governmental agencies assumed this role.

In many rural communities of Japan, an association connected with the payment of the numerous kinds of taxes imposed upon citizens has existed for decades. Streamlined today and operating under the direction of a municipal office, this "association" has become a governmental service agency. One local representative of the association serves the entire ward of over 1,000 persons in which Takashima is included. The limited activities of the so-called Self-Rule Association are similarly old and were once conducted through other associational channels, including the ward and hamlet associations. Today, one representative serves the entire ward.

Of the two semiassociations under the P.T.A., the Councillors' Association is an organizational device, and it is further divided into four subgroups concerned with specialized functions dealing with health, moral guidance, traffic safety, and cultural activities. This development, which informants were unable to pinpoint clearly in time, occurred well after 1951 and indicates increased participation by parents in the P.T.A. as well as changing functions of the P.T.A. Traffic safety, for example, was not a matter of concern in 1951. The Insurance Association is at best only nominally an association. In return for selling life insurance issued by the national postal service, the P.T.A. receives fees on a percentage basis, which it uses in its activities. Anyone who buys postal insurance is presumably a member of this nominal association.

Overall examination of the associations of Takashima in 1951 and 1974 shows several trends of change and points to influencing factors that reflect local and national circumstances. As a type of social group, the associations certainly show no overall diminution in number or importance. If consideration is given to the growth of expressive associations and labor unions, all connected with industry, their number and probably their importance have increased considerably. Individual associations have risen, declined, disappeared, or changed, a trend that appears to be characteristic of any culturally changing industrial society which allows its members any freedom of action to create such social groups. This pattern of emergence, disappearance, and change also illuminates the fundamental nature of common-interest associations: They have much latitude in which to appear and disappear without serious disruption to other social groups, such as the family and other groupings of kin, and their viability as a type of social unit is fostered by these traits.

One trend of change that is evident applies to voluntary associations having goals that are wholly or partly instrumental. Actions of certain of these associations in attempting to reach their goals have resulted in the assumption by one branch or another of the government of the responsibility for bringing about the desired ends. The result is that the associations undergo functional changes if only part of their goals are involved, as exemplified by the present state of the Hamlet Association. If their goals are entrusted to governmental agencies, as exemplified by the Takashima association connected with problems of environmental pollution, the associations go out of existence. This course of emergence, change, and disappearance has been followed with great frequency in the United States, often resulting in the establishment of governmental bureaus or agencies. Perhaps because these events have been so common in the United States, the tendency to form voluntary associations with aims of improving civic welfare or of social reform has sometimes been regarded as characteristic of democratic governments. Since common-interest associations of these kinds often result in increased governmental authority, however, a question arises as to whether or not they can be regarded as ultimately democratic.

An associated direction of change has been toward specialization of functions, a trend that is congruent with national conditions of increased specialization in economic and in all other matters. For example, the once generalized functions of the Hamlet Association are now largely performed by a variety of other associations and governmental agencies. The fishermen's and farmers' cooperatives formerly also had a broad scope of functions. Once the only financial institutions available to community members, the cooperatives in many Japanese communities often also tended to include expressive, leisure-time activities, especially in farm communities. Some years ago, their financial functions shifted largely to banks and to other commercial channels, and the activities of these associations for over a decade have progressively tended to center directly on the occupations they represent. The greatest numerical development of specialization in associations has come through the large number of distinct labor unions and expressive clubs associated with different industrial concerns.

Increased specialization in the goals of associations and the increased number of such groups relate, in turn, to another trend of change in their functional import. In times long past, the majority of Takashima's associations were in-hamlet groups, either as independent organizations or as united subdivisions of larger units, and hamlet membership in any group was relatively large. In this form, they served strongly to promote communal solidarity. The thin dispersal today among a large variety of associations having no identity with the community and the weakening of the surviving in-hamlet groups may be seen as operating in the opposing direction eventually to discourage communal solidarity.

RELIGION

A casual inspection of the religious scene at Takashima might suggest an increase in religiosity since 1950–51, and similar circumstances apply elsewhere in the nation. Evidence that seemingly supports this view is in several forms. Everywhere, sales of *Butsudan*, Buddhist altars for the home, and other Buddhist religious paraphernalia are greater than formerly, and commercial enterprises specializing in these products are thriving. Buddhist funerals, the prevailing national ceremony at death, have become more elaborate. New religious sects with a variety of dogmas arose in abundance in the late 1940s and 1950s, and many of these sects continue to survive. One of the new sects, *Sōka Gakkai*, has perhaps the largest number of adherents of the approximately 400 sects, old and new, in the nation. Proselytizers for foreign religions, of which the most obvious are young Americans promoting membership in Hare Krishna and the Mormon Church, are active in all sizeable cities including Kurashiki. Noted shrines and temples of the nation are well main-

15. *The dying god of fishermen, his protective shrine destroyed and not repaired.*

16. *The aged preserve tradition: a woman performs a home rite honoring her ancestors.*

tained and thronged with visitors. Groups of formally organized pilgrims bearing identifying pennants are a common part of the scene on trains, in the streets and hostelries, and at the religious sites. Great festivals attended by thousands of people are annual events in most cities. Buddhist priests, who for many years after the end of World War II could not support themselves and their families from the compensation for their priestly services and therefore became part-time priests, are often once again full-time religious specialists with many calls for their services.

But these apparent indications of religious intensity are illusory, reflecting improved economic conditions and other circumstances that are not indications of piety. Attitude surveys conducted over a period of many years by a governmental bureau, university sociologists, and sociologists employed by great newspapers with national circulations have uniformly reported a national trend away from affiliation with organized religious sects. Less than one-third of the adults of the nation declare themselves as members of religious sects, and the majority of the nation's population appears to be indifferent to religion. The ownership of religious paraphernalia is to a considerable degree an instance of conspicuous consumption. Shrines and temples are visited chiefly by vacationing sightseers, who make use of every resource for recreation that the nation has to offer. Municipally sponsored festivals are colorful pageants for tourists and a source of income.

The new sects arose after religious freedom was extended to the nation by law after World War II, and their great number represents in part a backlog of fission among established sects that could not formerly divide and some later additional fission among truly new sects. The old, established sects of the nation have been slow in adapting to changed conditions of life and views of the universe. Without any substantial changes in dogma, the new have features of organization and activity that are different from the past and congruent with the lives of a part of the nation's population.

All except a few of the new sects are small in their number of adherents, and as a group they are attractive to only a limited part of the population. Members are principally industrial workers and other people of the economically least favored urban occupations. Even *Sōka Gokkai*, the largest of these sects, has won few converts among rural people. The members of the new sects represent the least educated segment of the Japanese population and the people who have the least possibility of finding social identity as members of groups, a matter of importance to all classes of Japanese. The new sects offer a dogma that is intellectually acceptable to their adherents, but not to the rest of the nation. They also offer multiple opportunities for group identification that are satisfying and equally fine opportunity for group participation in pleasurable secular activities. The large sects all have as a feature of their organization many voluntary associations centering on sports and on all branches of aesthetics.

The upper echelons of employees of the industrial and business world form firm emotional attachments with their places of employment which consciously and strongly encourage them to do so. A college graduate who has entered employment ordinarily expects to remain with the same firm his entire working life, and he ordinarily need have no worries about being discharged except for outright misdeeds. The lower echelons of industrial workers may change employment and even occupations, and they have less opportunity for psychological identification with the concerns which employ them. Many industrial workers are former rural residents who lack relatives in the cities, are not community members in the sense applying to rural people, and lack affiliation with urban counterparts of the associations to which they belonged in the country. In the early years of the development of the new sects, faith healing was also an attraction, but the growth of socialized medicine has made this feature of their doctrines less appealing. Most of the Japanese nation looks upon the sects with suspicion as havens of the lowly and misguided.

The national circumstances relating to religion that are described in the preceding paragraphs are clearly evident in Takashima, and an account of the religious changes there since 1950–51 is principally a history of the decline of beliefs and practices of supernaturalism only slightly obscured by the seeming evidence of religiosity described earlier. Takashima people have purchased elaborate Buddhist altars and gravestones, and they conduct grand funeral ceremonies. The local Buddhist temple is well maintained by periodically fixed contributions of parishioners for this purpose, and its priest, who is very busy with religious tasks, is financially prosperous. In the 1960s, he was able to resign from his position as elementary school teacher. Shinto shrines in the area are similarly kept in good condition. Six Takashima people, five of them members of the same family, are members of *Sōka Gakkai*. But the traditional ceremony calendar has shrunk to a small fraction of its former size; the list of moribund and extinct supernatural beings is great; and informal beliefs and practices of supernaturalism have similarly waned.

Such survival as exists of most events of the old ceremonial calendar consists principally of observances by aged people, usually tokens of the former rites. Many of the young do not know even the names of the old ritual occasions. Twelve days of the year are official national holidays, but, like the holidays of the United States, these are fundamentally days of rest and most were never religious occasions. Many Japanese calendars still list ten additional days as events of the "folk ceremonial calendar," but these old festive observances have essentially disappeared, except where some of them are kept alive by municipal sponsorship.

For most people, the annual cycle of religious events consists of only two, the rites at Obon and at New Year's. The religious observances at these times are a minor part of the festivities, however, and, for most people, are obscured by the importance of these seasons as great secular holidays.

Buddhist rites of the home in honor of all deceased people are performed at Obon by all households including those converted to membership in *Sōka Gakkai*, which is a lay sect of Buddhism, and simpler rites are conducted at New Year's. At these times, within a period of fifteen days, the local Shingon priest unfailingly calls at each home, except those of the *Sōka Gakkai* converts, to conduct sectarian ceremonies honoring deceased members of individual families. Dancing at Obon, a tradition abandoned long ago in Takashima and in most other communities of the nation except as a professional or semiprofessional performance, has a small survival in the city of Kurashiki as a secular event of entertainment. In the neighboring suburb of Shionasu, immigrant industrial workers from other provinces initiated dancing in 1973, borrowing a microphone and loudspeaker from one of the chemical firms nearby, but Takashima people have not participated. Downtown, in the heart of Kurashiki a dozen miles away, elaborate dancing is sponsored by the city administration as a gesture of goodwill and a tourist attraction. Dancers are well-practiced amateurs, members of associations in different parts of the city composed of children, youths, mature women, and old people and of still other associations such as clubs composed of the employees of department stores.

Shingon households also continue to observe the major rites other than those at Obon and New Year's that are connected with the death of individual people. Funerals have grown to be so relatively elaborate that the wife of the local priest described them as often being "gaudy." At a funeral in the fall of 1974 for an aged woman, two wakes were conducted at which food, beer, and *sake* were supplied by a professional catering company. Members of the funeral association aided in serving food and fulfilled other simple roles connected with the ceremonial and burial. The principal rite was conducted two days after the death in the home and yard of the deceased woman, which was decorated with many large paper wreaths on easellike stands that bore the names of their donors. Rites were conducted by two priests, a luxury impossible in former years when only one priest officiated. Close relatives of the deceased sat formally in rows in the house near a casket holding the body of the deceased, which was packed with dry ice. Shutters of the house had been removed so that the performance of the rite was visible to others in attendance, who stood in the yard.

As guests arrived, they signed their names in a register presided over by a receptionist to whom each presented an envelope containing "incense money," a sum fixed by the community association at about $1 for nonrelatives. The guests each received in return a small towel wrapped ceremonially with paper on which the name of the deceased was inscribed formally. Final rites at the home consisted of each guest's paying respects to the deceased by placing a pinch of incense in a burner set beside a large photograph of her. Close relatives then performed a brief ceremony of farewell before her body. Most of these ritual events were continuances or only small modifications of tradition.

Ritual then followed that had not existed in 1950–51. Although uncommon elsewhere in Japan, inhumation had been the custom of Takashima people, who often lacked the money to pay for cremation. Today cremation is required by law. Two hired buses carrying guests, a hearse bearing the body of the deceased and her close relatives, and several private automobiles in which relatives and friends rode then proceeded to a crematorium several miles away. There a brief final rite was conducted, which featured the ceremonial igniting of the flames by the eldest son of the deceased by means of setting a match to some ceremonial paper. Actual cremation was done by gas in a device resembling a large hospital autoclave. A simple rite of burial of the ashes was held several days later. The cost of the funeral and burial, borne by a family that was formerly abjectly poor and now no more prosperous than the average, was estimated to have exceeded $1,000. If purchase of a grave site had been necessary, the cost would have been much higher.

Commemorative rites for individual ancestors are conducted by the local priest at the homes of their descendants on the anniversaries of death designated by Shingon doctrine. As in the past, the number of years during which these rites are conducted varies from household to household, but, according to the priest, the length of time is no shorter than in his past experience. A pleasant and well-liked man, the priest is careful to remind all parishioners of these anniversaries beforehand by sending them postcards. These rites are attended only by close relatives, but attendance at a funeral by a representative of every household is still regarded by most people as required. In other respects, as noted earlier, a funeral is no longer an occasion for cooperation by all households of the community.

As stated earlier, the shrine to *Kōjin-sama*, the tutelary god of Taka-shima, is no longer the scene of any communal ritual observances, and it had seen little joint use in 1950–51. As before, some old women perform brief individual rites there. Like the many thousands of Shinto shrines elsewhere in the nation, however, it retains some emotional importance as a symbol of identity. Shrines are of distinctively Japanese architec-tural style, and, although most people do not visit them, the shrines appear to be regarded as a pleasing and familiar part of the scene that should continue to exist. At the annual meeting of the association of Takashima households in 1974, a decision was made to renovate the shrine of the tutelary god within the next year or two, the cost being borne by a levy against each household.

As measured by the attention given to them, most of the super-natural beings of the past are neglected, moribund, or dead. Only *Gautama Buddha* appears to be in good health. Other gods and spirits have lost their usefulness or credibility under modern conditions of life. In the views of young people, the God of the Toilet, somewhat comical even in 1950–51, is an absurd belief of the past. The spirits of the wells and the spirit of the mountain have no existence for most people. *Funadamasama*, the God of the Boats, has similarly lost his usefulness and slipped into limbo.

The year of 1974 saw the death of *Ebisusama*, a Chinese-derived spiritual being adapted centuries ago to the Shinto beliefs of Japan and, in Takashima, the special God of Fishermen. Represented by a small wooden statue housed in a miniature, protective shrine, *Ebisusama* had stood beside the old pier and had been placed beside a well-traveled modern road near the new harbor when the landfill covered the pier. Although waning in importance as fishing drew to a stop, *Ebisusama* was not entirely neglected. From time to time, old men and women left sprigs of pine needles and seashells as offerings before his statue, an aesthetically pleasing object about 9 inches high, charred on one side as the result of a conflagration in about 1850 that is said to have consumed most of the dwellings of the community. In July 1974, the wooden shrine protecting the statute was demolished by a miniature landslide from the cut above the road by which the statue stood, and the undamaged statue was left to lie on its side exposed to the sun and the rain. The accident was quickly noted and brought to the attention of one of the elected community leaders, but no plans were made to spend the small amount of money needed for repair for the stated reason that Takashima people were no longer fisherfolk and *Ebisusama* was therefore no longer im-portant to them. In October the statue disappeared, presumably into the hands of a fancier of antiques. Some old people who regretted the loss consoled themselves by saying that at least he now probably had a more comfortable home.

Ideas of supernatural pollution resulting from blood and death remain alive only among the aged and the practices associated with them have generally disappeared. Modern mothers, who give birth to children in hospitals rather than in a symbolically isolated room of their homes, place no credence in the old beliefs of which they know very little. The prohibition against their visiting Shinto shrines during menstrual periods has long been irrelevant since they rarely visit shrines. Some people go into isolation for a brief time after the death of a close relative, but this behavior is usually looked upon as private mourning.

The traditional division of labor with regard to religious acts continues to apply. Most religious observances are conducted by the aged, especially by women, and these people may still conduct some of the lesser traditional rites of which other members of their households are unaware or scarcely aware. Pilgrimages to near and distant shrines and temples by aged women and by some men have become fairly common for those who can afford to do so. These are admittedly "half amusement," that is, pleasurable events that are, at the same time, acts of piety. Many houses contain talismans purchased on these occasions.

The large traditional inventory of Shinto rites of the home and informal beliefs and practices of supernaturalism of former times has similarly shrunk. The practice of changing one's given name to bring a change in fortune has disappeared, and few people have faith in diviners and traditional lore having to do with cardinal directions. Certain beliefs and practices survive, sometimes in transmuted, modern form. In 1974, a traditional rite of Shintoism was performed at the junior high school attended by Takashima children before use began of a new swimming pool. Called by the traditional Shinto name *o-harai*, literally "exorcism," and performed by a Shinto priest, the rite was generally regarded as a blessing or protection rather than an exorcism of harmful supernatural forces. Shinto rites of consecration of the ground before the erection of a house or other building are also performed and are generally observed everywhere in the nation. A similar Shinto rite that includes the distribution of rice cakes by throwing them from the rooftop to participants assembled below is usually performed when the roof beams of a house have been installed. This rite is conducted by the carpenters, and some informants state that its survival is due to the carpenters, who are superstitious and who enjoy the ceremonial food and *sake* that are served. Most people regard the roof-beam ceremony as a pleasurable event if the family can afford its cost.

The strongest survival is in beliefs having to do with auspicious and inauspicious days of the year, years of the calendar by old Chinese reckoning, and years of the life span. Calendars listing lucky and unlucky days for certain activities are consulted by some people. Marriages are generally avoided in years that are traditionally inauspicious for them, and attention is often given to the calamitous years of the human life span, when one should be cautious in all undertakings. None of these retentions of past custom is exceptional in other communities of Japan.

PROBLEMS OF ADJUSTMENT

This account has so far been principally a record of successful adaptation to vastly changed conditions of daily life, adjustments that many people seemed eager rather than reluctant to make. The men and women of Takashima learned their new occupational roles quickly. Employees of the shipbuilding firm and its subcontractors who gave professional instruction in their new occupations to Takashima men were pleased with their performances, describing them as being unusually attentive, quick to learn, and otherwise also untroublesome in their behavior. They were said to be a welcome contrast with the often difficult men at the other yard of the shipbuilding firm, which recruited most of its employees from the area of its location, the district named Nishinariku in Osaka, an area of slum and near-slum housing nationally noted as a place of riots and crimes of violence.

Takashima men who abandoned fishing in earlier years had not suffered in the transition. Middle-aged women who first entered employment in the 1970s found their tasks easy to master. Young, unmarried men and women, who, as time passed, turned to white-collar employment, neither expected nor had problems of adjustment to workaday lives in their occupations.

Adaptation to suburban life was often a pleasure for most people, and it included little that had not in some way become familiar. Newspapers and other news media, occasional visits to Okayama City and Osaka, and, especially, television programs of various kinds had made many of the conditions of urban life thoroughly familiar. Any interested person knew about urban living quarters, clothing styles, foods, entertainment, and much else. And, after all, Takashima was not a backwater. For many years it had been a detached part of a small city, and for several years now, after the amalgamation that formed modern Kurashiki, a suburb of a fairly large city. Although rural in flavor, Kurashiki had many of the characteristics of large urban centers.

With the outstanding exception of environmental pollution, the vexing problems of Japan's great cities affected Takashima lightly or passed it by. Beyond a few minutes of daily inconvenience for those who commuted to work by car, the rush hour was not a problem. By national standards, their living quarters were spacious. Urban crime was no special hazard for a variety of reasons, including the small size, isolation, and lack of obviously expensive dwellings or other indications of wealth in Takashima. The crime rate in Kurashiki was low, and, although crime was an ever-present problem of urban life, the crime rate in the entire nation had become remarkably low in the 1970s. Juvenile delinquency was not a problem. As in former times, the behavior of daughters was carefully supervised, and it was usually safely taken for granted that young adult sons would conduct themselves in ways that brought no serious problems to themselves or to others. Of course, traffic accidents were a worry, but children were taught caution both at school and at home, and Takashima drivers, nearly all of whom were male, had never had a serious accident. Although some people felt that life now proceeded at too fast a pace, this circumstance was generally regarded as an inevitable part of the human condition that was offset by the desirable things it brought.

Problems of adjustment nevertheless existed, obscured by general economic prosperity and, often, by silence on the part of the troubled people. The transition to urban, industrial life brought no serious problems to the young or even to most of the people of middle age. Among those of greater years, problems of adjustment were common, if not always severe. Among these aged or aging people, two distinguishable groups were affected by problems that are shared by many of their age- and role-mates in other communities of Japan. Both categories suffer from age, but only sometimes from age combined with infirmity. Their principal problem is the modern conception of the attributes of people of advanced chronological age.

The lesser of the two categories is composed of a small group of men of middle and advanced middle age who are still healthy and able-bodied. Under the conditions of the past when they were fishermen, these men might continue working for many years. They are heads of households and, as such, have held positions of leadership and esteem in their families and in the community. Unvalued, if not entirely rejected, by industry, they are able to find employment only in the least desirable occupations, generally as unskilled laborers, and usually only by the least desirable employers. Their sons and daughters who only recently finished high school have greater incomes and, of course, have steady employment with good future prospects. The prospects of these men are poor, a matter of which they are acutely aware. Their wives, who had lower expectations in employment and less distance to fall in status and self-esteem, have fared better. Usually a few years younger than their husbands and thus, as a group, somewhat more desirable as employees in industry, they were able to find employment as food handlers and custodians, occupations that are congruent with their domestic roles and are not regarded as demeaning. A man's wife might even earn more money than he if only part-time employment is available to him.

The families headed by men troubled by these circumstances are not in financial need. All the men who were still fishermen in 1974 had received large compensatory payments that would support their families for some years. All affected families owned their homes, and some had earlier become well-to-do or wealthy by community standards. The community as a whole is little affected by this group of men troubled by loss of their old occupations and accompanying problems of status and role because their number is small and the men are generally silent about their misfortunes.

The heads of the three wealthiest households of the community illustrate the problem and also show a range of responses. Two of these household heads are over seventy years of age and are thus chronologically aged rather than middle-aged, but their circumstances are otherwise similar to those of the younger men. All three men were active fishermen until 1974. None wished to relinquish his status as household head, and two were able to maintain these positions and also obviously to maintain their self-esteem, by means of retaining control of familial wealth and operating as financiers. The third household head has found no satisfactory solution to his problems. In his early sixties and in good health, he does not suffer from lack of money, but his wealth is not really great and he has no talent or ability that might allow him to become a financier or an entrepreneur of any kind. His days of unwelcome idleness are broken only now and then by part-time employment by the prefecture, using his old fishing boat in tasks connected with maintaining a flow of watercraft in the neighboring ship channel. His status as one of the two elected heads of the community offers him no solace, since he knows that the position is no longer regarded as desirable.

Poorer men are similarly troubled, and no answer for their problem seems available. Among these men, nostalgic yearnings for the old days when they were fishermen are sometimes expressed. The good things they describe are matters which anyone who has fished can understand— the feeling of freedom and of mastery of the boat and fishing operations, the excitement of lifting nets when the catch was good, and the peaceful, relaxed nights of spring, summer, and fall spent sleeping on the decks of the boats lulled by breezes while the gill nets did their work of entangling fish. Even men and women who abandoned fishing years earlier sometimes expressed these feelings.

The second category of troubled people, the most elderly in the community, is more numerous and their circumstances affect a larger number of other people. As a class, they constitute a great and growing social problem in the entire nation. National awareness of the problem began in the 1960s and has since grown as the circumstances became obviously more troublesome. Similar problems affect every industrialized nation of the world, of course, but the conditions in Japan appear to be especially severe because of the speed with which they arose. In the Western nations, life expectancies had increased relatively gradually in twentieth century. In Japan the rise was dramatically swift. Until World War II, life expectancy had not quite reached fifty years. By the 1960s, it had risen to a figure comparable with that of Western nations. In 1975, it was slightly higher than that of the United States, and, as in other industrialized nations, the life expectancy of females exceeded that of males by several years. In 1974, approximately 7.5 percent of the population of Japan was sixty-five years of age or older, a figure well below the approximately 10 percent of the United States but nevertheless a great increase over the past, and demographic forecasts made the proportion seem ominous in future years. Awareness of the problem struck general consciousness in Japan somewhat earlier than in the United States, in part because of the sharp contrast with the past brought by the speed of its emergence and perhaps also in part because of the contrast with the past of the change in relations between old and young that is involved in the problem. The aged became the themes of popular novels by famous Japanese writers in the late 1960s, and since that time they have been a topic of increasing attention by politicians and news media, urging remedial action. According to Japanese tradition, old age was a time of carefree leisure after ceremonially observed retirement took place, a time of no serious responsibilities when much freedom of behavior was tolerated or even expected. Age had also traditionally brought respect, and the terms "grandmother" and "grandfather" carried this connotation. This traditional attitude is dimly echoed in the official postwar designation of a "Respect for the Aged Day." The expression "ecstasy years," which spread through the nation in the early 1970s as a ruefully humorous name for old age, derived part of its humor from comparison with the ideal conditions of the past.

The traditional attitudes and ideals have not entirely disappeared, but they have weakened and are often impossible to maintain. The prin-

17. *A retired man in traditional work clothes, helping to build a garage.*

cipal, immediate problem of the aged is poverty, but many other problems also exist. Steps to end poverty taken by the nation so far have been small, consisting of an inadequate welfare program and free medical care for people of age seventy or older. Even when money is not a consideration, where to live and how to live are problems with which the aged must contend. These circumstances are not limited to Japan, of course, but the emotional disturbances they bring may be greater there than in some of the Western nations where the traditional nature of familial relations and conceptions of the roles of the aged differ. Among the Japanese, emotional ties with family members have been and continue to be intimate. They are perhaps especially so for the elderly, who grew up when traditional social arrangements for the aged had been less altered by changing times.

Nearly a century has passed since the birth of the oldest resident of Takashima, a woman whose family maintains her in traditional fashion without feeling apparent distress. Other aged men and women are less fortunate, sometimes because they themselves no longer think it suitable to follow tradition. Some of the grandparents of Takashima expect and are expected to live with their children. Others wish to live independently, and their feelings against living with their children are sometimes strong. All are aware that the mature young people of the nation generally strongly prefer to live apart from the parental generation. The expressed views of one Takashima woman of seventy years represent one extreme of sentiment among the aged. Despite repeated invitations, she has firmly and persistently declined to live with any of her three well-to-do children, who live with their spouses and children in other communities. She lives alone in the small house which she owns and subsists by a combination of the produce of a kitchen garden which she cultivates and two small pensions, one as a war widow and the other from a small firm by which she was employed for a dozen years as cook and housekeeper of a dormitory for young male employees. She described herself only half humorously as being "one of the lucky ones — because of the two pensions, the house, and the garden, I don't have to commit suicide."

Like various other Takashima oldsters, she regards loneliness as her most difficult problem, and she believes that her loneliness would be much greater if she lived away from Takashima, where she has cousins and other more distant relatives and childhood friends. Like other able-bodied old people of the community, she takes pleasure in briefly visiting her children and their families and talks with them frequently by telephone. By means of thrifty use of her money, she is able, from time to time, to join other aged women and men in making festive trips to shrines and temples that are not too expensively distant, traveling by bus and train and spending a night or two in hostelries en route.

No aged person of Takashima is without adequate food or medical attention, and, as a group, the aged of the community appear to be more fortunate than many others of the nation, particularly the many living in the largest cities, where cramped conditions of housing make it difficult or impossible for them to live with their children. But no Takashima grandparent wants to be a "burden" to others, an idea that scarcely existed when they were young, and all are aware of the bride famine and other problems that living with their offspring may bring to their families.

Some fear senility and the trouble it brings to relatives and even the whole community. Everyone knows of the senile behavior of old Kotomi, the grandmother of a well-to-do household, who turned eighty years of age in 1975. In former years, she had been well liked and highly respected for her refined, kindly nature and for her skill as an altruistic go-between in arranging marriages. Today her mind wanders and, in unguarded moments, she slips away from home, sometimes wandering into the kitchen gardens and the remnants of the forest on the hill, where she sees things that could not exist — fire engines, foxes, and other apparitions. At other times, reverting to her youth, she is a bride-to-be or an expectant young mother. In response to worried telephone calls from shopkeepers, she must then sometimes be retrieved from shops in neighboring communities where, as a shy bride or expectant young mother, she is selecting clothing and equipment for her wedding or for her expected first child.

Except for a hospital for the infirmly aged, nursing homes and residences for the aged do not exist in Kurashiki and are rare elsewhere in the nation. Admission to the hospital is said generally to be looked upon with dislike as the last interval before death, when one is torn away from all that is familiar and comforting.

As exemplified by the aged people of Takashima, the "work ethic" that has long characterized the Japanese appears to have become extended far past the boundary of its former limits. Of the twenty-eight men and women of sixty-five or more years of age in 1975, nine were in part- or full-time employment. Of the nineteen unemployed people, six were senile or infirm for other reasons. The remaining thirteen were active with household tasks and, especially, with tasks as kitchen gardeners. In former times, Takashima grandmothers had often enough done some horticultural work, but the industry with which gardening is done today by these women and a number of men, who had not traditionally been gardeners, does not appear to be simply a matter of personal interest or a way to fill one's days. It is also a way to prove one's usefulness and lighten the burden on kin.

CHAPTER III

Continuities and Discontinuities

THE SOCIAL REALM

The opening pages and various subsequent passages of this study have referred to both cultural continuities and discontinuities during the nearly one-fourth century that the community of Takashima was observed. The grand, overall change noted has been a rapid and seemingly successful shift, without migration, from rural to urban life. Subsumed under this general statement are many specific changes that reach into all aspects of human activity.

Poverty has been replaced by relative affluence which, in turn, has had many effects. Educational levels have risen and, together with other changes, have altered views of human society and the nature of human existence. Changes of several kinds have taken place in the structure of social groups and in the relations of their members. New groups have arisen and old groups have become modified or have disappeared. The social networks of individual people — the mesh of human contacts they have in daily life — differ substantially from those of the past, now including a larger and more diverse aggregation of distinguishable social categories. Attitudes and sentiments forming the complex set of explanations and supporting rationales for the standards and conventions of human relations have changed in congruence with the new circumstances to which they refer.

The preceding generalized statements are applicable in varying degree to most of the world during the past quarter-century, and, in one way or another, they have often been stated by observers of trends of change. It is clear that the fundamental factors fostering the changes have everywhere been economic, but this statement is also broadly general and embraces a varied category of specific paths of economic and related social change among the many societies that have been affected. The history of cultural change for each society is, of course,

335

unique. Although general trends of change in the United States and Japan are much alike, they differ in their particulars, and the ways in which they differ are of special interest.

Stated in broadest summary, the outstanding cultural changes, all interrelated, that have occurred in varying degree in both nations during the nineteenth and twentieth centuries have been greatly heightened industrialization and urbanization, a growth of egalitarianism, accelerated scientific development and the dispersion of knowledge to an increased part of the population, affluence as nations — an essentially new status for Japan and a heightened status in the United States — and in both nations relative affluence for the average person, a shrinking of the scope and functions of kinship, an increase in the number and importance of social groups not based upon ties of kinship, and changes in views of the proper and the improper, the desirable and the undesirable in human relations and other matters of human life.

Popular opinion in the United States has often seen other, undesired trends of change regarded as defects or hardships of modern life which, according to varying opinion, must be endured or for which remedies may and must be found. These undesirable developments notably include tiresome uniformity or homogeneity in national culture, a depersonalization of human relations, a rise in psychological stresses and strains caused by the conditions of "modern civilization," and the emergence of an associated set of psychological-social problems especially related to urban life. As the preceding pages of this study state or imply, none of these ideas or the circumstances to which they relate is unfamiliar in Japan.

The culture of Japan has long been unusually homogeneous in fundamental ways that make it everywhere easily recognizable as Japanese. Until recent times, however, this basic homogeneity allowed considerable regional diversity in customs and items of material culture, a diversity fostered by geographical and social isolation, differences in climate, and differences in the products of human endeavor that were possible under varying local conditions. Regionally, people took pride in their *meibutsu*, "famous products," and in variations from the standard or from their neighbors in tutelary gods, cuisine, and other matters of everyday life and in the annual cycle of ritual events. Like the local gods of Takashima, most of the formerly great host of supernatural beings of Japan have lost their roles and, thereby, their existence. Ritual has become more uniform than in former years by the loss of most rites except those connected with death. The growth of large industry and the elaborate, efficient system of transport and communication associated with it have discouraged diversity in more than one way. Local products have become more uniformly distributed throughout the nation; small-scale enterprises with distinctive products are being eliminated in economic competition by mass producers of a limited range of products, and the public has been educated by intensive advertising to desire those products. Many Japanese lament the modern decline of local specialties in such things as foods, handicrafts, and ceremonial events and, in particular, deplore the uniformity of modern urban housing, the great aggregations of tiny, monotonously similar apartments.

Japan and the United States are thus much alike in the trends toward increasing cultural uniformity and in the reactions to it of their populations, although Japan has so far changed less markedly. Impersonality in human relations, however, does not accurately describe modern Japan. To be sure, relations with the hordes of strangers with whom one lives in any urban area are impersonal, and migrants from country to city live at first in a state of social isolation, but, as later discussion will bring out, highly personalized relations are still characteristic of Japan and appear to be an essential ingredient of its industrial success.

The soundness of the contention that modern life imposes individually trying stresses and strains is surely questionable if it implies that such conditions did not previously exist. The emergence of this idea must depend in part upon the modern growth of science which, in the form of the social sciences, has directed attention to the human psychological condition and factors which affect it. The notion that civilized life is stressful has existed in Western scholarly circles since at least the time of Rousseau. Before the middle of the twentieth century, it had become a view of the general population of at least the United States, now made thoroughly conscious of its psychological state. But human stresses and strains are doubtless ancient, and anthropology has presented much evidence of them in the small and culturally simple societies of the world. Modern times have simply brought their own species of such problems, which are internationally similar and manifested in many ways that can be quantified, such as the incidence of "nervous" ailments and a variety of social problems. Like Americans and Europeans, the people of Takashima and of other cities of Japan often complain of the new social problems of modern life and of its exhausting pace. Nevertheless, conditions of health are better than formerly and life expectancies are longer. In Tokyo and adjacent Kanagawa Prefectures, the region of Japan most densely populated and most seriously plagued by environmental pollution, life expectancies in recent years have been the greatest in the nation.[1] Thus the stresses and strains appear to be tolerable, per-

[1] *Japan Report*, XXI, No. 4, 1975.

haps offset by desirable modern conditions bearing on health and well-being.

Other difficulties associated with industrial, urban life in Western nations, unplanned developments which are regarded as great social problems, also emerged in Japan after the pace of its industrialization quickened in postwar years. Generally the least severe among the large, industrial nations, their relatively small development is one of the many markers of Japan's success in industrializing.

Instability of unions of marriage is one of these common problems. The rate of divorce in Japan has risen somewhat annually for the past several years, although it is far below its highest peak in Japanese history, which occurred in the late nineteenth century when industrialization had just begun.[2] A related problem of Japan in recent years, familiar elsewhere, is called *jōhatsu*, literally, "evaporation," the desertion of spouses and children by men and, in very recent years, sometimes by women. Men who have evaporated have been principally migrants from rural areas who have taken presumably temporary employment in cities. Apparently impelled by a desire for the freedom from irksome traditions of country life which the city offers, they "disappear."

Although greatly increased over conditions existing before World War II, rates of both crime and juvenile delinquency in Japan are much lower than in the United States and, after decreasing in the early 1970s, have since risen only slightly. The incidences of alcoholism, drug addiction, crimes connected with drugs, and crimes of violence are much lower than in the United States. As in the United States, crimes of violence by women increased in the 1970s, but the rate continues to be low. In 1975, over 90 percent of the recorded crimes were nonviolent, and 84 percent of the crimes consisted principally of larceny.[3] Several factors are thought to account for the remarkably low rates.[4] These include the lack of any large minority groups, strict governmental control over narcotics, guns and other weapons, high average levels of education, the continuing strength of family ties, and economic prosperity shared by most citizens. Lengthy traditions of obedience to law and to superiors of any kind and strong disapproval of physical violence are sometimes also cited as additional factors, although these may be tautologous statements that "explain" conditions by restating them. The low rate of drug addiction and alcoholism may similarly reflect anciently established

---

[2] In 1890, the divorce rate in Japan was 2.7 per 1,000 marriages, compared with a low of 0.63 in 1938 and a rate in 1971 of 1.00. These figures are well below that of the divorce rate in the United States which was 3.72 in 1971. (Sofue, 1976.)

[3] Japan Report, XXII, No. 10, 1976.

[4] Sofue, 1976, 261–62.

ideals of asceticism and avoidance of any extremes of behavior. Even the religious thrill in Japan has traditionally been a tempered state that avoids transports of ecstasy.

The rate of suicide in Japan has long been one of the highest in the world and follows its own patterns according to sex and age.[5] As in other nations, males commit suicide more frequently than females, but the proportion of suicides by males in Japan is the highest in the world, about twice that by females. The suicide rate by females is highest among women of sixty years of age and older, and the highest rate for both males and females is among those of ages fifteen to twenty-five. Urbanization has brought no significant increase in the rate of suicide since the end of World War II, although a small temporary increase for a few years in the 1950s made the Japanese incidence the highest in the world for that period. In Western nations, suicide is most common in urban areas and is therefore possibly linked with urban life, but in Japan urban and rural areas vary in their rates and the urban are not always higher than the rural.

As earlier passages of this study have stated, these national social problems have so far been felt lightly or not at all in Takashima, which only recently became urbanized and where unity of the family and the community are relatively tight and other factors earlier described as serving to diminish the severity of social problems are still forceful. In the last century, only one suicide seems to have occurred in Takashima, by a young man in the early 1960s. Divorce has been uncommon, and no incidences of desertion, juvenile delinquency, crimes of violence, and drug addiction have occurred.

As they are conceived by most of the urban population of Japan, the greatest difficulties of everyday life today are none of the international problems described above. They are instead the congestion and cramped living quarters of the cities and the problems of what to do with the aged. The first of these problems is, of course, imposed chiefly by a combination of conditions which do not exist in the United States. Consisting of nearly 85 percent mountainous land unsuited for urban-industrial use, Japan has concentrated well over one-half of its population into a small fraction of its small total area of land, in a region where industrial development was economically possible. The problem of providing adequate living quarters is made additionally acute by Japan's lack or inadequacy of timber, metals, and almost all other natural resources, which must be expensively imported, and by the continuing movement away from agricultural employment to urban occupations and urban resi-

[5] Naka, 1973.

dence. The shift from rural to urban occupations, as revealed by censuses taken at five-year intervals by the Ministry of Agriculture-Forestry, reached its greatest height between 1970 and 1975.[6] In 1975, agricultural households constituted 15 percent of the total number of households in the nation, but only 12.4 percent of these households drew their incomes solely from agriculture. For many years, a large proportion of the members of farm households have held employment in nearby cities to which they commute, and many rural males have taken presumably temporary urban residence and occupations. Agriculture has often humorously been called *san-chan nōgyō*, three-*chan* farming." *Chan*, a suffix attached to names that indicates intimacy, in this instance refers to mother, grandmother, and grandfather, who do the farming while father works in the city. In full-time equivalent, the proportion of the national labor force engaged in agriculture in 1976 was below 10 percent. Other rural occupations, such as off-shore fishing, have also declined.

As noted earlier, some of the distinctive circumstances connected with the industrialization of Japan are the result of noncultural conditions unique to Japan and, as exemplified by Takashima, unique local conditions. Other circumstances of change, such as those in social groups, are global events that generally characterize industrial nations. The conditions bringing these about are primarily cultural; that is, similar cultural circumstances have everywhere produced similar results. Similarity does not imply identity, however, and close examination reveals differences of various kinds which do not become evident in data on such matters as changes in the size and composition of families. These words are to say that the paths to industrialization may differ and that, within an unclearly defined compass, the social conditions accompanying industrialization also differ. Japan set out on its route of industrialization under social conditions markedly different from those of Western nations at the time. The result today is vastly greater similarity among the nations than existed in the past, but also notable differences that reflect unique cultural conditions at the outset.

The nature of some of the outstanding differences and similarities may be illustrated by discussion of three related topics as they apply to conditions in Japan in general and in the community of Takashima. These are motivation toward economic and other achievement, a vital ingredient of successful industrialization which has not yet been explicitly discussed in this study, and two familiar subjects, the nature of the Japanese family and of social groups composed of nonkin. In these matters, strong continuities as well as changes are evident.

6 *Japan Report*, XXI, No. 6, 1976.

The industry, thrift, and drive to achieve of the Japanese has struck the attention of foreign observers since the nineteenth century and has often been seen as an analogue of the Protestant ethic of northern European nations and the United States. Modern interpretations of the genesis of the Japanese motivation toward achievement have generally seen no close link with religion and, setting aside the question of the ultimate origin of this long-established trait of character or personality, have concentrated on psycho-cultural factors in Japanese life that establish and reinforce the desire to achieve. These factors encompass child rearing, the nature of social and emotional relationships in the family and in other social contexts, and the sanctions imposed for meeting or failing to meet expectations of behavior.[7] Much of the interpretive reasoning may be summarized in the statement that, among the Japanese, emotional dependency upon others is very strong and that this dependency is first instilled by modes of rearing children.

As noted earlier, childhood in Japan is a time of indulgence by parents, especially by the mother, and by other adults. Bonds between mothers and their children are close and long-lasting. Under circumstances such as these, sanctions for behavior of whatever kind imposed by the mother or by other adults with whom a child is associated have much force, since they threaten to reduce or put an end to the affective satisfactions derived by the child from the human relations involved. Social and emotional isolation from others is hard to bear, and the well-nurtured child becomes the well-behaved, conforming adult who is anxious to meet expectations. The affective bonds and the condition of psychological dependency thus created in infancy and childhood are life-long traits that are revealed in features of the social relations of people of all ages.

Associated with dependency as one of its aspects is the desire to belong to or affiliate with human groups. In the abbreviated terms of psychologically-oriented anthropology, this linkage is referred to as "dependency-affiliation," and the Japanese are then described having strong needs of dependency and affiliation. Japanese society supplies these needs in a number of ways, notably in familial relations, in which the bonds with the mother, the principal nurturing figure for the child, are the most intimate.

One illustration of the nature of the mother-child relationship is provided by conceptions of the Japanese mother that have emerged since World War II. Traditionally, the Japanese mother has been a figure of consummate human virtue, self-sacrificing, gentle, kind, patient, loving, and deeply devoted to the welfare of her children. This idea has much

[7] De Vos, 1973; Doi, 1973.

life today, but it has been accompanied for nearly twenty years by another view of certain, and perhaps many, mothers as unconsciously evil beings who harm their offspring.

Especially by her techniques of "quiet suffering," the mother may drive her offspring to heights of striving to achieve, to meet ideal expectations that are often beyond the capabilities of the children and therefore destructive to them.[8] In her worst form, the driving mother became typified by name in connection with the postwar competition for advanced education and for the excellence in earlier school performance necessary to reach this goal. Since the late 1950s, this version of Japanese motherhood has been known as the *kyōiku mama*, "education mama," the mother who unremittingly drives her children to excel in school. Often seen by scholars as resembling a stereotype of the Jewish mother current in the United States, the education mama, like her Jewish counterpart, has become a figure of derisive humor, a development beyond imagination in the past when the tensions imposed by her conception and performance of her role appear to have been less severe.

Education mamas are extreme examples of the role of the mother in Japan, however, and, rather than illustrating a trend toward the weakening of familial ties, they appear to show the strength of the bonds. The Japanese family, reduced in the number of its members and in the length of years of economic dependency between eldest sons and their parents, continues to be an emotionally intimate unit. Perhaps reduction in its size has brought more, rather than less, emotional intensity and dependency among its remaining members during at least the years of their most intimate contact.

Opportunities for social-emotional affiliation with other human beings are still abundantly available in the family and, much more than in the past, elsewhere in Japanese society. It is noteworthy that psychiatry as private practice has almost no development in Japan, although psychiatrists are well represented in hospitals treating neurosis and psychosis and, as scientific representatives of modern medicine, in the nation's leading universities. A large part of the roles of psychiatry as it operates in the United States is met in Japan by ties with one's associates of daily life — family members, unrelated confidantes, comembers of the numerous social groups of the world of industry and commerce, and, for part of the nation, by membership in intimate subgroups of the new religious sects.

As implied in the foregoing paragraphs, the traits of dependency and affiliation are seen as being linked in complex ways with the Japanese drive to achieve and with the great modern development in Japan of

[8] De Vos, 1973.

associations composed of unrelated people. Japan's success in international competition as an industrial, trading nation has not come from fierce individual competition among its citizens, but from an emphasis on team work or group endeavor. Entrance examinations of universities are, of course, individually competitive, since talent must be recruited on an individual basis, but, once admitted to a university, the competitor studies in an atmosphere in which competition is greatly toned down. In commerce and industry, as in competitive sports, groups rather than individuals compete, and the competitive strivings of individuals, which unquestionably exist, are tempered by the emotional sustenance they draw from group membership and by the ideal of joint activity.

More than the population of the United States, the Japanese appear to be joiners. A discussion of the nature of common-interest associations and a review of the history of the associations of Takashima illustrate the circumstances in Japan and also point to the role that these social groups may perform in large, industrialized societies.

For reasons that are obvious, such as their inability to provide the offspring needed for social continuity, common-interest associations are never a lone kind of social group in any society. They have no place in very small tribal societies where populations are relatively minute and social organization is based upon kinship. Their strong development correlates with the growth of societies to large size and cultural complexity, conditions under which kinship and political organs cannot meet all the demands of human existence. Japan and the United States are both large and culturally complex societies, and in both nations common-interest associations have proliferated so greatly that merely compiling a list of their types, names, and numbers would be a monumental task. In broad view, the circumstances surrounding the associations of the two nations are similar. They had become such a common phenomenon in the United States in the nineteenth century that de Tocqueville[9] regarded them as a striking development of democracy. Although ancient in Japan, their greatest development there has been in modern times, after social units based upon ramified ties of kinship had become unviable and after the old scheme of social hierarchy had lost much of its rigidity. In both nations, the associations have ideally been egalitarian groups in which leadership was by guidance rather than by command. In historic Japan, egalitarianism has existed chiefly in the form of membership in its associations. Their existence was possible, however, only for activities that did not appear to threaten hierarchy, which existed in the family as well as in politics and economic enterprises. Accordingly, the degree of development of associations in Japan differed regionally; the tech-

[9] 1898.

nologically most advanced regions and those in which large, united kin groups were least developed had the greatest growth. Associations appear to have existed everywhere, however, in connection with religious matters and communal affairs that required joint activity, such as irrigation.[10]

The long history of associations in Japan as egalitarian groups has been one of complementary enmeshment with lines of hierarchic organization. This complementarity has increased in modern times and is so common and outstanding that Japanese social scientists have often described their nation's social order on the basis of *tate-sen*, "vertical lines" and *yoko-sen*, "horizontal lines." [11] Vertical lines are administrative and other chains of authority, such as those in governmental and commercial affairs and also in family life. Horizontal lines apply among members of common-interest associations and, informally, among unorganized groups of equals in age and status.

Both lines commonly coexist within any single, identifiable organization of substantial size. The large industrial firms of Japan provide one outstanding example in which patriarchal administrative hierarchy exists along with the egalitarianism of the abundant, company-sponsored associations centered on activities of leisure time. Outstanding examples of the skillful blending of vertical and horizontal lines are also afforded by the internal organization of the most successful of the new religious sects. Clear lines of authority certainly exist in these organizations, but they are intertwined with the horizontal lines of expressive associations of every conceivable kind connected with sports, aesthetics, hobbies, and personal problems.

Examination of the past and present associations of Takashima from the standpoint of horizontal lines makes it evident that egalitarianism was well developed at both times. Except for some years before and during World War II when the national government took control of all associations, the groups on Takashima appear always to have been consciously democratic. I have noted that, in the twenty-three years covered by this combined report, the tendency to form associations has not slackened, although individual groups have risen and declined.

As is readily obvious, the changes in social organization represent chiefly the influence of changes in economic matters, which, in turn, have affected family life, communal unity, religious ideas, attitudes, ideals, and a host of related customs. Although Takashima is probably atypical of the nation in retaining considerable communal identity and solidarity because of special circumstances of physical isolation and

10 Norbeck, 1962, 1976.
11 Nakane, 1970.

bonds of kinship previously discussed, the trends of change in its associations as well as in the family conform with those of the nation in general,
and, as such, they reflect past as well as modern conditions. For example,
ancient associations of Japan prominently included age-graded societies
with both instrumental and expressive aims. Such associations continue
to be common in Japan today, although their existence seems to be
nominal and their goals principally expressive. Takashima today lacks
children's, youths', and women's associations, but these organizations
continue to exist at least nominally in some neighboring communities.
In the larger cities of Japan, such groupings have generally long since
disappeared. The former instrumental goals of these associations have
become the tasks of professionals, and expressive activities are similarly
either commercially available or, for industrial workers, available
through membership in the clubs of their places of employment. Although a recent innovation, the token existence in Takashima of the Old
People's Association seems to be simultaneously an echo of the past and
a reflection of the present and future. Established as a result of encouragement by the municipal government, which often echoes the past in
its paternalism, this association points to a current national problem and
represents a token attempt to handle it.

Other lingering echoes of tradition are also evident in the modern
associations of Takashima. The Fire Prevention Association is redundant, but, for what appears to be emotional reasons, there is reluctance
to abandon it. The Funeral Association and the Farmers' Cooperative
Association are both approaching redundancy, but their nominal life
spans will doubtless continue until some time after they have lost their
utility. The Hamlet Association is much weaker than in former times,
but so long as the community remains isolated geographically and
retains communal property, it will likely endure. The semiassociations
that operate as service groups appear to illustrate the Japanese tendency
toward paternalism, another survival of the past, and, at the same time,
the trend toward continuing expansion of governmental control over
human affairs.

The preceding statements intend to point to changes in specific
associations and, as previously stated, contain no implication that associations are dwindling as a form of social organization. The contrary
applies. Although no quantitative account can be made, it is clearly
evident that on the national level common-interest associations continue
to grow in number and to be increasingly important in modern industrial
life. The number of labor unions in the nation, for example, is huge,
about 64,000 in 1973.[12] Newspapers and other mass media of com-

---

[12] Bureau of Statistics, 1974: 118.

munication — organs that report what is regarded as newsworthy —
give great coverage to activities of the labor unions and numerous other
kinds of associations. For some years, federations of unions have conducted "spring offensives." In 1974, a "fall offensive" was added, and
both individual unions and federations are prominently active at all
other seasons of the year. The rural and older counterparts of the labor
unions, the agricultural and fishing cooperatives, also assert themselves
forcibly when causes such as environmental pollution arise that threaten
their interests. A national teachers' union is powerful in matters relating
to the profession it represents, and earlier pages have referred to national
associations concerned with the status of women.

Even the world of professional crime in Japan is principally organized in associations (called *kumi*), much less egalitarian than other
associations, which operate in all sizeable cities of the nation. Beyond
these newsworthy associations is a great collection of others, less politically vociferous or otherwise noticeable, that center on finance, merchan-
dising, and other economic concerns. Expressive associations concerned
with pursuits of leisure time are also more abundant than in the past.
They appear to be a vital feature of industrial firms and other organizations with primarily economic or nonexpressive goals and also of the new
religious sects which, although regarded by their members as being
expressive, in their roles as sects competing with other sects have instrumental goals.

The foregoing discussion has aimed to give some notion of the factors
involved in Japan's success as an industrial nation and, at the same time,
of the factors involved in Takashima's easy conversion to industrial,
urban life. The social relations and associated standards of behavior
that are seen to have been influential in easing the process of industrialization have not disappeared. The value placed upon achievement has
similarly not decreased in modern times; instead it has seemingly gained
strength and importance. Today, striving by the ordinary citizen brings
to him or to her visible, tangible results that are rewarding, a condition
which did not often exist in premodern times when little change for the
better was possible in social or economic statuses. Success has thereby
served as a strong stimulus for continued and greater striving.

The cumulative change in Japanese culture since the end of World
War II is dramatically striking, but no cultural revolution has occurred.
Following a pattern observed since ancient times, transition in Japan has
been by means of synthesis and resynthesis in which the adaptation of
old forms to new conditions stands out prominently. These circumstances doubtless apply also in the United States, since no large society
obliterates its past culture, but Japan appears much more clearly to have

tended toward retentive modification of the old to serve as the new. As we have seen, old and seemingly fundamental features of the social order that are distinctively Japanese have been modified in both form and function. In their modified forms, they are both congruent with the new economic circumstances and give support to them.

THE FUTURE

Because the train of events which compose and are associated with the industrialization of Japan have varied from region to region and from community to community of the nation, neither Takashima nor any other urbanized rural community of the nation presents a precisely modal example of Japanese urbanization. Takashima has peculiarities of several kinds that have been noted, but the main outlines of the changes it has seen have been those of the nation. Moreover, as a suburb of a recently expanded city that is composed of settled people long in residential association with each other and as a residential area which cannot provide living space for strangers, Takashima doubtless represents a common type of modern Japanese community.

Since the life line of Japan depends upon international commerce and therefore upon conditions elsewhere in the world, more than for any other powerful nation its future depends upon conditions external to the nation. Forecasts about the future of Japan and Takashima are therefore risky. Provided that no catastrophic events seriously disturb the international scene, however, it seems reasonably safe to make certain statements.

In its nuclear rather than extended form, the Japanese family shows no sign of quick disappearance. The personalized bonds of the past are strongly alive today in the family and in relations formed through identity with other social groups. Operating in complementary relationship with the ideal of achievement as important elements of the process of industrialization and urbanization, they may be expected to continue.

An additional trend for Takashima and the nation appears to be toward an increasing growth of common-interest associations, which will rise and, after they become useless, disappear without disruption to the general social order. Enlarging incomes and increased leisure time will foster the further development of expressive associations. The extent to which the activities of instrumental voluntary associations will result in greater national control by the central government is uncertain; governmental organs and activities also become outdated, and new causes that give rise to new voluntary associations continue to develop. For Takashima, it seems predictable that nearly all the specific associations of

1951 will disappear before many years pass and that the now existing associations which will have importance at that time are the labor unions and the expressive company clubs. These are, of course, examples of an old social form in modern garb.

The social structures, ideals, and psychological traits discussed in the preceding pages have been described as being both old and new. In foods, clothing, entertainment, religion, and much else, the old has often disappeared or is not clearly visible today, but what is modern in social life may generally be seen as remodelings of old forms. As for the community of Takashima, now drawn increasingly into the urban life that represents most of modern Japan, more than in the past its trends of change may be expected to accord with those of the nation with decreasing variation from the mode.

A question now arises about the importance today and in the future of Westernization, a subject to which the first part of this study, done in 1954, gives considerable attention. Much of the modernization of Japan since its beginning in the nineteenth century might indeed be called Westernization, if this term means the adaptation of a vast amount of Western culture. Westernization of this kind continued until after World War II, and the Japanese still examine, and often accept, foreign innovations in culture. For perhaps two decades, however, Japan has been an internationally important innovator of culture in the fields of science and industry as well as in the realm of aesthetics, and Westernization has ceased to be an appropriate word for the state of Japanese culture. Together with many other nations, Japan is today an active participant in an international cultural pool of diffusion and exchange. From all indications, the importance of its role in this capacity will continue to grow. Perhaps the appropriate term for culture change among the various nations thus sharing their innovations is internationalization of culture.

Glossary

bēbi būmu: baby boom, from the English term

bonneto: hood of a car

bunke: branch household

burakukai: community association

burakumin: literally, "people of the hamlets"; customary name for people of the outcast group of Japan

Butsudan: Buddhist altars for the home

-chan: a suffix indicating intimacy attached to given names, surnames, and terms of kinship

chō: head, of any organized group

chōnan: eldest son

daikon: white radish used for pickles

danchi: housing developments composed principally of apartments or such housing provided by industrial firms for their employees

demo: demonstration, abbreviation of the English term

gasu rēnji: gas range, from the English term

generaru sutoraiki: general strike, from the English term

genesuto: general strike, abbreviation of the English term

hanare-beya: separated rooms

honko: permanent employee

honsaiyōin: permanent employee

ishūgyo: foul-smelling fish

itai-itai byō: a disease caused by cadmium

jōhatsu: literally, "evaporation"; desertion of their families by men or women

kōgai: damage to living things and the physical environment caused by environmental pollution

koresto: cholesterol, abbreviation of the English term

korestororu: cholesterol, from the English term

kumi: club or association

kurabbu: club, from the English term

kuzu: a vine that is a common garden weed

kyōiku mama: literally, "education mama"; a mother who strongly pushes her children toward the goal of success in school

kyūka: vacation

mantan: full tank (of gasoline), a combination of Chinese and English terms; sometimes used jocularly to mean a full stomach

matsutake: a mushroom

meibutsu: famous local product

miruku: milk, from the English term

nintei kanja: official invalids, suffering illnesses caused by environmental pollution

o-harai: rite of exorcism or purification

oya-tsuki: literally, "parent(s)-attached"; a young man responsible for the support and care of his parents

renai kekkon: love marriage

rinjiko: temporary employee

ronin: originally, masterless samurai; now aspirants to university study who have failed entrance examinations

sake: rice wine

-san: a suffix of moderate politeness attached to names of persons

sanchan nōgyō: agriculture done by wives and aged parents of ostensible household head, who has urban employment

sandai fūfu: three generations of pairs of spouses living together

shita-uke: abbreviation of *shita-uke kaisha* (companies), firms serving as subcontractors for large industrial firms

subarashii: splendid, magnificent

sokobiki: literally, "bottom trawler," a demeaning name for a community of former fishermen of low social status

sukiyaki: dish of meat and vegetables

sumo: Japanese wrestling

tanku: gas tank of a car, from the English term

tate-sen: vertical lines

tokushu burakumin: literally, "people of the special hamlets"; customary name for people of the outcast group of Japan

yew-tahn: U-turn, from the English term; rural people who return to their country homes after some period of urban residence

yobikō: cram schools which give instruction to high-school graduates in how to pass university entrance examinations

yoko-sen: horizontal lines
yōshi: an adopted son
yuinō: a gift of money
yukata: traditional cotton garment worn in the home

Bibliography

Abegglen, James C. *Japanese Factory: Aspects of Its Social Organization*. Glencoe: The Free Press, 1958.

Azumi, Koya. *Higher Education and Business Recruitment in Japan*. New York: Teachers College, Columbia University, 1969.

Beardsley, R. K., J. W. Hall, and R. E. Ward. *Village Japan*. Chicago: University of Chicago Press, 1959.

Befu, Harumi. *Japan: An Anthropological Introduction*. San Francisco: Chandler Publishing Co., 1971.

—————, and Edward Norbeck. "Japanese Usages of Terms of Relationship," *Southwestern Journal of Anthropology*, 14, No. 1 (1958), 66–68.

Bennett, John W., and Iwao Ishino. *Paternalism in the Japanese Economy: Anthropological Studies of Oyabun-kobun Patterns*. Minneapolis: University of Minnesota Press, 1963.

Blood, Robert O. *Love Match and Arranged Marriage: A Tokyo–Detroit Comparison*. New York: The Free Press, 1967.

Chiku Seikatsu Kenkyūkai. *Mizushima Rinkai Kōgyō Chitai ni Rinsetsu suru Chiku Jūmin no Seikatsu no Jittai to Shōrai ni Kansuru Sōgō-teki Chōsa Hōkoku, Kurashiki-shi Yobimatsu, Matsue, Takashima Chiku no Jirei* (Comprehensive Research Report on the Present and Future Conditions of Life of Residents of Regions Adjoining the Coastal Mizushima Industrial Area: The Cases of Yobimatsu, Matsue, and Takashima, in Kurashiki City). Kurashiki: Kikakubu, 1972.

Chūgoku Shimbunsha, hensha (compiler). *Setouchi kara no Hōkoku, Kōgai ni Mushibamareru Ningen to Shizen* (Report from the Setouchi Region: The Despoiling of Man and Nature by Environmental Pollution). Tokyo: Miraisha, 1972.

Cornell, John B., and Robert J. Smith. *Two Japanese Villages*. Ann Arbor: University of Michigan Press, Center for Japanese Studies, Occasional Papers, No. 5, 1956.

De Vos, George A. "Achievement and Innovation in Culture and Personality," in Edward Norbeck, Douglass Price-Williams, and William McCord, *The Study of Personality: An Interdisciplinary Appraisal*. New York: Holt, Rinehart and Winston, 1968.

—————, with contributions by Hiroshi Wagatsuma, William Caudill, and Keiichi Mizushima. *Socialization for Achievement: Essays on the Cultural Psychology of the Japanese*. Berkeley and Los Angeles: University of California Press, 1973.

—————, and Hiroshi Wagatsuma. *Japan's Invisible Race: Caste in Culture and Personality*. Berkeley and Los Angeles: University of California Press, 1966.

Doi, Takeo. *The Anatomy of Dependence*. Trans. by John Bester. Tokyo: Kodansha International, Ltd., 1973.

Dore, Ronald. *British Factory–Japanese Factory*. London: George Allen and Unwin, 1973.

Fukutake, Tadashi. *Japanese Society Today*. Tokyo: University of Tokyo Press, 1974.

Hall, John W., and Richard K. Beardsley, eds. *Twelve Doors to Japan*. New York: McGraw-Hill, Inc., 1965.

Japan Report. New York: Consulate General of Japan, XXI, 4, 1975; XXII, 6, 10, 1976.

Kurashiki-shi Tōkeisho (Statistical Handbook of Kurashiki City). Kurashiki: Municipal Office, 1972.

Lebra, Takie S., and William P. Lebra. *Japanese Culture and Behavior: Selected Readings*. Honolulu: The University Press of Hawaii, 1974.

Mannari, Hiroshi. *The Japanese Business Leaders*. Tokyo: University of Tokyo Press, 1974.

Marsh, Robert M., and Hiroshi Mannari. "Lifetime Commitment in Japan: Roles, Norms, and Values," *American Journal of Sociology*, March 1971, 795–811.

————. "Pay and Social Structure in a Japanese Firm," *Industrial Relations*, 12, No. 1 (1973), 16–32.

Matsuda, Michio. *Nihonshiki Ikujihō* (Child Rearing in Japan). Tokyo: Kōdansha, 1964.

Mizunoe, Suehiko, and Shōzō Takeshita. *Mizushima Kōgyō Chitai no Seisei to Hatten* (The Establishment and Development of the Mizushima Industrial Region). Tokyo: Kazama Shobō, 1971.

McClelland, David C. *The Achieving Society*. Princeton: D. Van Nostrand Co., 1961.

McFarland, H. Neill. *The Rush Hour of the Gods*. New York: The Macmillan Company, 1967.

Naka, H. "Jisatsu" (Suicide), in K. Ōhashi, T. Shikata, and J. Ōyabu, eds., *Gendai Shakai Byōrigaku* (Contemporary Social Pathology). Tokyo: Kawashima Shoten, 1973.

Nakane, Chie. *Japanese Society*. Berkeley and Los Angeles: University of California Press, 1972.

Nakayama, Ichiro. *Industrialization of Japan*. Honolulu: The University Press of Hawaii, 1965.

Norbeck, Edward. "Postwar Cultural Change and Continuity in Northeastern Japan," *American Anthropologist*, 63, No. 2, Pt. I (1961), 297–321.

————. "Associations and Democracy in Japan," in R. P. Dore, ed., *Aspects of Social Change in Modern Japan*, pp. 185–200. Princeton: Princeton University Press, 1967.

————. "Human Play and Its Cultural Expression," *Humanitas*, 5, No. 1 (1969), 43–55.

————. *Religion and Society in Modern Japan*. Houston: Tourmaline Press, 1970.

————. "Japanese Common-Interest Associations in Cross-Cultural Perspective," *Journal of Voluntary Action Research*, 1, No. 1 (1972), 38–41.

————. *Changing Japan*, 2d ed. New York: Holt, Rinehart and Winston, 1976.

————, and Harumi Befu. "Informal Fictive Kinship in Japan," *American Anthropologist*, 60, No. 1 (1958), 102–17.

————, and George A. De Vos. "Culture and Personality: Japan," in F. L. K. Hsu, ed., *Psychological Anthropology*, new ed., pp. 21–70. Cambridge, Mass.: Schenkman Publishing Co., 1972.

————, and Susan Parman, eds. *The Study of Japan in the Behavioral Sciences.* Rice University Studies, Vol. 56, No. 4, 1970, whole number.

Okayama-ken Kōkōbu Kōgyō Kaisatsuka. *Mizushima Rinkai Kōgyō Chitai no Genjō* (Actual Conditions of the Coastal Mizushima Industrial Region). Okayama: Okayama-ken Kōkōbu Kōgyō Kaihatsuka, Vol. 1, 1971; Vol. 2, 1972.

Okochi, K., Bernard Karsh, and Solomon B. Levine. *Workers and Employers in Japan.* Tokyo: University of Tokyo Press, 1973.

Passin, Herbert. *Society and Education in Japan.* New York: Teachers College, Columbia University, 1965.

Plath, David W. *The After Hours: Modern Japan and the Search for Enjoyment.* Berkeley and Los Angeles: University of California Press, 1964.

Reischauer, E. O. *Japan: The Story of a Nation*, rev. ed. New York: Alfred A. Knopf, 1974.

Smith, R. J., and R. K. Beardsley, eds. *Japanese Culture: Its Development and Characteristics.* Chicago: Aldine Publishing Co., 1962.

Smith, Thomas C. *The Agrarian Origins of Modern Japan.* Stanford: Stanford University Press, 1959.

Smith, W. Eugene, and Aileen M. Smith. *Minamata.* New York: Holt, Rinehart and Winston, 1975.

Sofue, Takao. "Psychological Problems of Japanese Urbanization," in George A. De Vos, ed., *Responses to Change: Society, Culture and Personality.* New York: D. Van Nostrand, 1976.

Statistical Handbook of Japan. Tokyo: Bureau of Statistics, Office of the Prime Minister, 1974.

Vogel, Ezra F. *Japan's New Middle Class.* Berkeley and Los Angeles: University of California Press, 1963.

Wallace, William McDonald. "Cultural Values and Economic Development (A Case Study of Japan)." Ph.D. dissertation, University of Washington, 1963.

Weber, Max. *The Protestant Ethic and the Spirit of Capitalism.* Trans. by Talcott Parsons. London: George Allen and Unwin, 1930.

Whitehill, A. M., Jr., and Shin-ichi Takezawa. *The Other Worker: A Comparative Study of Industrial Relations in the United States and Japan.* Honolulu: The University Press of Hawaii, 1968.

Yasuda, Saburō. *Shakai Idō no Kenkyū* (Studies in Social Mobility). Tokyo: Tokyo Daigaku Shuppan-kai, 1971.

Yoshino, M. Y. *Japan's Managerial System.* Cambridge, Mass., and London: The MIT Press, 1968.

Index

Adoption, 298, 304

Aesthetics, 294

Aged people, 265, 266, 276–77, 279, 280, 285–86, 293, 294, 295, 315–16, 339; and poverty, 333; problems of adjustment, 329–34; *see also* Family, changes in

Agriculture, 245, 247, 257, 260, 266, 286–87, 312, 334, 340

Alcoholism, 338–39

Asceticism, 294

Associations, 261, 301–2, 307, 308–20, 343–48; characteristics of, 319, 320; egalitarianism of, 308; Buddhist Parish Association, 314; Farmers' Cooperative Association, 312, 320, 345; Fishermen's Cooperative Association, 312, 320; Fire Prevention Association, 310, 345; Flower arranging club, 316; Freight Boat Operators' Association, 312; Funeral Association, 312, 313–14, 345; Hamlet Association, 312–13, 345; Old People's Club, 315–16, 345; Pilgrimage Association, 310; P.T.A., 308, 314–15, 317, 318–19; Takashima Special Association for Meeting Problems of Public Damage, 315; Ward Hamlet–Representatives' Association, 310, 313; Women's Association, 311–12; Young People's Association, 309–11; *see also* Clubs, *Chupiren*, Labor unions, *Sōka Gakkai*, *Shufuren*

Baseball, 294

Bēbi būmu, 277

Beer, 282, 288, 304

Birth control, 304–5

Birthrate, 279

Bizen pottery, 253

Bonuses, 266–67

Bowling, 294

Buddhism, 320, 324–26

Bunke, 302

Burakukai, 307; *see also* Associations, Hamlet Association

Burakumin, 254

Butsudan, 320

"Bride famine," 300–1, 334

Cemetery, 305; *see also* Communal property

Ceremonial calendar, 323–24

Chickens, 287–88, 291

Child care, 285

Chōnan, 275, 300–1

Chupiren, 301

Cicadas, 259

Clothing, 288

Clubs, 316

Commemorative rites, 325

Communal property, 305, 312

Communal relations, 305–7

Communal ties, 270–71, 281, 305–20, 344–45; *see also* Associations

Competition, 343

Continuities, cultural, Chap. III, 335

Cosmetics, 288–90

Crime, 329, 338, 339; organized, 346

Culture change, Chap. III, 335; summarized, 336

Danchi, 252, 267, 281

Deities. *See* Religion, Tutelary gods

Demographic changes, 274–81, 340

Dependency and affiliation, psychological, 341–43

Diet, 290–92

Discontinuities, cultural, Chap. III, 335

Divorce, 338–39

Drug addiction, 338–39

Dwellings, 245, 279, 283–84; remodeling of, 284–85; as a social problem, 339

Ebisusama, 326

Ecologic changes, 257–60

Economic changes, 260–71

"Ecstasy years," 331

Education, 270, 271–74, 307–8, 314–15, 342–43

"Education mama," 342

Egalitarianism, 343

Employment, 260–71

English words in vocabulary, 295–96

Entertainment, 293–95

Environmental pollution, 242, 247, 254–60, 269–70, 315, 329, 337

Eta, 254

"Examination hell," 272, 343

Family, changes in, 296–305; composition of, 279–81; extended, 297–300; nuclear, 301, 347; size of, 277; *see also* Aged people, Kinship
Family ties, 341–42
Festivals, 295, 312–13, 322–24, 327
Financial institutions, 320
Fishing, 255, 260–61, 312, 330–31
Flowers, 245, 316
Funadamasama, 326
Funerals, 302, 312, 313–14, 323–25

God of the Boats, 326
God of the Toilet, 326
Gossip, 306

Hairdress, 290
Hanare-beya, 298
Handicrafts, 288
Hare Krishna, 320
Health, 247, 255, 260, 270, 277, 292–93, 317–18, 334, 337–38
Hierarchy, 343–44
Honko, 261–62, 263, 316
Honsayōin, 316. *See Honko*
Household appliances, 283

Incomes, 266–68
Individualism, 343
Industrialization, history of, 249–57, 261–66; problems of, 328–34
Illiteracy, 274
Internationalization of culture, 348
Ishūgyo, 255
Itai-itai-byō, 255

Jōhatsu, 338–39
Juvenile delinquency, 329, 338, 339

Kinship, changes in, 296–305, 343; ties of, 302, 305; *see also* Family, Dependency and affiliation
Kin terms, 306
Kitchen, 284–85
Kōgai, 255–57; *see also* Environmental pollution
Kojima City, 249, 252, 253, 256, 265
Kōjin-sama, 326
Koreans, 254
Kōrenchū. See Associations, Funeral Association
Kurashiki, development of, 250–57
Kuzu, 257
Kyōiku mama, 342

Labor unions, 316–17, 345–46, 348
Life expectancy, 270, 277, 331, 337
Lucky and unlucky days and years, 328

Male–female statuses, 301–2
Marriage, 303–4
Matsutake, 291
Medical care. *See* Health
Meibutsu, 336
Minamata disease, 255
Minority groups, 254, 338
Mizushima, 242, 243, 250, 252, 253, 256, 260, 268
Mormon Church, 320
Mother role, 341–42
Motivation toward achievement. *See* Work ethic

New Year's, 282, 291, 295, 324
Nintei kanja, 255
Nutrition, 291

Obon, 282, 291, 295, 324
O-harai, 327
Okayama City, 253, 273, 328
Oya-tsuki, 279

Pollution, environmental. *See* Environmental pollution
Pollution, supernatural, 327
Population, of Takashima, 275–77; sex and age distribution of, 276
Protestant ethic. *See* Work ethic
Psychiatry in Japan, 342
P.T.A. *See* Associations

Religion, 314, 320–28
Religious belief, decline of, 322–23
Religious sects, new, 322–23; *see also* *Sōka Gakkai*
Respect for the Aged Day, 331
Rinjiko, 262, 263
Ronin, 272
Roof-beam ceremony, 327

Sake, 282, 292, 324, 327
San-chan nōgyō, 340
Sandai fūfu, 297
Sanoyasu, 245, 262–63, 267, 268
Senility, 334
Sex roles, 287, 301–2, 334; in religion, 327
Shinto rites, 327–28
Shipbuilding. *See* Sanoyasu

Shita-uke kaisha, 263, 265
Shrines, 245, 305, 313, 317, 320–22, 326, 327
Shufuren, 302
Social change, Chap. III, 335; in the future, 347–48
Social problems, 329–34, 336–40
Sōka Gakkai, 317, 322, 323, 324,
Sokobiki, 308
Suicide, 333, 339
Sukiyaki, 291
Sumo, 294

Tate-sen, 344
Television, 293–94
Tokaido Megalopolis, 274
Tokushu burakumin, 254
Tutelary gods, 312, 326; *see also Ebisusama*, *Kōjin-sama*, Shrines

United States and Japan compared, Chap. III, 335

U-turn, 274, 279, 280

Voluntary associations, 319, 347; *see also* Associations

Weddings, 302
Wells, 288
Westernization, 348
Women, and crime, 338; in industrial employment, 264, 265–66, 330; *see also* Family, Mother role, Sex Roles
Women's liberation movement, 301–2
Work ethic, 334, 336, 340–41; and the family, 341

Yew-tahn. See U-turn
Yobikō, 272
Yoko-sen, 344
Yōshi, 298
Yuinō, 303

A colophon for Part One of this volume, "Takashima: A Japanese
Fishing Community," will be found on page 233.

Manuscript editor for *Country to City: The Urbanization
of a Japanese Hamlet*, was Suzanne Shetler.

The volume preliminaries and Part Two, "Takashima Urbanized,"
were designed and set in Intertype Baskerville
with handset Baskerville Foundry display type by
Donald M. Henriksen.